AN ECCLESIASTICAL HISTORY OF ENGLAND
THE LATER MIDDLE AGES

AN ECCLESIASTICAL HISTORY OF ENGLAND

The Later Middle Ages

FROM THE NORMAN CONQUEST TO
THE EVE OF THE REFORMATION

J. C. Dickinson

M.A., B.Litt., F.S.A., F.R.Hist.S.
(former Fellow of Emmanuel and Pembroke
Colleges, Cambridge)

ADAM AND CHARLES BLACK
LONDON

First published 1979
A. & C. Black (Publishers) Limited
35 Bedford Row London WC1R 4JH

ISBN 0 7136 1948 1

© 1979 J. C. Dickinson

Dickinson, J C
    The later Middle Ages.—(Ecclesiastical history
    of England).
    1. England—Church history—Medieval period,
    1066-1485
    I. Title   II. Series
    274.2   BR750

    ISBN 0-7136-1948-1

Printed in Great Britain by
Page Bros (Norwich) Ltd Norwich

CONTENTS

To
FRANCE
with great gratitude

PREFACE

THE provision in one volume of an adequate portrait of the vigorous and variegated life of the English Church during the four and a half centuries which separate the Norman Conquest from the Reformation is an enterprise which engenders many problems, great and small, on whose solution no total agreement is to be expected. I trust and believe that teachers and students alike will mostly approve my allotment of a fair amount of the limited space to depicting the medieval background, since this was so markedly different from that of today and is likely to be very largely unknown to those who seek to study in some depth the area of history with which this work is concerned. Victorian historians, obsessed by the political and constitutional strands of history, neglected social and economic factors to an extent which makes ecclesiastical history lop-sided and lacking in vivacity; hence my attempt in the final section of the book to stimulate interest in this fascinating area.

Minor but trying problems occur in the field of terminology. On the period of time called 'medieval' professionals are not of one mind: here the term is used to cover the thousand years between the collapse of Roman rule in Western Europe and the Reformation, and 'late medieval' for the latter half thereof. For the Sacrament of the altar I have utilised Mass rather than Holy Communion, Lord's Supper and Eucharist, partly because the latter each stress only one aspect of this complex rite and also because the former was the terminology used in the period with which the survey is concerned. The enormous mass of material available renders the Bibliography highly selective, especially in the topographical studies included.

'And what should they know of England who only England know?' Modern conditions enable us to realise the importance of Kipling's question far more adequately than did our Victorian ancestors. I am immensely grateful to the Leverhulme Trust for financing my widespread researches in Italian archives which, whilst not producing adequate supplies of material for the book I had hoped to write, incidentally greatly expanded my comprehension of that medieval Italy to which contemporary England owed so much. With France of course, during the period under consideration, our history was inextricably mixed to our enormous profit—as the colourless history of medieval Scotland plainly suggests. Now, as ever since the days of Abelard, if a man would experience the spirit of enquiry in its most passionate and comprehensive form, it is to France that he must go.

Finally, I must express my grateful thanks to Mrs M. Richards, whose skill and patience produced an immaculate typescript from a trying script; to the printers for their considerable competence and to the staff of my publishers for valuable aid, as well as to Dr K. Major and Fr B. Hackett for each improving the text of several chapters.

PART ONE

The Background

CHAPTER I

GENERAL FACTORS

HISTORY is one and indivisible. Convenience may suggest that it be split up into separate categories—political, social, economic, ideological and the like—but such divisions are unreal and tend to mask the inherent complexity of the subject. The notorious definition of history as 'past politics' has died the inevitable death which attend all such gross over-simplifications. Much to be preferred to it, despite its literacy inelegance and potential anti-feminism, is the memorable declaration 'history is about chaps', for this puts first things first, reminding us that history is primarily about people, not about politics, processes or philosophies. And since, as modern knowledge shows us ever more luminously, people's thoughts, actions and inactions are perennially liable to be influenced by a very wide range of factors operating in varying combinations and degrees, it follows that no one aspect of history can be studied effectively if it is studied in isolation. Ecclesiastical history must be regarded not as an independent entity but as history studied from the ecclesiastical viewpoint.

In the case of Christianity the involvement of religion with things and people crudely called 'secular' is particularly evident, owing to the built-in dualism of its way of life, which demands from its followers devotion to both the natural and supernatural world, requiring them to love not only God but Man. Thus with electrifying rapidity the first Christians at Jerusalem displayed a deep concern for the poor quite alien to the pagan Romans, no few of whom, like the Emperor Julian the Apostate, were forced by the facts to pay unwilling tribute to Christian 'benevolence to strangers'. In the area and period with which this volume is concerned the social conscience of the Church was immensely strong and pushed ecclesiastics into shouldering a huge part of the functions now in the hands of the Welfare State. As we shall see, they fostered assiduously the frail plant of literacy, dispensed stupendous patronage to the visual arts and displayed an immense concern for the poor and needy. As a result, in medieval times more than in most others, matters ecclesiastical and non-ecclesiastical were so extensively intertwined that it is totally unrealistic to consider one without the other.

However, this does not mean that it is advisable to discard the modern practice of distinguishing between 'theological' and 'non-theological' factors in church history. Clearly in the Middle Ages, as always, there were various developments such as the Black Death and the revival of urban life which, being purely secular in origin, belonged to the latter category, whilst others, such as the devotion to the monastic ideal and the rise of the chantries being fruits of religious experience were theologically motivated. But it is important to appreciate that what separates the theological from the non-theological is not a clear-cut ditch but a very hazy no-man's-land.

The medieval barons who founded monasteries, like the Victorian magnates who backed the work of missionaries in 'darkest Africa', so acted, not only because of their strong conviction that the Christian ideology provided the correct answer to the mighty question 'What is Man?', but also because the monks and missionaries brought with them those social by-products which are the almost inevitable concomitant of Christian living—care of the sick and poor, and education. These latter activities the modern pagan may regard as 'social', but to those who fostered them they were an essential element in Christian living and therefore religious. If we look at the often exaggerated persecution effected under Christian auspices we see something of the same complexity, religious bigotry working alongside financial, political and social factors. Results, like motives, similarly may appear to be both theological and non-theological. Thus the immense devotion to the monastic life in medieval times incidentally gave great fillip to both agriculture and architecture. In our own day the problems of pacifism and abortion provide obvious modern examples of the impossibility of squeezing all human action into either 'theological' or 'non-theological' categories. Bearing this in mind let us look first at the machinery of that Church whose history is this volume's concern.

The Machinery of the Church[*]

EASTERN AND WESTERN CHRISTENDOM IN THE EARLY ELEVENTH CENTURY

The word Church has so often been hazily employed as to have lost all clarity of meaning. To use it to signify solely the papacy or the bishops or the clergy as a whole, is to misuse it, for it properly denotes the whole body of those who have received Christian initiation and seek to follow the Christian way of life. In the eleventh century none of the splits in the fabric of Christendom with which we are familiar today yet existed. The Church of the West was at one with itself and, at least in theory, at one with the prestigious if somewhat battered 'Eastern' or 'Orthodox' Churches which inhabited the eastern and southern sides of the Mediterranean.

At a very early stage the universal unit of Christian government had become the diocese, a territorial area which varied greatly in size and was in the charge of a bishop, and were now grouped into five large units known as 'Patriarchates'. Of these the universally acknowledged senior was that of Rome which sprawled over the very considerable part of Europe then Christian. The bishop of Rome was now claiming sole right in the West to the title of 'pope' (*papa*), though in the East the equivalent word was (and still is) used to denote any parish priest. The primacy of the Roman see was principally grounded on the fact that the two chief apostles of the early Church, St Peter and St Paul, had been martyred and buried there, but also, to a degree difficult to assess, on the non-theological fact that Rome was then the unchallenged capital of the Empire to which all roads led. Although its seniority was admitted, the precise powers of the Roman see *vis-à-vis* the other patriarchs and general councils of the bishops of the church had not yet been very much discussed, and papal authority was mostly exercised in a helpful paternal spirit that aroused very little opposition.

Second to Rome ranked the Patriarchate of Constantinople, the imperial city founded in the ancient town of Byzantium by the first Christian Emperor, Constantine (d. 337). From the fourth century it

---

[*]Brief definitions of technical ecclesiastical terms are noted in the Index; for fuller details see *The Oxford Dictionary of the Christian Church*.

had been the capital of a separate 'Eastern' or 'Byzantine' Empire and came to be known as 'the second Rome'. Standing at the centre of a most elaborate network of trade-routes, with a flourishing capitalist economy, a superb fortified site and close links with the fertile cultures of the East, it was now incomparably the greatest city in the Europe within whose bounds it only just stood. Of the other patriarchal centres those of Alexandria and Antioch were huge cities with a vigorous past, whilst Jerusalem had been added to the number because of its unique connection with the life of Christ, but by the eleventh century all these three were of much less significance than in early times.

Between Eastern and Western Christendom in these times there existed no major doctrinal differences, though some minor divergences on matters of discipline had grown up. Thus in the East, bishops were chosen exclusively from monasteries, the use of statuary was excluded from the churches in favour of mosaics, paintings and icons and the Western tradition that the parish clergy should not marry had not been paralleled. Unhappily however, almost entirely because of deep-rooted non-theological factors, by the eleventh century effective contact between Eastern and Western Christians had become very restricted indeed, barbarians by land and Moslems by sea having done much to shatter that astounding Pax Romana which for so long had made the Mediterranean a Roman lake. Partially because of this, the bilingualism and trilingualism which had been so fruitful a feature of the life of Imperial Rome had now sadly decayed. The Eastern Empire had largely lost interest in Latin, whilst the West's ignorance of Greek was such that by the twelfth century the phrase 'it is Greek to me' was already current to indicate a state of utter ignorance. Happily for human civilisation the Latin tongue continued to dominate France, Italy and Spain, albeit in versions which would have shocked the literary purist of Cicero's day.

By the early eleventh century that flow of personal contacts which does so much to give Christian unity its full potential had dwindled to a paltry trickle so far as relations between Eastern and Western Christendom were concerned. Emperors, kings, popes and patriarchs might still have sporadic top-level contacts and more pilgrims than might be expected were still making their toilsome way to and from the Holy Land whereon Christ had walked, but there were no strong and widespread links between Eastern and Western church life. These might have followed in the wake of the great economic and cultural renaissance of the late eleventh and twelfth centuries had it not been for that major ecclesiastical disaster known as the Crusades, which reached its appalling climax in the Fourth Crusade (1202–4) when unscrupulous Westerners, turning viciously on their Eastern allies carved up amongst themselves most of the European lands of the Byzantine Empire. The antagonisms which the earlier Crusades had been steadily building up now exploded with consequences that were nothing less than disastrous for Christian vitality. Although no formal separation of Eastern and Western Christendom ever occurred (that long ascribed to 1054 is now known to be mythical) relations between the two were henceforth poisoned by profound and mutual mistrust. Dispassionate and intelligent interest in the Eastern Churches was scarcely to be found in the West until it was kindled in the aftermath of World War I, principally by Orthodox refugees, notably some most stimulating Russians living penuriously in and around Paris.

In recent years there has developed a deep if still much too small appreciation of the baleful negative influence on Christian history of this unnatural divorce of the mighty traditions of the Eastern and Western Churches. The former are seen to have undermined their vitality by too often turning a very blind eye to the vigorous scholastic tradition and spiritual inventiveness of Western Christianity, while both Catholicism and Protestantism have developed certain lopsidednesses that might have been avoided had they taken full account of important insights of early Christianity which Eastern Orthodoxy devotedly preserved. Thus, for example, if the Western Church had retained the early Eastern tradition that the papal primacy was desirable but limited its scope, it would not have put its sixteenth-century members in the improper situation of having to choose between a highly despotic papacy or none at all. Similarly, as we shall see, certain dangerous Western usages of the Mass created a most controversial situation which would not have required reformation had the Western theologians involved taken full account of the much more balanced thought of the Eastern Churches on the matter. It is today becoming increasingly clear that the mighty rift which steadily developed in medieval times between the life and thought of Eastern and Western Christendom was much the most important cause of the tragic fragmentation of Western Christendom which men call the Reformation. Be this as it may, to medieval England, as to almost all the rest of the medieval West, the venerable traditions of the Eastern Churches were almost totally unknown.

THE ORGANISATION OF THE WESTERN CHURCH IN THE EARLY ELEVENTH CENTURY

In most of those parts of Western Europe which had been Christianised in Roman times the Church survived the barbarian invasions which followed, albeit not without some battering in the process. In certain areas like Britain extensive re-conversion was needed and provided, whilst from the eighth century onwards East of the Rhine persistent missionary effort, albeit sometimes of a much too muscular variety, steadily extended the bounds of Christendom. In the West, respect for the Roman see was universal but hazy, and by this time often did not mean very much in practice, largely for non-theological reasons. In the early eleventh century, through no fault of its own, the papacy was in a very unhappy state. Chronic local disorders, which seemed almost as eternal as the city itself, ravaged Rome, with local families being ever ready to fly at each others' throats in attempts to acquire or dominate the papal office and its attendant possessions. However, in 1046 the then German Emperor, Henry III, intervened to stop this local racketeering and established an eminently respectable line of popes which quickly and confidently assumed vigorous leadership of a reform movement that rapidly acquired massive proportions.

The Clergy

The clergy who staffed the thousands of churches which now so liberally studded the landscape of Western Europe belonged to an elaborate hierarchy which came to comprise seven ranks or 'orders'. The lower of these, which were known as 'minor orders', had the legal status of 'sacramentals' and were conferred either by a bishop or by some lesser ecclesiastic who had episcopal authorisation so to do. The higher ones, termed 'major orders', ranked as sacraments and could only be received from episcopal hands.

These 'orders' had to be received one by one, starting with the lowest of them, but before receiving any of them the candidate had to take the preliminary step of receiving the tonsure in a ceremony at which his head was shaved so as to leave the tonsure (a bare circular patch on the top of it) which, at least according to some liturgical pundits, should be increased in size each time he received an additional order. Although it is tempting to regard this tonsured person who was known as a 'clerk' as the ancestor of the modern clergy such a comparison, as we shall see, is misleading, for in medieval terminology this title—*clericus*—was ambiguous.*

Owing to a passion for religious symbolism which leaves the modern descendants very unimpressed, medieval church folk had a curious devotion to the number seven which led them, not without doing some violence to the unobliging facts of history, to assign this number to various sets of holy things including the Sacraments, the Corporal Acts of Mercy, the Deadly Sins and the grades of Holy Orders, which latter ultimately came to consist of four minor orders and three major orders. In ascending order of importance the former ultimately were doorkeeper, lector and acolyte. These titles derived from early Christian times and indicated their original duties, which were mostly concerned with assisting in the conduct of Christian worship in various ways. Until 1207 the 'minor orders' were headed by that of subdeacon, who made preparations for Mass and aided the deacon.

By the period with which we are concerned these titles were mostly not used in any very strict sense and, in any case, in practice included other functions. Men in minor orders had probably rather more piety and a little more learning than the contemporary laity as a whole, but it is essential to realise that they were not clergy in the modern sense, since by no means all of them went on to take priest's orders and devote themselves to full-time pastoral duties. They were certainly known as *clerici*, but this term should be translated 'clerks' rather than 'clergy', for in medieval times it did not

---

* It is convenient and now common to use 'clerics' or 'clergy' to denote all those in minor or major orders who are not following the monastic life or something very similar to it, though in the following pages, in accord with medieval usage, such folk will be termed 'secular clergy'.

A useful note on the functions of a clerk is given by William fitzStephen who served Becket in this capacity. 'I was draughtsman in his chancery, subdeacon in his chapel when he celebrated, reader of letters and instruments when he sat to hear [law] suits, and in some of these, when he so ordered, advocate.'

have a purely parsonic connotation, being frequently used merely to denote people who had some smattering of learning, in times when this was far from usual. Thus King Henry I of England, who dabbled somewhat in matters literary, was termed 'the fine clerk' (*beau clerc*), whilst, long after, Chaucer terms the great Petrarch 'the laureate poet highte (called) this clerk'. To this day the Church of England has 'lay clerks' and 'bible clerks' who are not necessarily in holy orders. The modern use of the word clerk to describe white-collared workers is a relic of this usage, even if collars and ties are not. In our medieval context the term 'clerk' does not necessarily denote anything more than a man who has taken the tonsure.

The 'major orders', in ascending order of importance, were sub-deacon, deacon, priest and bishop, their functions being both pastoral and liturgical ones. The deacon was the major assistant of the celebrant of a high Mass, but could not administer any sacraments save that of baptism in cases of grave emergency—a privilege he shared with the laity on such occasions. The priest was the lynch-pin of parish church life and normally dispensed the sacraments which formed the core of its worship—baptism, Mass and confession. He was bound to lead a series of daily offices, when possible, in his church. He had to visit, encourage and, when necessary, rebuke the individual members of his flock, to aid especially the poor, the sick and the dying to whom he would administer the last rites. To preach he was also bound, though here-on in the medieval West there was often a considerable gap between theory and practice.

At the top of the ladder was the bishop. In these times he almost always had charge of a diocese, though assistant bishops became more numerous as time went on, late medieval England attracting no few episcopal strays from the Emerald Isle. The diocesan bishop had to administer his diocese in accordance with the laws of the Church. He alone chose those who were to be admitted to holy orders therein, ordaining those concerned himself or sometimes delegating the function. (Very ancient custom dictated that he himself be consecrated as bishop by at least three other bishops.) He was expected to assure himself of the worthiness of those whom he ordained and of those nominated to serve in parishes by the appropriate patron or patrons. For preaching and instructing the faithful he had a special responsibility. He had also to visit the monasteries of his diocese, except those legally exempted from this, seeking out anything amiss and providing for its cure. The confirmation of laity seeking to become communicants was also one of his duties, as was the task of consecrating altars, churches and churchyards, and reconsecrating any of them defiled by bloodshed—a contingency which was very much more common than the well-behaved laity of today would expect. He also solemnly blessed new heads of monasteries, consecrated holy oil and chrism used in certain sacraments and blessed for sacred use a wide range of objects. His high office involved him in attending major church councils where possible and presiding over diocesan ones. On top of all this, as we shall see, he was involved, willy nilly, in a trying set of secular responsibilities. Dioceses were grouped into local units known as provinces, each usually headed by an archbishop. At this time England had two of the latter—at York and Canterbury—but Wales and Scotland had none.

Church and State

In the eleventh century almost all the governments of Western Europe outside Italy were monarchies, though these were very much less puissant in both theory and practice than those which succeeded them in the sixteenth and seventeenth centuries. Usually a deceased monarch was succeeded by his eldest son, but the latter's unpopularity or incompetence might lead to him being passed over in favour of some close male relative. In England the choice of the new sovereign was made by a not very clearly defined body of lay and ecclesiastical magnates, headed by the archbishop of Canterbury who then, as now, ranked as the first subject of the Crown outside the royal family. He it was who conducted the all-essential finale of the process of king-making—the majestic and elaborate coronation service. In this the new sovereign was solemnly vested with the official robes and emblems of his office and anointed with holy oil in a ceremony somewhat resembling that used at the consecration of a bishop. The grand climax of the rite came with the imposition of the crown on the king's head by the archbishop, after which the magnates present, headed by members of the royal family, solemnly swore allegiance to the new sovereign, who was also vociferously acclaimed by the very motley multitude present. Finally came the celebration of Mass at which the king received holy communion.

In view of the foolish talk of 'medieval despotism' to which we are still so often subjected by journalists and members of Parliament, it is important to stress that the power held by the king in these times was very far from being absolute, either in theory or practice, though under exceptional circumstances and with exceptional skill the ruler might acquire considerable freedom of movement. Unlike the rulers of the Byzantine Empire or the Islamic states, medieval Western monarchs, and not least those in England were bound by a strong tradition not of absolutism but of what it is tempting to term 'Social Contract'. At the coronation ceremony the people through their social leaders swore to accept the king as their lawful ruler and to render him due but not absolute allegiance, whilst on his part the king pledged himself to give his people good government, a commitment which a Norman chronicler defines as seeking 'to defend the holy churches of God and their rulers, and further to govern all the people subject to him with royal foresight, to enact and maintain good laws and utterly prohibit robbery and unjust decisions'. Thus whilst the people accepted the new ruler as their rightful sovereign and pledged him the considerable respect which such a position demanded, this allegiance was conditional on his observance of rules of good government which, if somewhat hazy, were far from insubstantial.

In practice royal power in these times had major limitations. Taxation in the modern sense was barely existent, since in times of peace a monarch was expected to largely 'live of his own', i.e. pay his own way from his traditional revenues. Major matters of policy, of which war or peace was much the most prominent, had not to be settled without consultation with the magnates of the realm, who in fact themselves largely controlled the considerable parts of the country which they held from the king. The naive and brittle machinery of government, however, depended very much on effective royal management if there was to be preserved that law and order without which men could not go freely about their lawful occasion. Of this hard fact ecclesiastics and traders were particularly conscious, and because of it when civil strife threatened were mostly apt to give the monarchy their backing. Further, because medieval baronial revolts, like modern trades union strikes, so often seemed to be inspired by purely selfish motives, they often swung popular support behind the monarchy, though from the late twelfth century

onwards in England the inflated power of the Crown inspired a
school of thought which, in a somewhat Irish way, held that opposition to government was normally an act of piety and its leaders
men of God. Western monarchies might and usually did substantially reinforce their power through the ecclesiastical patronage
which they held. This was much the case in England where the kings
controlled most of the high ecclesiastical appointments, as well as
nominating to scores of lesser ones.

At the opening of the eleventh century the papacy was much too
heavily bogged down in local disorders to concern itself with
advancing contentious claims which would challenge this royal
control, and good relations between ecclesiastical and non-ecclesiastical authorities had long been strengthened by the fact that the
former had for so long undertaken invaluable social functions which
the latter had neither the wish nor the means to assume. For long
centuries the monasteries, especially, had been a civilising force
of immense value over many parts of Western Europe. In the
material sphere they had displayed the means, the will and the
patience to reclaim huge areas of the wood, scrub and marsh which
covered so much of the contemporary landscape, gradually con-
verting it into invaluable agricultural land. At a time when few lay
magnates showed much interest therein ecclesiastics extensively
patronised the visual arts and almost monopolised such interest as
there was in literacy, whilst their exhibition of that tranquil disciplined life without which a society cannot go on its way in profit
and peace was invaluable. Profound devotion to the Catholic way
of life now united all from labourers orderly or disorderly to
hermits gentle or *outré* and barons cantankerous or non-cantankerous.
But although throughout the early Middle Ages Church and State
had lived in amity, the eleventh century was not to get far along its
course before this *entente* began to show very ominous cracks.

THE IDEOLOGICAL SITUATION

Although it is undeniable that, until recently, historical writing
has often grossly underestimated the influences of non-theological
factors on the course of human affairs, it is also incontrovertible
that down the ages the course of events has been perennially and
potently influenced by the ineradicable tendency of men to seek out

and propagate answers to the major problems involved by the fact of his existence. Does the supernatural exist? If so, how is it revealed to Man? In any case what is Good and what is Evil? How far is it legitimate to enforce particular answers to such questions on those who think differently? Medieval Catholics, like modern Marxists, were well aware that such questions were far too fundamental to society to be pushed into the background, and came to hold equally clear-cut, if very different ideas, about the correct solutions to them which should be proclaimed and practised.

Today human society is sundered by irreconcilable opinions on the most socially influential of all human questions—the existence or non-existence of the supernatural. As an effective ideology atheism is barely two centuries old, and medieval man found it as unconvincing as had the great thinkers of Greece and Rome. Medieval man perceived that the supernatural emanated from a single deity and not from the childish collection of gods and goddesses so venerated in ancient Greece and Rome, and was as convinced as Beethoven that 'He who is above exists, without Him there is nothing', and as certain as Simone Weil that 'only God is worth concern: nothing else is.'

Two minority groups in the medieval West would not go along with the further Christian conviction that the one God had revealed Himself supremely and uniquely in Jesus Christ. The Jews worshipped the God of the Old Testament, holding that they themselves were the Chosen People round which its writings are focussed, and that the Christian revelation was an aberration. Small in numbers and mostly living in very scattered communities, they had no interest in proselytism and constituted a minor social influence. Their tightly knit and exclusive organisation, the never-to-be-forgotten part which some of their leaders had long ago played in securing the crucifixion of Christ, and their interest and skill in making money (a pursuit regarded with some suspicion in these times) all made them the subject of deep and mostly undeserved suspicion in the medieval West, wherein from time to time erupted very nasty local outbursts of anti-Semitism, albeit never on the modern scale. In much of Spain and in the extreme south of the Italian peninsula and Sicily, existed a sizeable Moslem population which, whilst venerating Christ as a valuable religious leader, refused Him the unique position as the Son of God basic to Christian belief, the Koran written by their founder Mahomet being their supreme authority. By the eleventh century their power over the Spanish peninsula was crumbling and it continued to do so.

With these exceptions in the eleventh century all the West was Christian, and almost all followed the historic common core of belief and worship which need not be here detailed. Because Christianity is by nature both static and dynamic, and because the relative stress on its very complex characteristics given by the faithful varies from age to age, no two periods of Christian history look exactly alike, even though all have strong family resemblances. Hence in the ecclesiastical life of the medieval West there existed certain major characteristics which were then very much more prominent than they are today.

Very dominant in it was immense concern over the question of life after death. Then, as always, Christian folk were clear that what St Francis of Assisi termed 'our brother death of the body' opened the way to a new life which was potentially very much fuller than life on earth, but in which the capacity of the individual soul to find full union with God was judged. What was the nature of this judgment? This majestic question which inspired Dante to produce the world's greatest poem and Michelangelo to paint the world's greatest picture, dominated the minds and action of the medieval West to a degree which it is most difficult for the semi-pagan society of our day to visualise, and had enormous repercussions in both theological and non-theological fields.

In their search for full understanding of the eternally difficult question of divine judgment, medieval thinkers of the West were severely handicapped by very considerable complexities of the New Testament texts on the subject which only modern research has fully revealed. Further trouble was caused by their inadequate knowledge of the very sophisticated thought of the Eastern Church. Understandably but unfortunately, medieval Western thought was much too interested in the strong legal traditions of Roman times which was a main factor in that passion for over-definition which dogged Western theology now and later. It also suffered severely from a semi-idolatrous respect for St Augustine of Hippo. His works they treated very much as a theological encyclopedia, though they combined immense and invaluable insights with some highly debatable affirmations from which the Church has suffered understandable discredit, such as the belief that those dying unbaptised would suffer serious spiritual deprivation. Similarly, if Western pre-occupation with an after-life too often verged on the neurotic, this was in no small degree because of the great concern with Purgatory in the writings of Gregory the Great, which ought to have been balanced by the much more cheerful thought of Eastern Christendom.

Over the prospects of the individual gaining a favourable verdict when finally subjected to divine judgment the mass of medieval Western opinion both literate and illiterate was decidedly pessimistic, a point which had immensely important repercussions on social life, since it led folk to take continued and elaborate precautions to ensure as far as possible that in due course they were ranked with the Blessed whose place would ultimately be on God's right hand. Without this conviction medieval almsgiving and support of the monastic life and chantries, for example, would have been much less massive than it was.

Medieval men of the West were profoundly concerned with the nature of their own fate after death. In the over-confident way of their tribe the theologians of the period gradually constructed a picture thereof which went far beyond what the historical evidence could justify. There were, they held, in all five habitats in the after-life:

(i) *Limbo of Infants*—where abode children who died unbaptised, deprived of the full vision of the Divine Being in Heaven but not subject to pain.

(ii) *Limbo of the Fathers*—where abode the Old Testament Saints with limited happiness, awaiting Christ's coming and the redemption of the world.

(iii) *Purgatory*—for souls not guilty of mortal (i.e. very grave) sin, where they underwent 'temporal' (i.e. temporary) punishment that served as reparation for wrong-doing and a means of purification.

(iv) *Heaven*—for those who needed no purification or who had been cleaned through Purgatory.

(v) *Hell*—where those who had died unrepentant of mortal sin lived in torment by eternal fire.

This picture, which today is far from being universally acceptable, was built up not on irrefutable statements in Scripture but largely by theological deductions from the very scanty biblical texts on the subject. Belief in the two Limbos is especially open to criticism and, it is to be noted, was never incorporated into the official teaching of the Church. Even more controversial is the belief that God, Who is above all things Love, would condemn individuals to live in eternal punishment. In words on this difficult question which many modern Christian thinkers would commend, the medieval author of *The Book of the Poor in Spirit* writes 'it is frequently said that God damns Man. Rather, Man damns himself, for by wilfully turning himself towards sensuality and living in it he chooses death and forgoes life. Were God to grant him life he could not accept it for he has no space in which it may be received.'

On the other hand, many besides medieval Catholics regard as not unreasonable the idea that at the time of their death no few folk would lack sufficient degree of sanctity to achieve unity with God, so would require some subsequent discipline, which is primarily constructive, not punitive. St Catharine of Genoa (d. 1510) writes 'Paradise has no gate . . . but whosoever will may enter therein, for God is all mercy and stands with open arms to admit us to glory. But, nevertheless, I see that the being of God is so pure—far more pure than can be imagined—that should a soul see in itself the least speck of imperfection, it would rather set itself in a thousand hells than go with that spot to the presence of Divine Judgment. Wherefore, seeing Purgatory established to remove such blemishes, it plunges therein and deems it great mercy that it can thus remove them. . . . The greatest pain which the souls in Purgatory endure proceeds from their being sensible of something in themselves displeasing to God.' Once purified 'they rest in God without any alloy of self; their very being is God.' Dante and many lesser men wrote of Purgatory 'where the human spirit is purged and becomes worthy to ascend to Heaven.'

To be fair to medieval theologians it is to be noted that their teaching only threatened with eternal punishment those who died unrepentant of mortal sin, so that in the last resort the individual's own repentance even at the moment of death was all that was needed. Complete freedom from the pains of hell was guaranteed to those who with sincerity confessed their sins to a priest and obtained through him divine absolution therefrom. The importance of death-bed confession was, therefore, very heavily stressed in medieval times and as most of the faithful lived in small communities with a priest at hand and none of the great variety of possibilities of sudden death provided by modern technology, the proportion of the faithful who died unconfessed must mostly have been small.

However, in these times the perennially dangerous gap between what the Church officially taught and what the laity in fact believed was certainly very pronounced over this question of the nature of life beyond the grave, and there is not the slightest doubt that the latter maintained extraordinary misapprehensions on the question, notably through frequently failing to distinguish between the pains of Hell and those of Purgatory. Of the manifold illustrations of these gross misapprehensions which abound in medieval Western literature a case detailed by the very reputable chronicler William of Malmesbury is worthy of consideration here.

He relates that two men were so gravely concerned about their fate after death that they agreed that the first of them to die should report back to the other on his situation in a dream. This duly came to pass. The dead man opened with the reassuring declaration (which one would have thought unnecessary in a Christian context) that the Platonic tenet was correct in asserting that death does not extinguish the soul and lead it to 'vanish into the air or mix with the wind' as believed by 'the sect of the Epicureans', but he went on to create despondency and alarm by declaring 'I am doomed by a sentence which has been pronounced and ratified to eternal punishment.' Rather gratuitously, he proceeded to display a message written on one of his hands in black characters wherein Satan and 'the whole infernal company' sent their thanks from Hell to the whole body of ecclesiastics, both for denying themselves no single pleasure and for, by their neglect of preaching, sending more of their souls to Hell than any other age had ever witnessed. The crudities of this anecdote need no stress, and could be very easily paralleled from similar literature which leaves us in no doubt that many medieval Catholics developed the same sort of 'hellfire complex' which afflicted no few Victorian Protestants.

On this it may be observed that a crude society is bound to swallow crude ideas, and also that in crude times crude ideas may not be without salutary effects. Certainly the deep trepidation with which medieval men viewed the approach of death and judgment again and again led them to turn to good behaviour. The undisciplined king William Rufus 'supposing himself to be at the point of death ... vowed to God, as the barons suggested to him, that he would amend his life ... that he would abolish unjust laws and enact just ones.' Of such amelioration many similar instances can be found. The recipient of the dream just noted was so affected by the horrifying message which he received that he accepted also the advice added to it by the visitant to give all his properties to monasteries and to the poor, and to spend days in fasting and prayer and to 'change your habit, change your disposition, become a monk at Rennes in the monastery of St Melania.' The argument of modern authorities that the prevalence of crime in recent days owes much to the fact that those implicated in it see no resultant disadvantage beyond the possibility of being caught, could not have been urged in the medieval West.

However, though medieval men regarded the acquisition of eternal bliss in the after-life as hard to come by, they did not regard it as beyond their reach. In its attainment prayer was a major weapon. Especially to be valued were the prayers of top people in the world spiritual. Did not the *Epistle of St James* declare 'tremendous power is made available through the earnest prayers of a good man'? And were not the obvious good men the saints, no few of whom, in friendly fashion looked down from the walls and windows of men's parish churches? To the folk of these times such saints were every bit as beloved and helpful as are the pop-stars and athletes of television to modern audiences. Specially to be venerated was the patron saint of a man's local community. The medieval folk of Durham never doubted that the Almighty had put in perpetual charge of their welfare St Cuthbert, whose bones lay treasured in their cathedral. The Venetians had exactly the same confidence in St Mark, whose bones had been so brilliantly smuggled through the customs at Alexandria *en route* for their city, and whose emblem of the lion they persistently splattered all over the town—'I cannot help thinking that the Venetians went a little queer about lions' writes an admirable exponent of Venetian life 'for the profusion of stone lions in Venice is almost unbelievable' (J. Morris). Immensely valuable were the prayers of Our Lady, for every good son pays special attention to his mother's requests and Christ could properly help a man further than mere justice would allow through love of His earthly mother. But all holy people were not dead people. There were the monks and nuns giving themselves so totally to God in the monasteries all over the West. They were good people whose prayers too must be sought. As time went on, in their search for outside spiritual help medieval Western folk increasingly added to the prayers of holy people, living and departed, the spiritual benefits of private Masses—celebrations of the Mass attended by few or none save the priest and his server, in which special intercession was made for a certain specified person or persons.

But to medieval folk prayer alone was always inadequate—it must be accompanied by its spiritual twin, almsgiving. 'As a body is dead when there is no breath left in it, so faith divorced from deeds is lifeless as a corpse,' declared the *Epistle of St James*, and this medieval men believed with the very greatest intensity, as is shown in Chapter 13. To term almsgiving 'the favourite pastime of the middle ages' as one expert once did, is to misunderstand and under-rate it, for it was not to men of the time a minor pre-occupation resulting from hazy feelings of social goodwill, but a most funda-mental element in the life of the followers of Christ, who must be simultaneously lovers of God and helpers of Man. Like most actions, of course, it could be performed from purely selfish motives but at its best it was of much wider scope, as is illustrated by the foundation charter of St Paul's hospital set up in Norwich by Bishop Losinga. Herein he declares that he has founded the place 'for the maintenance of the poor of God ... for the good of my soul and the good of all the benefactors of that place' and orders 'let all the people dwelling in the said hospital ... hear the service of God in the aforesaid church of St Paul and securely praise God for us and for all Christians alive and dead.' (The prayers of poor people who, after all, were 'poor as Christ was poor' seem to have been specially valued by medieval folk—the idea that a wealthy society was automatically a good society they would regard as semi-crazy.)

A further distinctive characteristic of the medieval Western Church was its very profound admiration for what is known as 'asceticism'. This word and practice had originated in pre-Christian times amongst thoughtful pagans who perceived that a fruitful and lofty life could only be achieved through constant acts of self-discipline, and has been defined as 'a system of practices designed to combat vice and develop virtue such as were employed not only by many philosophers but also in some Eastern religions, especially Buddhism.' The very far-reaching demands of the Christian way of

life, with its insistent call to perfection, inevitably demanded a
corresponding high degree of discipline where the things of this
world were concerned. 'If a man would come after Me let him deny
himself,' said Christ, and St Paul early stressed the immense importance of nurturing the spirit of self-denial by constant discipline.
'Every competitor in athletic events goes into serious training' said
he. 'I run the race with determination, I am no shadow boxer, I
really fight, I am my body's sternest master'—words of which the
incomparable Muhammad Ali would approve. These words inaugurated and inspired that comparison of the disciplined life of
the Christian to the disciplined life of the athlete, that was much
used hereafter and led, *inter alia*, to Christian saints being sometimes
termed 'athletes of God'.

What did this discipline involve for the Christian? To this
question experience soon showed that there was no single answer.
Obviously all were called to such obligations as almsgiving and
fasting, to a use of sex which did not enslave the individual concerned or infringe the happiness of others, and above all to the
discipline and delight of systematic worship. But St Paul was only
the first of a long and fruitful line of Christian enthusiasts who found
himself called to happiness through a much less extensive use of the
things of the world. Celibacy he found fundamental to his work
and commended it vigorously to his followers. Perception of its
value grew steadily in Christian circles and from the late Roman
times onwards was marked. By this time also voluntary poverty
was found a useful asset to the minority thereto called, whilst the
spiritual fruitfulness of a communal life was also so much appreciated
that by the fourth century it had come to be regarded as the life *par
excellence* of the Christian, following the reference in the *Acts of the
Apostles* to that first church at Jerusalem having 'one heart and soul
and all things in common'. If, as Eastern and Western Churches alike
steadily did from now on, we put together celibacy, voluntary
poverty and the common life, we have all the ingredients of the
monastic life and this form of Christian living enjoyed in the
medieval West a high prestige which our sex-ridden age finds hard
to visualise. Medieval man realised that costliness was an essential of
the Christian life and here was Christian costliness on a grand scale
presenting challenge and inspiration. Throughout our period,
though somewhat less at its close than at its opening, the monastic

life reigned over men's hearts as the supreme Christian way of life, offering greater facilities for self-realisation and a more sure and safer route to salvation than any other. Though only the enthusiastic minority might adopt it, the rest would admire it and give vigorous support to those men and women who lived what was often equated with the 'apostolic life' (*vita apostolica*).

Non-Theological Elements

Various of the non-theological elements present in medieval Western life are of little or no import for the comprehension of contemporary church life, but others to greater or lesser degree significantly influenced the course and shape of ecclesiastical developments.

Of these latter, in various ways most important, was that illiteracy which dominated such large sectors of the society of Western Europe at this time. By the eleventh century it had long become an accepted fact of life that the ability to read and write was by no means a universally desirable attainment but, like knowledge of nuclear physics today, was a specialised skill, and only appropriate for that element of society almost all of whose members in one sense or another could be regarded as ecclesiastics. This illiteracy was not due to the desire of the wicked clergy to keep the laity ignorant so as to render them more amenable, but was the result of deep-rooted and widespread non-theological factors which had very severely sapped Western interest in that devotion to literacy which had been one of the corner-stones of the way of life of classical Greece and Rome. The aristocracy (if such it may be called) of Western Europe in the Dark Ages were dominated by a barbarian outlook which saw no obvious value in literacy, the more so since this did not seem particularly relevant to that agricultural way of life which had so widely supplanted the urban life of Roman times. As Alfred the Great and Charlemagne both discovered, the task of interesting their nobles in the strange arts of reading and writing was more than even their own immense enthusiasm and vigour could achieve.

Although written transactions in these times could not be entirely written off by the laity, they were now minimal. That the now very frail plant of learning survived effectively in the West was very largely because it was recognised as indispensable to their work by the great ecclesiastical institutions of the time, notably the cathedrals (though their interest was very apt to be sporadic and shortlived) and the much more important and vigorous monasteries whose now very elaborate round of daily worship could not be conducted without much recourse to reading and whose varied activities demanded also a knowledge of writing. The very widespread illiteracy of society at this time was intensified by what moderns must regard, at first sight, as the curious conviction that Latin was the only respectable medium for literary communication, a belief which had for some time a good deal to commend it (page 384).

A second non-theological factor which had major repercussions on ecclesiastical, as on non-ecclesiastical life, was the extreme inadequacy of communications in the medieval West. There was now nothing to replace the Roman signal stations whose transmissions had ceased so long ago, whilst if some old Roman roads stayed in use, their condition in medieval times too often resembled those of eighteenth-century England which a contemporary pamphleteer pleasingly described as 'what God left them after the Flood'. The maintenance of bridges was often equally neglected, with the result that only too often, both figuratively and literally, they let people down. Water transport tended to be easier and pleasanter but had obvious limitations. The result was that travelling was an immensely time-consuming process; numerous medieval itineraries show very clearly that even if a man rode instead of going on foot he often could not count on averaging much more than about twenty miles a day.

Immensely important also for ecclesiastics, especially the highest of them, were the effects of the insubstantial governmental machinery which in England, as in most of the West, prevailed throughout much of medieval times. Social and economic factors here prevented the existence of the massive central governments and powerful local bureaucracies to which we are now conditioned. The machinery which served William the Conqueror and his successors for long to come, though not unimpressive by contemporary standards, was far from puissant and inescapably left the charge of considerable sectors of government to great local magnates, both lay and ecclesiastical, with the result *inter alia* that, as has been well said, 'medieval England was a confederation' (Jolliffe).

Intimately intertwined with this constitutional fragility was the prevalence in these times of what is termed a natural economy, a fact which had immense ecclesiastical repercussions. In much of the medieval West the old Roman economy with its capitalistic characteristics of huge supplies of currency and massive loans and taxes, had been largely replaced by a set-up in which trade and industry played a relatively small part. In medieval England the life of the great mass of the population was local and agricultural and had very limited use for coinage, which for some time existed only on a very minor scale. Instead, payments great and small were made in kind, involving a wide range of things from lands and buildings to corn, wine, eggs and manual labour. Thus William the Conqueror's rewards to the magnates who helped him to take and hold the kingdom of England did not take the form of fat cheques or clinking money-bags, but were principally gifts of property which often had attached to them legal privileges that enhanced their value.

The king himself drew little of his revenues in cash in Norman England. 'Our fathers have told us that in the original constitution after the Conquest no sums of gold or silver were paid to the king from crown lands but victuals only', notes a twelfth-century Exchequer official, and a document of about 1136 shows us that the Chancellor of England received as part salary 5s. a day, three loaves of simnel bread, an allowance of wine, one large wax candle and forty candle ends, the latter being much more desirable adjuncts than might now seem feasible in ages which knew not electricity or gas. The same document shows us that some creditors paid their dues to the Crown in the form of hawks, though these were not to be presented at Easter 'because there is so little use for them in summer'. Lowly folk like clerks and cooks might be paid in part by doles of food and clothing, as were the manifold pensioners attached to medieval monasteries. As is well known, many peasants fulfilled obligations to their lords in the form of labour services and renders of agricultural produce, whilst medieval clergy received a major part of their income in the form of tithes (tenth parts) of produce.

Three other points are to be noted, though none of them is peculiarly medieval in character. The first of these is the continued dominance of the conviction so strong in ancient Greece and Rome that men are born unequal. 'Some men are born to be slaves,' the mighty Aristotle had declared, and although the medieval West showed remarkable pertinacity in getting rid of its slavery, men accepted social inequality as unquestioningly as the author of the post-Reformation jingle 'God bless the squire and his relations, and keep us in our proper stations.' They themselves divided society into three groups, 'Those who fight, those who work and those who pray.' The first of the categories comprised the king, the barons and lesser dignitaries whose primary function it was to maintain the good order of society. The second (curiously anticipating Marxism on the point), reserved the title of worker to those who used their hands much more than their brains, a forgivable lapse in days when society was overwhelmingly agricultural. The third consisted largely of clergy, monks and nuns by whose labours man would find union with God. Like all such midget social definitions, this one oversimplified the situation, allotting no place to the small but growing class of lawyers and civil servants or to tradesmen (a group which now, as in Victorian times, was regarded with some distaste). In practice these distinctions were very far from absolute. A clerk might be in effect a layman even if technically an ecclesiastic. Able lads from back-of-beyond villages, like Thomas Beckington, could rise to hold mighty bishoprics and bright sons of the bourgeoisie like Thomas Becket and Thomas Wolsey achieve top posts in Church and State. Public schools were not reserved for the well-to-do.

Secondly, there should be noted that there now prevailed an important negative factor which has characterised almost all human history until very recent times—the very minor interest in the study of the theory and practice of economics, a subject which only came to attract serious attention under pressure of the immense complexities of modern industrial society. To reproach medieval men for their neglect of this would clearly be absurdly anachronistic, though it may be admitted that some delving into it would have lightened the heavy burden of poverty or semi-poverty with which they tended to be faced, and with which they battled in most vigorous but very unskilled fashion.

Finally, it is most important to appreciate how little superfluous wealth there was around in medieval England. The more closely we scrutinise its society the clearer it becomes that though the folk of these times were mostly not faced with the grinding poverty of Victorian industrialism many of them were placed in that condition of 'living and hardly living' which T. S. Eliot so acutely ascribed to the people of Canterbury in the days of Becket. Of this widespread absence of high living standards indications are very visible in all levels of society. At first sight the majestic castles, cathedrals and monastic ruins still so evident in England would appear to contradict this, but close scrutiny shows that this is not the case. So far as the middle classes are concerned, their fascinating wills which survive in great number show clearly how very limited were the personal possessions of even the comparatively well-to-do. Very few of them indeed have more than a tiny number of books or pieces of plate (which last were of course a primitive form of investment), their other personal effects were mostly far from extensive and loose cash in very short supply. In the countryside where most people lived, in many areas, despite the high death rate, as for long before and long after, it must often have been quite impossible for a farmer to provide all his children with their own separate ménage, whilst in high society, for different reasons, baronial estates could not be split up indefinitely amongst children and children's children, provision for daughters and younger sons being often meagre. The very minor proportions of industry in medieval England, the very small-sized staffs of both central and local government and the very minor part played by education in these times meant that the wide range of employments today available simply did not exist, and there can be not the slightest doubt that the proportion of the population whose members could at this time hope to have their own house and everything handsome about them was minute.

NON-THEOLOGICAL EFFECTS

The influence on the social and religious life of the medieval West of that high degree of illiteracy which therein prevailed was very considerable indeed. The allied contemporary difficulty of adequately checking much of the information current often rendered it immensely difficult for even intelligent folk to distinguish between fact and fiction, and allowed currency to a considerable amount of knowledge which was bogus, not least in the field of history. Thus Oxford University was now said to have been established by King Alfred three centuries before, in fact, its first scholars assembled, whilst its rival at Cambridge was claimed to have had as its founder the much more venerable Prince Cantaber who, however, suffered from the not inconsiderable disadvantage of never having existed. This disability he shared with several of the minor saints of England including the aptly named St Uncumber, whose statue may still be seen in Westminster Abbey. She was believed to have been entrusted by the deity with the delicate task of removing to the next world, with all reasonable speed and due regard to divine law, husbands whose continued presence here below was found by their spouses to be undesirable.

Similar disregard for historical reality was much evident in the struggle for pride of place between the great abbeys of Glastonbury and Westminster. After both had claimed foundation by the mythical second century King Lucius, the former produced as its trump card the claim that no less venerable a person than St Joseph of Arimethaea had preached and expired on its premises leaving behind the Holy Grail (the cup used by Christ at the Last Supper). In the field of zoology also, men firmly believed in the unbelievable, such as the existence of colourful creatures like the dragon, the unicorn, the griffin and the salamander. Now, and for long to come, it was held that an elephant had no joints in its legs, and so could be captured by sawing half-way through the tree against which it was accustomed to lean during slumber. This would, of course, lead to it crashing helpless to the ground, thereby providing a useful spiritual comparison with Adam who also 'fell through a tree'. With today's tales of spacemen and flying saucers, its manifold astrological asininities and the fascinating myths about the British royal family to be found in various week-end papers, medieval men would feel much at home*.

On contemporary church life this illiteracy had major effects. Thus, in combination with the allied high cost of books, it made it quite impossible for the mass of the congregation to follow the complex services of the times in the modern manner. As a result, the visual side of worship was shrewdly developed in a way which made it perfectly possible for the illiterate to follow its general course.

Now, as ever, the fact that illiteracy was widespread among the

---

* The ignorance of contemporary conditions caused by the huge gaps in official documentation could have remarkable results. When under Edward III it was decided to tax the parishes of England it was airily held that these numbered about 40 000 though investigation showed the total to be under 9000!

laity inevitably did much to limit the learning of the clergy who so unhappily had to emanate therefrom, even though it must be admitted that the situation here was rendered far worse than it need have been through the disinterest in the important matter of training the clergy shown by many bishops of the times, which Knowles has properly termed 'always the blindspot of the medieval religious world'. Though literacy is by no means the sole necessity for a priest and is no inevitable guarantee of true piety, its absence of course entailed serious problems which were much magnified through the contemporary insistence on conducting public worship in Latin. Of clerical ignorance in this field many a story is told. When a thirteenth-century English bishop unsportingly decided to test his clergy's Latinity and enquired of one of them what governed the first word in the sentence of the Mass which begins *Te igitur*, he elicited the wildish response 'God for he governeth all things.' Amongst the clergy of Archbishop Becket's diocese was one whose piety so exceeded his learning that the only form of the Mass which he felt competent to employ was that for the feasts of Our Lady which he proceeded to use on all other occasions. However, it is at least to be remembered that such gross ignorance as this appeared very much less reprehensible then than it does now, since with all their inadequacies, the clergy were indubitably much more literate than almost all the laity they served.

Quite different were the disabilities which the clergy suffered through the fact that most of them received so much of their income in kind, a situation aggravated by the necessity to arrange for the collection thereof themselves. The payer might be obstreperous or forgetful or both, and the question of assessment was not always easy—who, for example, was to have the tithe of sheep which spent the day munching in one parish but slept the night in another? Again and again we find the question of payment of such clerical income causing frustration and friction. The noted intellectual Peter of Blois, having, somewhat imprudently, accepted the archdeaconery of London, wrote dolefully to the pope that, although the city had 40 000 inhabitants and 120 churches, he could obtain neither tithes, first-fruits nor offerings but had to live 'like a dragon on wind'. Yet he fared better than poor Bishop Adam of Caithness whose diocese lay in a land notorious for what a contemporary bishop of Worcester termed 'unmitigated barbarity'. In 1222 some of the flock of the bishop proceeded to demonstrate their disapproval of ecclesiastical exactions in very unambiguous fashion by roasting to death their unfortunate father in God. Not altogether reasonable objections to paying tithe were to last as long as tithe itself, totally abolished in England only in recent times.

The complications introduced into medieval ecclesiastical life by the conditions traditionally termed feudal were very far-reaching and very galling even if for long there was no very obvious way of phasing out most of them. Very undesirable indeed were the strains imposed on major ecclesiastics—largely diocesan bishops and the heads of great monasteries. They were saddled with a variety of secular responsibilities similar to those incumbent upon lay barons, which repeatedly produced undesirable complications and distractions. Thus in post-Conquest England such major ecclesiastics might be laden with judicial responsibilities which could involve the very onerous task of acting as justice of assize. Some might have charge of royal castles and royal treasure and, as time went on, many got heavily involved in the assessment and collection of both royal and papal taxes. From the late thirteenth century onwards all the diocesan bishops of England and a variable selection of the heads of English monasteries were liable to be summoned to the new thing called Parliament, thereby being liable to involvement in tedious travel which usually brought them little or no advantage. From the royal angle various of such labours had the advantage of saving the Crown considerable expense and obtaining the service of men who were like to have greater integrity and much less concern for family interests than the lay barons—three bishops appointed royal justices in 1179 owed their selection to the conviction that 'as hearers of God they would not oppress the poor or accept bribes.' But from the ecclesiastical angle such responsibilities were highly disadvantageous, diverting from the matters ecclesiastical to which such prelates owed primary responsibility much valuable time, thought and money.

The time factor, indeed, was of great importance in these times, unavoidably slow travel and lack of such things as the telephone creating very undesirable complications. Post-medieval kings, bishops and barons might live happily in some central residence on resources drawn from afar, but under medieval economic and social conditions it was often necessary for them to go to their resources, not their resources to them. Thus medieval kings might move around the country not only for political reasons but to reside on outlying estates. Bishops similarly were much on the move in their over-large dioceses and out of them, for both business and economic reasons. 'A medieval bishop was seldom long in one place,' writes Hamilton Thompson, and he goes on to point out that the archbishops of York had regular residences within their archdioceses at Cawood, Bishopthorpe, Bishop Burton, Bishop Wilton, Ripon, Otley, Bishop Monkton, Southwell, Scrooby and Laneham-on-Trent, as well as two others in Gloucestershire and two in Northumberland. The bishops of Lincoln had nine such bases in their sprawling diocese and even the somewhat penurious bishops of Carlisle had five, of which three were within their diocese, one in Derbyshire and one in Lincolnshire. Of Bishop Richard de Swinfield of Hereford the editor of his fascinating account roll of the year 1289-90 comments 'looking at his wanderings as set forth in his registers and in this roll, and the many roofs beneath which he sheltered, it is difficult to answer the question which was really his home.'

Some, though not all, of the travel thus involved was both inevitable and useful, since without it the bishop would have been unable to carry out major functions in his diocese which only he could perform, but under contemporary conditions the travel involved was immensely time-consuming and created in the larger dioceses problems to which no satisfactory solution was feasible. Thus the large number of monasteries in the populous diocese of Norwich could not possibly be visited by their father in God with the frequency desirable without making impossibly large inroads into his limited time, so they were unlikely to see their bishop more than very rarely. If the archbishop of York chose to visit the parts of Cumbria and Lancashire which belonged to his diocese he would engross a very large amount of time in visiting a very thinly populated area. When Archbishop Wickwane did this in 1281 it took him two whole months, as well as involving travel which, even by medieval standards, was highly unpleasant, including the crossing of three tidal estuaries. Unsurprisingly, the archbishops of York largely handed over spiritual responsibilities of this area to the archdeacon of Richmond and assistant bishops, so that the proportion of the medieval faithful therein which ever saw their archbishop must have been microscopic. The same problem of shortage of time was largely responsible for the archbishops and bishops confirming candidates for the confirmation not by laying hands on them individually as good ancient custom demanded, but in a very abbreviated form and often greatly neglecting to perform it. However, it is worth noting that the primitive communications of medieval times did have the major spiritual advantage of sparing bishops the plethora of telephone calls and committees which plague their modern successors and tended to confer on clerical assemblies a commendable brevity.

SECULARISATION AND REFORM

THE PROBLEM OF SECULARISATION

Of all the problems which confronted the medieval church in the West, very much the most serious and most stubborn was that of 'secularisation', a term which denotes the diversion to private profit of ecclesiastical appointments and revenues. This was endemic and was effected pertinaciously by various methods, of which some were very crude, whilst others contrived to keep within the letter if not the spirit of the law.

At its worst secularisation might be carried out by force or threat of force, a man being intruded into an ecclesiastical office or emolument and maintained in possession thereof contrary to the reasonable rules of the Church and spiritual interest of the faithful. In other cases appointments great and small as well as ordination were obtained by means of financial payments to the relevant authority—a practice known as 'simony'. But it was also feasible to secularise things ecclesiastical without such flagrant breaches of the law, since contemporary ecclesiastical practice did not rule out automatically any participation of the laity in the making of ecclesiastical appointments.

So far as the appointment of a cleric to a parish church was concerned it had long been accepted by medieval Westerners that the initiative in filling the vacancy came from the 'patron' of the office concerned, who was either its founder or, very much more often, the founder's legal representative. The patron was often a layman but might also be a cleric or an ecclesiastical corporation such as a cathedral, secular college or monastery. The office of the holder of a parish church was mostly known as a 'benefice' and the legal right to nominate to it as the 'advowson'. The first move in filling the benefice was the nomination of a candidate to the bishop of the diocese concerned by the patron. This person the bishop could only refuse to accept if he found him unsatisfactory on one or more of several counts. Of these heresy (i.e. major theological dissent) was one, but was very rare in medieval England. After the Conquest marriage was gradually established as another bar with considerable if not total success. Much more troublesome and common was the lack of that good character or education essential if the holder of a parochial charge (who came to be known as the 'incumbent') was to be an effective pastor. But if the bishop turned down a nomination on these grounds he might find himself in an awkward position. He would certainly thereby offend the patron and he himself had no legal right to put in a more suitable candidate of his own. In any case very suitable candidates were often so rare that it might seem advisable to accept the nominee and hope that he would improve with time. Certainly medieval bishops accepted no few clergy who today would be regarded as very sub-standard.

The much more lucrative appointments in secular cathedrals and colleges were usually made by nomination, and were also legally benefices with all the complications which such status involved. The heads of these places, as well as those of monasteries, were theoretically chosen by the brethren of the place at a meeting of their 'chapter'. The head of a monastery (most of which were houses of men) was however a person of importance and, in cases of great monasteries, of great importance, so it is not surprising that the patron of the place concerned often showed interest in the selection of a new head. When the post (whether of abbot or prior depending on whether the house ranked as an abbey or a priory) was vacant a fairly complex procedure for electing his successor got under way which entailed some degree of consultation with the patron, and the same was the case with vacant bishoprics of all of which in England the king was patron, though for legal reasons consent of the chapter was essential.

The extent of royal influence over church appointments varied very greatly with the position of the monarchy concerned. In England from a very early stage the kings were very much masters in their own country, and as a result, had extensive rights of patronage, in practice sweeping into their net appointment of all the bishops of the country and of the heads of almost all the major monasteries and many lesser ones, as well as of scores of parish churches of which some few had revenues at which their rising civil servants might not sniff. Barons might be patrons of one or more monasteries and of parish churches in very varying degree, whilst in the countryside now, as throughout subsequent English history, the local lord of the manor was often patron of the parish church that stood on the far side of his garden wall.

It is thus evident that medieval practice was very far from excluding lay participation in the making of ecclesiastical appointments. Though there was in the eleventh century an extremist element which disapproved of this, it was never influential, since realism dictated recognition of the harsh fact that lay patronage was much too firmly embedded in the structure of contemporary society to be dislodged. What was very open to criticism and received it in no small measure in post-Conquest England as elsewhere, was the fact that at all levels there were far too many people being appointed to ecclesiastical offices who had no deep interest in clerical life and few of the requisite qualifications for it.

In cases where the higher appointments were bought and sold or simply grabbed by some local miscreant the consequences for the work of the Church might be very severe, with ecclesiastical property being temporarily or permanently lost and the likelihood of one bad appointment leading to others, thus stifling interest in reform. Such catastrophes were very common in certain parts of the eleventh-century West, such as Italy and southern France, but apparently were much less grave in England.

Besides the spiritual shortcomings bred by secularisation a bad appointment (e.g. of a non-resident clerk) might lead to serious diminution of that hospitality which was a major responsibility of medieval clergy high and low. Herein the resources of most parish churches were not of a kind which would be extensively alienated permanently, but with major posts like deaneries, canonries and bishoprics, the endowments and property pertaining to them could easily be passed to others by an unworthy holder and might be difficult or impossible to regain after his death. In this connection it is most important to note that increased impetus was likely to be given to secularisation when, as was long the case, a considerable proportion of the clergy were married. The temptation for a priest or bishop with a quiverful of children to provide married portions and the like out of the possessions pertaining to his office was obviously much too strong to be uniformly resisted, and such possessions once alienated might also be most difficult to recover at a later stage.

Although a massive campaign against secularisation was mounted which was by no means without success, it is quite certain that despite it, in England as elsewhere, secularisation of ecclesiastical offices and revenues went on to some considerable degree, albeit sometimes in a disguised form. Major cathedral appointments in England were steadily and heavily utilised to support royal servants by kings who, though almost all in principle on the side of the angels, persistently picked ecclesiastical pockets in a series of ways. Lower down the scale, reasonably pious nobles and squires were accustomed to put into their parish churches people quite untrained for the work involved and sometimes not even in priest's orders.

What were the reasons for this curious paradox? The complete answer cannot be made without much more knowledge of certain aspects of medieval life than we now have, but certain explanations may be tentatively suggested.

In the first place it can be fairly argued that the royal intervention here can up to some point be excused as being one of those 'special cases' so beloved by the trade unionist of our day. Certain royal exactions, as we shall see, could not be regarded as very baneful, given the circumstances of the time, whilst others might be excused by them. An advocate of royalty might argue with some reason that since great magnates like the English bishops were in fact barons, and mostly very wealthy ones at that, it was reasonable that their resources should be markedly tapped for the needs of the Crown. The good order and fine justice which the English kings steadily built up in post-Conquest times was an expensive commodity, and the crude economic and social structure of the time for long made it impossible for the Crown to raise great sums in the modern fashion from the mass of the populace, whilst its own revenues were not intended to run an elaborate machinery of government and were utterly inadequate for such a task. These things being so, it seemed excusable if not theoretically commendable, that the Crown should lessen the undoubtedly heavy strain on its own resources by utilising ecclesiastical appointments and resources in various ways, provided, as was usually the case, that adequate provision was made for the maintenance of the ecclesiastical duties attached to the post.

A second reason for the insatiable secularisation of ecclesiastical resources in medieval times may be tentatively advanced, though it is as yet little explored. If, as seems likely, contemporary social and economic conditions in medieval England produced amongst other things only a very limited number of posts which would provide both a reasonable income and an independent household it is likely enough that a main reason why so many men drifted into the ranks of the parish clergy without any strong sense of vocation, was the fact that they found therein one of the very few comparatively easy ways of acquiring employment which gave them a house, income and security of tenure. Certainly we find indications that a family living was regarded as a useful social perquisite. Mostly these are implicit, as when a younger son of the local squire is found holding the benefice of which his father was patron, but sometimes references are more explicit. Thus the will of the Earl of Arundel (1392) provides that if at the time of his death a particular living in his patronage should be vacant, it should be offered to either of his sons, if they were content to be ordained, otherwise to a certain clerk on his staff, but should he be dead or unwilling to accept nomination 'then I will that it be presented to my next of kin who may be able to hold it.' But it must be admitted that we know so very little about the social backgrounds of the vast majority of the secular clergy of medieval England that most generalisations on the matter must contain a large element of uncertainty.

However, it would certainly be unrealistic to regard the extensive medieval secularisation of church property as due principally to these extenuating factors. Unless, as can scarcely be argued, human nature then was very different from what it has been before and after, there can be little doubt that the principal factor at work was that love of money which an Old Testament writer found to be 'the root of all evil'. History shows very clearly that where money and position are to be had there will men be fighting for them. The wave of lust for wealth which swept over English society at the time of the Dissolution of the Monasteries, the insistent wage claims of our own affluent society, the corruption found at so many royal courts down the ages as well as in no few modern governments,

all illustrate this ever-present passion for wealth in human society—
'where the carcase is there will vultures be gathered together.'

The absurdity of believing that medieval secularisation was
primarily due to poverty can easily be spectacularly illustrated. In
thirteenth-century England one Bogo de Clare was the greatest of
all contemporary English pluralists, holding at one time no less than
twenty-nine ecclesiastical appointments, yet he was no penurious
parvenu but a son of the Earl of Gloucester and Hertford. A century
later there followed in his footsteps William of Wykeham who, as
Chancellor and bishop of Winchester held what were probably the
two wealthiest posts in the realm, but found it necessary to make
much more than doubly sure that the necessity of plain living did
not rear its horrid head by collecting two dozen other ecclesiastical
appointments.

THE UNDERTAKING OF REFORM

One of the principal reasons for the non-arrival of that demise of
the Christian Church which has so often been confidently predicted,
is her ever-present capacity to seek out and remedy her imper-
fections. Christian history is, indeed, an unbroken process of reformation, though the scope and durability of this has varied greatly
down the centuries. In the five centuries which followed the collapse
of Roman rule in the West the Church there was confronted with
very massive problems, mostly due largely to non-theological
factors. These her enthusiastic members strove manfully to solve,
though the instability of contemporary society inevitably greatly
circumscribed the effects of much of their work.

But in the course of the eleventh century the various rivers and
rivulets of local reform which survived, were steadily united and
reinforced by a powerful new movement of ecclesiastical renewal
which, if it did not achieve all that its more extreme proponents
desired, certainly purified and strengthened most remarkably the
life of the Western Church. For such an advance circumstances were
now favourable. The long series of barbarian invasions which had
caused so much chaos were now terminated. Everywhere Christianity was the supreme ideology and its strength was unsapped by any
great theological conflicts. Local monarchies had neither the power
nor the will to enslave the Church. Catholic worship inspired an

attachment that was widespread and profound and in no few areas a flourishing monastic life flashed out to the thoughtful believer its perennial reminder that, in the last resort, the kingdom of God is a kingdom not of this world. But now, as always in religious crises, the decisive factor was the personal one—the appearance of a remarkable body of enthusiasts who have come to be known as the Gregorian Reformers from the fact that their most famous devotee was the formidable Pope Gregory VII (1073–85). Its early members were a small band of Italian ecclesiastics, mostly monks, who worked in close liaison with the reformed papacy and united with utter devotion to duty, as they saw it, no small shrewdness and a truly magnificent capacity for fulmination.

The passionate attack on a wide front which they now launched was inspired by the noble ideal of raising the spiritual standard of living of their Church, principally by securing far better ecclesiastical appointments than the often scandalous ones which confronted them in their own country. So far as the nominations of parish clergy were concerned they had little room to manoeuvre, since the rights of lay and other patrons were much too deeply rooted to be removed. Appointments of bishops and monastic superiors were much more important, both in their own right and because of the influence which their holders had over lesser posts. They were also somewhat easier to attack since, at least in theory, they were effected through election by a chapter of ecclesiastics and not by mere nomination. The Gregorians fought vigorously to ensure that these capitular elections should be as free in practice as they were in theory. However, to effect this involved attacking a mighty array of vested interests, financial and social.

Opposition to the Reformers was much intensified at lower levels by their equally vigorous claim that henceforth, with very minor exceptions, all clergy in major orders should be unmarried. This contention they pushed so far as to forbid the laity to attend the Masses celebrated by married clergy by a very questionable line of argument which was vigorously opposed. To the question of clerical celibacy church history shows that there is no obvious and easy solution. As has been noted, from the time of St Paul an influential stream of Christian opinion greatly admired the celibate life, principally because of the freedom which it gave to devote to good works the time, thought and money which married life inexorably demands, though celibacy amongst the clergy had moral but no legal authority in the West until in the fifth century. Then gross abuses of secularisation of things ecclesiastical similar to those which faced the Gregorian Reformers six hundred years later, led the papacy to insist that clergy in higher orders should not marry either before ordination or after it. This rule was never current in the Eastern Church and in the West was far from uniformly accepted in practice. Certainly by the early eleventh century in many areas marriage of the clergy was very widespread indeed. Inevitably, the attempts by the Gregorian Reformers to enforce once more celibacy of the clergy in major orders led to storms of protest both from conservative laity—and in medieval times the great mass of laity were conservative—as well as from many clergy undispassionately urged on, one may suspect, by their spouses. The legal precedent for banning marriage of the higher orders of clergy was, of course, not overwhelming Christian practice hereon, but under contemporary social conditions clerical celibacy certainly provided invaluable safeguards against gross abuses and appealed strongly to some.

Further opposition to the Gregorian Reformers was excited by the very radical conception of papal authority *vis-à-vis* local churches which they propounded with all their usual extremism. Though they did not regard the papacy as an absolute despotism—there were various non-theological matters which were unlikely to come within the range of its authority—the pope they held to be the God-given guardian of the morals of society with the inalienable duty of checking evil behaviour, notably at top ecclesiastical level where local authority might not prove effective. Further, the Roman court or 'curia' was the final court of appeal in all matters of Christian belief and conduct, and to it all the faithful should be allowed unhampered access. The official representative of the popes, notably the top-ranking ones termed 'legates', had the right to visit unhindered any local church and there hold councils, publish decrees, carry out enquiries and effect reforms without let or hindrance. The pope himself as the Vicar (i.e. legal representative) of Christ could summon councils whose decrees were binding on the faithful, could call bishops to his presence and depose them if they failed to appear. Such a concept of papal authority involved nothing less than a revolution in Western machinery and, for better or for worse, could scarcely be justified on grounds of ancient practice.

With the blithe disregard for the *via media* which makes them at once so colourful and so infuriating, the Gregorian Reformers proceeded to an equally radical thinking of the place of monarchy in Christian society. Downgrading the deep-rooted traditional view that monarchy was a great and God-given thing, they regarded kings as not much more than high-grade policemen. 'Human pride has created the power of kings,' blandly declared Gregory VII, and went on to insist that the pope had the right and duty to punish rulers who seriously and stubbornly transgressed. As the *Dictatus Pape* put it, the pope could 'release subjects from their allegiance to wicked men' and 'is at liberty to depose emperors.' For such sweeping powers as this neither past precedent nor the pages of Scripture provide anything remotely approaching a clear-cut precedent, though a not untenable case might be deduced therefrom by the more self-confident type of theologian. But this concept was inevitably under very heavy fire at every level of society, not least because it contravened the immemorial custom that kings were unmade as well as made by their subjects. The fact that this right to depose rulers was intended as very much a last resort, and in fact was very seldom used indeed, even against the admittedly trying German Emperors, did not greatly diminish its unpopularity.

Although the Gregorian Reform met with much welcome and did much to strengthen Western Christendom, its extremism in an ultra-conservative age inevitably evoked widespread and often very violent opposition, on a scale not to be challenged until Martin Luther crashed onto the ecclesiastical stage. The attacks on secularisation upset many top people who were profiting from Church resources in one way or another, whilst no small sector of Western clergy regarded with apprehension the attempt to impose on Christendom a highly centralised government which gravely threatened the traditional freedom of local bishops to have all but major affairs settled locally—'this man orders us about as if we were his bailiffs,' said one of them of Gregory VII, and herein was not all that far from the truth. For obvious reasons the attempt to enforce clerical celibacy as a universal rule upset many, both within and without the ranks of the clergy, challenging a great mass of vested interests of more than one kind.

However, pragmatically the Gregorian Reform can be strongly defended along certain lines. In view of the corruption, inefficiency and worldliness of local bishops in many parts of the West and their frequent subservience to local interests, to leave the enforcement of the major reforms so desperately needed in their hands would have been in the highest degree foolish optimism. Dispassionate and full enquiry into major abuses might be had where, as in England, the local rulers were effective and conscientious, but Italy had no monarchy even in name, that in France had very little power at this time, whilst that in Germany, for reasons by no means wholly to its credit, was increasingly at loggerheads with the Gregorian Reform's supporters. Even in England, as the reigns of the intemperate Rufus and John demonstrated, non-stop good behaviour from the monarchy was not to be had. In major confrontations of Church and State at this time the papacy was the only institution in society which could be expected to supply a dispassionate court of appeal to which aggrieved ecclesiastics could refer with some reasonable hopes of redress, though, as we shall see, its efforts to settle matters great and small from clerics all over the West ultimately created disadvantages liable to criticism on both theological and non-theological grounds. But the Gregorian Reform inevitably raised very fundamental questions on the nature of authority in the Christian society, and like all such major programmes split contemporaries sharply between the 'little liberals' and 'little conservatives' into which Gilbert sagely divided mankind. To the latter category much of the Gregorian Reform programme was indefensible because it broke with tradition, to the former such a contention was utterly unconvincing for, as Becket infuriatingly pointed out, 'God did not say I am Tradition but I am Truth.'

CHAPTER 2

THE ENGLISH SCENE

CONSIDERATIONS of space do not allow any detailed consideration of the English Church which the Conqueror found in 1066, but a miniature picture of it is needed if its subsequent development is to be seen in perspective.

PARISHES AND CLERGY

A parish has been defined as 'a definite area of land the inhabitants of which have the right to the religious offices of an incumbent who is normally in priest's orders, and the duty of accepting his services.' By 1066 the English Church had long been divided into such units though their number was not quite static nor their area at all uniform. In early Anglo-Saxon times a parish (*parochia*) was often of considerable size and centred on a mother church which was either a monastery or a college of secular clergy, around which were scattered a varying number of dependent chapels (later known as 'chapels of ease') mostly founded either for the benefit of a particular village or particular family or for both. Before such a chapel was established the need for it had to be shown and the necessary provision made for the erection of the building and the maintenance of its priest. The principal function of such a chapel was to provide the local faithful with facilities for frequent attendance at the Mass, but baptisms, weddings and funerals had to be sought at the mother church of the parish.

For some time before the Conquest new developments had, however, eroded much of this pattern, especially in the richer and more populous parts of England such as Norfolk and Suffolk. Here for some time there had been growing up in considerable numbers parishes which were very much smaller in size and which often had no daughter churches. In the country these often consisted of little more than a village with the lands around it worked by the locals, whilst the very small number of them in towns were often minute in area. We have, unhappily, next to no information on the dates of foundation of English churches and chapels established before the late twelfth century, but there can be no doubt that a large number of them had come into existence in the two centuries which immediately preceded the advent of the Normans, and that an indeterminate proportion originated as chapels but went on to acquire parochial status.

In the poor and scantily populated parts of England then so evident in the north and west, huge unwieldy parishes long persisted. Of these Halifax in Yorkshire has been claimed as the largest; in later days it was estimated to measure some seventeen miles long and have an average width of eleven miles. In such parishes the religious inconveniences in times of ultra-slow travel on ultra-bad roads might clearly be considerable, especially where lack of resources severely limited the number of chapels of ease. Even where chapels existed they might not remove the necessity of long and toilsome journeying to the mother church for baptisms and burials. Any acquisition of the rights of baptism and burial for a local chapel inevitably diminished the rights and revenues of the mother church, so could never be obtained automatically and was sometimes very slow in arriving. As late as 1445 answer was made to a recent complaint by the inhabitants of Eskdale in Cumbria that their dwellings were ten miles from the mother church of St Bees and separated from it by two broad stretches of water and three becks (*rivulis*) 'which swell in rainy and wintry weather so that they [the parishioners] cannot conveniently go thither for christenings, burials, divine offices, sacraments and sacramentals.' The strength of this case was now admitted and permission given to them to elevate their chapel to the status of a parish church, with rights of burial and baptism, and the concomitants of a cemetery, font, bell-tower and bells. This is, however, a late and spectacular example of a process which in southern areas had been under way on a large scale a very great deal earlier. In vivid contrast to this was the very small size of many town parishes in England, as, for example, at York where at the end of our period the population of about 8000 had no less than 40 of them. The reason for these very small units is not obvious; perhaps a realisation that the liveliest communities are small communities was a major factor.

At the time of the Norman Conquest the erection and maintenance of the place of worship and the production of an adequate
endowment for the cleric who served it had long been a local
responsibility, but associated with it went the right of the legal
representative or representatives of the person or persons who had
provided the original endowment to nominate to the bishop the
person who should take charge of the church when this post was
vacant. As we have seen, such a right of nomination was legally
regarded as a piece of property and came to be known as an 'advowson'. The post itself was known as a benefice, the holder as the
incumbent, and his nominator as the patron.

Unhappily here, as elsewhere in the West, only too often this
right of presentation to a benefice instead of being carefully used
for spiritual ends was regarded as little more than a useful perquisite
which would provide a stable position and income for friend or
relation of the patron, or for that great menace, a friend of a friend.
Century after century, before and after the Reformation, there
were thus nominated, especially to the more lucrative benefices,
men who in varying degree lacked both the vocation and the
training required of an effective priest. In medieval England it was
very far from unknown for the incumbent not to be in priest's
orders as the law of the church demanded, and to be therefore incapable of fulfilling his fundamental duties to celebrate Mass and
hear confessions.

The value of the income which a medieval English parish priest
received varied very considerably. Clergy who served small back-
of-beyond parishes where the soil was hostile and the population
scanty must have found it as hard to make ends meet as did no small
number of their post-Reformation successors. At the other end of
the scale were the incumbents of the few large parishes in town and
country who might be affluent. In between these extremes were
probably many parishes which would provide incumbents with a
standard of living that was reasonable but not luxurious. The most
lucrative appointments to which a medieval cleric could aspire
were the principal posts in the very small number of secular cathedral
churches and the canonries of some collegiate churches, though these
last were not very numerous and mostly not immensely lucrative.

Unlike modern Anglican clergy or medieval English Benedictines, the parish clergy of these days derived little or none of

their income from endowments. Much their most important source of revenue was the 'tithe', a tenth part of the agricultural produce of the parish, payment of which by the faithful had been made compulsory long before the Norman Conquest. Ultimately these tithes came to be categorised under three heads, though these should not be regarded rigidly;

(i) *Predial tithes*—the fruits of the earth, notably grain, hay, fruit and wood.

(ii) *Mixed tithes*—the produce of animals, notably calves, lambs, chickens and eggs.

(iii) *Personal tithes*—the produce of labour, notably milling and fishing.

Tithes often came to be divided into 'great' or 'rectorial' tithes and 'small' or 'vicarial' tithes. The former might consist mainly of corn, beans, hay and wood and it was originally paid to the 'rector' who, as we shall see, was holder of a benefice which had not been 'appropriated' (page 170); the latter, consisting of any remainder of the predial tithe and mixed and personal tithes, being often paid to the 'vicar', i.e. the rector's deputy in a duly appropriated benefice, but there were no strict rules on the matter and an immense variety in details of such arrangements.

This income was augmented by certain occasional payments and dues. Charges for the sacraments were strictly forbidden, but the better inclined and better endowed might make voluntary offerings therefor. Several times a year there were made what were, in effect, compulsory collections for the incumbent, who could also augment his income by celebrating private Masses for some special purpose, mostly the good of the soul of a person or persons departed this life, though as he was not allowed to celebrate more than one Mass a day, income from them was limited. Perhaps now, as often later, in poorer parishes he might be provided with some meals by some of his parishioners. For taking a funeral the parish priest was entitled to a bonus known as a mortuary (page 347). In rural parishes, in the case of families able to afford it the offering was often a horse or ox, which might have the pleasing privilege of leading the funeral procession. Less wealthy folk and those not engaged in agriculture might yield their best garment or a sum of money.

In most parishes the incumbent had also a little land and sometimes also a building or two which together constituted his 'glebe'.

He was entitled to a place of residence, but this did not always materialise, though by late medieval times some of these clergy houses were quite capacious, as the few surviving examples of them show. As time went by the incumbents' revenues were often threatened by the rapid spread of 'appropriation', which might allocate to other ecclesiastical uses some fraction of the income of the richer benefices.

Before the thirteenth century contemporary documents tell us very little about the staffing of the English parishes. Obviously the smallest parishes would neither need nor be able to afford to pay more than one priest, but any sizeable parish would have one or more assistant clergy who were often known as chaplains (*capellani*). Legally these were at a considerable disadvantage, since they were not beneficed clergy and did not enjoy the security of tenure which was one of the legal privileges of holding a benefice. Such a chaplain would often be paid partly in cash but might have also certain perquisites such as accommodation. By English law an advowson was regarded as a piece of property which, as such, could be bought, sold, bequeathed or given away, whilst its holder could not normally be removed, save by death or resignation or deprivation for some grave offence once he had taken legal possession.

How was this last effected? The process in its final form, (which probably was not quickly established) was quite involved. It began with the patron of the living making a formal nomination to the bishop who could only refuse to accept it if the candidate concerned was clearly unsuitable in character or attainments. Nomination led on to the ceremonies of 'institution' and 'induction'. In the first of these, in the presence of the candidate the bishop officially announced the institution of the former into the benefice, an act which came to be recorded in an official document sealed with the episcopal seal. The effect of this act was to terminate the vacancy of the living and convey to the nominee the duties and privileges of his office. There followed the 'induction', a picturesque but routine affair whose conduct the bishop often delegated to one of the clerical officials of his diocese. The epoch at which this took its stock form is not clear, but in this the officiating ecclesiastic took the new incumbent by the hand and placed it on the ring or key of the main church door and pronounced the formula of induction, after which the incumbent entered the church, rang the church bell as a sign of his having taken possession of his church, and took possession of his official seat in the chancel. He was now the legal holder of the profits and emoluments of his benefice. In cases where the bishop himself was patron of the living a slightly different procedure combining presentation and institution and known as 'collation' was the rule, the absurdity of a bishop presenting a candidate to himself being thus avoided.

THE LOWER CLERGY

We have very little useful evidence regarding the English clergy at the time of the Norman Conquest, even their total number being highly uncertain. The total number of English parishes in later times came to be in the region of 9500 of which the great majority were certainly in existence by 1066, but more than this cannot be safely averred. Of the number of clergy at this time no reasonable guess can be made. Comparatively recently an American scholar has asserted that at the time of Domesday Book (1086) 'an estimate of 4,500 includes all of the secular clergy except those in minor orders', but this is very likely to be a considerable underestimate. It can however be safely assumed that most parish priests of Norman times had certainly got flocks of very manageable size as their successors had. About 1380 roughly 9000 beneficed clergy with 14 000 assistants tended a population of perhaps 2 200 000 in the sharpest contrast with some 23 000 parish clergy in England today who face a population of 45 000 000. The extent to which English incumbents in 1066 were in priest's orders is yet another of the questions to which only very vague answers can be given. Low as the standard of education was amongst the clergy, it was certainly appreciably lower amongst the laity. In late Anglo-Saxon times there was at least a small band of enthusiasts who preached the cause of celibacy but it is certain that in 1066 there was no lack of married clergy and a very strong body of opinion which regarded their position as a perfectly proper one.

PROVINCES AND DIOCESES

Unlike areas such as southern France and Italy where dioceses were very small and very numerous, in 1066 in England there existed but fifteen of them, which were grouped into two provinces, a southern one headed by the archbishop of Canterbury and a northern one under the archbishop of York. Now, and indeed right down to the advent of the Industrial Revolution, the southern one was immensely superior in wealth and population, principally because of its more fertile soil and better weather, so important in days of an agricultural economy.

THE PROVINCE OF CANTERBURY

The see of Canterbury, established in 596 in what was then the capital of the kingdom of Kent, was the oldest in England, and, quite accidentally, had from the first held the primacy which Pope Gregory the Great's blue-print for the re-conversion of England had intended for London, already the most important English city. From an early date Benedictinism flourished mightily in Kent, and in 1066 monks of this order constituted the chapter of Canterbury Cathedral and also held the majestic abbey of St Augustine just down the road, in whose church no few of the early archbishops were interred. The diocese was small, since it shared the county of Kent with that of Rochester, established in 604. The latter was far from grandiose, and in 1066 its small cathedral was in the hands of a chapter which consisted of five secular canons. Westward was the county of Sussex, unevenly populated but of very manageable size, with its cathedral at Selsey. Bordering it was the large and flourishing diocese of Winchester. Its cathedral stood in the ancient capital of the great kingdom of Wessex, whose rulers had been the principal agents in the unification of England and patronised Benedictinism lavishly. Monks of the order had been re-established in the mighty cathedral in 964 and simultaneously in the sizeable church known as the New Minster, which had inconveniently been set up on the north side of the cathedral by King Edward. The diocese stretched from the south coast and Isle of Wight right up to the south bank of the Thames, where the bishops had useful access to London from their estate at Southwark. For reasons not fully explored, the bishopric of Winchester became the most lucrative in England, a fourteenth-century magnate noting 'Canterbury hath the finer stable but Winchester the deeper manger.'

In the far west the sparsely populated counties of Devon and

Cornwall formed a single diocese whose see had recently (1050) been moved to the substantial town of Exeter where the Roman walls were still very usable, as the Conqueror found to his cost when he attacked the place. This largely infertile area had more than its full share of over-large parishes and in it, alone in England, old Celtic traditions still flourished mightily. In Cornwall most curious place-names were legion and there luxuriated deep devotion to the memory of no few local holy men of Dark Ages times, whose un-official canonisation by the locals would probably not always have won nods of approval from the tough curials at Rome who in later times were to settle such demanding matters. Amongst various remarkable feats attributed to some of these local saints was a capacity to peregrinate even when they had literally lost their heads and ability to chug about the Channel on chunks of local stone. To the north lay Somerset, where a cathedral established at Wells in 909 with a chapter of secular canons had recently been reformed. The site had charming countryside and marvellous building stone but was ill-placed for through traffic, whence came in later days its curious distinction of being the only cathedral city in England with no great railway station.

In neighbouring Dorset the cathedral of Sherborne had a line of bishops stretching back to 705, and recently (1058) had been made highly cumbersome by the addition of the diocese of Ramsbury. Stretching from Portland Bill to the upper Thames it covered much pleasant country but had few towns and no obvious centre. At the southern end of the Welsh border was the diocese of Worcester, whose cathedral stood in what was by Anglo-Saxon standards a major town. No small part of the fertile countryside around it belonged to the Benedictines, who had held the cathedral and the sizeable abbeys of Evesham and Pershore. Its bishop since 1062 had been the monk Wulfstan, the most attractive prelate of the day and a product of the cathedral, where monastic life was flourishing mightily. Further north was the diocese of Hereford, the county of that name still being termed 'in Wales' by royal officials a century after the Conquest. From the wildish inhabitants of the local Principality it tended to suffer no little. North of it stretched the rather colourless diocese of Lichfield, with its see long established in the little village of that name which was remarkable only for its possession of the shrine of the great St Chad (d. 672): its largish limits stretched from the Avon to the Ribble. The Anglo-Saxon veneration for holy men which gave little Lichfield its cathedral accounts also for that at Dorchester-on-Thames, where lay buried St Birinus, one of the great apostles of the re-conversion of England. But this site was immensely inconvenient, since the northern boundary of the diocese was the Humber, well over a hundred miles away. Much of the area was sparsely inhabited, but in the Fenland were a group of substantial abbeys—Ely, Croyland, Ramsey and Peterborough.

From Dorchester a man might easily pass by water to the land's unchallenged capital of London. Its line of bishops stretched back to 664; the diocese comprised Essex, Middlesex and parts of Hertfordshire. To the east were the counties of Norfolk and Suffolk, with a flourishing agriculture supporting what Domesday Book shows to be a population that was, by contemporary standards, very dense. But now, as in Roman times, it had no effective town life, though for some time Thetford had been expanding from very small beginnings. Rather curiously there was only one cathedral for the whole region. This was situate at the back-of-beyond village of (North) Elmham where its unpretentious foundations are yet to be seen; the bishop apparently also carried out some episcopal functions at the equally unprestigious village of Hoxne.

THE PROVINCE OF YORK

In 1066 northern England was very much a poor relation. The arch-diocese of York was certainly vast in area, covering, as it did, not only the huge county of Yorkshire but also substantial portions of what were to become the counties of Cumberland, Westmorland and Lancashire. But the climate was not very friendly, and much of the land consisted of hostile moor, mountain and fell, so that the population of most of the area was very scanty, much of it being widely scattered in lonesome farms where cattle and rather scraggy sheep were much more prominent than products of the plough. Despite modern suggestions that the Vikings on their raids on England were little more boisterous than Victorian Sunday School children on their annual outing, there can be no doubt that Northern England suffered heavily from their invasions which pounded both its eastern and western seaboards and swept far inland. Amongst other things, the Vikings seem to have done much to eliminate the formerly splendid monastic life in the area, and certainly helped themselves to much church property. This is possibly mainly responsible for the poverty of the archbishopric of York, which led to its holders in the sixty years which preceded the Conquest finding it necessary to hold the see of Worcester 'in plurality' (e.g. holding the two appointments simultaneously) with that from which they took their title, a thing only permissible under very special circumstances.

The only other diocese in northern England at this time was that which had been set up in 995 on the noble, river-girt rock of Durham which provided a highly defensible home for the greatest ecclesiastical treasure of these parts, the body of St Cuthbert, which here found a permanent resting-place after having been much trundled around to escape Viking troubles. The area was notably far from rich and was perennially in danger of Scottish raids.

In north-western England there was no English diocese, the area having been for long a no-man's-land between English and Scots, who had utterly failed to agree on a frontier to replace that which the painstaking Romans had constructed here almost a thousand years before. The fact that there were thus but two dioceses in northern England entailed various disabilities, as, for example, the difficulty of implementing the long-established rule of the Church that at least three bishops should participate in the consecration of a new bishop. It has been very properly remarked that 'at the time of the Norman Conquest there was a northern metropolitan but no northern province' (Hamilton Thompson). It was smallish consolation that there yet survived rather frail links with the see of Whithorn which were to be maintained in post-Conquest days.

THE BISHOPS

Thanks to the immense inspiration which Anglo-Saxon England steadily derived from Benedictine monasticism, by the time of the Norman Conquest the English Church had long maintained a venerable tradition of Eastern Christianity, now largely neglected in the West, that the most suitable people to be bishops were monks, since they sought more scientifically and sacrificially to acquire that high degree of personal holiness to which the Christian is called. Knowles has shown that in the period 960–1066 of the 116 bishops in England no less than 67 are known to have been monks and only 15 secular clergy. Of the great mass of these we know next to nothing, but the attractive biography of St Wulfstan, the monk of Worcester who held the see there from 1062 to 1095, gives us a vivid picture of a lovable, sanctified man whose work as a bishop could scarcely be bettered. The fact that at that time of the Norman Conquest Benedictine communities held the prestigious sees of Canterbury and Winchester and also those of Worcester and Sherborne was probably largely due to the same deep respect for the Benedictine life, though it may also have been partially inspired by the realisation that the monastic cathedral chapter was very much less likely to alienate property than a secular one, in days when so many clergy were married.

THE ENGLISH MONASTERIES

The immensely significant part played by the monasteries of the early Anglo-Saxon England had been most severely damaged by the Viking invasions, but with the aid of God-fearing kings, with whom England was now well supplied, a very valuable monastic revival had got under way in the tenth century which left the Benedictine life here again firmly rooted, at least in the southern province, and highly regarded by the time of the advent of the Normans.

By 1066 all English monasteries had for long followed a single monastic code—the *Rule of St Benedict* which had long ago vanquished all its old competitors and was not yet faced by the new ones which flooded into England after the Conquest. This *Rule*, written about 540 in central Italy for the monastery of Monte Cassino by its abbot St Benedict, had gained its supremacy largely by its own superlative merits. It had three principal assets. Firstly, unlike some of its main competitors, it gave a very detailed and systematic survey of the whole monastic programme. Secondly, its elaborate provisions were marked by a shrewd moderation, demanding of its followers neither an unpracticable degree of severity nor leaving large loopholes for laxity. Thirdly, it was not content to offer merely a series of concrete regulations but everywhere sought to expose the basic spiritual qualities from which a stable and joyous life would spring. Although the Benedictines of these times did not normally aim at undertaking missionary or pastoral work, they by no means closed their eyes to secular society, stressing especially the importance of hospitality to travellers—'let a guest be received as if he were Christ,' says the *Rule*.

As Domesday Book shows us, in 1066 there were in England 48 monasteries of men and 13 of women. Their differences in size were very marked, especially in houses of monks. At the top of these was a small band of abbeys which now certainly held a very great deal more wealth than their reasonable needs demanded. Such were Glastonbury, Ely, Christchurch, Canterbury, Bury St Edmund's, St Augustine's Canterbury, the cathedral of Winchester, Westminster, Abingdon and the New Minster at Winchester. At the bottom end of the scale were houses like Athelney, Buckfast and Horton, which lived very far from affluence. Of the nunneries Ramsey, Wilton and Shaftesbury all were rather fashionable and well-to-do, but little Swavesey's tiny income put it at the bottom of the whole list. The total wealth of the English monasteries surveyed in Domesday Book (1086) was certainly very considerable, being about a seventh of that there recorded, but this famous record bristles with technicalities, gaps and obscurities, and it would be most unwise to conclude that monasteries then owned this fraction of the total English wealth.

The geographical distribution of the monasteries was very uneven, owing to a variety of non-theological factors which need not here be analysed. 'There was no monastic house in 1066 west of the Severn nor north of a line drawn from Worcester to Burton on Trent and thence to the Wash; in the large Danish counties of Lincoln, Norfolk and Suffolk and Essex there were only Cnut's two recent foundations at Bury and Holme. Sussex had none nor had Oxfordshire and Buckinghamshire; in the extreme West, Cornwall had no houses,' notes Knowles. In the disorderly north and impoverished west of England the magnificent monastic tradition of Anglo-Saxon times had capsized almost without trace. Of the size of the Benedictine population of England on the eve of the Conquest we have no very precise evidence but a recent estimate suggests that these were then some 200 nuns and 850 monks, figures which were soon to be stupendously swollen.

In England, as elsewhere in Western Europe, the Benedictine monasteries played an immensely important rôle in the social and economic development. Economically they led the way in reclaiming moor, fen and forest and in the large-scale farming, which their major financial resources and their skills facilitated. Socially, their concern for the poor and needy led them to perform no few functions which have now slid into the hands of the Welfare State, whilst their primary concern with the maintenance of an unceasing round of stately and beautiful worship made them incidentally major patrons of the arts in times when these were very thin on the ground. But then, as always, the principal attraction of the monastic life for the faithful believers was not its by-products but itself—its God-centred life so disciplined, so peaceful, so charitable. The greatest historian of Anglo-Saxon England has written 'every ecclesiastical statesman regarded the monastic life as essential to the life of the Church ... the motive of escape from a violent world will not explain the enthusiasm with which men and women of all classes entered religion ... it was the appeal to the imagination of the ordinary man which gave vitality to early English monasticism' (F. M. Stenton).

The condition of the English Benedictine monasteries on the eve of the Norman Conquest has recently been thus summarised: 'While a few of the smaller ones were apparently dwindling to extinction and two or three of the greatest houses had become relaxed, the majority were, it would seem, living a life distinguished from all save the most observant Norman houses not so much by degree of departure from the monastic rule, as by the national characteristics of a less enclosed life and wider external relationships, though there is some evidence that regular silence and regular food had to some extent given way to relaxations. At a few, and especially at Evesham and Worcester, a standard of fervour was maintained upon which the Norman model could not improve ... the monasteries of England on the day when King Edward "was alive and dead" were as a body living and powerful. There was no trace of serious moral decadence, nor of that lay encroachment which in previous centuries had had such disastrous consequences both in England and abroad. ... No great spiritual leader however, whether bishop or abbot, existed ... and there was little in England of the new intellectual life of France, while the English abbeys wholly lacked the great and regularly planned churches and conventual buildings that had sprung up all over Normandy within the last generation' (Knowles).

ENGLAND AND THE PAPACY

The tendency to talk historical and theological nonsense about the relationship of the medieval English Church to the papacy so obvious in Victorian times, is of late much diminished, under the twin influences of modern historical research and the very remarkable upsurge of ecumenical feeling which in very recent decades has swept away so much dessicated prejudice. The Anglo-Saxon Church, like that of most of the rest of Western Christendom, had long been isolated and insulated from effective contact with the Eastern Churches, and in the process had lost effective knowledge of the Eastern conception of the papacy as being the natural leader of Christendom but not possessing extensive unique authority. English folk had certainly long manifested a very real veneration for the Roman see. The Eternal City was the place of pilgrimage *par excellence* to which no few who could afford it and perhaps no few who could not, made their laborious way. English nuns and prin-cesses—categories which in these days notably overlapped—plied pious needles to confect embroideries for one who was regarded as being in very real sense 'the Holy Father', whilst kings brought or sent to him appropriately regal gifts. In theory, though not always in practice, English householders paid to Rome small annual tributes known as 'Peter's Pence', whilst newly-appointed archbishops were accustomed to visit Rome and obtain from the pope the 'pallium' (a small woollen vestment worn round the neck) which symbolised their unity with the see of Peter.

For two very good reasons there was as yet no sign of any con-frontation between English nationalism and papal power. In the first place, at this stage in English history nothing existed that could be regarded as even incipient national feeling. The England of 1066 was a collection of localities with widely different dialects and no effective common feeling. Thus those who lived north of the Humber had strong links with Scotland and with Scandinavia and little interest in a south-country king whom they almost never saw and who could not count on any automatic loyalty from them. Secondly, it is to be noted, papal intervention in English affairs at this juncture had long been so very intermittent and so very gentle that it could not conceivably be regarded as baneful by any reasonable person. Only in very much later days did there arise that vigorous anti-papalism which ultimately triumphed in the Anglican Reformation. The number of occasions on which papal legates visited England in Anglo-Saxon times was very minute and their acts here largely uncontentious. The popes of this period never thought of levying regular taxation on the English Church and seldom sought to influence local church appointments, whilst appeals from England to the Roman see were equally rare. If there was no anti-papal sentiment here it was mainly because that pragmatic animal known as the layman found nothing to criticise in the very limited papal intervention in English affairs and was much too illiterate to think of analysing the theological *raison d'être* of the Eternal City, which he viewed through a beneficent religious haze.

THE ENGLISH MONARCHY

As we have seen, monarchy was the principal form of government in medieval Europe. Nowhere had it been more valuable than in England in the days when the Vikings' raids tested to the full the strength of governmental institutions, flattening weak ones as tanks flatten tins. From the time of King Alfred the Great (848–899) an almost unbroken line of competent and vigorous rulers reduced the invasions to manageable proportions. In the early eleventh century the attacks were renewed in less massive form and Danish kings held the English throne from 1013 until 1042. In the latter year Edward the Confessor succeeded them. Like some other medieval rulers he would have been far happier as a monk than as a monarch, and his neglect to provide the heir to the throne, so essential in those days of naive and brittle governmental machinery, led to the famous crisis which saw the nine-month reign of the Anglo-Saxon Harold and his removal by Duke William of Normandy at Hastings on 14 October 1066.

These changes in the tenure of the English throne were not of immense significance in contemporary church affairs since, as we have seen, almost inescapable conditions in these times gave to the leaders of Church and State a very real community of interests. Thus all rulers, even those from Scandinavia, were assiduous in church attendance, Cnut even taking himself off to Rome, and all seem to have been little prone to engagement in that simony which was ravishing so much church life on the Continent—a chronicler notes that in the days of Edward the Confessor 'the trafficker in benefices and the covetous man never found anything to forward their designs.' Similarly the appointment of very secular minded men to bishoprics now so obvious in certain parts of the Continent was little known here. Symbolic of the close alliance of king and people was the august coronation service of late revised. As the future was to show clearly, the English monarchy was fortunate in being called to govern a land where there were arising next to none of the great cities such as dominated medieval Italian history and few of the mighty aristocratic families which already and for long to come made the power of the French monarchy so much less considerable than the public weal demanded.

The Laity

In the Middle Ages, as ever, the gross numbers of the laity and their very diverse degrees of spiritual enthusiasm and insight were such as to defy definition in a thumbnail sketch, any conjecture in any case being rendered particularly obscure owing to the immensely scrappy information regarding their comportment. As has been noted, they were certainly very few in numbers by modern standards, and the huge proportion of them were country dwellers. Almost all were totally illiterate and had no interest in matters intellectual. Religion to them meant largely Catholic worship and the immense increase in the numbers of parish churches in the two centuries which preceded the Norman Conquest is proof enough that their affection for this was very much more than formal.

If lay religion had its crudities it was by no means without its sacrificial side and had the huge advantage of being ubiquitous. As has been attractively written: 'For all lay people, ealdorman, thegn and peasant, in the late Old English period, the Christian faith and the practices of religion were a built-in part of society. It made no difference whether the layman had any personal sense of possible contact with God or not; whether he was a good man or a bad man; whether he were stupid or intelligent; whether he hung round the ale-house and disliked his wife and contemplated pushing her into the mill stream one day . . . or paid his tithe and followed the procession of the litany and hoped that his five-year-old little Aeswige would one day be a little clerk, for to all these men the Christian faith was sure and certain. He might not, like Pope Gregory, ever hear time's winged chariot echoing near, but certainly before him lay deserts of vast eternity. But this did not depress him, whether he were good or bad; doomsday, the parson said, when the Lord came with fire, and the sun shone seven times brighter than it now shines, would be very alarming, but the saints were kind, all men knew the mild-heartedness of Our Lady; there was always confession for wife murderers and men going to be hanged, and though no man wanted to be hanged, death was over in a minute, whether you died on the gallows or in your bed, all was not lost, ever' (M. Deanesly, *The Pre-Conquest Church in England*).

ENGLAND AND THE CONTINENT

Life in the medieval West was characterised by a very profitable combination of localism and cosmopolitanism. At the bottom of the social scale, and by no means solely there, most men led a life which was obstinately local, involving few journeys far from home and usually depending for knowledge of anything more than news of the vicinity on gossip which was often scrappy and unreliable. Food and clothing were largely locally produced and local edifices built of local materials in the local style of architecture. Only a very small fraction of the population of medieval England can ever have set eyes on their king and, at least in certain areas, even the prospect of a diocesan bishop and his suite must have been a rarish sight.

On the other hand, in certain ways medieval English life was very cosmopolitan. Trying as it might be to acquire the Latin tongue, once he had so done a man might travel over all the West with a language problem infinitely less acute than it is today, whilst the fact that in post-Conquest England French was also widely spoken, at least in the upper strata of society, made the problem of communication even easier. The stupendous devotion to hospitality shown by the medieval church (see Chapter 12) made it comparatively easy for those of very restricted means to carry out journeys which until very recently they would never think of attempting, a steady trickle of Englishmen plodding pertinaciously to such distant shrines as Compostella, Rome or even Jerusalem.

By the time of the Norman Conquest England was already showing abundant signs of that interest in trade for which some medieval puritans were later to reproach her. In days when water transport tended to be much easier than carriage by land she was very far from isolated. In the century before the Norman Conquest the English Church had various contacts with Flanders and north France as well as with Scandinavia. Thus Edward the Confessor's wife was Flemish and the king himself, brought up in Northern France, was uncontaminated by the public-school conviction that 'niggers begin at Calais.' In his historic rebuilding of the abbey of Westminster he took as his model the Norman church of Jumièges and also imported various foreign ecclesiastics, one of whom he made archbishop of Canterbury. His successor, King Harold, in setting up the great college of Waltham was aided by a native of Liège and in the previous century an archbishop of Canterbury had established fruitful links with Ghent. In northern England a major element in the population was of Scandinavian origin, and by no means lost touch with the lands of its forefathers. In the south, London, already one of the major cities of Western Europe, owed no small part of its importance to the wide trading network which it had built up. 'In the first half of the eleventh century London was a place of frequent resort for traders from every country between Norway and Northern France,' notes Stenton. As has been well said, 'in the middle ages the Channel was a high-road not a tank-trap' (Wormald). Having crossed this high-road, William the Conqueror and his very competent successors welded England into a domain which by the late twelfth century stretched from Scotland to Spain, and immensely facilitated English participation in the mighty renaissance in matters ecclesiastical and non-ecclesiastical which in these times was so greatly enriching the life of Western Europe.

PART TWO

The Age of Reconstruction

c.1066 - c.1199

CHAPTER 3

THE SECULAR CHURCH AND REFORM

The Conciliar Revival

FOR the 'secular' (i.e. non-monastic) sector of the English Church
the century and a half which followed the Norman Conquest was a
period of immense importance, in which its life was elaborated and
rationalised by a remarkably comprehensive series of reforms.
This, along with other good works, was principally the result of a
very intense renewal of activity by ecclesiastical councils both local
and national. Fundamental was the very great concern for reform
evinced by the series of councils convoked by the popes, mostly at
Rome, which met very frequently from the middle years of the
eleventh century and continued so to do for long to come. Most of
these were of limited size but those held at the Lateran in 1123, 1139,
1179 and 1215 were so important as to rank as General Councils in
the Western though not in the Eastern Church. The Council of 1215
was indeed the mightiest gathering of its kind for centuries, and
produced an immense series of 'canons' (i.e. decrees) covering a
huge range of matters ecclesiastical. Meanwhile papal activity was
vigorously manifested in other ways. Legates visited local areas to
carry out reforms, the curia became increasingly utilised as a court
of appeal in all sorts of matters both major and minor, whilst as
the twelfth century progressed the papal court unloaded part of
the stupendous amount of business which flooded in on to local
ecclesiastics, who were appointed 'judges delegate' and had power to
hear and settle specified controversies in their area. The sheer bulk
of Roman ecclesiastical legislation and judgments became quite
stupendous and was augmented by unofficial commentaries on them
compiled by the now rising class of professional ecclesiastical lawyers.
Meanwhile in England there was taking place a major local revival
in conciliar activity, whose initiation was due in no small degree
to the interest in reform shown by the pious if conservative King
William. Between 977 and 1066 only five English ecclesiastical

councils are known to have been held, whereas in the following hundred years there were no less than thirty-five.

Before the process of ecclesiastical reform could get vigorously under way there was need of a tidying-up operation to remove no less a person than the archbishop of Canterbury, one Stigand. This man had shown no interest in reform and a very gross interest in accumulating money, whilst by breaching the canon law in more than one way, notably by supporting the pope's illegal rival, he made it feasible for William to satisfy an understandable desire to replace him by a man whom he knew and trusted. Before launching his attack on England, William had cultivated friendly relations with the pope of the day, who had approved his enterprise and sent him a specially blessed banner in token thereof. In 1070, when the political situation had calmed somewhat, with William's concurrence, three legates arrived from Rome and proceeded to hold a council at Winchester. Stigand was removed from office and a few months later was replaced as archbishop of Canterbury by William's close friend Lanfranc, a totally admirable Italian who had thrown over a brilliant career to become a monk in the then little-known Norman abbey of Bec (Hellouin). He found the prospect of his new position very far from welcome. 'In vain did I plead my own incapacity, my ignorance of the language and the barbarous people,' he wrote to the pope, going on to request, 'permit me once more to return to the monastic life which above all things is my delight.' Very happily for the English Church this plea was rejected. From now on the king and archbishop, bound together by deep mutual respect, saw to it that a series of councils quickly initiated a variety of very necessary reforms.

Understandably, the great majority of these councils were held in London or at nearby Westminster, where the mighty abbey, rebuilt in unparalleled scale on the eve of Conquest, was adjoined from the end of the century by William Rufus' hall which was then as mighty a palace as Western Europe could show. The facts that London was already incomparably the largest town in England and that the mass of the English population at this time was concentrated in the south and east, combined with the obvious need of William to live largely within easy reach of the Norman coast, made any other meeting-place much less desirable. Of the composition of these early councils our knowledge is scanty. The all-essential core of the gathering was formed by the diocesan bishops, to whom were added certain of the higher members of the diocesan staff and what was probably a rather arbitrarily chosen selection of the heads of monastic houses of men. How far the lower clergy and the laity were represented is not clear. Proceedings seem not yet to have been formalised—one chronicler writes of a council at this time 'the bishops having been disposed in order of the precedence of their sees, the people in confused and tumultuous mass, as is their wont, thrusting themselves in everywhere', a comment suggesting that not all those who attended were pedantic enough to await an official summons thereto.

The agenda of these early councils seems often to have been short and uncontentious, with previous canons, whether local or Roman, often being reiterated. The fact that the highly controversial question of ecclesiastical taxation was not yet a major issue must have saved a great deal of time. Education attracted next to no attention, as did the question of heresy, which was not at this stage a vital problem in England. A very large part of conciliar activity was concerned with two major problems so deep-rooted as to remain such for long to come—the secularisation of church property and appointments and the considerable room for improvement in the education and comportment of a quite unknown proportion of the clergy, which inevitably resulted from so many unsuitable men being pushed into ecclesiastical posts for which they had inadequate spiritual qualifications.

The canons of the important legatine council held at Westminster in 1126 illustrate major preoccupations of this time. Ecclesiastical ordination was not to be conferred for money, nor was a fee to be exacted in connection with administering of the sacraments of baptism, confession, extreme unction, Mass and communion or for burial. There were to be no compulsory gifts (apparently to bishops) at episcopal consecrations, the blessing of abbots and dedication of churches. No abbot, prior or monk or clerk was to accept tithe or benefice from a layman without the consent of his bishop. Appointments to churches and prebends were not to be treated as hereditary possessions. Clerks holding churches or benefices 'who avoid being ordained in order to live with greater freedom and continue to treat holy orders with contempt' despite episcopal injunctions, were to be deprived of their posts. The offices of deans and priors should be given to those in priests' orders, and arch-deaconries to those in deacons' orders. No one should be ordained priest or deacon without a 'title' (i.e. a guarantee of the means to maintain himself with the necessities of life, either by ecclesiastical appointment or private means or some other reliable source). No abbot, clerk or layman was to eject an ordained person from his church without episcopal authorisation, on pain of excommunication. Clergy were to be ordained and judged by the bishop of the diocese and no other, and 'one who has been excommunicated by another was not to be received'. No one was to be allowed to hold more than one archdeaconry or similar appointment. Priests, deacons, subdeacons and canons were forbidden to live with any women, except a mother, a sister, an aunt or other 'female free from suspicion.' To clerks of every degree was prohibited 'usury and filthy lucre.' Sorcerers, fortune-tellers and those who dealt in divination of any kind were excommunicated and were declared 'branded with perpetual infamy.' Marriages up to the seventh degree of consanguinity were forbidden and the separation of offenders ordered, but men were not allowed to urge this accusation against their wives.

It is to be noted that in these times about half of the councils were 'legatine', that is to say, were presided over by a papal legate or legates. At first these legates were exported from the Continent, but fairly soon, by a tactful gesture to local feeling, the papacy conferred legatine rank on a local prelate. The archbishops of Canterbury were the obvious and usual recipients of this privilege, though the pushing and well-bred Bishop Henry of Winchester (1129–71) held it briefly. Soon this link with Canterbury became usual, but it was long before it became officially permanent and the canny papacy retained the right to overrule local action by use of a legate *a latere*, an official with superior powers. An obvious adjunct to the new active conciliar machinery in England was the old diocesan synod, an ecclesiastical council held by each local bishop for his diocese, wherein the canons of higher bodies could be rehearsed and enforced, and local matters discussed and settled. These now became increasingly important and by the early thirteenth century were meeting fruitfully and frequently.

THE ENGLISH PROVINCES

William the Conqueror was a tidy-minded man and in some major respects the Church which he found in England could do with being tidied. A striking example of this is the fact that in 1066 men were not agreed as to the course of the boundary line which separated the two provinces of Canterbury and York into which the country was divided. In 1070 the northern archbishop claimed that the diocese of Lichfield belonged to his jurisdiction, but his case was not strong and in 1072 a local council considered the matter at papal behest and decided against him. The boundary line was to be the river Humber (the southern frontier of the arch-diocese of York) and the northern frontier of the diocese of Lichfield. But in kindly medieval manner the loser got a consolation prize—Nottingham-shire was added to his arch-diocese, which made it even more un-wieldy than it already was. The same council of 1072 decreed that the archbishop of York and the bishop of Durham (the only two diocesan bishops in the northern province) should attend councils summoned by the archbishop of Canterbury and accept all council decisions which did not challenge their position.

Odd as it may seem today, at this time the southern province of Canterbury included the three Welsh dioceses then in being—Llandaff, Bangor and the venerable St David's. In 1143 a new diocese was established at St Asaph. Under medieval conditions to allow Wales to be a separate province was out of the question, and from 1107, if not earlier, at their consecration bishops of Welsh sees made profession of canonical obedience to the archbishops of Canterbury just as did the bishops of the southern English province. The English kings exerted the same extensive control over Welsh episcopal appointments which they did over English ones, but the former were not much sought after by those with worldly ambition, as they were scantily endowed and their local flocks curious and incomprehensible. Sometimes nomination hereto was accepted as a lowly step on the ladder of promotion, but the curial element here was small.

The northern archbishopric of York enlarged its bounds through the creation of the diocese of Carlisle in 1122–33 (page 76) and at first claimed primacy over the Scottish dioceses. To the English, however, the Scots were a barbarous lot of whom the less said and seen the better, and the frequent and bloody-minded raids which originated from both sides of the Border rendered out of the question any prospect of English and Scottish churchmen being of one mind in a house. In 1192 after many legal comings and goings this hard fact was wisely recognised at Rome, and Scotland made an independent province though without its own archbishop. Once again the archbishop of York was given a consolation prize, in the shape of the little diocese of Whithorn, which in the ancient days had had ties with York and where the see had been revived in 1125,. though as time went on it drifted away from its English allegiance. Off the western coast was the little diocese of the Isles with its see in the Isle of Man. Here there was little interest in the new canon law and hazy links with both England and Scandinavia. Early in the twelfth century the King of Man innocently but incorrectly gave the right of appointment to the bishopric to the abbey of Furness, but this arrangement was much challenged and in later days the diocese acquired rival lines of English and Norse bishops.   .

CANTERBURY VERSUS YORK

Very quickly in the Conqueror's reign there arose one of the longest and most entertaining of the major ecclesiastical disputes in medieval England—the question of the relative positions in the hierarchy of the two archbishops. Were their positions equal or not? This question was not a trumpery one of ecclesiastical fussiness, for it had unavoidable practical implications, e.g. on the answer to it depended which archbishop took the seat of honour on major public occasions, and whether or not the northern archbishop had the right to have his primatial cross borne before him when he appeared in public in the southern province (the reverse question seems not to have arisen owing, presumably, to the archbishops of Canterbury tending to give the northern province a very wide berth). To northerners it was self-evident that the position of their archbishop was fully equivalent to that of the southern one, to the southerners it was indubitably inferior to it.

There were few things which medieval men enjoyed more than a really good law-suit which, like no few Victorian novels, tended to sustain interest by going on for a very long while and reserving the climax to the last moment. History and law combined to make this dispute one of immense complexity and guaranteed it a long and contentious course.

What were the powers of a primate? To this major question there was as yet no neat answer, as the Continental practice showed. Some primates, like those of Lyons and Bourges, claimed supremacy over other archbishops, but others, like that of Rheims, limited their authority to their own province. What about local English tradition on the matter? Here history, as so often, refused to provide a clear-cut answer. So far as non-theological factors are concerned, Canterbury certainly was much the more populous and important of the two provinces, but York had a very long tradition of virtual independence. In any case a famous letter of Pope Gregory the Great preserved in Bede's great *History*, laid down specifically that the English Church was to be organised into a northern and a southern province, the former under York, the latter under London (which second proviso never took effect). Here also an eminently sensible rule prescribed that a new archbishop of one province should be consecrated by that of the other, militating against the school of thought which exalted the position of Canterbury.

Inevitably the matter came up for settlement soon after the new Norman king had ensconced himself in England. Lanfranc, ignorant of local precedent, egged on by his convent and putting faith in unconvincing precedents derived from Spain (where the primate of Toledo had extensive powers over all other dignitaries in his kingdom) naturally urged the supreme position of Canterbury and, in token of this supremacy of Canterbury, he demanded that the northern archbishop should make a profession of obedience to him. This position was taken over by his illustrious successor, Anselm, another Italian who could be forgiven for not grasping all the niceties of English life. There followed a colourful battle, both sides displaying much skill and great devotion to duty as they saw it. Soon the Canterbury side produced at the papal court some charters which they had confected but the astute officials there, well-used to such things, were not caught napping—'some smiled, others turned up their noses and others laughed aloud,' noted a York chronicler. In 1119 Rome declared that the archbishops of the two provinces should consecrate each other when need be, but neither should demand a profession from the other. However this did not satisfy all the archbishops of York. In order to avoid giving their colleagues of the southern province the chance to think more highly of themselves than was proper, between 1256 and 1373 all but one of the new archbishops of York not in episcopal orders at the time of his election were at pains to be consecrated at the Roman court.

What might seem to be less important was the question of whether the northern primate could have his cross carried before him in public when in the southern province, which, partly because it was less important, went unsettled for a very long while. Neither side could lose face by yielding, and at least one archbishop of York earnestly demonstrated his rights when sailing back from France by having his cross erected on board ship once what corresponded to territorial waters were reached.

Only in 1353 was the dispute ended and then with typical Roman finesse. The archbishop of Canterbury was accorded the title of 'Primate of All England' and the archbishop of York that of 'Primate of England'—a settlement still in operation. Each had the right to visit the province of the other and to have their crosses carried before them in procession. If their processions met in a narrow road or entry the archbishop of Canterbury should pass first. As a small sop to the southern primate it was ordered that within two months of entering the southern province for the first time a new archbishop of York was to send a gold statuette of an archbishop or some other costly object of gold to the shrine of St Thomas Becket at Canterbury. As has been wisely said of this matter, 'trivial as the dispute may seem to us, it was of great moment in an age when resentment at any infringement of personal rights was always compatible with eagerness to encroach upon the rights of others. . . . In process of time the northern primacy has justified its existence, it has become no mere antiquarian curiosity but a necessity' (A. Hamilton Thompson). We may note in passing that in the mid-twelfth century an attempt was made to elevate the see of Winchester to provincial status but very quickly collapsed.

THE ARCHBISHOPS

In medieval England, as in later times, the archbishops and bishops of England were mostly in practice, though not in theory, nominees of the sovereign, as we shall see. For understandable non-theological reasons the Norman kings were particularly careful to see that all who took such offices were loyal and efficient servants of the Crown. Of their appointments none is more difficult to fault than that of Lanfranc as the first Norman archbishop of Canterbury. Shrewd, intelligent and very pious, after a fracas with Duke William he finally built up the most cordial relationship with the Conqueror, who paid him the somewhat embarrassing compliment of appointing him regent of his new realm during royal absence in Normandy.

Lanfranc's heart was in the monastic life and this he aided substantially in his new milieu, revitalising the conventual life of his cathedral of Canterbury with the aid of carefully compiled observances and a massive rebuilding scheme, giving generous alms and patiently effecting a difficult reform programme in the English Church. Of him the chroniclers speak in nothing but most glowing terms—'a man worthy to be compared with ancients in knowledge and religion', says one, 'of whom it may truly be said that Cato the third descended from heaven so much had a heavenly savour tinctured his heart and tongue.' He died in 1089, to be succeeded after a four-year vacancy by another Italian who had been a monk at Bec, the illustrious St Anselm (c. 1033–1109). He shared with Lanfranc a profound devotion to the monastic life and at the time of his election was celebrated over much of the West for his sanctity and immense theological insight—'the most luminous and penetrating intellect between St Augustine and St Thomas' he has recently been designated. But he had no interest in the feudal chores inseparable from his office and no great savoir faire herein. Circumstances drove him into exile both under William Rufus and Henry I.

Ancient tradition at Canterbury demanded that the archbishops there be chosen from men living the monastic life, and this custom was by no means allowed to lapse in post-Conquest times. Of the eight archbishops who followed St Anselm in the chair of St Augustine five were Benedictines, one Cistercian and one an Austin canon. The only secular was Thomas Becket (1162–70) who was holier than he appears at first sight and had intimate links with the priory of Merton, where he had been educated.

The contemporary archbishops of York were of a very different type. Here was no monastic chapter nor any ancient monastic tradition lingering on, but a cathedral set in a region where local feeling was very strong and trouble from Scots and Scandinavians by no means a thing of the past. Here the king must put men with a capacity to govern whose loyalty to him was beyond doubt. (It is worthy of note that even the obliging King Stephen vetoed the appointment to the archbishopric of York of the saintly St Waltheof in case his relationship to the Scottish king should undermine his support of the English one.)

It is not surprising to find that in the century which followed the Norman Conquest only one archbishop of York came from a monastery, most of the rest being royal chaplains of proved administrative ability, albeit by no means without piety.

The first Norman archbishop, Thomas of Bayeux, learned and competent, 'tried boldly and honestly to do his duty. . . . When he was defeated he cherished no ill-will against his opponents' says Raine, whilst he was not without musical skill: 'if he chanced to hear any light or trivial air he would parody it, as it were, with marvellous (may I say unfortunate) facility into a hymn.' After his short-lived successor, Thomas II, came the noble Thurstan (1119–40) a royal servant and one of the most impressive ecclesiastics of the century, whose industry, piety and good sense did an enormous amount to restore to the northern province its ancient vitality. His death was followed by a disputed election, some backing Henry Murdac, the saintly abbot of the newly established Cistercian monastery of Fountains, others William fitzHerbert, a chaplain of King Stephen who posthumously outshone his rival by being canonised. His immediate successor was Roger Pont l'Eveque (1154–81) who, like Becket, had previously been one of the bright young men in the household of Archbishop Theobald of Canterbury.

An unparalleled vacancy of almost ten years separated his death from the consecration of the unconventional Archbishop Geoffrey (1191–1212). An illegitimate son of King Henry, he had been nominated to the see of Lincoln at the age of fourteen by a scandalous decision of a type to which England was not accustomed. But before having taken priest's orders he resigned to become chancellor, a most wealthy and prestigious post which he lost on his father's death (1189). Rapidly, as a result apparently of local initiative, he was elected to the long-vacant see of York which he at first refused on the commendable grounds that he was fonder of dogs and hawks than books and priests. To this, as Raine notes, 'the Yorkshiremen made a characteristic reply; they told him that it was not necessary that he should altogether abandon those tastes when he came into the north.' Hereby they won his consent. However, his very stormy career hereafter showed clearly that he was much more suited for the chase than the choir. After the Conquest, as before it, the northern province was animated by a very strong local feeling, which was reinforced by the fact that it was very seldom visited by the kings of England. The august city of York maintained the position it had held in Roman times as something like the northern capital (albeit never vying in size and wealth with London), now with the cathedral as its focus.

THE ENGLISH DIOCESES

Although English diocesan organisation was not to be very radically altered in the century which immediately followed the Norman Conquest, there then occurred two developments worthy of note. Of these the first was the transference of certain sees to places more suitable than those which they had occupied in Anglo-Saxon times. This move was not the result of a newish brain-wave but had very ancient precedent. Long ago the councils of Sardica (347) and Laodicea (366) had ordered that episcopal sees were not to be in villages but in cities (*civitates*), the difference between these two categories being not only one of size but the fact that the latter mostly had central and strongly-walled sites, which the former had not. Such a rule was obviously sensible, since it placed the bishop in a vicinity where many of his flock resided, and where others could reach him easily by the roads which radiated from it, whilst the walls provided protection in times of disorder. In the Dark Ages this rule had been much disregarded in outlying areas like Britain, though the justification for it was still valid.

The move to 'translate' certain sees began officially as early as 1075, when a council at London ordered three such removals. The see of Sherborne was to be transferred to Salisbury, a somewhat surprising decision since at this time the latter name belonged, not to the present town which was not yet in existence, but to the hill of Sarum a few miles away where the old prehistoric fort that topped it had recently been reinforced by a Norman castle. Here was no urban community but strong walls, a fairly central site and remains of an excellent road system left by the Romans. The site, evidently given by the king, presumably cost nothing, but was very

cramped and made more so by the fact that it was shared with the
castle and its garrison which latter, presumably, innocently generated
the eternal, uninhibited barrack-room atmosphere. Understandably
one writer rather impolitely termed the arrangement a case of 'the
ark of God shut up in the temple of Baal.' The first bishop of the
new see was consecrated in 1078 and a minuscule cathedral erected.
But experience adequately confirmed the unsuitability of the place
and the good Bishop Richard Poore (1217–28) transferred the
cathedral to an unencumbered site two miles away, the foundation
stone of the later magnificent Gothic cathedral there being laid in
1220.

Much more sagacious was the order of the council of 1075 that
the see of Sussex be moved from the little village of Selsey to the
old Roman town of Chichester, also a fairly central, well-walled
place, which was easily reached from the useful port of Bosham and
from most of the parish churches of the diocese. At the same time
the see at the village of Lichfield was translated to Chester—at first
sight a commendable move, since the latter place still retained
evident remains of its erstwhile rank as one of the principal cities of
Roman Britain. But in 1102 the then bishop decided to move this
see to the Benedictine abbey of Coventry, a step perhaps principally
due to his desire to acquire part of this monastery's resources,
though further incentives may have been the unpleasant garrison
town atmosphere of Chester (which was now the principal fortress
of the Welsh border) and the residence there of the very powerful
and none too placid Earls of Chester. Various complications built
up, and by the middle of the century the three chapters of Lichfield,
Coventry and Chester were all claiming the right to participate in
the election of new bishops. The very title of the bishop was un-
fixed. Bishop Walter Durdent (1149–59) took his from Coventry,
after his two immediate predecessors had used that of Chester. But
Lichfield with the body of the famous St Chad on the premises
was not to be left in the cold. The inevitable protracted and complex
legal proceedings which ensued ended in 1228, when both Coventry
and Lichfield were declared to be sees and their names used jointly
as the title of the diocese, with monks of the former and canons of
the latter combining to elect new bishops.

By the time the council of London had taken up the question of
translating certain English sees other initiatives to the same end had

already been manifested. At the time of the Norman Conquest easily the most inconveniently placed see was that at Dorchester, a small town of Roman origin, pleasantly sited by the Thames and having within its venerable church the body of St Birinus, one of the great missionaries of Anglo-Saxon England. But it suffered from the immense disadvantage of being situated at the extreme end of the largest diocese in England, whose northern boundary, the river Humber, was some hundred and fifty miles away. The obvious site for the new cathedral was Lincoln, one of the greatest cities of Roman Britain with a noble and central position. Details of this transference have not been worked out fully, but it was certainly effected by Bishop Rémy (1067–92), who got to work before the council of London on what was probably a rather complicated problem, the actual removal apparently taking place in 1072. The new cathedral was planned in magnificent style—'strong as the place was strong, beautiful as the place was beautiful, that it might be pleasing to the servants of God as, according to the necessities of the time, it should be invincible to their enemies', writes a contemporary.

Although East Anglia in 1066 was one of the richest and most populous parts of England, its cathedral arrangements at this time were by no means satisfactory, the pocket-size cathedral (of which interesting remains are yet visible) being situated at the village of North Elmham. In 1071 the new Norman bishop moved the see to Thetford, one of the curiously few major centres of population which East Anglia possessed at this time, but went on to hope to solve the question posed by its apparently inadequate endowment by seeking to transfer it to the immensely rich abbey of Bury St Edmunds. This move inevitably stirred up immense opposition from the monastery, which understandably wanted neither the complications of having a bishop and his household on the premises nor the implied necessity of yielding him an important part of their revenues. As so often when a great Benedictine abbey got down to major legal business, it got its way and the scheme was dropped. Later on, in 1123, the abbey shrewdly obtained a papal privilege ordaining that if the church were converted into a cathedral (a step which from the financial angle seemed commendable) only monks should be bishops thereof—a move which must have greatly damped down any secular interest in such a change. Meanwhile in 1095 the pious Bishop Herbert of Losinga, a Benedictine monk from

Fécamp, began the protracted task of establishing a new cathedral at Norwich, though that at Thetford continued in use until about 1113. Steadily a great Romanesque church was here constructed and endowment built up, the establishment being put in charge of a monastic community whose first members were drawn from the abbey where Herbert had formerly been a monk.

Of these translation of sees, the last to come into effect was that which concerned the people of Somerset, whose cathedral at the time of the Conquest was charmingly but remotely set in the tiny town of Wells. Here recently the life of its secular canons had been vigorously reformed. But the rather tough Bishop John de Villula (1088–1122) bought from the king the abbey and city of Bath, another of the old Roman cities of England, and in 1090 established his see there, taking the title of bishop of Bath. However, the canons of Wells were not to be written off in this way. Legal action rumbled slowly on, until in 1245 the question was settled—episcopal election was to be made by the two chapters jointly and the bishop was to have the title of 'Bath and Wells'. Half a century before this—in 1197—the powerful Bishop Savaric of Bath, who boasted some useful connection with no less a person than the German Emperor Henry IV, had got the English King Richard to permit him to establish his see in the most venerable and most plutocratic abbey of Glastonbury. Such a step must rank as amongst the most temerarious of such actions in the century. The convent rapidly and pertinaciously brought into action all their very heavy artillery. Rome, understandably, for some while played for time, but in 1218 Pope Honorius cancelled the arrangement and in the following year the new title of 'Bath and Glastonbury' was dropped.

It is to be noted that these largely laudable attempts to translate sees to convenient places were very greatly handicapped under contemporary circumstances by the lack of any very obvious source of revenue to cover the very considerable expenses involved, notably that of providing resources adequate to maintain the bishop and his now far from inconsiderable household. Medieval churchfolk did not hold with central ecclesiastical funds and none existed that could be tapped for this purpose, whilst it may be doubted whether the laity of the time would have shown much interest in supporting a special campaign for this kind of 'good cause' which would fetch them very little advantage. The only places where large accumulations of superfluous revenue could be found were the limited number of very large Benedictine monasteries. However, these were most unlikely to welcome being mulcted of their money and site for this purpose. To have a cathedral on their premises would undermine the placidity of their life by having their church put to a double use and a large secular establishment in operation near their cloister, whilst in days when private property was accorded a degree of sanctity today fast becoming extinct, it was thought a form of spiritual treason to surrender for secular use resources specifically given for the support of the monastic life. From the episcopal angle, of course, the problem looked very different, the use of what was, at least arguably, superfluous wealth providing the obvious answer to a difficult and important problem, at a time when quite unavoidably, the size of a bishop's staff was steadily expanding to keep pace with his ever-growing commitments, ecclesiastical and secular.

THE NEW ENGLISH DIOCESES

Despite the considerable interest in ecclesiastical reform in post-Conquest England and the obvious unwieldiness of most of the medieval English dioceses, the number of the latter was only increased by two in pre-Reformation times. Of these one was on reclaimed territory, the other carved from the indefensibly vast diocese of Lincoln.

The latter was set up at the venerable and very rich abbey of Ely. The idea of this conversion was apparently first mooted by Richard, abbot of Ely, (d. 1107), not so much to increase pastoral efficiency as to render his house immune from the jurisdiction of the local bishop (a privilege whose acquisition no few English Benedictines seem to have regarded as the acme of spiritual one-up-manship). At the time of his death the matter was unsettled, but soon afterwards a council gave the scheme official approval and the first bishop was installed—one Hervey, who had been bishop of Bangor but had recently been flung out by his wild flock. He contrived to acquire for his use and that of his episcopal successors a very substantial share of the abbey's revenues, which made the convent very cross and the bishopric one persistently coveted by worldly people.

The second new cathedral was of a very different type, having, like the Welsh dioceses, financial resources which were very far from being tempting, and being set in a diocese perennially liable to be disturbed by the raids of intolerable Scots. This was the diocese of Carlisle which was, without doubt, planned by Henry I following his visit to the city in the winter of 1122–3, though it is just possible that attempts to re-edify the church which became the cathedral had begun as early as 1102, without getting very far. He now established at the church of St Mary a priory for Austin canons, colonised from Nostell Priory near Wakefield and having as their head its prior, Athelwold, who was the king's confessor. But there was no great endowment here to inherit and little to be expected from an infertile and scantily inhabited area, though it acquired useful if distant estates at Horncastle and Melbourn. Only in 1133 was Athelwold consecrated as the first bishop of Carlisle. The place's poverty in 1136 led Pope Innocent to urge King Stephen to give the house financial aid and a decade earlier had caused his predecessor, Calixtus II (1119–24), to authorise Athelwold to continue to hold his priorate of Nostell after his translation to Carlisle— a most unusual privilege. In his time the diocese was much disturbed by warfare in the course of which it passed for a time into Scottish control and after his death (1157), largely because of the disorderliness and poverty of the area, no successor was found for long. Ultimately in 1203, perhaps in a fit of perverse humour, King John gave the bishopric to a vagrant bishop of Ragusa who is unlikely to have regarded Cumbria as a home from home.

MONASTIC CATHEDRALS

An interesting and unusual feature of the medieval cathedrals of England was the fact that a significant proportion of them had chapters which consisted not, as was usual in the West, of secular canons, but of men who lived together as a monastic community. This custom had a venerable history in England before the time of the Norman Conquest, and persisted thereafter to an extent difficult to parallel elsewhere in the Western Church in these times. By 1066 chapters of Benedictine monks had long been installed at Canterbury, Worcester, Winchester and Sherborne. The last of these lost cathedral status soon after but, contrariwise, in 1077 Lanfranc established monks at the little cathedral of Rochester and six years later brethren of the same order were installed in the mighty northern cathedral of Durham. Soon after, as has been noted, another Benedictine chapter came into being at the newly-founded cathedral of Norwich, whilst Ely had long belonged to the same order. Thus no less than seven cathedrals had Benedictine chapters, whilst Carlisle had an Augustinian one.

Of the seven dioceses whose cathedrals had a chapter of secular canons, York, London, Lincoln and Salisbury were all establishments with posts which were a perennial attraction to medieval English go-getters; those of Chichester, Exeter and Hereford were less attractive from this point of view. The two other English dioceses—'Coventry and Lichfield' and 'Bath and Wells'—had twin sees, one having monks, the other secular canons. Although the high proportion of monastic chapters was probably partly due to the strong affection for the Benedictine life which had long prevailed in England, it is to be noted that the existence of a monastic chapter had the invaluable indirect result of not having those valuable preferments of a deanery and canonries that were so coveted by the worldly-minded who, as we shall see, did not always feel obliged even to reside at the church from which they drew such revenues. Here the common revenues were held in common by brethren pledged to a life of individual poverty.

THE BISHOPS

The most notable and unfortunate characteristic of the English episcopate in the century and a half immediately following the Norman Conquest was the very rapid drop in the proportion of them who were monks. The conceptions of a bishop being above all a holy man and the monastery as being much the best place wherein to learn holiness, were both very venerable, and by this time had long ago led to the Eastern Churches insisting that their bishops should be monks. In the crude feudal conditions of Western Europe this tradition never got more than limited acceptance, but in Anglo-Saxon England it was very alive, thanks partly to the fact that Bede's great *Ecclesiastical History* made it very clear that the conversion of England was very largely the work of monks; partly to the great affection for the Benedictine life shown by the English of the period. As we have noted, a huge majority of the later Anglo-Saxon bishops of England were Benedictines.

Although the Normans themselves had no small affection for the latter, William the Conqueror was understandably clear that in view of the precarious nature of his hold over his new kingdom (the battle of Hastings by no means put all England into his control); of the very large size of so many dioceses and of the strong local feeling of northern England, his bishops should be above all men on whose efficiency and absolute loyalty he could count, a view dominant after his time. The local tradition that the archbishop of Canterbury should be a monk was respected, but from now on other such monastic appointments constituted a small proportion of the whole. As Knowles has shown, in the period 1066–1215 a mere twenty-five bishops (about a sixth of the total number) were drawn from monasteries, of whom nineteen were Benedictines, four Austin canons, two Cistercians and one Carthusian. The number of such bishops varied now from three to six at any one time, with peak periods for special reasons immediately after the Norman Conquest and in the reign of Stephen. Even this limited number is less important than it looks, for seven of the appointments were made to the see of Canterbury in accord with the ancient tradition which we have noted, and three more to the small see of Rochester, which was very much a satellite of mighty Canterbury. But it is very significant that the four bishops of this period whom posterity has venerated for their great piety were all monks—Wulfstan of Worcester whom William inherited from Anglo-Saxon days, Lanfranc, Anselm and Hugh of Lincoln.

What sort of people were they that constituted that high proportion of the English episcopate in early post-Conquest times who were not monks? We must be chary of giving too absolute an answer to this question, partly because many have left very little information on their activities and character, partly also because, far more than is now usual, social characteristics were hazy and civil servants unregimented by tradition. Thus some royal servants there were whose severity made even tough sheriffs quake when they came to render their account at the Exchequer, but others had no difficulty in winning the affection and respect of their cathedral colleagues in their episcopal days, like William of Warelwast, who as bishop of Winchester was highly esteemed by his monastic chapter, as the *Winchester Annals* plainly show us.

NORTHERN BISHOPS

In the northern province there are few bishops to analyse. Carlisle had first a monastic bishop of repute, followed by a long vacancy and then a makeshift appointment. The bishops of the lordly see of Durham were wealthy and had a high degree of power and responsibility which ranks them alongside the puissant prince-bishops of Germany. Here good government was essential and was mostly forthcoming. William of St Carileph, bishop here from 1081 until his death in 1096, replaced the none too active chapter of secular canons by a community of Benedictine monks and eternised his name by his planning and commencement of the cathedral church in a style which put it amongst the pioneers of that Western Romanesque architecture which blossomed into early Gothic (page 417): its foundation stone was laid on 11 August 1093. His immediate successor, put in by the unpleasant William Rufus, was Ranulph Flambard (1099–1128), also an unpleasant man, who showed no signs of knowing what holiness was all about. Like his successor the toughish Bishop Hugh of Puiset (1153–95) he acquired the curious episcopal distinction of having done time as a prisoner in the Tower of London. Of Puiset his recent biographer comments, 'patently not of that dedicated class of good pastors, he was at least a popular and a good administrator' (Scammell), words applicable to no few other bishops of post-Conquest England.

What of the very numerous non-monastic bishops in the province of Canterbury in these days? A handful of them were scholars, in an age when the founts of Western learning were at long last showing clear signs of replenishment. Amongst them were Gilbert the Universal (bishop of London 1128–34), Robert of Melun (bishop of Hereford 1163–67) and the canonist Bartholomew (bishop of Exeter 1161–84). But nothing is more obvious than the fact that at this time the high road to episcopal office lay through the little bureaucracy of clerks who worked at the royal court and were given what today seems the misleading titles of 'chaplains' or 'clerks'. This staff was headed by the chief justiciar and the chancellor, and repeatedly holders of these offices went on to hold lucrative and prestigious episcopal appointments which, of course, cost their royal master not a groat. Thus all the four holders of the post of chancellor under William the Conqueror acquired bishoprics in due course and his three chief justiciars all died in episcopal orders, as did William Rufus' two chancellors and most of those holding this office under Henry I and Henry II, including, of course, Thomas Becket. Less eminent but still important was William Warelwast, a faithful royal servant who died bishop of Exeter; Alexander, bishop of Lincoln whose expensive tastes won him the title of 'the Magnificent'; his brother Nigel, bishop of Ely, and their uncle, Roger of Salisbury, all of whom showed a good deal more interest in secular matters than was appropriate.

Here were court bishops of a type which was to dominate, at times virtually to monopolise, English episcopal appointments down to the outbreak of the Reformation. Of the mode of living of one of them, Bishop Robert of Lincoln (1094–1123), we get a most revealing glimpse recorded by a contemporary—'I had opportunities of closely observing the splendour in which our bishop Robert lived. I saw his retinue of gallant knights and noble youths; his valuable horses, his vessels of gold or silver-gilt; the magnificent array of his place, the gorgeousness of his servitors, the fine linen and purple robes, and I thought within myself that nothing could be more blissful.' However, it must be remembered that this high standard of living amongst high ecclesiastics seems to have been a social convention which did not shock the man in the street provided there went along with it almsgiving (page 345) and beneficence. Our writer continues, 'bishop Robert was humane and humble, he elevated the fortune of many and crushed none: he was the orphan's father and beloved by all who surrounded him.'

It is to be noted that in these times it was by no means unknown for a bishop to be expected to hold major secular responsibilities concurrently with his ecclesiastical ones. Understandable, if not laudable, was the royal habit of leaving the kingdom in charge of some trusted ecclesiastic during the king's absence elsewhere, such a person being far less likely than a lay baron to get up to mischief when his master's back was turned. Thus Lanfranc for a time acted as regent here for the Conqueror; the bishop of Durham and arch-bishops of Canterbury and Rouen were acting as chief justiciars in England, and the bishop of Ely as chancellor, whilst Richard I exhibited royal absenteeism of proportions unchallenged before or since. Richard fitz-Neale, treasurer from about 1159 to 1196, held with it ecclesiastical preferment which culminated with the see of

London and is remembered not for episcopal solicitude but for his authorship of 'The Course of the Exchequer', a fascinating and very early example of a tract written by a civil servant to explain to the uninitiated the machinery of his department.

This promotion of civil servants to bishoprics and the conflation of episcopal and political responsibilities which, as we have seen, was to some degree under contemporary circumstances inevitable, meant that the bishops of the age were mostly such as to leave little mark on the spiritual history of their time. Not only had too much of their limited time to be devoted to secular purposes largely irrelevant to their office in the Church of God but, what was worse, they were often by temperament apt to put holiness in the background and business efficiency in the foreground of their priorities. Significantly, few of them felt called to establish that personal contact with their flock which is of such overwhelming importance. The pious Wulfstan of Worcester (d. 1095) had this deep pastoral sense as had the saintly Bishop Hugh of Lincoln (d. 1200) who, as a historian of the diocese has noted, gave it 'a type of pastor hitherto almost unknown.' Social conditions, of course, made the establishment of wide personal contacts difficult, but few bishops tried to do the best they could herein. A similar lack of pastoral sense was seen in the almost total lack of interest in the training of the clergy for their demanding work which long tradition had very properly regarded as a major episcopal responsibility. The inevitable result was the establishment of an episcopate which, whilst it was morally respectable and often intelligent, hard working and administratively efficient, must often have seemed to have presented the Christian life in an uninspiring form, through missing out its prime essential —the search for holiness.

Of this defect much testimony could be quoted. The recent biographer of Archbishop Hubert Walter admits that he was 'without any pretentions to saintliness.' Of the bishops of Lincoln of this time it has been written that they were 'men of secular aim and character, whose weight and ability left its mark on the history of their country, but did little for the advancement of the religious life within the diocese.' Speaking more generally of the English episcopate at this time A. L. Poole declares, 'piety in matters of religion was seldom the primary qualification in the selection of bishops, they continued to be men of affairs and administrators.'

More recently it has been said of the episcopate of late twelfth-century England 'their distinction lay, if not in spiritual qualities, in intellectual and administrative abilities revealed in the routine of diocesan life as well as in the direction of national affairs or the operation of these legal and administrative reforms which mark the reign of Henry II' (Scammell). Such things as 'administrative abilities revealed in the routine of diocesan life' are not apt to spark off much deep religious enthusiasm, and it may very well be that one reason why for so long so many of the more lively souls sought to serve God in the monastic life was because of the uninspiring guise in which Christian living was represented by many of those who ruled English secular life at this time.

However, this type of bishop did have one far from inconsiderable asset. With industry and high competence they developed in post-Conquest England a most impressive and effective machinery which, within its obvious limits, was of significant advantage to the Church. Of this machinery the main elements were those ecclesiastical officials known as archdeacons and rural deans, the which in England survived the Reformation to carry out after it most of the functions with which they had been laden by medieval English bishops. Unfortunately the early evolution of these major offices is obscure.

ARCHDEACONS

The early history of the office of archdeacon is ill-documented and ill-explored. So far as concerns England it seems likely that the principal factor in its rise to importance was the decision of William the Conqueror to terminate the hazy-minded Anglo-Saxon habit of having admittedly ecclesiastical business settled in the local courts. In or soon after 1072 he ordered that such matters should be heard 'in the place where the bishop has selected and nominated' and be there settled 'according to the canons and episcopal laws' without any lay intervention. Before the early decades of the twelfth century mention of archdeacons is mostly sporadic. At first they did not have that special territorial area of the diocese for which they became responsible and which was known as an archdeaconry, but by the middle of the century convenience suggested that this should be so, though the chronology of this development is uneven and obscure. Naturally the number of such units varied largely according to the size of the diocese. By the end of the eleventh century the huge diocese of Lincoln may already have acquired the eight which became its norm. Ultimately, populous London and far-flung Exeter got four, but for Canterbury, Carlisle, Ely and Rochester one sufficed.

The office of archdeacon was administrative and not pastoral and because of this, as the name implies, the archdeacon need not be in more than deacon's orders and frequently was not so in medieval times. He was a major member of the staff of the diocesan bishop, responsible for so much of its business that he was sometimes termed 'the bishop's eye'. He usually drew part of his income from a prebend or portion of revenues of the cathedral of the diocese but this was apt to be considerably augmented from other sources. The prebend was legally a benefice—though a benefice without charge of souls (*sine cura animarum*)—which gave the holder security of tenure, so that he could not be removed without his consent, except for some very grave defect.

The duties with which archdeacons were entrusted by their diocesan bishops were not uniform. The over-busy archbishop of York understandably gave his archdeacon of Richmond a degree of power highly unusual, whilst 'just as the archbishop of Canterbury had functions transcending those of the ordinary diocesan bishop, so the archdeacon of Canterbury was not wholly as other archdeacons' (I. J. Churchill). This latter archdeacon had, amongst other things, the privilege of enthroning every new bishop in the southern province and took for this fees which, it has been claimed, 'were no small part of an income which made him one of the wealthiest of English dignitaries.'

The extent and degree of variety of the duties of other English archdeacons in the early post-Conquest period is very far from clear at present, but may well have quickly assumed the traditional range partially sketched by Chaucer in his characteristic fashion (page 181). They included responsibility for the instruction of clergy below the rank of priest and for parish clerks. An archdeacon had also to ensure that the fabric (i.e. structure) of churches was kept in good order, having power to impose for this purpose a church rate or tax on the inhabitants of the place concerned, and had also to see that all the necessities for the conduct of public worship were duly provided.

He might induct new incumbents into their benefices and had a not unprofitable concern in matters concerning wills.

Two other rights were responsible for much of the unpopularity which, from an early date, attached itself to holders of the archidiaconal office. The first of these was reception of a payment known as 'procurations' due to him from the parish clergy and, theoretically at least, intended to reimburse him for the expenses he incurred in the course of his official visitations of their parishes. Two factors made this especially unpopular. Firstly, the fact that for some time these fees were not carefully regulated allowed some of the archdeacons to be neither modest nor scrupulous hereon. Here a notable offender was the archdeacon of Richmond who on one occasion, inspired intervention by Pope Innocent III by descending on Bridlington Priory to claim hospitality for himself, ninety-seven horses, twenty-one dogs and three hawks as well as for a staff of unspecified dimensions, with the result, so the priory claimed, that the visitors consumed 'in a brief hour more than would have maintained the monastery for a long period.' However, this abuse was fairly soon ended by the establishment of an official 'rate for the job'. This was by no means uniform but in some places came to be 1s. per head for a maximum of six attendants and 1s. 6d. for the archdeacon and his horse.* Procurations were even more unpopular when, as sometimes occurred, the archdeacon drew his fee but did not carry out the visitation.

But the greatest cause of the unpopularity of medieval archdeacons arose from the fact that they were entrusted with seeking out and punishing major moral offences amongst the laity, an engagement which—as Anglican and Calvinists found in later times—was inevitably troublous. His intervention in affiliation cases, for example, was perennially liable to cause great offence, which was aggravated by the fact that for serious breaches of morality the punishment might now include very humiliating acts of public penance with the guilty person parading scantily clad in the traditional white sheet at some major Sunday service in view of the faithful, sometimes receiving, into the bargain, a public beating. Unfor-

---

* This payment long survived in certain English parishes, in one of which, quite recently, the parishioners boggled at paying the archdeacon 6d. annually for a horse which he had not got, and floated an attractive but ultimately unsuccessful scheme to provide him with a steed (which he was known to be incapable of riding).

tunately, rightly or wrongly, from an early date archdeacons' courts had a widespread reputation for corruption, false charges being made or veritable ones withdrawn to obtain financial profit by or with the aid of informers, a situation made worse by the very fact that the procedure of the court apparently allowed much scope for such abuse, whilst successful appeal from its verdicts seems to have been difficult.

The medieval passion for hyperbole being as vigorous as it certainly was, it is difficult to know how seriously to take the complaints thus aroused, but there is no doubt that very soon and for very long the archdeacon was regarded as a highly extortionate and therefore unpopular figure. In 1158 King Henry II, himself no anti-clerical, asserted that archdeacons and deans extorted by their fines more money in a year than he acquired revenue—a highly unlikely thing. A little later, more credibly, a local council accused archdeacons as a class of harrying the laity with false charges of crime and the clergy with undue exactions. About the same time the learned John of Salisbury opined that archdeacons lived by robbery on the sins of the people and were barred from salvation, though this did not prevent him from going on to become an archdeacon himself. His contemporary, Gerald of Wales, admittedly a man almost pathologically devoted to denouncing other people's shortcomings, said that in the popular ear 'archdeacon sounds like archdevil' and two centuries later the entertaining Chaucer asserted 'Purse is the archdeacon's hell'. On the other hand the evidence of that nice and reliable man Henry of Huntingdon, regarding his fellow archdeacons in the diocese of Lincoln, does nothing to confirm such attacks on their probity. It is quite likely that no little of the bribery and corruption was due to minor officials of the archdeacons, and not to their masters.

RURAL DEANS

Below the archdeacon in post-Conquest England ranked the rural dean, an official often termed 'arch-priest' across the Channel and in certain areas of this country known as 'the dean of Christianity'. The origins of this office, which in a less significant form apparently existed in pre-Norman times, are immensely obscure, but it perhaps acquired no little increased importance after the Conquest. Like the archdeacons, rural deans early came to have charge of a specified territorial area, which was known as a rural deanery. This consisted of a group of adjoining parishes, an archdeaconry having within its bounds several such units.

Unlike the archdeacon the rural dean usually was expected to be in priest's orders and held a parish in his area. He was elected by his local clergy though his appointment required confirmation by the bishop. His primary responsibility was to supervise and aid the clergy of his deanery in their work. He had to see that they duly administered the complex round of worship to which they were bound; that they respected their obligations to maintain a celibate life; did not dress frivolously or omit to maintain a tonsure and avoided such perennial and obvious pitfalls as drunkenness and gambling.

The rural dean had also to keep an up-to-date list of the clergy in his deanery in times when change was often quite frequent and, at first, was expected to hear their confessions, though this duty soon came to be shared with others. He had to put into effect the wills of deceased clergy and take charge of the property of vacant benefices. As liaison officer between his clergy and the diocesan bishop he announced to the former episcopal visitations and excommunications, and enforced episcopal sentences on delinquents. In process of time he might have to aid in the collection of ecclesiastical taxes. Like the archdeacon, he might be empowered by the bishop to carry out institutions or inductions to benefices in the diocese. He was also to some degree involved in the trying task of punishing what the Anglican *Book of Common Prayer* later termed 'notorious and evil livers'. Archbishop Hubert Walter ordered that a person strongly suspected of evil living should be admonished if necessary by the rural dean and if this proved ineffective be put on trial by the latter, who was to assign an appropriate penance to one found guilty.

The Secular Cathedrals

Although there is as yet unclear indication how far the secular cathedrals of England attracted in post-Conquest times the considerable flow of benefactions which greeted the monastic renaissance of this period, they certainly shared in the very vigorous and effective reorganisation now so dominant. The most notable example of this came in 1090–1, when the three major secular cathedrals of

York, Lincoln and Salisbury adopted a very elaborate series of 'customs' or observances which laid down in very great detail the way of life to be adopted by their members. To some degree these were based on past local experience, but they were also very strongly influenced by the regulations which governed the life of their opposite numbers in Normandy and its neighbourhood. The sagacity of these new customs made them invaluable for the future, and those of Salisbury were quickly utilised in revised customs drawn up for the lesser cathedrals of Wells, Chichester and Lichfield.

The governing body of these cathedrals consisted of a 'chapter' or official body of senior clergy, each of whom was known as a 'canon' and sooner or later acquired a 'prebend' or portion of the common funds of the place which made them full members of the chapter. Their number varied considerably from place to place and for long was not finally fixed. Ultimately at the top of the list was Lincoln with fifty-eight and Wells which, rather surprisingly, had fifty-five. These were followed by Salisbury with fifty-two. York had thirty-six, Chichester thirty-one and at London St Paul's early acquired what became its traditional thirty. At the bottom of the list were Hereford with twenty-eight, Exeter with twenty-four and Lichfield with twenty-five. It has been suggested that housing all the canons at one of the larger cathedrals would have been immensely difficult but unhappily we cannot tell at this stage what proportion of them tended to reside elsewhere at this time.

As Dr Edwards had shown, by a process not unreminiscent of Parkinson's law the English medieval secular cathedrals gradually built up a stupendously large staff of clergy, servants and dependants of various kinds, some of whom must have worked very much harder than others. At the top of the hierarchy was, of course, the cathedral chapter which was headed by four dignitaries who became responsible for much of the heavy burden of business which the maintenance of the cathedral demanded.

THE DEAN

At the head of them was the *Dean* whose ancient title had originally no special ecclesiastical flavour. On the nature of his functions there was not very great uniformity. A fifteenth-century writer noted 'that which pertains to the office of dean is found to be little defined by law, indeed it consists of different things in different places.' His principal commitment was to lead the activities demanded by the care of the cathedral church and its possessions. If, as was commonly but not invariably the case, the dean held a canonry, he summoned and presided over the chapter and in any case its decisions required his consent. He was the main though not the sole leader of the cathedral's majestic services, supervising its staff and inspecting its churches and manors, though he had little legal power over them. His freedom of action was sternly hedged in by the authority of the diocesan bishop on the one hand and that of the cathedral chapter on the other. As medieval cathedral business tended to increase in process of time, the dean might acquire a personal assistant known as the *Subdean*.

THE PRECENTOR

Early on, the second place in the cathedral hierarchy came to be allotted to the *Precentor*. As his title suggests, his main concern was with the maintenance of the very elaborate music employed in the public worship of the cathedral. He appointed the members of the choir, sang major parts of the services and supervised other sides of its work, as well as being responsible for the provision and maintenance in good repair of the very expensive service books. In his duties he also had a personal assistant, known as the *Succentor*.

THE CHANCELLOR

Third in rank in almost all English cathedrals ultimately came to be the *Chancellor*. His title was of very secular origins, being derived from the screens (*cancelli*) by which the large churches and halls of medieval times were often sub-divided, and was shared with the highest royal official of England, the Chancellor. He had the important duty of directing the schools maintained by the cathedral in accordance with very ancient church law (page 389). Because of this he was sometimes termed 'master of the schools' (*magister scholarum*). He also had charge of the cathedral library and archives, and was responsible for the secretarial side of the chapter's business and for arranging the readings at public services. Inevitably he built up a substantial staff.

THE TREASURER

The fourth of the great quadrilateral of English cathedral dignitaries of the medieval English secular cathedral was the *Treasurer*
who acquired his title and rank somewhat tardily. He had the very
important duty of seeing to the safe custody of the often considerable treasures of the cathedral (mostly plate of silver and sometimes
of gold) used in its services, which was valuable, beautiful and
easily turned into cash if a financial emergency arose. His also was
responsibility for the care of the often numerous and precious
vestments, as well as for other adjuncts of worship such as heating,
furniture, bells and incense. Inevitably he also had an assistant staff.

Below these ranked the other canons who belonged to the cathedral
and beneath them assistant clergy of various kinds, as well as lay
assistants like vergers, a biggish domestic staff and sometimes also
a number of almsmen supported by the cathedral. The financial
history of English cathedrals in the century which immediately
followed the Norman Conquest is obscure, but there is no doubt
that none of them lived anywhere near the poverty line.

A major problem incapable of quick agreed solution was the
nature of the common life to be expected from members of the
chapter of a secular cathedral, a matter on which Christian theory
and practice had never reached any unanimity. The uncompromising
St Augustine of Hippo had insisted that the canons of his cathedral
should live what was in effect a monastic life, expecting them to
add to the obligation of celibacy, individual poverty and a common
life. This went notably further than long church precedent on the
matter demanded, and for long seems to have been little followed
but much admired. In England, as elsewhere at this time, the highest
norm at which most secular cathedrals aimed was that of a life
involving a common refectory, a common dormitory and a common fund from which they drew their revenues. But this was not
popular for several reasons. In the first place it conflicted with a wish
for privacy which cannot be condemned as patently improper.
Further, since most canons' share of the revenue included that from
one or more parish churches, some of their holders preferred to
reside there rather than at a cathedral which must often have been
overstaffed in any case. What was difficult to defend was the practice

already noted, whereby a canon of a cathedral treated his post as merely a convenient way of lining his pocket, paying little attention to the need to reside on the spot and farming out ecclesiastical responsibilities to one or more of those clergy who so abounded in medieval times. As we shall see, prolonged and variegated attempts to enforce an effective common life in English cathedrals had little success, despite the fact that they were unencumbered by the problem created by marriage of clergy.

Secular Colleges

The establishments just considered besides being cathedrals were also 'collegiate churches', i.e. managed by a chapter of secular clergy, not by an incumbent with paid assistants. To this latter type belong a number of other English churches which have also come to be known as 'secular colleges'. In Anglo-Saxon times they had been comparatively numerous and quite important, but as time went on their influence decayed, owing partly to the piecemeal establishment of hundreds of parish churches which absorbed no small part of their pastoral responsibilities and income. After the Norman Conquest a number of them, including no small proportion of the wealthier ones, were given over to the monastic life which to men in these days seemed so much more edifying than the sometime slackish life which the secular occupants exhibited. Chief amongst the colleges thus lost was the great college of Cirencester, which Henry I transmuted into the wealthiest houses of Austin canons in England, and the college which Harold had set up at Waltham which Henry II gave to brethren of the same order. Notably dotted about the West country existed various others which were now put to similar use, such as Bodmin, Launceston, Plympton, Taunton, St German's and Hartland.

This diminution in the number of English secular colleges was not off-set at this time by any significant addition to their number, largely because admiration for the monastic life was now at one of its peak levels in Christian history. As a result, by the close of the twelfth century English secular colleges numbered only about seventy-five, a paltry figure to set against the hundreds of monasteries newly set up in the land. Most of the colleges were small or mediocre in size, but a few ancient giants there were. Amongst these we must class the ancient East Riding twins of Ripon and Beverley, both immensely affluent, and Southwell not far away. Of the internal life of such establishments in the century and a half which followed the Norman Conquest we know very little. By what seems to us a curious arrangement, several of the smaller secular colleges were set up alongside or inside castles, as at Bridgnorth, Hastings, Leicester, Oxford and Tickhill. Such places had often very restricted sites and responsibilities and very restricted incomes, and of course, no great hierarchy of officials.

Parish Churches

Evidence on the history of English parish churches in the first century and a half after the Conquest is scanty and very limited in its scope, mostly consisting of isolated details regarding the ownership of advowsons and names of incumbents. Now, as down to quite recent centuries, various interesting aspects of parish church activities went unrecorded so that large gaps in their history will permanently remain unfilled, such as the number and nature of public services, and the attendance and alms thereat.

Much to be regretted is the inadequacy of the evidence regarding the actual number of the parish churches and of the clergy who served them at this time. The increase in wealth and population of rural England by the late twelfth century almost certainly led to an increase in both, but neither can be estimated with any clarity. Establishing new parish churches was an expensive and difficult business apt to arouse strong legal opposition, so one may doubt whether very many more of them were now founded, but chapels of various kinds were much easier to set up and probably a largish number was established from the late twelfth century onwards for some time to come, whilst in these times, as later, existing chapels acquired parochial status. Our earliest useful statistics suggest a total of about 9500 English parish churches by the end of the thirteenth century. Evidence regarding the number of clergy in medieval England is mostly so very scanty that estimates of it are mostly unwise.

Two developments in the history of English parish churches at this time are, however, quite clear. The first of these is the immense amount of rebuilding of them which took place, mostly in or around the last half of the twelfth century, a development which is clearly to be associated with the contemporary increase in wealth, population and probably also in piety about this time. That church building in England was active even in the late eleventh century when non-theological factors operated against such things, is evident from the *Life* of St Wulfstan which shows him dedicating various new places of worship, but archaeological evidence in the shape of literally hundreds of so-called 'Norman' doors still in use in English parish churches is a useful pointer to immense architectural activity here in the latter half of the twelfth century.

Also very evident is the fact that the advowsons of an enormous number of parish churches were given to English monasteries and, to a much lesser degree, to cathedrals and collegiate churches in the generations which immediately followed the Norman Conquest. As we have seen, the Gregorian Reform had successfully launched a vigorous campaign on a broad front to diminish lay control of church appointments, and it was partly the direct or indirect influence of this which led to no few private owners in these times to hand over advowsons to ecclesiastical institutions. Notably was this so in the case of those establishing new monasteries, barons, for example, often conveying to their new foundations the patronage of all the churches which they owned. Such gifts had obvious advantages. They much diminished the dangers of appointments thereto of unsuitable people, since the monastic chapter which presented such livings had not the same selfish temptation to put in a friend or a relation as had a private patron. As we shall see, contemporary church law made it perfectly possible to arrange for some fraction of the income of such benefices to be syphoned off for the use of the monastery owning the patronage, a matter of real advantage in the case of no few of the later monastic foundations which were often poorish ones established by people of moderate means. Such arrangements at first seem to have been made informally and not always fairly, but, as we shall see (page 170f), from the late twelfth century onwards such transactions came under strict official scrutiny.

CLERICAL CELIBACY

As we have seen, the Gregorian Reformers regarded as an essential element in their programme imposition of the celibate life on clergy who belonged to the higher grades of the ministry. Such a demand was bound to arouse very vigorous opposition in England and in Normandy, for in both areas clerical marriages at all levels had long been very widespread. As a dutiful archbishop, Lanfranc had no alternative but to take up the matter, though his wisdom and moderation restrained him from seeking to impose rapid and radical measures. In 1076 he took major action, ordering that unmarried candidates were not to be ordained to the grades of priest or deacon unless they pledged themselves to the celibate life, but married clergy were allowed to retain their wives. The degree of success this achieved in practice is uncertain.

Anselm was temperamentally unable to compromise on such a question and at a major council at London in 1102 he led a major attack on married clergy. No archdeacon, priest or deacon could marry. Any of them who were married could not retain their wives, nor could subdeacons who had broken their pledge to the celibate life. Such a harsh measure caused no little suffering for some who could hardly be regarded as criminals and was not likely to be universally accepted. The fact that by now the faithful were ordered not to attend Masses celebrated by married priests caused additional indignation. Rome was not unaware of the complexities caused by its new claims and the pope informed Anselm that sons of married clergy were not automatically to be refused ordination. But in a council at London in 1108 the hard-liners were on top. Disobedient clergy were to be suspended and a married priest was only to see his wife in the open air in the presence of two reliable witnesses. Deprivation of function and benefice was to rapidly fall on the disobedient. In effect there was the option of abandoning either one's spouse or one's ministry, but the law was widely broken, sometimes aided by bribes to officials ecclesiastical and non-ecclesiastical. The fact that before 1130 seven bishops as well as a brace or two of other cathedral dignitaries were married men did not help the reformers cause, though the fact that Richard, bishop of London, gave prebends of his cathedral to two sons and nephews was no good advertisement for clerical marriage. Very effective, however, seems to have been the drastic action by Calixtus II, partially because half a century of Roman propaganda had now dimmed the image of married clergy. In a great council at Rheims in 1123 any relations with wives or concubines was forbidden, continuance in this after expulsion being punishable by excommunication. At the same time the allied practice of hereditary church appointments being countenanced was vigorously prohibited.

This measure seems quickly to have achieved a considerable success in England, and very quickly in subsequent decades traces of higher clergy being married very largely disappear. However, human nature and contemporary social conditions combined to prevent total disappearance of any form of married life among the clergy, indications of its existence showing up from time to time. Some of the ladies in question, enjoying a status which though unofficial was also stable, were roughly termed 'concubines' or 'hearth women' (*focarie*), a term probably implying more than a passing relationship. It is totally impossible to assess the size of this underground movement, but almost certainly it was small and is likely to have been found mostly in remote rural areas, though this we cannot prove. Of the mass of the parish clergy at this time we have next to no useful information. They were certainly ill-educated, but this would not prevent them being pastoral-minded. Celibacy and the poverty of many benefices would put off some secular-minded.

CHAPTER 4

THE MONASTIC RESURGENCE

In England the century and a half which followed the Norman Conquest witnessed a stupendous resurgence of monasticism, the number of monasteries here which in 1066 was a mere 61 jumping to the region of 700 a century and a half later, and increasing notably even thereafter. At first, for several decades, this increase was not very marked, but soon came the deluge—a chronicler notes with accuracy that there were more monasteries founded in England in the reign of Stephen (1133–54) than in the previous hundred years. Concurrently the monastic population of England which was about 1100 in 1066 had increased to about 12 500 later, and went on to reach its peak of about 17 500 on the eve of the Black Death. What were the reasons for this very great and protracted expansion?

Clearly the considerable increase in English wealth and population in the period contributed to it indirectly, by providing far more resources, human and financial, than those on which the Anglo-Saxons could draw, but equally clearly such increases by no means guaranteed the creation of more monastic houses and inmates. The massive support for monasticism in these days had more fundamental causes.

In some instances a monastery was founded after military victory either as an act of thanksgiving or in reparation for the lives lost therein, or both. Thus William the Conqueror established the abbey of Battle on the field whereon he had been vouchsafed his momentous victory. Similarly, over a century later King Philip Augustus of France set up the abbey of La Victoire near Senlis after triumph at the most crucial battle of Bouvines (he ascribed his success here to the mercy of God, the prayers of the Cistercians and the courage of his soldiers). Other monastic foundations originated as an expensive form of apology, like the noble twin abbeys which the Conqueror set up in Caen because he had married a wife who was more closely related to him than the rather fussy rules of the Church on

95

the subject permitted. Similarly, Henry II founded three abbeys in England as part of his penance for his involvement in the tempestuous events which culminated in the murder of Thomas Becket. The Earl of Albemarle founded the abbey of Meaux because old age and corpulence prevented his fulfilling his vow to journey to the Holy Land.

There can be no doubt, however, that such special reasons as this lay behind the establishment of only a small proportion of English monasteries—such contingencies as gross corpulence amongst the English baronage must have been rare, as also were very major victories and very major transgressions.

None of the problems which face the historian is apt to present more difficulty than that of discovering the motive, or motives, which inspired particular human acts, for these are so often mixed, are by no means always what the person in question believed them to be and are mostly incapable of scientific demonstration. A politician may be adopting a policy for a reason quite different from that which he announces in public, and a magnate who makes a great benefaction to charity may do so from various not necessarily incompatible motives—the wish to aid society, a desire to help his home town, the hope of enhancing his chance of obtaining a peerage, the advisability of placating his wife—are but a mere selection of the possibilities which may be operative in some degree or another. Similarly, for the foundation of English monasteries in the Middle Ages motives were certainly varied, and might occur in various combinations; evidence is too scanty to allow conclusive diagnosis of the huge majority of cases.

There can be little doubt that the social services which the monasteries supplied was one reason which impelled their foundation, though it was almost certainly a subsidiary one. In many areas the hospitality offered to traveller and others (see Chapter 12) was of very great value to the general public, as various of the protests against the Dissolution illustrate. For tenants of the local monastery there were often perquisites which were well worth having, like the schooling which Furness Abbey gave local lads, along with various material bonuses. Perhaps the chief advantage of a monastic presence was the example of disciplined behaviour given by its inmates which to some degree permeated local society. A chronicler notes that when Norman monasticism began to flower in the ravaged lands of Yorkshire 'the inhabitants thereof began to alter their behaviour for the better from their uncouth life ... many also abandoning worldly life entered upon monastic warfare.'

The principal inspiration of monastic foundation was undeniably religious in nature. It is expressed in what became a stock form in the foundation charters of post-Conquest religious houses. Herein the founder asserts that he did what he did 'for the good of my soul' (*pro bono anime mee*), it being sometimes further laid down that the gift was also made for the spiritual good of his ancestors and successors. What does this imply? It can denote more than one thing and did not necessarily mean exactly the same to all those who employed it. But it certainly inspired the desire to establish a community which would be under the strictest obligation to remember regularly in their worship and in other ways the souls of such benefactors. Thus for the founder of Wigmore Abbey the house had a Mass said daily by one of the canons and each week the office for the dead. In addition, weekly doles of bread and beer were made to the poor and strangers, whilst on the anniversary of his death a hundred poor were 'plentifully fed'. When the founder's son became fully aware of all this he abandoned the hostility he had shown to the abbey and gave it a very fertile piece of land called 'Mortimer's treasure', declaring 'I will give it to keep for me to a treasurer who will put it in a treasury from which no robber may steal it, where no moth will eat it, and where it will not be stripped bare by beasts but it will bear fruit for my soul.' As we see repeatedly, medieval opinion had no doubt that the acquisition of regular intercession and the dispensation of alms on a scale which hurt were the common spiritual responsibilities which any man who took his religious obligations seriously would inevitably accept and which would bear fruit for his soul; to expect to obtain ultimate union with God merely through orthodox belief and pious intentions was absurd.

But men being as disparate as they are, such actions, as always, might be rooted in motives of very varying quality. To crude people, for example, extensive almsgiving might spring from the conviction that this had the same capacity for producing automatic rewards in the spiritual world as a penny-in-the-slot machine has in the material one, but more sensitive minds might regard it as an invaluable exercise in unselfishness whereby a man could beat off that temptation to greediness which cuts him off from his Maker. However this may be, it is quite certain that a principal and probably in the huge majority of cases the dominant motive for founding a monastery in these times was the desire of the individual concerned to improve his spiritual status and often also that of close relatives.

However, along with this worked another potent religious factor —the profound contemporary admiration for the monastic life as the form of Christian living which, by and large, produced appreciably more successfully the virtues which a man must seek to acquire. This sentiment at this time almost certainly was based on solid fact. In the eleventh and twelfth centuries too many clergy had at their disposal facilities for building up a firm and well-balanced Christian life which were very far from being adequate. Books they could mostly not afford to buy, and systematic instruction was notably deficient. The sacrament of confession with its associated asset of counsel on the individual's need they used little. For spiritual sustenance they had to rely very largely on frequent attendance at Mass and use of their daily round of public prayer—(how assiduously the latter was employed it is impossible to tell). Under such circumstances it is not surprising that their life was not free from crudity.

If monastic piety was much more virile and refined than non-monastic piety in these times it was for the simple reason that it undertook the perennial responsibilities of the Christian life much more seriously and scientifically—after all, no-one whose Christianity was merely skin-deep would be likely to seek to lead the monastic life, with its searching demands for self-sacrifice. Within the monastery the brethren regulated their lives by a carefully planned and detailed programme. Here was an intensive and regular round of worship having vitality and variety. Here were comparatively frequent opportunities for communion and confession with Mass daily and spiritual advice to be had for the asking from folk likely to be competent to give it. Here were daily readings from the Bible and other spiritual writings, together with abundant time and quiet wherein a man could give some thought to his personal problems. Here, in short, the Christian life was strong because opportunities for its cultivation were sedulously and scientifically organised.

In later medieval days there were to be found certain major saints who were seculars, but in the first century which followed the Norman Conquest in England, as we have seen, the only bishops whom the future was extensively to remember for their sanctity were all monks. 'The monastery' wrote a twelfth-century intellectual, 'is the school of love wherein the study of love is pursued, love's disputations held, love's questions answered.' At bottom it was principally because of this that monasticism was so beloved by the general public.

Again and again men threw up all to embrace the monastic life through being entranced by the quality of Christian living which they saw therein displayed, like Hugh of Fleury, a kinsman of King William Rufus, who wrote off his military career to become a monk at St Augustine's, Canterbury, after beholding there 'the love of the saints and the cleanness of life of the monks.' Equally significant are the unsolicited testimonials to the impressive characters of those living the monastic life that occur in the chronicles, like that to William, abbot of the Norman abbey of Bec. Magnates, we are told, entrusted him with their affairs and clerics 'found in him the mirror looking into which the ecclesiastical orders should study to conform themselves.' In him were united 'the weight of consummate wisdom and the prerogatives of a pure holiness . . . he is reverenced by venerable abbeys, synods and courts as a prudent and eloquent man, as just as he is discrete. . . . He tastes the delights of authority but does not feast on them; neither money nor influence does he fear but speaks his mind whether in giving sentence or tendering advice. As change of circumstances demand he shows himself now gentle, now severe . . . a calm enemy to every vice but to no individual.' Similarly warm is a contemporary testimonial to the nuns of Shaftesbury, 'it is hard to know whether to applaud more their assiduity in the service of God or their affability . . .; assent is thus properly accorded to those people who say that the world, which has so long tottered under the weight of its sins, is entirely supported by their prayers.' Of the theological factors of these times the value attached to monastic living and monastic praying is perhaps the chief, and the one which most potently influenced contemporary social life.

THE BENEDICTINES

As we have seen, the monasteries to be found in England on that day when King Harold was alive and dead were very unevenly distributed over the face of the country and varied greatly in size and wealth. All of them based their life on the so-called *Rule of St Benedict*.

The primary purpose of the Benedictine life was the maintenance of an elaborate round of communal worship. This began in the very early morning with the long office of Matins and then, after a brief return to the dormitory, continued at intervals throughout the day. Both the text of the services and the music which in varying degree accompanied it, tended to become increasingly complicated as time wore on, the latter developing the majestic 'Gregorian Chant' or 'plainsong' which was to long outlast the Middle Ages. Later medieval Benedictines did not normally undertake missionary work (St Gregory's famous mission to England had been a highly exceptional venture) and they scarcely ever took charge of parish churches in our period. Their milieu was appreciably more literate than that of the outside world, especially before the rise of the medieval universities, but it was no part of their function to provide schooling for the outsider. On a modest scale they collected and copied books in days when both of these were very rare pursuits, and from time to time fostered the aptitude of brethren with scholarly and artistic interests of one kind or another. They provided various useful amenities for poor of the locality and showed special regard for travellers (Chapter 12).

The important expansion of Benedictinism in England which followed in the wake of the Norman Conquest was powerfully aided by several local factors. It was useful that for several decades to come the Benedictines here were without that major rivalry for patronage that was innocently offered by the new monastic orders now making progress in certain other parts of the Western Church. Also important was the entirely coincidental fact that the duchy whence came William the Conqueror and his followers, was, like England, one wherein Benedictinism was very highly in favour and also as yet unrivalled by monastic competitors. Thirdly, religious conventions of the age made it very likely that the *nouveau riche* baronage of England in Norman days would display their piety by founding monasteries here, many of which would be linked with those of their homeland.

The question of whether the Normans who established themselves in England after 1066 should be classed as 'goodies' or 'baddies' still excites historians, and they have not produced a unanimous answer to it. Certainly their influence was not uniform in every field of their activity. It has been declared that 'in the minor arts the Norman Conquest was little short of a disaster' and the same is held true in the fields of vernacular literature. But so far as monastic life in England was concerned, the verdict of one highly qualified to judge is highly favourable. Writes Knowles, 'The Norman monasteries were in a position to give England a literary culture and enthusiasm for at least a modest amount of learning to which no parallel, even the remotest, could be found at home.' If the new abbot of Glastonbury staged an inappropriate display of muscular Christianity when he set armed men on his monks who disliked some of his ways and who proceeded to fight an unconventional rearguard action in their conventual church with candle-sticks and benches, this was highly exceptional—'the new rulers appointed during the Conqueror's reign were an unusually able and exemplary body of men' affirms Knowles. Certainly the reorganisation of local monastic life under the leadership of the archbishop Lanfranc made fruitful progress and helped to enhance the already considerable prestige of Benedictinism in England.

The increase in the number of Benedictine houses in England after the Norman Conquest was certainly pronounced. By 1215 the 61 houses which existed in 1066 had increased fivefold to 225 houses of men and 75 of women.* In size these varied considerably. A few new abbeys, like Battle and Selby, were large, but many others were of mediocre size and some quite small. A notable feature now in northern England was the restitution there of the monastic life, which included its re-establishment on one or two sites of famous Anglo-Saxon monasteries now long derelict, like the erstwhile illustrious abbey of Whitby on its noble cliff.

Some 78 Benedictine houses were what came to be known as 'alien priories', i.e. monastic establishments whose mother-houses were situate on the far side of the Channel. For obvious reasons the latter were almost all French and mostly Norman, notable being the popularity of the great abbeys of Fécamp, Jumièges, Bec-Hellouin, Boscherville and Mont St Michel. Unfortunately, however, a sizeable proportion of these alien priories were poorly en-

---

* These and similar monastic statistics which follow are unavoidably only approximate.

dowed and so able to maintain only a very small number of brethren; such houses were often little more than farmsteads with a chapel attached. Such gifts often originated naturally enough through the wish of new Norman rulers to establish a link with their native heath and must have been very difficult for a mother-house to refuse without giving offence. As was clear from the first, such small establishments produced little financial profit and entailed the residence in areas whose language they knew not of brethren who were effectively deprived of that full common life that was of the essence of Benedictinism.

THE CLUNIACS

By the end of the twelfth century there had taken firm root in England several new monastic orders which combined observance of the *Rule of St Benedict* with acceptance of elaborate new observances and forms of government that gave each its own special ethos. Of these the first to arrive in Norman England was the order of Cluny whose name derived from its mother-house, founded in 909 deep in the beauteous land of Burgundy. Here was gradually evolved an elaborate and somewhat novel approach to monastic life.

The now traditional Benedictine insistence that nothing was to be given precedence to the maintenance of an elaborate round of worship was much amplified by the adoption of an immensely complex music and various expansions in the text of the offices which led to communal worship completely dwarfing all other aspects of the Cluniac monastic life—a visitor to the abbey in the mid-eleventh century concluded that the length of the services left little time for any sins save those of thought! Allied to this was an immense stress on visual beauty and magnificence. After a good deal of rebuilding in its early history the abbey church of Cluny apparently became the largest church in Western Christendom and so remained until the fanatics of the Renaissance rebuilt St Peter's, Rome, its total length falling little short of 600 feet; of it little but a mighty transept with twin towers remains. Cluniac furnishings were similarly splendid, including giant candelabra, exquisite tapestries, paintings and vestments along with most precious, gleaming altar vessels, and its carving was lavish and of the highest quality. Behind the provision of such things lay the firm Cluniac conviction that nothing was too splendid to be used in the service of God.

A very novel feature was the highly centralised constitution which was gradually developed. Until the widespread expansion of the order made the practice impracticable, it was expected that monks of Cluny's daughter-houses should make their profession at their mother-house, and the abbot of Cluny had the right to visit and correct anything which he found amiss in other houses of the order; understandably the abbots of Cluny helped themselves to the proud title of 'abbot of abbots', though in due course the firm hand of the papacy made them disgorge it. The Cluniac régime left very scant opportunity for intellectual and literary activities, nor did it allow more than minimal attention to that manual labour which from the first had been regarded as a major element in Christian monastic life. But again and again visitors stood spellbound in the immense mother church, staggered by its artistic richness and the sonorous chant which its huge choir of brethren sent reverberating through the majestic vaults—surely here was 'none other than the House of God.'

In France the Cluniac order was immensely popular, but in England its progress began late and was never extensive. The first house here was the lordly abbey set up at Lewes by William of Warenne, one of the leading barons of the day, in 1077. To this thirty-six more were added, the last of these being founded in 1222. Among them were Montacute, Pontefract, Thetford, Bermondsey, Castle Acre and Much Wenlock, all of which were sizeable places. The architectural remains of the last two illustrate the high artistic standards in which the order delighted, as do the attractive capitals from Reading Abbey recently revealed.

THE CISTERCIANS

Very much more influential in England was the Cistercian order, which in its first half-century of existence generated in Western Europe an intense emotional appeal that engendered massive and instantaneous if rather short-lived expansion, and attracted huge numbers of men of every class to its cloisters.

Their name came from their mother house of Cîteaux (*Cistercium*) set up in 1098 on a lonely site beyond Dijon. The early years of the house's history were precarious, but it soon went on to hit the ecclesiastical headlines in no small way, principally through the witness of its most celebrated member, St Bernard of Clairvaux, one of the most magnetic personalities in Christian history. His high intelligence, profound sensitivity, golden eloquence and deep mystical experience combined to make him the most influential preacher of the century; his spiritual writings posterity has found good reason to cherish. The overwhelming value of the Cistercian way of life he preached persistently with electrifying effects—it was said that the mothers hid their sons when they heard of his approach lest he swept them off to the cloisters. The important but less spectacular task of organising the new form of life in effective shape was providentially and superbly undertaken, principally through the efforts of an Englishman, Stephen Harding, abbot of Cîteaux from 1110 to 1133. With most remarkable speed and vigour the order expanded, acquiring no less than 300 houses by 1153. Thereafter its increase declined rapidly and after the early thirteenth century in many parts of Western Europe, including England, was very limited.

The dominant characteristic of their programme was very conservative—the maintenance of an austere, contemplative life in places isolated from human society. It was characterised by considerable austerity on such major matters as the use of food, artistic decoration and the scope of silence. Their first *Rule* started with the injunction that houses be constructed in 'places remote from human habitation', and, with very rare exceptions, Cistercian houses were established well away from towns, mostly in remote valleys or on lonely plains. Involvement in pastoral work was rigorously eschewed and, with minute exceptions, no parish altar was attached to their houses, preaching or administering the sacraments to the outside world being largely limited to the little chapel which stood near the main entrance of the house and which was provided for the use of their dependents and visitors. Returning vigorously to primitive practice hereon, the Cistercians laid very great stress on the importance of brethren making manual labour a significant element in their daily life, and for some time tended to refuse gifts of tithes or advowsons. Food was simple and largely vegetarian, inexpensive both to acquire and cook. Meat was largely reserved for the use of the sick; fish, eggs, vegetables and bread forming the staple diet. During much of the day silence was strictly observed. There was only one room with heating available for the monks, and access to this was only to be had at limited times of the day during the colder portion of the year. At first the cloisters in which they spent no little time had unglazed windows; existence therein seems to have been alleviated by very effective underclothing.

A major social change in Western monastic life came with the very extensive use which the Cistercians made of the 'lay brethren', folk who had no aspirations and usually no qualifications for taking holy orders, but gave themselves wholeheartedly to divine service in simpler ways, notably through manual labour of various kinds for their house. Hitherto, lay brethren had tended to be few and little regarded, but the Cistercians made them an invaluable element in religious life, as well as one which offered the faithful laity a fruitful form of spiritual endeavour. They had their own often extensive living quarters, and were allotted the western part of the church for what was, inevitably, a comparatively simple round of worship. Many of them, however, were to be found working on the outlying farms of their abbeys. Unfortunately we have few reliable statistics to illustrate the immense popularity of this vocation in early Cistercianism. A contemporary asserts that in the time of Ailred (d. 1167) Rievaulx Abbey had no less than 600 of them, but medieval use of large statistics is often pictorial rather than mathematical and this figure may not be accurate. The claim that in 1249 Meaux Abbey had ninety lay brethren is more credible; Waverley is said to have had one hundred and twenty in 1187. That the lay brothers were termed *conversi* ('the converted') is an interesting illustration of the revivalist spirit behind their life.

In some ways the most remarkable feature of the Cistercian order is to be found in their constitution. The old Benedictine tradition which regarded each abbey* as an independent unit was jettisoned, as was the centralisation adopted by the Cluniacs. Instead, the Cistercians early established a system of annual general chapters which was oligarchic in that all members were abbots, but democratic in that all were of equal importance. These 'general chapters' had complete control of the order, laying down new regulations and enforcing or modifying old ones, as well as dealing with partic-

---

* All Cistercian and Premonstratensian houses ranked as abbeys as did a minor proportion of Benedictine ones and a very few English houses of Austin canons, others ranking as priories.

E

ular local problems as they arose. They began in 1116, being held at Cîteaux and were attended by all abbots as far as possible, though because of the wide expansion of the order it was sensibly laid down that those in far distant parts were not expected to attend every year.

This system, unlike so much medieval regulation, was never a dead letter in practice, but functioned vigorously and efficiently for very long to come, being reinforced by the visitations by individual abbots which did much to ensure that its work was relevant and respected. It was a notable indication of the good sense of the Cistercians in the field of monastic organisation that they insisted that no new houses should be founded with a colony smaller in size than the 'full convent' of an abbot and twelve brethren (symbolising Christ and His apostles). By this rule they avoided the persistent and trying problems which afflicted Benedictine and Augustinian orders, which were prepared to permit the establishment of a new monastic house with a mere handful of brethren whose size was often quite inadequate to ensure a stable future for the place. A further novel feature in Cistercianism was that all houses of the order were exempt from the traditional visitation by the local bishop, a sensible enough decision in view of the effectiveness of their own machinery and the unlikelihood of most of the bishops of the time being of any great use in solving various of their problems. Instead, each abbey was liable to be visited by the abbot of the house which had provided the brethren which first colonised it, whilst the abbey of Cîteaux itself was liable to visitation by the heads of its first daughter-houses.

Partially to make adequate space for manual labour, the Cistercians severely limited the length and complexity of the programme of monastic worship, laying down a scheme which was comparatively short. Further, although they never thought of abolishing use of those visual aids so beloved in the medieval West, they much reduced their luxuriance. They had no scruples about constructing for their worship those lordly conventual churches which were now very much *de rigueur*, and they readily accepted the glories of the new Gothic style whose rise coincided with that of their order. On the other hand they reacted against the richness of late Romanesque ornamentation with a vigour similar to that shown by many moderns in their rejection of Victorian luxuriance. In a famous diatribe which is more psychologically interesting than artistically convincing, St Bernard inveighed in his usual vigorous way against the artistic lusciousness of Cluny, their candelabra 'glittering as much through their jewels as their lights' and cloister sculpture with its 'disgusting monkeys, spotted tigers or fighting soldiers'.

Early Cistercian art was, in contrast, characterised by a certain austerity, albeit one which was far from flat and uninspired as the superb remains of Fountains and Rievaulx bear eloquent witness to this day. Buildings were lofty and graceful but ornamentation was very restrained. As with Islam and Judaism, use of the human figure and of animals was frowned upon, motifs of Cistercian decoration often consisting of geometrical patterns and foliage. Few or no wall-paintings and precious fabrics glowed on the walls of their churches, which were apparently often simply whitewashed, and for some time no tombs entertainingly decked with sculpture were allowed admittance. The colourful stained glass windows now rapidly coming into fashion were banned, whilst the use of gold and silver for such things as altar vessels was strictly limited and crucifixes were made only of wood. Of much of this austerity the Quakers would have approved, as they would of the very important place in Cistercians' programme of periods of silence though this did not, of course, mean that the latter in any way neglected that primacy of the sacraments which has always characterised Catholic worship. To many moderns such a programme seems forbidding, but many church folk of the twelfth century found it immensely fruitful since it excluded so many things that can divert attention from man's main aim 'to know God and enjoy Him for ever' and provided so many facilities to do this. Potently it recalled Christ's saying, 'my kingdom is not of this world.'

In the middle decades of the century in England, as elsewhere, the popularity of Cistercianism was nothing short of astounding, with substantial new abbeys being established at a remarkable rate. The first English house was that founded at Waverley in Surrey in 1128, but it never attracted much attention and the centre of gravity of the movement lay in the long neglected north. About 1132 on a gracious hillside north of Helmsley in North Yorkshire was established the abbey of Rievaulx with no less a person than St Bernard's secretary, one William, as its abbot. As, apparently, had been planned, the house quickly became the main centre of the order's expansion in England. Massive recruitment enabled it to establish no less than five daughter-houses within fifteen years and it is thought to have had no less than 140 monks by 1167. Its fourth abbot, Ailred, was canonised and ranks amongst the very limited number of important medieval English writers on spiritual matters.

The same year that saw the community established at Rievaulx witnessed another abbey begun at Fountains, near Ripon, where the narrow valley abounded in the springs (*fontes*) from which its name derives. Here also progress was remarkable, six daughter-houses being set up by 1150, of which one was in Norway. The original great church and its attendant cloister buildings, though now roofless, remain to an extent unparalleled elsewhere in Western Europe, and include a huge range for the lay brethren. In course of time Fountains became the richest Cistercian abbey in England, with much property in Yorkshire and the Lake District. Between 1128 and 1154 no less than fifty-one Cistercian abbeys were founded elsewhere in England, the final total being seventy-six, all of which started with at least thirteen members and most of which probably for some time steadily increased the number of their brethren and the extent of their possessions. Although the houses were widely dispersed, few counties being without one of them, a very substantial proportion of them were to be found along the Welsh border, in Lincolnshire and in the lands north of the Humber, where monastic-ism hitherto was little to be seen. In such areas as East Anglia the multitudinous villages and shortage of massive baronial estates were unfavourable to more than very limited Cistercian colonisation, since their way of life demanded a remote site and a substantial area of land by cultivation of which the brethren maintained themselves.

Quite accidentally the Cistercians gave to English agriculture its first major fillip since Roman times. They were happy to settle in poor, uncultivated lands, quickly setting to work to remove their marsh and scrub. For this task they possessed assets which were literally incomparable. They did not require immediate returns but could await patiently for profitability to an extent which barons and squires could not, whilst from an early stage they built up amounts of capital to finance agricultural expansion on a scale at which some local lay magnates and farmers may well have looked with envy. Their numerous lay brethren gave them a labour force which worked for God and no pay and because of this was very much less likely to strike than most labour forces, whilst the value of such agricultural labours was usefully enhanced by a papal privilege which exempted them from payment of tithe on land which they cultivated with their own hands.

Although part of their farming was to provide their own food and clothing, very quickly many English Cistercian houses showed major interest in the wool trade which was now developing very rapidly here and ultimately became much the most important element in English exports of late medieval times. Great tracts of land were bought up or sometimes created by enclosures (though these, as always, were liable to cause hardship to locals) and stocked with large flocks of sheep. The wool which these produced was not of the ultra-fine quality needed for the rich fabrics for which contemporary people were ready to pay great prices, but was nevertheless in great demand, notably by Italian merchants who, from the early thirteenth century onwards shrewdly trekked around England to buy up the local crops. So rapid and important was the rise of this trade that when, at one stage in his reign, Richard I found himself in especially dire need of much money at short notice, he found some solution to the problem in confiscating the Cistercian wool crop. From the depredations of his successor, King John, Cistercians also suffered much.

On a smaller scale, but much more important to contemporaries than it might seem to us, was the revival of mining which in England, as in other areas of Western Europe, was getting under way at this time. If the prize find of the century in England was the royal silver and lead mines at Alston, more sustained was the development of the iron trade in which the Cistercians played a useful and profitable part. The abbots of Furness, Calder and Holme Cultram all developed iron mining in parts of Cumbria, as did Byland Abbey in Yorkshire.

In the first decades of their history the English Cistercians had very often been confronted by much hardship and poverty, partly through lack of means, partly through being too ready to accept for new houses sites where the weather was often bad and the soil poor, which forced a fair number of their houses to abandon the original site of their abbey for a more suitable one. The early days of Fountains were made very anxious ones for the community by starkest want, and a colony sent from here to establish an abbey at Barnoldswick was so greatly troubled by robbers and by what the chronicler calls 'the importunity of the climate' which almost every year spoilt their crops (British weather in the mid-twelfth-century seems to have been pestilential) quickly moved elsewhere. But the Cistercian ground record in respect of removal was held by Byland Abbey which, for one reason or another, had had to change the site of its house no less than three times.

However, by the end of the twelfth century all such troubles were very much past history and an indeterminable number of English Cistercian houses were faced by the problem of possessing not too little wealth, but too much. Their situation was subjected to some little criticism, with a degree of accuracy not easy to assess, for solid evidence on the matter is scanty and the accusers too often display the same penchant for extremist language as do some modern journalists. Certainly by the early years of the thirteenth century an unascertainable proportion of Cistercian houses had become well-to-do and of these some were at times behaving in a way of which the founders of their order would not have approved. Thus various abbeys of the order were now adding to their revenue by accepting the advowsons of parish churches and deriving financial profit therefrom by appropriation (see page 170) or by securing annual pensions from them. To what extent the fact that other ecclesiastical bodies also did this justifies it, is a matter of opinion. In some ways more serious was the accusation that, like the Tudor landlords in later times, Cistercian houses were adding to their profits by enclosing land for sheep farming and expelling therefrom harmless peasants; it is not feasible to determine the extent of this malpractice. However, though a number of the Cistercian houses came to acquire more money than their elementary needs demanded, it would be very improper to conclude that they had become unpopular. As locals of the late twelfth century must have been well aware, the foundation of an abbey in an area brought with it very real social benefits of various kinds, whilst the fact that the number of Cistercian monks in England increased very steadily throughout the thirteenth century is irrefutable proof that their way of life had not lost its considerable grip on popular imagination.

THE AUSTIN CANONS

Some twenty years before the first Cistercian abbey was established in England there arrived here members of another monastic family, which was destined to have more houses in England than any other, though few of these were very large and many were very small. These newcomers were ultimately to acquire the cumbrous title of 'regular canons of St Augustine', abbreviated in non-legal contexts to 'Augustinian canons' or 'Austin canons' or 'black canons' (from the colour of the outer cloak which they wore). These complicated origins have only comparatively recently been unravelled, and were not dominated by any great religious personage but by somewhat general factors.

By late Roman times, as we have noted, the monastic ideal had come to be greatly venerated in both Eastern and Western Christendom, though it had not been closely connected with the life of the diocesan clergy. However, this link came to be forged notably through the efforts of the ultra-famous St Augustine, bishop of Hippo (d. 430) who, sharing to the fullest the now deep-rooted belief that the apostolic church had lived what was in effect a monastic life and discerning its obvious practical advantages, insisted that the clergy of his own cathedral should live what was in effect the monastic life—a left-wing move which attracted much attention and produced some admirable results. Memory of it was destined to survive the troubles of the fifth century through enshrinement in various writings well known in the West from the eleventh century onwards.

But the original impetus towards renewal of this form of clerical life which Augustine had supported with such vigour was not directly inspired by his example but by the Gregorian Reformers who so vigorously stressed the importance of raising the standards of clerical life. This revived interest, first visible in Italy and slightly later in the extreme south of France, received the all essential stamp of official approval in synods held at Rome in 1059 and 1063, and quickly gathered a good deal of support in these areas. Obviously it was important to produce a title which would clearly distinguish those leading this new form of life from those who followed the old less demanding régime of collegiate churches and fairly quickly the title of 'regular canons' was coined for this purpose. The phrase, derived from two Greek and Latin words both denoting 'a rule', became established by the early twelfth century, and canons of the old type came to be known as 'secular canons' since they lived in the secular world (*seculum*). Slightly later, because of the value of having an official precedent linked to a great leader of the Church, regular canons gradually adopted the so-called *Rule of St Augustine*.

What the *Rule* gave was prestige and legal respectability but not much detailed guidance on the details of the monastic programme, its few provisions on this latter being mostly quite out of date and soon often omitted from its text. This meant that a house of regular canons adopting it must acquire also a detailed set of observances to regulate their régime. For a considerable time, provision and revision of this was left very largely to the individual house concerned, which understandably often copied in varying degree customs in existence in other houses of the order or, to some extent, in Benedictine houses. The result was that observances of houses of Austin canons showed a marked lack of uniformity and contained some quite important differences of custom with regard to such matters as diet and silence, a minority, for example, following important parts of the Cistercian tradition but most others following a programme similar to that of the old Benedictines, though rather less exacting on certain points.

The Austin canons had for some time no common machinery of government and, as we shall see, when they were given one did not find it immensely useful. By the ancient law of the Church all monastic communities were subject to the bishop of the diocese in which they were situate, unless specially exempted therefrom, a privilege vary rarely accorded to individual houses, though it had already been given to the Cistercian order and to that of Cluny. It was unfortunate that there was no official minimum size for a new house of Austin canons. Episcopal approval for its establishment was all that was required and seems to have been easily obtained, partly, perhaps, through optimistic hopes with regard to expansion in the near future which were very often not realised. As a result there came into existence a very large number of priories of Austin canons whose personnel was much too small to maintain a very strong monastic life.

What was the relation of the Austin canons to parish work? This question has been much discussed and no easy answer is feasible, since for the period with which we are here concerned the evidence on the matter is very scanty. It is quite certain that no few houses of the order were given the patronage of a very considerable number of parish churches, though there were others which had few or none of these. It is also certain that in later times we find regular canons occasionally for shortish periods serving or one two of the parish churches which their monastery owned and also sometimes the parish altar attached to it, where there was one, though even in the fourteenth and fifteenth centuries this usage was far from widespread. It is possible that in the eleventh and twelfth centuries where canons held a collegiate church with a comparatively small parish attached, as was common in southern France and Italy, pastoral work was more substantial but this cannot be taken as proved, even though probably in practice most of their members were in major orders. One look at the code of observances which regulated their life, of which no few examples remain, suffices to show that their daily programme did not differ in any major essential from that of contemporary Benedictines, being focussed on a complex round of common worship which, together with their other responsibilities, could have left them very little time for pastoral activities. Operating to the same end is the fact that, in England at least, a number of the houses were much too small to undertake outside responsibilities, the more so since, very wisely, the authorities normally insisted that a regular canon should not be exposed to the intense strain of living without that common life to which he was called, but should have company. Thus in 1280 the archbishop of York ordered that canons of Bridlington Priory were not to dwell alone in any manor or elsewhere and above all not at Blubberhouses, the which must seem a very proper and understandable provision to anyone who knows the latter's isolated position. Long before this it had become usual for papal privileges which (fairly frequently) permitted Austin canons to serve a parish church whose advowson their monastery owned, to order that in such cases there should be at the place a community of at least three or four canons, a sensible enough provision but one which was almost certainly found too demanding to be invariably fulfilled.

Although one or two small houses of regular canons had originated in England in the last years of the eleventh century, the effective expansion of the order here began with the foundation of the important priory of Holy Trinity, Aldgate, by the queen of England in 1107–8, and gained further impetus with the establishment of Merton Priory in 1114–17. These two houses were immensely popular and inspired no few magnates to found others. As time went on their example was increasingly followed by people in rather lower income groups, many of whom were able to found their own private monastery instead of merely making benefactions to someone else's by the simple and quite legitimate expedient of using a wealthy parish church of which they held the patronage as the nucleus of a new monastery. By the early thirteenth century there were in England some 260 houses of Austin canons of one kind or another. In the following century and a half their expansion was appreciably greater than that of other orders (notably that of the Cistercians which, as we have seen, slackened abruptly) and ultimately reached the massive total of about 300, though many of the houses of Austin canons here were fairly small. English houses with very large complements were very rare indeed, few even remotely approaching the sixty or more brethren to be found in the largest Benedictine abbeys of England. The abbey of Cirencester which at one time had forty canons was one of the largest, but a very large proportion of English houses of Austin canons had convents of about one or two dozen and many others are not known to have attained even the modest target of double figures. Differences in income were as marked as differences in size. At the time of the Dissolution of the Monasteries only a very few houses of Austin canons had financial resources at all comparable with those of the wealthiest Benedictine houses, and a number of the smallest houses had already been closed down.

The sites of the houses were of various types. A small minority lived in remote spots of the kind preferred by the Cistercians. Such were the priories of Bushmead and Llanthony (Mon.) which had originated as hermitages. Others began in great collegiate churches like the West Country ones already noted, lordly Waltham, Cirencester and little St Oswald's, Gloucester, but very many more houses were set up in existing parish churches like Bridlington and Breamore. In such cases, sometimes as at Blythburgh and Butley, although the church provided useful endowment it was found convenient to acquire privacy for the monastic community concerned by building the priory clear of the town or village concerned. The very real inconvenience of having two churches under one roof might also be solved by giving the parishioners their own place of worship near the monastery gate, as at Kenilworth and Cirencester.

The houses of the Austin canons were spread very widely indeed, being found in every county except Westmorland and Durham. In the populous counties of Norfolk, Suffolk and Essex, and to a lesser degree in Lincolnshire, they were very numerous though mostly of only mediocre size, and the order dominated much of the West Country through a smallish number of substantial ex-collegiate churches.

Like the Benedictines, the Austin canons of these times developed independent orders which, whilst observing the same general *Rule* as the rest of the order, had their own special customs and organisation. These were not very numerous and, so far as England is concerned, only two of them were of much significance. The first of these was the order headed by Prémontré, an abbey near Laon; its members were known as Premonstratensians. Their observances had been much influenced in certain major respects by those of the Cistercians but they pursued an interesting double aim. Some of their abbeys were set in the sort of remote sites of which the Cistercians would approve but others were planned as mission centres with preachers based therein and early began a tradition of undertaking some parish duties. The Premonstratensians acquired, in England, thirty-one houses of which the first was that of Newhouse (1143). As with the Cistercians, all houses of the order ranked as abbeys and were exempt from episcopal visitation. Just as the Cistercians were known as the 'white monks' so the Premonstratensians were termed 'white canons' because of the colour of their outer raiment. The second order to be noted is the order of Sempringham. Its founder was St Gilbert, originally of the parish of Sempringham, who in 1131 founded a small convent by his church. This became a 'double monastery' with communities of men and women living in the same precinct but having entirely separate living quarters and places of worship. The total number of houses of the order was only twenty-four, all of which, with a minor exception, were in England, none being very large.

MONASTIC BUILDINGS

For a mixture of social and economic reasons the buildings of these medieval monasteries were much more complex than those of their modern successors. They were set in an enclosure which, except in some cases where a monastery was established, in a large town (as few were) was of considerable extent, often covering several dozen acres.* This enclosed area, or precinct, was surrounded by a massive curtain wall which did much to exclude undesired visitors —a very wide-ranging category in which were included dogs (which were evidently apt to be refractory) and on rarish but lively occasions, high ecclesiastical officials claiming a right to visit the monastery which its brethren viewed with more than suspicion. Such were the representatives of the abbot of Cluny who, in 1279, sought to inspect the priory of Monk Bretton and had to retire from the scene unadmitted since its gate-house 'remained persistently closed'.

Within the monastic precinct a good deal of the land was open ground and might include gardens, orchards and a field or two, but the area was dominated by a largish number of buildings arranged around two or three courts. There might be one concerned solely with barns, shippons, stables and the like, but the major and indispensable one was that which included the great gatehouse, through which ran the main entrance to the monastery, a broad passage which crossed its ground floor. This was closed at its outer end by massive doors with a porter's lodge adjoining it on one side, similar to the arrangement still preserved in some Oxford and Cambridge colleges. On the first floor of the gatehouse was a large chamber which was sometimes used as a courtroom, to which might be added some guest accommodation. The gatehouse usually stood athwart the centre of the west wall of the enclosure. East of it, on the far side of the largish court, reared up the west front of the great conventual church, in which was its principal entrance. This was usually exactly opposite the entrance of the gatehouse, thus facilitating the processions to and from it that were usual on certain occasions such as the visits of important personages. Elsewhere around this courtyard were lesser buildings, often providing accommodation for guests and stabling for their horses and, in some cases, an almonry to serve the impecunious.

Much the most important court was that of the cloister court, which constituted the heart of the monastery. Probably for symbolic rather than practical reasons, the cloister was generally square in

---

* English monastic buildings of this period are considered in some detail in J. C. Dickinson, *Monastic Life in Medieval England.*

plan and centred round a 'garth' or enclosed area; around it ran four broad alleys covered by a lean-to roof. Its outer ends were supported against adjacent buildings and the inner ones rested on low walls which were pierced by ranges of small windows placed close together. Usually, because of sound practical reasons, the cloister court adjoined the south side of the conventual church. Its northern alley would thus receive maximum sunlight, and was used to some degree for study, there being set along it desks that were sometimes set in alcoves. On the north side of the cloister ran the south wall of the nave of the conventual church which, because it was masked by the cloister, contained no windows in its lower part, but might have smallish ones above.

In post-Conquest England the cruciform plan was very greatly favoured for monastic churches of the time, though, for unknown reasons, in France this was not very popular. The western limb of the church was always longer than the others, unless the church was unfinished, as was more frequently the case than is generally realised, and in the case of great abbeys might be very long indeed, as we see at St Albans and Winchester. This limb or, more often, part of it, was cut off from the eastern part of the church by a complex screen termed the *pulpitum*. In the case of the Cistercian houses the part west of the screen was originally reserved for use as the lay brethren's chapel though later times occasionally brought in additional uses for it. Where Augustinian and Benedictine monasteries had a parish altar pertaining to the conventual church this western area might be used for it by the parishioners, as at Dunstable and Bridlington, though the obvious inconvenience of having two quite different rounds of services going on in a single building at the same time often led to different arrangements. Either at the time of its foundation the monastery itself was erected outside the town or village concerned, as at Butley and Blythburgh, or a parish church was built outside the gates of the monastery, as at Kenilworth and Cirencester. In the case of the Cistercians there was no such parish altar to complicate matters, but usually a small chapel was built outside the main entrance for the use of dependents of the monastery and such visitors as it had. Houses of nuns usually did not have such complications, and because of the lack of means of most of them, the conventual church was often a small rectangular edifice with no aisles or transepts.

The *pulpitum* was a complex structure. On its western side was a screen of wood, often elaborately carved and painted; it had a central doorway and sometimes also side ones. A few feet to the east of it were the western sides of the choir stalls, with the entrance to the choir between them. The intervening space was left open at ground level, but covered overhead by the floor of what was known as the 'rood loft', since over it towered the 'rood', which were large sculptured figures of the Christ crucified on the cross with Our Lady standing on one side and St John, the 'Beloved disciple', on the other. On the loft might perch the organ or sometimes one organ, for larger churches had more than one. Durham Cathedral, never pinched by penury, had three organs in its huge choir, including one which was 'never playd uppon but when the 4 doctors of the Church was read . . . being a fair paire of large organs called the cryers'.

The eastern limb of the church quite often had small aisles to the north and south. At its eastern end was the high altar, behind which was usually an elaborate window or set of windows, the high altar standing on the floor immediately below. Between the high altar and the choir stalls was a largish open area. On either side of the eastern and western limbs of cruciform churches were transepts projecting to north and south with the 'crossing' uniting them, and often having above it the belfry.

South from the south transept ran the eastern range of the cloister. This contained the main buildings required by the brethren. On the ground floor was a little parlour wherein for good reason conversation (which was not allowed in the cloister) could take place; south of it ran the chapter house, much used for monastic business, and a largish and curiously anonymous room which was probably a form of living-room for the brethren. Overhead was the long dormitory, with the beds set against its eastern and western sides, that of the head of the house being at the southern end unless, as often came about, he had acquired a private apartment. From the north end of the dormitory a doorway gave access to the choir with the aid of a staircase which led from it down into the western corner of the adjoining south transept.

Along all or most of the south side of the cloister ran the great refectory in which the brethren took their meals. It was generally a graceful and lofty room with large windows in its south wall which let in the noonday sun and had a pulpit at its eastern end, near the high table, from which edifying literature was read during meals. Beneath it was often a vaulted cellar, used mostly as a store. In the west wall of the refectory was a hatch or hatches communicating with the adjoining kitchen, which might also serve meals to folk in the western range.

This latter in the case of the Cistercians was largely given over to the use of the lay brethren, though later on when their numbers declined, parts of it were put to other uses. In the case of the Benedictine and Augustinian houses, the ground floor of this range was usually given over to guest accommodation and a largish parlour, within which, when good reason so required, brethren could converse with people from the outside world. The top floor might be taken up by domestic offices connected with the kitchen, a large guest hall with a high table where might sit the head of the house (whether abbot or prior) behind which sometimes was what was in effect a flat for him, adjoining the church. To the south-east of the cloister court, in what was usually a quiet and undisturbed part of the precinct, was the monastic infirmary. Herein might be found brethren too old to cope with the exacting régime of the cloister, the sick and those who had recently undergone one of those periodic blood-letting operations in the efficacy of which medieval men had great faith. In the case of very large monasteries the infirmary might be one of several buildings which edged yet another court-yard on the south-east side of the cloister.

As we shall see, the erection of this complex series of monastic buildings in their final form (which after the Conquest mostly implied construction in stone) was apt to be a very protracted process indeed. The completion of the grandiose churches that were so much desired from Norman times onwards often took half a century or even more, whilst the major buildings which encircled the cloister in many cases were not finally finished in less than a hundred years or so; subsidiary buildings might wait even longer to attain their final form.

MONASTIC HOUSES OF WOMEN

One of the most marked social differences between medieval and modern monasticism is the fact that whereas in the former a very high proportion of the monastic population was men, in the latter the exact reverse is the case. It has been estimated that towards the middle of the fourteenth century there were in England about 146 nunneries with some 3300 nuns as against some 890 houses of men which had about 14 000 inmates. How is this remarkable difference to be explained?

Probably the main reason for it lies in the fact that in these times, as for so long before and so long after, society felt very strongly that the woman's place was the home. Certainly medieval English law allotted them a markedly inferior position, e.g. in practice often a woman was not held to have any absolute right to choose her own husband (it was perhaps partly to provide a safeguard against older women being re-married against their will, that the medieval Church provided widows with a special status by a rite wherein they took the veil and a vow to remain unmarried). Another quite different factor which worked to the same end was the fact that in the West increasingly from the twelfth century onwards, it became very usual for members of male monasteries to be in holy orders, notably in the case of the friars, much of whose work could only be done by those ordained priests, but also with members of the older orders whose members were increasingly bound to say Masses for benefactors and others. The unbroken tradition of the Church denied ordination to the priesthood to women, and thus barred them from such activities. Finally, it is to be noted that the very crude social conditions of the times may well have rendered dangerous feminine participation in such activities as pastoral visiting,* whilst the very limited medieval interest in schooling (especially for the fair sex) deprived medieval nuns of an activity in which their modern successors have engaged so fruitfully over most of the face of the earth. As a result the monastic life for medieval women was inevitably very largely confined to the precincts of their monasteries.

Much too common amongst English nunneries was a marked lack of this world's goods—a thing that is not surprising when we reflect that their life had such limited scope and that they could not go round begging like the friars nor celebrate Masses for their

---

* It is worthy of note that only a century ago when the formidable Florence Nightingale and the inadequately appreciated 'Aggie' Weston felt called to engage in visiting the poor, their families felt that they should not do so unless accompanied by a footman.

benefactors like monks and regular canons. Several of the English convents had already faded out before the Reformation began and a very high proportion of the rest were living on microscopic incomes of a few dozen pounds a year. There were finally just under 140 houses of nuns in England, of which almost half, including the few very wealthy ones like Romsey, Wilton and Shaftesbury (all of Anglo-Saxon origin) were Benedictine, 29 were Cistercian, 26 houses of Augustinian canonesses, and 15 of the order of Sempringham. Inevitably many of their conventual buildings were very modest, and by no means always in excellent repair.

THE MILITARY ORDERS

One of the very few products of medieval asceticism which did not permanently enrich the life of the Church but, in effect if not in name, has disappeared from modern life, is that of the Military orders. These, curious as it seems to us today, combined military activity with monastic discipline. Certain of them sprang up in Spain and East Germany with the primary aim of pushing back Moslem and Slav domination in those areas. The only two which concern England both focussed their activity on the Holy Land and originated as part and parcel of the Crusading movement.

The Order of the Temple was so called because it had its headquarters on the site of Solomon's Temple in Jerusalem. It originated about 1118 and sought to provide much needed protection for pilgrims in the area. Its knights rapidly acquired popularity and no little wealth, of which much was in the West. To help organise and store this the Templars set up 'Temples' or local headquarters. That in Paris has been totally demolished, but of that in London there remains intact the notable round church, which, like some few other twelfth-century churches copied the circular shape of the Holy Sepulchre at Jerusalem, and wherein are yet visible military effigies of some of the top people who sought burial there. Handling their business affairs with great competence, the Templars quickly contributed to the contemporary rise of banking in Western Europe. Most of their English houses were small. They were known as 'preceptories' and finally totalled forty-five, of which two-thirds had been founded before the end of the twelfth century, by which time events were clearly heavily undermining the *raison d'être* of the order.

The second military order in medieval England was that of the Hospital of St John of Jerusalem whose members were known as 'Hospitallers'. It came into being a little earlier than that of the Templars, and had as its original aim provision of care for the sick and hospitality for pilgrims and crusaders. Some of the brethren were, in effect, male nurses, but almost inevitably the order went on to develop a military side to its activities to help to shore up the increasingly shaky Western hold on the Holy Land; also inevitably, their personnel included a body of chaplains. The Hospitallers acquired just over fifty houses in England (preceptories) of which almost all were small and situated in remote spots. It seems unlikely that the impact on English society of either of these military orders was more than very minor.

HERMITS

Modern historical research has demonstrated with certitude the considerable part played by hermits in the life of the medieval Western Church. Unhappily their history is so very scantily documented that it will never be feasible to reconstruct its main outlines with the degree of detail feasible for that of the great monastic orders of the period. All we can produce are occasional pictures of individual hermits, some longish lists of their names and abodes (which are, however, very far from complete) together with a few invaluable texts displaying the details of their daily life. But to ask to know, for example, the rate of their expansion in medieval England and their total numbers here at various stages is to demand the impossible. A further real, if lesser, historical problem is caused by the fact that the word 'hermit' can be used both in a wide sense and in a particular sense, thus denoting both or only one of the two sets of people who lived the eremitical life. Like the monks and nuns, some hermits followed a comparatively moderate régime, others a very strict one. The latter are sometimes termed 'recluses' but much preferable are the ancient terms 'anchorite' and 'anchoress' to denote the men and women respectively who were pursuing this exacting mode of Christian living. Like the naval implement whose title closely resembles theirs, such people had a marked propensity for staying very firmly in the same place. To denote those following the less austere régime the word Hermit is also used, and for it there is no obvious alternative, but sometimes it also includes the stricter category.

Unlike the monk or the nun, the hermit or anchorite was not bound to a community but could and mostly did live a solitary life, though occasionally more than one of them lived together for reasons of convenience. There was no single *Rule* which they followed and they formed their own time-table which was probably often fluid. Though some of their establishments had a little endowment, this was never very great and the large majority of them lived wholly or largely on the alms of the faithful.

The sites of hermitages varied very greatly. From early times hermits had regarded desert places as highly desirable habitats. Thus the most beloved hermit of Anglo-Saxon England, St Cuthbert, for some time lived a most austere life shut up in a stone hut on the isle of Farne, near Lindisfarne, until he was persuaded, albeit with great unwillingness, to leave it to become a bishop. His friend Herbert, much less eminent, settled on an island in Derwentwater in times when the floods of tourism were a thousand years and more away from it. Other hermits lived in caves which, if chilly, were at least proof against wind and rain: thus did St Robert of Knaresburgh (d. 1235), whose habitation is still to be seen, and a Derbyshire baker, who after performing many kindly works for customers and others found the call to solitude irresistible, so retired to a marsh 'exceeding dreadful and far from human habitation' where he carved himself out a rock dwelling in which he served God 'in hunger and thirst and cold and nakedness', until he 'passed from the prison of the body to the Lord.'

It is unfortunate that no systematic study of the dwellings of English medieval hermits has yet been made, for the material, if scanty, suffices to provide an outline picture. The modern habit of terming the place where a hermit lives a 'cell' is to be deplored, since this tends to be taken to mean that he had only a single room. The facts of life demanded something much more like the accommodation now to be found in a small flat, though a hermit's dwelling was almost always detached from other buildings, save in the case of certain anchorages which were constructed against the wall of a church. Anchorites, living an enclosed life, of necessity had to have some domestic service, and for this reason often had a help who lived on the premises. With hermits in the narrow sense this was not necessary as they could, for example, effect their own shopping. But even in such cases an inner and an outer room with a lavatory was essential, which is what the noted Somerset hermit, St Wulfric of Haselbury, is known to have had. In some cases where the hermitage was set in a rock, there remains a chapel with its altar, to be used either by the hermit himself, if he were in priest's orders as some were, or by a visiting priest if he were not. When, however, a hermitage attracted followers more substantial accommodation, similar to that of a small monastery, was obviously essential. This came into existence at Markyate as a result of the high repute acquired by its anchoress, Christina (d. *c.* 1160). The surviving *Life* of her, though more useful for social than religious history, shows that she abandoned her very cramped quarters to live with other sisters in an establishment similar to a small nunnery, which had a dormitory, refectory and chapel, and a cloister-garth graced with flowers.

The background of these hermits varied enormously. Down the ages the eremitical life has often been sought by monks of ripe religious experience who found themselves irresistibly pushed thereto. Such was Sigar, who established himself in a Hertfordshire wood. Here, perhaps because he was a very musical man, he found over fascinating the singing of copious local nightingales, so prayed with success for their decampment, fearing 'lest he might seem to rejoice in the warbling of birds rather than the worship to which he was bound before God.' Very different was St Godric (d. 1170) who spent his early life adventurously as a sailor and trader, possibly even also as a pirate, and who in 1102 sailed from Arsuf to Jaffa in company with no less a person than king of the crusading kingdom of Jerusalem. After various long pilgrimages he too felt the fascination of the hermit's life. He retired for a time to the great royal forest of Inglewood in Cumbria. Here, 'desiring to follow the life of St John the Baptist in the wilderness, he lived on herbs and wild honey with acorns, nuts and crab apples', but finally removed to the forest of Finchale, near Durham. Like so many ascetics he lived to a great age, passing sixty years there before death took him, at which time men noted in his face 'a dignity and beauty unknown before.'

Unlike the anchorite, the hermit was free to come and go from his dwelling as seemed good for him and could, therefore, add to his meagre resources by doing odd jobs on the side; he could also visit those who had need of his counsel, as Friar Lawrence visited Romeo and Juliet, in times of stress.*

As the hermit had no need of domestic help he would normally live alone in what was often little more than a shack. The sites of their abodes vary greatly, some being in the heart of a town but many more were in the countryside, though not necessarily 'remote from human habitation' like those of the Cistercians. Some lived by bridges, perhaps partly because there was here more chance than usual of receiving the slender alms necessary for their living but, in certain cases, also so that they could look after repairs to the bridge and adjacent road, a responsibility which at least one hermit found to be quite compatible with discoursing to passers-by on 'the subject of temptation and sin'. Some others lived on the coast and are found acting as coastguards and light-keepers, in days when the absence of radar made shipwreck all too easy. On the handsome Plymouth Hoe was a hermitage perched alongside a cross that was used as a seamark, and on the coast near Winchelsea was another hermitage, which in 1536 was burnt by Flemish raiders who 'hewed an image of St George with their swords, bidding it to "call on St George for help".' However, the proportion of hermits who lived in such sites is likely to have been small. Many must have found the physical exercise which experience had long recognised as a valuable element in the religious life through looking after their little garden or seeking vegetarian foods in the countryside.

Such activities as these were not permitted to the anchorite or anchoress. After careful thought by the person involved and careful investigation by the appropriate ecclesiastical authority, the man or woman was ceremonially enclosed in a small dwelling which was henceforth not to be quitted except when very great necessity demanded it. This rite was effected by the local bishop and a form for it therefore is included in medieval pontificals. A fair proportion of such folk seem to have been women, and probably most of their

---

* The word 'friar', like its French and Latin equivalents *frère* and *frater*, can mean not only 'brother' in a general sense, but also is used to denote members of the mendicant orders like the Franciscans and Dominicans. Whether the Bard of Avon knew it or not, 'friar' Lawrence should be classed as a hermit, not a mendicant, since he clearly lived on his own and not in a religious community as did the members of the mendicant orders.

dwellings were built against a wall of the church, very often towards its east end. In this wall would be a small grated window, veiled by a curtain which made it feasible for the person concerned to hear Mass, receive communion and go to confession without leaving his or her abode. The window could also be utilised for conversation with members of the outside world, though it was expected that this was to be reserved for special occasions. There has happily survived a substantial handbook, written probably about the end of the twelfth century for the guidance of a small group of anchoresses in England. This is the *Ancren Riwle* whose considerable merits won it long popularity. Businesslike, shrewd and comprehensive, it is arranged in seven books, each with a topic systematically treated— that of confession is studied under sixteen heads! Its valuable spiritual guidance is backed up with very practical injunctions on mundane matters—'between meals do not munch either fruit or anything else', 'you shall not own any animal, dear sisters, save only a cat'.

As has recently been stressed, the *raison d'être* of this life was, like that of the Cistercians, the acquisition of a maximum understanding of the divine purpose. 'If only, went the idea, a man could shake himself free of the involvements of land, administration, legal complexities, logic-chopping, careerism, flattery, relics-mongering and all the things which seemed to have so signally developed or expanded in the twelfth-century Church, and indeed, concentrate his mind simply on God, then he could cut the Gordian knot of every social and spiritual problem. A man of prayer could see what was right or what ought to be done far more quickly than, for instance, a learned lawyer' (Mayr-Harting).

Such a vocation was never envisaged as the form of life to be adopted by more than a very small section of the Christian community, and by its stress on self-denial it provided an additional, useful reminder to the public of the fruitfulness of this. It was not an introverted one which displayed no interest in the outside world. There is no doubt that hermits were greatly valued throughout the thousand years of the Middle Ages as valuable sources of spiritual advice, especially by those with major problems to face, a sort of service likely to have been specially valued in the eleventh and twelfth centuries when monks did little pastoral work and the clergy were often too untrained to be always competent in this difficult sphere, and when the friars who were so to excel in it had not yet graced the scene. In post-Conquest times a *Life* of St Wulfric of Haselbury displays him as a source of much spiritual help and, in the best medieval way, of combining healing with religion, he having acquired 'an outstanding reputation in what would appear to have been disorders of sight and speech.' But no English hermit of Wulfric's century has bequeathed major spiritual writings of the same high value as those of Richard Rolle of Hampole (d. 1349), a Yorkshireman whose influence had very considerable popularity in late medieval England, or Julian of Norwich who, rather later, long lived as an anchoress at a church in Norwich. Her work entitled *The Sixteen Revelations of Divine Love* has a very valued place in our mystical literature.

Had a pious Anglo-Saxon, felled at the battle of Hastings, returned to survey the English scene a century and a half later, he would have found very large numbers of Englishmen living within sound of monastic bells. Frequently these rang out, sometimes announcing joyously some festive occasion, sometimes solemnly in memory of one who had sloughed off this mortal life, and always with frequency and great regularity in the course of the daily round of monastic worship, reminding the thoughtful that 'here we have no abiding city, we look for one to come', and inviting them to participation in prayer for living and departed.

Alongside these the new monasteries now offered society invaluable social amenities. In the lively and increasingly sophisticated society of the late twelfth-century England there were to be heard a few raucous voices criticising the monasteries of their day. It would be as unwise to believe that this criticism was incompatible with affection for it, as to believe that it should be accepted unreservedly, if only because contemporary social conditions made it impossible for a man to acquire accurate information on more than a small part of any sector of the human scene. Neither now nor later is there anything to justify the curious superstition so rampant amongst Victorians that a monastic programme cannot exist for more than a century or so without exhibiting indubitable signs of decay. Recruitment of men and women to the demanding life of the cloister progressed steadily in post-Conquest England for almost three centuries and this, together with the immense flow of benefactions to religious houses, in these times constitute undeniable illustrations of the profound popular esteem for the cloister and all its works.

However, at the end of the twelfth century there were two matters over which a keen supporter of the monastic life might feel some concern. The first of these was the fact that a small minority of English religious houses had acquired and were acquiring more worldly wealth than was good for their reputation. As stated earlier, the Cistercians were not guiltless here, but the chief offenders were a score or so of the ancient Benedictine houses which, as much by accident as design, had acquired far more wealth than their needs demanded. This must almost certainly have lowered the level of their spiritual life, since a very sensitive soul might well not wish to try his vocation there, and was certainly apt to excite criticism from laity to whom the brethren of such places might seem to be 'poor yet having all things' in a sense which the New Testament author of this phrase certainly did not intend.

Reading the long famous *Chronicle* of Jocelyn of Brakelond with its vivid picture of life at the venerable abbey of Bury St Edmunds gives the impression that the great increase in the house's possessions and privileges made it virtually impossible for an abbot, however well-intentioned, to avoid putting the care of these in first place at the expense of the pastoral responsibilities expected of him by the *Rule of St Benedict*, in the same sort of way as the increase in size and complexity of modern university life has rendered it equally all but inevitable that an increasing number of professors switch their priorities to administration and put on the shelf the writing and research which used to be regarded as their prime duty. Jocelyn shows us his newly-elected abbot Sampson going on a grand tour of his manors and demanding from them customary dues: 'daily he grew skilled in earthly knowledge and turned his attention to acquiring knowledge of secular affairs'. But they that touch pitch shall be defiled, and it is not surprising that Sampson went on to acquire the mentality of a business magnate so that when a rural dean without authorisation provided himself with a mill on abbey property, the abbot 'was so wroth that he would scarcely eat or utter a single word' and swore 'I will never eat bread until that building be overturned', which it quickly was. Again like a business magnate, the abbot welcomed the possibility of meeting top people, declaring that he would be prepared to spend the stupendous sum of 2000 silver marks in connection with the dedication of the new conventual church 'provided the king be present and the matter conducted with appropriate ceremony'. To the far-seeing St Francis of Assisi, charitable as he was, such an outlook would be nothing if not indefensible.

If these great Benedictine houses regarded care of wealth as important at least equally did they look after privileges, herein showing the same vigorous but unconvincing obstinacy in their defence which is now so often displayed by trades union leaders over pay rises and 'who does what' disputes. William Thorne's chronicle of the abbey of St Augustine's, Canterbury, is dominated by stories displaying the determination of local Benedictines to hold what they had, come what may. To modern eyes St Augustine's hard and pro-tracted struggle to insist that the archbishop of Canterbury should bless its new abbots in their conventual church and not in his cathedral seems petty in the extreme, as does their equally vigorous but unsuccessful fight with him over some minor church revenue. 'In this way,' concludes the chronicler of it, 'though it is shame to confess it, the archbishop holds and possess now £4 instead of 50s 7d'. Since St Augustine's ranked amongst the half-dozen richest monasteries in England, it could have spared the archbishop the extra 29s 5d without danger of drifting into bankruptcy.

It is, of course, true that the number of English monasteries sub-jected to the trials and criticism which great wealth inevitably brings in its train formed only a very minute proportion of the total number. They were very far outnumbered by hundreds of others whose inmates were living on paltry resources, but popular opinion then, as now, was not good at scientifically surveying the whole of the picture. As St Francis of Assisi was soon to manifest, the most satisfying way to rebut criticisms over wealth and privilege was to reject them.

The second factor which damaged the monastic image somewhat, albeit less than modern men might expect, was the considerable lack of extensive personal contact between monastic communities and the outside world. The fact that Augustinians and Benedictines in large numbers were living in the cloister, a dedicated life which men in the street found edifying, did not alter the fact that at this time there was an increasing population in the outside world whose spiritual needs were being inadequately met by a secular clergy which was mostly ignorant and by no means always edifying. Here was a major pastoral problem from which far, far too many bishops all over the West tended to avert their eyes, but whose proportions the friars were soon quickly and successfully to seek to diminish.

CHAPTER 5

CHURCH AND STATE

ENTIRELY fortuitously the beginnings of Norman rule in England coincided with the opening of a new and very spectacular chapter in the history of the relations between Church and State in this country. In late Anglo-Saxon times, as has been noted, the two had lived happily together in a condition of hazy and almost unbroken harmony. This accord had been principally due to the considerable overlap in both their interests and their ideologies, and the total absence of the powerful machinery needed to wage a major conflict. After the Norman Conquest and throughout the period under review a very substantial core of this common interest remained, which accounts for the fact that conflicts between Church and State, dramatic though they sometimes were, had largely died out in the latter half of the period and were only very sporadic in the earlier half. Nevertheless, in the century and a half which followed the Norman Conquest conflict was never very far away and at times assumed major proportions.

The main causes of this strife were three in number. Most important was the arrival on the stage of the Gregorian Reform, with its radical and novel views on the relationship between the Roman see and the local churches of Western Christendom, which were quite incompatible with the conservative views on this matter held by Western monarchies. But this would not have been of such major practical significance had it not been for the steady growth in the scope and effectiveness of the machinery of the Roman see which steadily tended to intervene in local Western life to a degree hitherto quite unparalleled, and the exactly contemporary growth in power of the English monarchy which for a century and a half after the Norman Conquest, with very little intermission, built up a most puissant government unparalleled elsewhere in the West, which could and did on occasion offer very vigorous and sustained opposition to papal intervention.

The disputes which now occurred between Church and State varied greatly in intensity and in duration, some blazing up into mighty conflagrations, others smouldering mildly on without often producing any great flames. But just as it is highly misleading to regard industrial relations in modern England as characterised by almost universal and unbroken conflicts, so in medieval England clashes between Church and State, whilst at times being spectacular and significant, were nevertheless far from being continuous. Most of the time the two existed side by side either harmoniously or exchanging baleful words rather than violent blows.

FINANCIAL CLASHES

The firm royal government of post-Conquest England was an expensive commodity requiring, for example, many grim stone castles that now for the first time became part of the English landscape, as well as an increasing number of civil servants and, somewhat more slowly, sizeable mercenary forces which limited dependence on the traditional often inefficient feudal levies. The *Anglo-Saxon Chronicle* (of late re-baptised as the *Old English Chronicle*) shows very starkly how back-breaking were the financial burdens which William the Conqueror imposed on his subjects. Later finances were made even more difficult by a gradual, pitiless price-rise, since in these times a goodish part of royal revenue came from sources which were fixed by long custom and could not be suddenly increased in the modern way. By the late twelfth century the royal machinery of government in England was running with great success but not much concern for the general public. Royal officials were far from scrupulous over modes of raising the revenue which they believed to be so essential for the public welfare, having anticipated certain modern trades-union leaders in persuading themselves that unpopular claims they made were justifiable because they were 'special cases'.

PILLAGING AND LOANS

Amongst the smaller but not unimportant actions of the Crown which irritated ecclesiastical authorities of post-Conquest England was the sporadic pillaging or borrowing of ecclesiastical wealth in one way or another by the former. Thus the Conqueror, pious though he was, finding himself desperately short of ready cash immediately after 1066, according to the *Old English Chronicle*, 'caused all the monasteries of England to be despoiled of their treasure', a statement which the judicious Florence of Worcester makes in less flagrant form, asserting that the king 'caused all the monasteries of England to be searched and the money deposited in them by the richer sort of English for security against his violence and rapacity to be seized and taken to his own treasury.' In 1096, when William Rufus required much money urgently in connection with the mortgage of Normandy, he took similar drastic measures —'the bishops, abbots and abbesses broke up the gold and silver ornaments of their churches and the earls, barons and viscounts robbed their knights and villeins.' When in 1139 Stephen arrived in Salisbury it can scarcely have been spontaneous joy at this approach which led the canons of its well-to-do cathedral there to loan him the enormous sum of two thousand pounds in return for what were, in comparison, some very minor concessions. At first ecclesiastical plate which, it must be admitted, in some of the greater churches existed in superabundance, was an obvious target, being one of the very few sources of ready money available to a penurious monarchy. By the end of the twelfth century, however, new riches had arrived through the rapid growth of the English wool trade, and the wool crop of the rising Cistercian abbeys was on occasion appropriated both by King Richard and King John. Under the latter (a man given to fury and anti-clericalism), arbitrary exactions of various kinds from churches reached its acme. Thereafter it declined, largely because, as we shall see, a highly efficient system of taxing English ecclesiastical wealth was developed.

The monarchs and officials concerned in this would not have sought to ascribe to it that legality on which medieval folk mostly felt so strongly, but probably felt that such type of action was excusable when special situations arrived which necessitated ready cash which the royal treasury simply could not produce. It may well have been thought, and not unreasonably, that the great ecclesiastical corporations of England (which were principally affected) were well able to supply this immediate royal need from their considerable possessions without their daily life suffering any very considerable hardship thereby, so that the pillaging of their possessions was a defensible solution to a problem where no thoroughly respectable course of action was available.

PROLONGED VACANCIES

The same sort of pragmatism may well have lain behind another habit of royal officials at this time which attracted some vigorous criticism, at least from those who bore the brunt of it. This was the practice of postponing immoderately steps to fill vacancies caused by the death, resignation or deprivation of diocesan bishops and the heads of certain monasteries which were in royal patronage. When such a vacancy occurred it was customary for royal officials to take charge of the sources of revenue attached thereto. If one reliable chronicler is to be believed, under William the Conqueror they ploughed back what must often have been a considerable surplus revenue, but, perhaps from Rufus onwards, royal officials quickly came to regard it as a legitimate rule of their game to delay filling the vacancy for longer than usual and to keep any profits from these ecclesiastical sources during a vacancy, provided that all necessary running expenses had been paid. In the case of a very wealthy abbey or cathedral this was a very easy way of obtaining large sums of money quickly.

Because good kings like Henry I were as short of cash as anti-clerical ones like Rufus, both to some degree resorted to this practice. Of it the most spectacular examples were the vacancy in the see of Canterbury which followed the death of Lanfranc (May 1089–Sept. 1093) and that after the death of his successor, Anselm (Apr. 1109–Apr. 1114). But Rufus certainly pushed this practice very much further than others; at the time of his death, as the *Old English Chronicle* notes—'he had in his own hands the archbishopric of Canterbury, the bishoprics of Winchester and Salisbury and eleven abbacies all let out to farm' (i.e. rent). Though purists might object to it, there was produced hereby a good deal of cash in quite a short space of time without creating any great financial hardship, whilst the damage which it caused to the government of the institutions which it affected can be over-estimated, at least so far as monasteries were concerned, for a large Benedictine monastery at this time had a huge staff of officials (the abbey of Ely at this time had twenty out of a total of seventy monks) which must have been perfectly capable of running the establishment effectively when their house had no abbot, just as can the equally large crew of a great modern warship when deprived of its captain. In the case of cathedrals, of course, the effect of a prolonged vacancy must have been more serious and all that can be advanced are pleas in mitigation. The number of dioceses likely to be affected by prolonged vacancies was not great, since with minor ones like Carlisle and Rochester the game was barely worth the candle. Certainly, a vacancy in the primatial see of Canterbury would deprive English ecclesiastics of their authoritative leader and the English realm of its first subject, but the diocese was a very small one and duties like its ordinations could easily be effected by the bishop of Rochester who lived so near at hand and had small responsibilities.

Although vacancies in English bishoprics were the more spectacular target of Norman kings, those in some monasteries were also affected. No systematic study of this aspect of the question has yet been carried out but it would appear likely that the houses largely concerned were that smallish group of plutocratic Benedictine abbeys to whose exceptional position we so often have occasion to refer. By the late twelfth century a very high proportion of the now large number of monasteries in the patronage of the Crown were smaller places, and it may well be that the profits from their vacancies were not considered enough to justify royal officials always taking action to obtain them.

LOCAL LEGAL CLASHES

An inevitable side-effect of the growth of papal and monarchical power was the steady growth at this time of rival codes of law. First in the field was the canon law of the Western Church, which from the mid-eleventh century developed remarkably in bulk and sophistication to attain ultimately an elaboration and fair-mindedness on which departed Romans of ancient days must have looked down with warm approval. The law which the English monarchy developed was, by comparison, very puny in size and much less carefully thought out. But it was demanding and clear-cut in its claims, and vigorously upheld by the royal bureaucracy so that clashes between the laws of Church and State were inevitable. Such disputes often had economic as well as constitutional repercussions.

LAY INVESTITURE

A problem which hit the headlines for a while in post-Conquest times but which, unlike most of the others, had an importance that was short-lived, concerned what was termed 'lay investiture', the title given to a ceremony which took place after a new bishop or abbot had been elected but before he was consecrated or installed. Herein the newly-appointed dignitary was ceremonially given the ring and staff which were the symbols of his new post* by a lay person and did homage before consecration. This ceremony was of comparative recent growth and was therefore somewhat suspect, even in the eyes of some conservatives, and was violently disliked by the Gregorian school of thought since it seemed to portray vividly that improper control of spiritual appointments by the lay powers of which, in England, the policy of William Rufus provided a most flagrant example.

The practice of lay investiture had been totally condemned by Gregory VII in 1075, but knowledge of this decision was slow in reaching England. Anselm discovered the ban during his first exile abroad and on his return (1100) announced his inevitable adherence to it, to the consternation of English conservatives, including the well-meaning and well disposed new king, Henry I. Despite their mutual respect king and archbishop could find no agreed solution to the matter, and Anselm went off into exile on the Continent once more. Complex and protracted negotiations ensued and finally in 1107 agreement was reached. The English Crown renounced the practice of lay investiture which henceforth lay discarded in history's junk-yard, but so far as the future was concerned the king got his way by one of those roundabout routes so necessary in the tricky conditions of the times, thanks to two archi-episcopal concessions. Anselm specifically undertook that a bishop-elect should not be denied consecration if he had previously done homage to the king, and it was accepted informally that, whilst the king did not in theory deny that election should be free, there should continue the old custom whereby these elections should be made by a delegation of the chapter concerned in the king's chapel, an arrangement which

---

* The ring symbolised marriage to the office concerned (at this time a diocesan bishop was not likely to be moved to another similar post whilst Benedictine abbots held office for life). The staff symbolised their pastoral duty as shepherds of souls.

implied, in effect, previous consultation with the king or his representative. With these two safeguards the over-all royal control of appointments was maintained without the fact being specified and, as far as circumstances allowed, honour on both sides was satisfied. As a contemporary correctly observed, the king might have lost a little in dignity but nothing in royal power.

EPISCOPAL ELECTIONS

The question of royal control over certain higher ecclesiastical appointments, notably that of English diocesan bishops was, of course, very much more crucial than the comparatively minor grievance just considered, and had a long and contentious history. As previously stated, the procedure for filling a vacant bishopric became a complex one. It began with the chapter sending messengers to notify the Crown of the existence of the vacancy and to request official leave to proceed to an election which was normally automatically followed by the latter granting what came to be termed the *congé d'élire* ('permission to elect'). Ecclesiastical custom allowed more than one form for the election which followed. It might be done by a rapid decision wherein the chapter concerned was unanimous or almost so. But in the cases with which we are concerned this was mostly rare, the usual procedure being for a sub-committee of the chapter (if it was a large one, as most were) being empowered to make the choice on behalf of all. The obvious next step, and one which prevailed in that great mass of English monasteries of which the king was not patron or in whose elections he was not interested, was for this body to reach its decision in its own house after due religious consideration and announce it to the awaiting brethren. But in the case of the episcopal appointments it came to be habitual for the election to be made in the royal chapel—a place of worship attached to the court wherever it then happened to be (royal households were as prone to itinerating as Victorian circuses). This might involve a long journey for the electors but this could not be avoided as only thus was the Crown in a position to exert the influence over the final choice which, as we have seen, it regarded as right and proper. Before the election took place at court the king or, in his absence, some one or more of his leading officials, would enter into discussion within the delegation sent by the chapter and make quite clear the nature of royal wishes on the election.

It is most unfortunate that in almost every case we know little or nothing of the nature of these preliminary discussions. It would be wrong to assume that almost always they ended with what was in effect an ultimatum to the electors to choose someone that they did not really want, though how often much outside advice was sought by the Crown and the extent to which it prevailed it is almost always quite impossible to tell. But preliminary soundings by the Crown was certainly not always absent. In archi-episcopal elections we have some indications of the Crown previously consulting outside advisers, whilst over the minor appointments it may not always have held very strong views. Under Stephen, the archdeacon Robert who was appointed bishop of Exeter was, a chronicler tells us, 'the choice of some few', and appointments to lesser bishoprics were probably sometimes made on the advice of the archbishop of Canterbury. Certainly behind these appointments, as with modern Anglican and Roman Catholic episcopal ones today, probably there was often no little preliminary activity on the back-stairs of which, for one reason or another, few or no details have survived.

Be this as it may, there is no doubt whatsoever that after the Conquest in England, as before it, the royal will on the matter was the final factor. It is very significant that when chroniclers of the period announce new episcopal appointments they almost always use some such phrase as 'the king gave the bishopric', not 'the chapter elected'. Writing soon after the settlement of the lay investiture question, Anselm asserts that in appointments King Henry 'does not use his arbitrary will but submits entirely to the advice of religious men', but this was, perhaps, a rather rosy view of the situation. Two factors made it highly unlikely that the Crown would relinquish its claims over these appointments. Firstly, the fact that by contemporary standards the income of most English bishoprics were so considerable (in late medieval times that of Winchester was asserted to be the richest in the Western Church). Secondly, the tight hold which the English monarchy was able to maintain over its kingdom made it perfectly feasible for it to exercise a high degree of control herein which was not possible in some other parts of the West.

For some time after the Conquest this royal control of major elections was the main target of criticism by the ecclesiastical left wing, notably after the scandalous behaviour of Rufus in the matter. His immediate successor, Henry I, at once sought to make a good impression by issuing a *Charter of Liberties* of which the opening article declared, 'Firstly I make free the Holy Church of God' and the promise was made not to sell or farm or tax the domain of a vacant church or its tenants. In hard fact, however, Henry's control over these appointments was maintained. Similarly, King Stephen on his accession in 1135 made vague promises with regard to ecclesiastical liberty, albeit with no specific mention of the question of episcopal elections, which also did not produce any great effect. But in 1164, when the conflict with Becket was coming to a head, Henry II in the *Constitutions of Clarendon* made precise reference to the matter. Article 12 declared that when a vacancy occurred in a bishopric or abbey or priory of which the Crown was patron, the king was to summon leading members of the body concerned who were to proceed to an election to fill the vacancy in the king's chapel 'with the assent of the lord king and the advice of the dignitaries (*personae*) of the kingdom whom he had summoned for this purpose'; and the person elected was to do homage and fealty to the king as his liege lord before he was consecrated. Such terms accurately mirror what had become the standard practice which made it as easy as possible for the king to control the election. Therefore what was here done was to define a procedure for election which, without saying so in so many words, left effective control of the appointment to the Crown. Diplomatic phraseology could not cover up the harsh facts of a matter on which no compromise was feasible; either the Crown controlled the appointment or it did not. In theory the right of freedom of election was never disputed, and it was implicit later on in the first article of *Magna Carta* which ordered that 'the English Church shall be free', but in practice by this time it was clear that the powerful English monarchy would insist on being consulted beforehand over the election and would expect its word hereon to be law. Such a solution to the problem was under the circumstances the only one that ever looked likely and was to remain very largely unchallenged throughout our period. Had English bishoprics been as small as Italian ones, this matter of appointment would have been much less serious.

ABBATIAL ELECTIONS

From the point of view of the English monarchy and its servants, control over episcopal appointments must have seemed very much more important than that over elections to the headships of those monasteries which were in royal patronage but did not have cathedral status, if only because the days had long gone past when a secular person, whether married or unmarried, could be intruded into the headship of a monastery. The English kings of our period were patrons not only of the wealthy Benedictine abbeys founded in pre-Conquest times, but of what ultimately became a large number of later houses of which no small proportion were of moderate means. Though the question has not yet been systematically explored, it seems likely that royal officials were as little concerned over exploiting the revenues of minor places during vacancies as of intervening over the appointment of their heads. But it was clearly important for William the Conqueror to be sure that abbots of the major Benedictine abbeys of England were loyal to him in the very exacting years which immediately followed the battle of Hastings and inevitably he saw to this, whilst Rufus desired control over them for gross financial reasons. But normally such control cannot have brought any enormous secular benefit to the monarchy, and it may have been largely exerted because of the intense legalism of the times—'what I have I hold'. As Knowles has shown, the Crown maintained tight control over major abbatial elections in the generations after the Conquest but without any serious ill effects. 'On the whole', he writes, 'it cannot be said that the royal control of elections was a source of injury to the monasteries. It is true that almost every king was responsible for a few wholly bad appointments ... but the great majority of the nominees were either members of the house whom the community had selected or monks of other monasteries at home or abroad whose abilities had made of them figures in the life of the Church ... the interchange between house and house, especially in abbeys of the second and third rank, did much to counteract the tendency towards isolation and stagnation which inevitably made its appearance at this time in the scattered and independent monasteries of England.'

WILLS

How was the steadily growing canon law of the Church to come to terms with the much less extensive but very deep-rooted and far-reaching law of the kingdom of England? This question became increasingly vital in post-Conquest times when both papacy and monarchy were gaining in power and ambition. Behind all disputes lay economic as well as constitutional factors, for then, as now, going to law involved expensive fees and the lawyers and royal officials of medieval England, like the rest of mankind, were mostly not disposed to see their sources of income reduced. The matters over which there was contention varied greatly in significance.

A minor but not unimportant example of them was provided by the question of testamentary jurisdiction, i.e. the legal control of matters pertaining to the proving of wills. Here was an area to which the authorities of both Church and State could put forward not unreasonable claims, though it is to be noted that its scope was much more restricted than it has since become. In our period very largely, though by the end of it not totally, it was the rule that wills could not dispose of such things as lands and buildings but confined themselves mainly to the bequest of what are known as chattels (i.e. movable possessions) of which the most frequently mentioned are clothing, articles of adornment, culinary and other utensils, furniture and, to a lesser degree, cash and plate.

Clearly it was arguable that the disposition of them was a matter for the civil authorities. But in these times the making of wills had a very profound religious significance which today is little evident. They were inevitably very deeply involved in with what was, in effect, almsgiving which was a religious responsibility on which the medieval Church laid major stress, so that it could be held that a will irreligiously made might damage the spiritual future of the person concerned.

The clergy were officially urged to ensure that the faithful did not die without making a will and the fact that a priest would normally be present when members of their flock were dying (for sudden death must have been comparatively rare in conditions which did not encourage thrombosis and knew not the motor-car) enhanced their position in matters testamentary. Under the circumstances it was not unreasonable to claim that since making a will was a major spiritual responsibility, matters concerning it should be in the ecclesiastical hands. In any case it is probably true that the financial pickings from testamentary business were not very considerable. The question was not one of major dimensions and the disputes over it prevalent for some time after the Conquest never reached substantial proportions. Recent study of the question has demonstrated that 'by 1230 a general extrinsic jurisdiction over chattels had been assumed by ecclesiastical courts' (Sheehan). Once the testator had died it was a legal necessity that the will should be proved, i.e. officially accepted as valid and registered in a court. This 'probate' of wills in medieval England was concentrated in dozens of local ecclesiastical courts of which the chief were the diocesan ones.

PAPAL JURISDICTION

Of all the disputes between Church and State in our period incomparably the most important and the most prolonged was the fundamental one over the rightful extent of papal jurisdiction. In 1066 in no sense could England be called anti-papal, but its relationship with Rome was very much less intimate than the Gregorian Reformers regarded as desirable. Conflict between the monarchy and the ecclesiastical authorities, or rather the left wing element of the latter, went on for very long and varied greatly in intensity though gradually tending to become much less violent. So far as the English monarchy was concerned the question, of course, was not whether papal authority should be rejected or not, but of what its rightful boundaries were. In view of the immense spread of papal authority in the West it is not surprising that as time went on this issue demanded much attention and became much entangled with various other problems.

THE NORMAN KINGS AND THE PAPACY

The attitude of William the Conqueror towards papal jurisdiction differed notably from those of both Victorian Protestants and Victorian ultra-montanists, being merely the usual attitude of Western monarchy at this time. Rome was the centre of unity and worthy of high respect, having certain major functions which no other ecclesiastical centre could properly claim. But papal intervention in the internal affairs of a local kingdom was not expected to occur very often, and of local appeals to Rome the same should be true. The idea that the popes could ever depose a sovereign was inconceivable.

William had carefully solicited and obtained papal blessing for his claim to the throne of England and, as soon as circumstances allowed, found it useful to have papal legates hold a council in England to clear up certain outstanding problems (page 62). In the reign that now opened he insisted on three rules in the sphere of Church-State relations, as a contemporary notes. In the first place, when there were two rival claimants to the papal title (as was occasionally happening in these times, largely through antagonisms between Rome and the German Emperors) William ordered that no-one in his realm should acknowledge either of them as genuine save by royal command, nor receive letters from such a person unless they had been previously shown to the king. Secondly, an archbishop of Canterbury who held a council of the English Church should not order or forbid anything therein without having previously obtained royal approval—an understandable safeguard against publication of new-fangled Gregorian ideas which might challenge traditional legal custom in England. The third royal order was the rather minor one that barons and royal servants were not to be involved in major legal charges, excommunicated or subjected to other ecclesiastical penalties without his consent. For one reason or another the chronicler here makes no mention of the important question of appeals to Rome from England. Almost certainly the king was strongly opposed to such things, save in highly exceptional circumstances and in business which did not threaten the royal prerogative.

Although William was a pious churchman who appointed an admirable archbishop of Canterbury and backed his extensive and useful reform programme, his relations with the new Gregorian papacy was inevitably difficult at times, the more so since the support of his invasion of England given by the Roman see was followed by claims that the new king owed feudal allegiance to the pope. This William curtly rejected, taking his stand firmly on local precedent.

William the Conqueror died in 1087 to be succeeded by his red-haired son, William Rufus, an unpleasant person and one of the very few kings of medieval England to be vigorously anti-clerical. He and his chief servant, Ranulf Flambard, worked unstintingly to extort ecclesiastical wealth by methods that few approved, notably by very extensive prolongation of vacancies in major church appointments. Very notable here was the long refusal to arrange for a successor to Archbishop Lanfranc who died in May 1089, action only being taken in March 1093 when serious illness had suggested to the king that the trials of purgatory might not be far away. The new primate was Anselm, as illustrious for learning as for sanctity, but unlikely to succeed in the almost impossible task of establishing friendly relations with the king. The situation was made even more difficult by the fact that there were at this time two rival claimants to the papal title, one of whom (Urban II) Anselm had already recognised, the other being supported by the king. This posed a major problem which was far from academic since venerable custom demanded that the new archbishop should, at an early stage, visit the pope and receive from him his pallium.

By somewhat naive diplomacy William Rufus sought to get Anselm displaced in return for transferring his own backing to Urban. The latter's papal legate sent to England to negotiate, in conciliatory fashion officially recognised the local custom that papal legates and letters should not circulate in England without previous royal consent, but with consummate ease defeated the royal manoeuvre to get Anselm removed from office. But the latter inevitably failed to establish friendly relations with William, and, when the king refused him permission to visit the pope to discuss the situation, went off without it in November 1097. His immense reputation brought him a rapturous welcome to the papal court, difficult to parallel, but, as so often in such situations, almost unavoidably papal diplomacy found it advisable to take no firm action against the king, and Anselm was still abroad when Rufus died on 2 August 1100.

He was succeeded by his brother, Henry I (1100–35), who rapidly urged the great archbishop to return, partly from pious reasons but also because his royal title was not as secure as could be desired. The new king was no despoiler of churches and founded various houses of Austin canons as well as the Cluniac abbey of Reading where in due course his mortal remains were deposited. Unhappily, hopes of a rapid and sound entente between king and archbishop were thwarted, for Anselm during his exile had learnt of the Roman ban on lay investiture which was wholly unacceptable to the king.

Despite sincere attempts on both sides to reach agreement, for some time this could not be attained and Anselm went into exile again until a satisfactory compromise was agreed in 1107 (page 136). The archbishop died two years later and was interred in his cathedral church of Canterbury, where his tomb remains.

So far as official visits by legates from Rome were concerned, Henry I took his father's line that these were only to take place under special circumstances. Of nine such projected visits to England, only one was effective, the most notable failure here being that which kept one unfortunate legate waiting in Normandy from 1116 to 1119. The successful visit was that of John of Crema who, for special reasons, was permitted to hold a legatine council of the English Church which concerned itself with useful unrevolutionary work, but caused some little hostile comment through the fact that in course of it the legate took precedence of the two archbishops. However, local feeling was speedily soothed by making the archbishop 'standing legate', though the permanence of such an arrangement could not be guaranteed.

Henry I's successor to the English throne was Stephen (1135–54), son of the Conqueror's daughter, Adela, who had married the Count of Blois. In his reign the royal control over relations with Rome showed very obvious signs of going into a marked decline. The obvious though by no means the sole major reason for this was the very insecure hold of the new king over his country, which made it necessary to conciliate ecclesiastical authorities to a far greater degree than hitherto, and also prevented him from having more than very partial political control of the kingdom.

Stephen's claim to the English throne was contested by Henry, son of Henry I's daughter, Maud, by Geoffrey Count of Anjou. Civil war ravaged the land, albeit very unevenly, in the course of which for most of the year 1141 Stephen was a prisoner. At no time had he that firm grip of the land so evident since 1066, and in his relations with Church leaders he was in an extremely uncomfortable position. On the one hand he wanted all the ecclesiastical support he could get; on the other, he also desired to maintain the old controls established by his immediate predecessors on the throne.

At the outset of his reign, when his succession was far from stable, the pope had come down firmly on his side and in return Stephen made the usual promise of good behaviour in brief and vague form at his coronation, confirming this the following year in a more detailed and much more unusual document. Its opening paragraph stressed that Stephen had been 'consecrated by William archbishop of Canterbury and legate of the holy Roman Church and confirmed by Innocent pontiff of the holy Roman see' and was followed by various promises for the good of the Church, including one which apparently implied that ecclesiastical elections should be free and not subject to royal pressure. In point of fact, more by accident than design, Stephen lost control of these. His brother Henry, bishop of Winchester, whom the king got made papal legate, was largely in charge whilst he held this office (1139–43) and for some time to an unprecedented degree chapters were left to their own devices at elections.

Whilst this decline of royal influence in certain top-level ecclesiastical matters was clearly a significant development, it is important not to over-estimate its influence in the major increase of contacts between the English Church and Rome which characterised this period, for there were major forces at work here which were quite unconnected with the new king's insecurity.

It must be appreciated that never since 1066 was it either feasible or even thought desirable to isolate England from the Continent with which it was now linked in so many ways. As the flight of distinguished refugees like Anselm and Becket illustrate, it was an easy task to slip across the Channel undetected in days which knew no radar or naval patrols. In any case, English and French ecclesiastical life at this time was inextricably interwoven in various ways which led to ecclesiastics frequently crossing and re-crossing the Channel. The growth of interest in learning was drawing Englishmen to the young university at Paris whose reputation the brilliant Abelard (d. 1142) was provocatively boosting, whilst copies of new treatises and new laws passed easily over to England. Especially important was the now very intensive interest in the new canon law which in the first half of the century greatly increased in substance, and was vigorously stressing the centrality of the Roman see in Western church life. Further, under Stephen, for the first and last time in history, we find a small band of Englishmen in high places in the Roman curia, including Nicholas Brakspear who in 1154 became the first and last English pope.

If canon law flourished so mightily now it was because it seemed so very relevant in an age when the ecclesiastical life of the Western Church was expanding so richly and so fast. Especially important at this time was the massive expansion of monasticism in England, which inevitably brought in its train a whole series of matters where aid from the Roman see was desirable. Thus, steadily from this time onwards, monasteries applied to the papacy for confirmation of their ecclesiastical possessions (which did much to eliminate the danger of trying lawsuits over them in the future) and sought also from Rome certain minor but useful privileges, such as the right to maintain their round of worship during an interdict or to establish a handful of their brethren at one of the parish churches in their patronage. It was becoming increasingly clear that Rome was much the best place to settle definitively major ecclesiastical disputes.

By the time of Stephen's death the relations between the English Church and the Roman curia had increased very greatly in volume since the Conqueror's day, even if very much of it was largely concerned with quite petty ecclesiastical matters which, though important to those officials and corporations immediately concerned, presented no significant challenge to the power of the Crown. Fears created by the extremism of early Gregorians had, so far as England was concerned, significantly diminished. Under Gregory VII no head-on clash threatened, the pope being unwilling to go to extremes against a ruler who, as he put it, 'neither persecutes nor sells the Church of God'. After Gregory, a similar attitude normally prevailed.

HENRY II AND THOMAS BECKET

It was thus apparent that when Stephen died in 1154 and (as had been previously agreed) was succeeded as king of England by his erstwhile rival, now Henry II, the monarchy was faced by a challenging situation. Significant changes in the Church and State relationship had developed. Were they to be accepted or challenged? The young and vigorous Henry was perfectly clear that ancient lost ground should be regained for, like most rulers of these days, he found it self-evident that the decisive factor in the relationship of Church and State was past precedent.

At first he had to move slowly and cautiously, seeking to reestablish control over high ecclesiastical appointments. The death of Archbishop Theobald of Canterbury in 1161 after a primacy that had lasted no less than twenty-two years seemed to make his task notably easier, and the fact that at this juncture the papacy was bogged down in yet another clash with the German Emperor meant that only minor trouble with the new appointment seemed likely. The essential was a new archbishop of Canterbury who was highly competent and deeply devoted to royal interest.

Such a man Henry II was quite certain he had already to hand in his Chancellor, Thomas Becket. This very colourful person was born in or about 1118, his parents being Normans who had emi-grated to London. Lively, highly intelligent, with a prodigious memory and a great capacity for administration, he had early joined the business staff of Archbishop Theobald who had sent him to study law at the great centre of Bologna and also at Auxerre. In 1154 the archbishop had appointed him to the very prestigious and lucrative office of archdeacon of Canterbury. The king approved of him greatly and the following year gave him the top office of his government, that of Chancellor. This post Becket filled with much success and no little worldly show, giving the king and many others the impression of being the civil servant *par excellence*, though there were depths in his character which Henry failed to note.

Pious he was, though not in any ascetic way, but it was not this which now caused him to show unwillingness to become archbishop, an attitude which bewildered and infuriated the king. Becket was no idealist sacrificing himself totally to an intense and clear-cut view of his Christian duty, like an Anselm or a Francis of Assisi. He was a servant, whose function it was to devote himself entirely to main-taining the dignity and interests of whatever office he held. As Chancellor he had upheld the interests of the Chancery, even if this involved the occasional fracas with ecclesiastical authorities. As arch-bishop of Canterbury and Primate of England he would be bound to maintain above all the interests of the Church. To Becket this was self-evident and he accordingly showed no readiness to accept the appointment, seeing that this could inevitably upset his relationship with the king, for whom he had a real regard. He informed Henry of this fact quite unambiguously. But the king, deficient as he was in psychological insight, failed to see this, and on the strength of Becket's admittedly efficient and loyal work as Chancellor success-fully pressed him to accept the bishopric.

Soon after his consecration Becket resigned his post as Chancellor, hereby aggravating King Henry, and went on to clash with him on several other comparatively minor matters, notably the question of 'criminous clerks', i.e. those who were accused of having committed major crimes such as manslaughter, assault and theft, and claimed the status of clerks (page 151), which entitled them to be tried in the ecclesiastical and not the royal courts. At a council held at Westminster in October 1163 Henry delivered himself of a hectoring harangue on the matter to which Becket responded with remarks that gave nothing away. No agreement was reached and Henry left abruptly in no friendly mood. Relations between king and archbishop steadily worsened, Henry unfairly accusing Becket of ingratitude and—very inaccurately—of being the son of a villein, whilst Gilbert Foliot, the trying and ambitious bishop of London, displayed a hostility to Becket which was to be deep and long-lasting.

Understandably and properly, Becket looked for aid from the pope, Alexander III, but at this time the papacy was in an immensely difficult position. The tough German Emperor, Frederick I, had set up an anti-pope so it was not politic for Alexander to alienate at this juncture anyone so immensely powerful on the Continent as Henry II. As a friend informed Becket, 'you must expect nothing from the Curia in anything that might offend the king'. As Lane Poole comments on Alexander, 'his halting, uncertain attitude is easily understandable and was, perhaps, the only one which he could adopt. But so far from assisting to bring about a settlement it had the effect of prolonging the dispute.' Much depressed, under papal and other pressure Becket now consented to give a purely general acceptance of the customs of the realm to which the king attached so much importance, albeit with the qualifying phrase 'saving the rights of his order' (*salvo ordine suo*), one of those contemporary hazy phrases which came in useful in times of legal trouble.

The king proceeded to overplay his hand in no small way, deciding to have these customs put into writing and officially accepted by the episcopate. To expect to settle anything so delicate as contemporary relations between Church and State in this clear-cut way was to push optimism to the point of lunacy, but work on the matter went steadily ahead, and at the now long demolished palace of Clarendon, the *Constitutions of Clarendon* (1164) was produced, giving the text of the customs.

The document was a brief one, its core consisting of sixteen articles whose total length barely covers a couple of pages. These varied greatly in significance. Of no great account were some of them, e.g. Article 16, which ordered that villeins' sons should not be ordained without their lords' consent (a claim reasonable enough since ordination conferred free status on those who did not already have it), and the previous article, which was concerned with certain pleas concerning debt. But three were of major importance.

Article 8 laid down that ecclesiastical appeals should go 'from the [court of the] archdeacon to that of the bishop and from this, if need be, to that of the archbishop', but if judgment in the latter's court was found deficient 'it must come finally to the lord king, so that by his precept the dispute be settled in the archbishop's court' and was not to go beyond this (i.e. to the papal court) 'without the assent of the lord king'. This provision, without saying so in so many words, clearly aimed to cut back severely the very heavy recent growth of appeals to Rome, and was reinforced by Article 4 which declared that archbishops, bishops and other dignitaries (*persone*) were not to leave the realm without having previous permission and giving security that when abroad they would do nothing which did 'harm or damage to the king and kingdom'—an unpleasantly vague phrase. Although this provision expresses accurately the royal attitude on the question of appeals to Rome traditional under the early Norman kings, it had now been completely overtaken by the passage of events, and in view of the now frequent recourse to Rome which had built up, was an attempt to put the clock back that was bound to create strong opposition and very unlikely to attain success.

Also dangerous was Article 12 which put down in black and white what had been the traditional English practice over elections to vacant bishoprics and monasteries in royal patronage, i.e. that these were to take place in the royal chapel and have royal assent, and that those elected should do homage and fealty to the king before receiving consecration.* To demand official recognition for this somewhat under-the-counter practice of election, or rather, selection, was to ask for trouble.

---

* In later legal language the term 'consecration' applied only to bishops, heads of monasteries receiving a benediction or blessing.

Accidental circumstances attached to the question of criminous clerks much more publicity and controversy than it inherently deserved. It was dealt with in rather tablet form in Article 3. In the trial of an accused clerk there were to be, in effect, three stages:—

(i) the accused person was to appear in the royal court and plead his clerical status;

(ii) if this plea was accepted he was then to be tried in the ecclesiastical court in the presence of a royal official;

(iii) if there he confessed his guilt or was found guilty, he was to be handed over to the secular authority for the appropriate punishment and, as the article puts it, 'the Church ought not to protect him further'. This implies that the clerk be 'degraded', i.e. officially stripped of his position in orders by the church authority, though this is not stated in the Constitutions.

In effect, therefore, the question of guilt of an accused clerk was to be settled by the church court, but if he was found guilty he was to be punished by the secular court according to its rules. Such an arrangement had much more to be said in its favour than Becket, in the violent heat generated by the controversy, was prepared to recognise, and had already been approved by such notable legal texts as the Code of the great Byzantine Emperor Justinian and that of the contemporary Italian canonist Gratian.

Becket based his opposition to it on the argument that a man should not be punished twice for the same offence which, he argued, this procedure demanded. It was at least arguable that degradation from orders was not a complete punishment but might be merely a legal preliminary which was necessary to allow the same punishment for a major offence to be imposed on clerks (who, as we have seen, were not necessarily clergy in the modern sense) as that to which laity were liable. On the other hand, as the very perceptive Hutton points out, under contemporary conditions 'for those who had received ordination from the Church the solemn and terrible act of degradation was a distinct and, to all but desperate criminals, must have been a truly awful punishment ... It would be difficult indeed, to exaggerate the awfulness to the medieval mind of degradation from holy orders ... To add to it, the chopping off of a hand or foot was ... to give a second punishment.' But the general public may well have found the privilege as indefensible as certain of those held by some trades unions today. No contemporary comment on this involved question of criminous clerks is more worthy of cogitation than that of the admirable historian, William of Newburgh: 'The bishops however, whilst anxious more to maintain the liberties or rights of the Church than to correct and root out their vices, suppose that they do God service and the Church also, by defending against established law those abandoned clergy whom they either refuse or neglect to restrain as their position demands by the strength of canonical censure.' If the atmosphere of the times had been less legalistic and the protagonists in the controversy less aggressive, a reasonable compromise could have been found, but quickly ill-temper and suspicion prevailed. Though Becket certainly was not faultless, no small share of the blame goes to King Henry who, like so many rulers before and after him, at bottom regarded the Church as not very much more than a useful branch of the civil service, not as the Bride of Christ whose claims were universal.

A great council of barons and prelates called by the king to consider the *Constitutions of Clarendon* met at Northampton (Oct. 1164). Henry, in most choleric mood, embittered the opening proceedings no little, and a tense atmosphere quickly built up amongst the bishops. Abruptly the king made the situation worse by ordering that all appeals to Rome be withdrawn and *inter alia* that Becket stand trial for alleged unfulfilled secular obligations of former days. The archbishop of York and the bishops of London and Chichester were scandalously vigorous in their opposition to Becket who, racked with worries, was very understandably on the verge of breakdown. Negotiation seemed useless and outside aid non-existent. Suddenly he fled to the near-by Cluniac priory on the outskirts of the town and bedded down in the church. When the monks arrived there for the night office they proceeded to sing it softly lest they should wake him, but by this time the archbishop had sought flight. After a difficult journey, part of it in disguise under an assumed name, he reached the coast and from Sandwich was rowed across to France by two priests expert in oarsmanship (2 November 1164).

After landing near Boulogne there came more hard journeying as Becket sought out the pope, then an exile himself at Sens, to whom he wrote beforehand to inform him of his plight. Henry, in a fury, further undermined his own reputation by ordering the expulsion from England of all Becket's relations, the aged and children in arms included, and seized his archiepiscopal property. Appeals to Rome were forbidden as was the giving of money or benefices to Becket's clerks. The archbishop of York, in Erastian mood, ordered his clergy to swear to disobey any papal injunctions regarding Becket.

There now followed for the latter a period of exile in France which lasted no less than six years, spent at first at the august Cistercian abbey of Pontigny where Becket sought, not very successfully, to acquire the ascetic spirit of its brethren, and then at Sens where his memory and various attractive relics of him are still cherished. More than one of his friends tried in vain to get the archbishop to take the situation with Christian placidity, but this was not in his nature and he relieved his feelings but not the situation by despatching a voluminous series of letters in which the spirit of compromise was seldom evident; to his mind when a thing was legally right to compromise over it was morally wrong. The situation was made worse as time went on by his excommunication of various major opponents. Henry was at least equally uncompromising, as no less than ten meetings between him and the king of France (who sought to act as peacemaker) plainly displayed, as did conciliatory efforts by the pope.

In 1170 Henry II, maladroit as ever, dropped no small brick when he had his eldest son crowned as his successor (a practice current in these times) by the archbishop of York (June 1171), though tradition, which then had all the force enjoyed by statute law today, assigned this prestigious function to the archbishop of Canterbury, and this royal action the pope had expressly forbidden. An interdict now threatened the king and under papal pressure in July Henry and Becket patched up a reconciliation at Fréteval. The king made no mention of the customs, demanded no oaths and returned confiscated lands. The two talked together for a while like the old friends they had been of yore and everything seemed set fair. But very quickly thunder clouds of controversy rolled in. The king's goodwill disappeared and Becket saw clearly that royal servants had lost none of their implacability. Very properly he planned now to return to his long desolate archdiocese but departed from France with a very strong premonition of the tragedy that was to come. To the pope he wrote, 'necessity drives me to my suffering Church'. To the king he said, 'my heart tells me that I shall see you no more in this life'; to the bishop of Paris he remarked, 'I go to England to die'.

THE RETURN

On 1 December 1170 he sailed to Sandwich and on the following day returned to Canterbury amidst manifestations of stupendous popular delight unparalleled before or since in any archiepiscopal progress, with garments being strewn before him and cries of 'blessed is he that cometh in the name of the Lord' ringing around. There can be little doubt that by now what corresponded to modern public opinion had had more than enough of the tough and ruthless rule of Henry II and his minions, and saw in the Primate of all England much the best hope of protection from this, as T. S. Eliot's play shrewdly manifests. Wildly enthusiastic crowds slowed the archbishop's progress as he walked barefoot through the streets of Canterbury, and men marked and wondered at his visage, 'for it seemed as though his heart afire showed also in his face'. Arrived at the cathedral he gave to each of its monks the kiss of peace, and then in the chapterhouse preached on the text, 'Here we have no perm-anent home but we are seekers for the city which is to come', one which mirrored perfectly that sense of the all-importance of things supernatural which had developed notably within him of late.

Quickly came signs of darkness. The sheriff of Kent and others arrived with violent demands; a little later the king's eldest son, whom Becket had taught and loved, refused to see him. Men at-tacked his servants and stole his goods. Preaching at the Christmas Day Mass Becket spoke meaningly of Alphege, his martyred pre-decessor. Meanwhile across the Channel complaints about him had sparked off the intemperate Henry: 'Fools and dastards have I nominated in this realm who are faithless to their lord and none of them will avenge me on this base clerk' he fulminated. Unsurprising-ly, four of his knights standing by took this as a broad hint and hastened to seek out the archbishop at Canterbury. On 28 Decem-ber they met there the archbishop who refused flight and had pre-pared for death by confession and scourging, followed by a meal at which he ate pheasant, remarking attractively, 'one who must go to his Maker should needs be cheerful'. The knights, on arrival, were politely treated. They railed at him furiously, demanding that he lift various excommunications, and then stormed out to collect men and weapons.

Calmly, with his primatial cross carried before him, Becket

proceeded through the monastic cloister to the mother cathedral of England, insisting that entrance to it be not barred. The knights, fully armed and ferocious, rushed in and found their archbishop, who faced them with that utter serenity which is the mark of Christian martyrs. As the ring on his finger reminded him perpetually, to his cathedral he was espoused and within it he was now determined to die, so he clung obstinately to a pillar therein, foiling efforts to remove him. Then, says the eye-witness account, 'the unconquered martyr, seeing that the hour was at hand which should terminate this miserable life, and give him at once the crown of immortal life promised by the Lord, inclined his neck, as one who is at prayer, and elevating his joined hands commended his cause to the Church of God, to St Mary and blessed martyr Denys.' Furiously the swords flashed at him, leaving a horribly mutilated corpse and a pavement bespattered with his brains and blood. Over the city crashed thunder and lightning. The assassins fled. Tenderly the monks took up the body with its calmly smiling face, and the following day buried it in the crypt. In the desecrated church the altars were stripped and for a whole year the majestic voice of cathedral worship was stilled.

This brutal and deliberate murder of a courageous archbishop in his own cathedral church sent a mighty thrill of horror over the West. Writes Lane Poole, 'no single event of this age so profoundly shook the Christian world ... Nothing is more striking than the almost instantaneous birth of the cult of St Thomas. And the cult grew and prospered; antiphons were composed and sung in his honour; miracles in plenty were attributed to him and representations of him in every medium in every European country in every age until the Reformation.' This cult for long enjoyed a prestige on the Continent which few other English developments of the period can rival.

With remarkable rapidity the first crowds of pilgrims to Canterbury came gathering round Becket's tomb to make their variegated pleas for help. Meanwhile the king was now held in deepest disgrace. Put under an interdict and refused papal audience he discreetly withdrew to Ireland whither few were likely to follow him. In May 1172 terms for peace were finally agreed. There was no total or dramatic abandonment of the *Constitutions of Clarendon*. As a basis for discussion it 'softly and suddenly vanished away', though various of its terms were by no means totally abandoned. In the devious diplomatic language so necessary Henry promised to abolish customs detrimental to the Church introduced in his reign, but these he not altogether inaccurately termed 'few or none'. The jurisdiction of lay courts where it conflicted with those of ecclesiastical ones was not immensely impaired. Control over criminous clerks had theoretically to be dropped, though sometimes exerted by devious routes; clergy were not exempted from the far-reaching Laws of the Forest which governed considerable rural areas of the country. In practice the traditional royal grip of episcopal and other major elections was not ended.

But so far as contact with the Roman see was concerned major change there was. Though the insistence that legates entering the country and prelates leaving it should obtain preliminary license so to do was not abandoned, it came to have little importance, largely because in the centuries about to ensue both Crown and papacy steadily found the value of exchanging squabbles for understandings to share ecclesiastical spoil, an accommodation which the lower orders of English society came to regard as far from gentlemanly. In general, access to Rome was henceforth very seldom impeded and at the lower levels for more than one reason steadily swelled to enormous proportions. Much of the routine business transmitted to it was of very little concern to the royal bureaucracy and was very useful to ecclesiastics great and small. So far as appeals to Rome were concerned, they were to be freely allowed with the minor proviso that any appellant suspected of seeking to harm royal interests thereby was to give adequate surety not so to do. This access to an outside tribunal with no local axe to grind, even if it required often a measure of greasing of palms to work effectively, was a valuable safeguard to local well-being, as the reign of John was to exhibit conspicuously. In the centuries ahead, relationship of Church and State was very close and increasingly free from more than sporadic and minor squabbles, largely because Rome now found it politic to grant the English Crown a very large part of its demands, which were predominantly financial, ideological differences of opinion being mostly kept discreetly in the background by both monarchy and papacy.

From the point of view of art and letters no event in the period covered by this book so caught the imagination of the future as

Becket's death. At once there sprang up a group of biographers of Becket quite without parallel in medieval England, the fullness and variety of whose work is not unworthy to be compared with that inspired by the celestial Francis of Assisi, whilst down the age artists paid massive tribute to Becket in a variety of media. Early came the noble mosaic of the archbishop in the tasteful cathedral of Palermo and the small statue of him still evident at Sens. Very frequently, as century followed century, his murder was pictured in wall painting, stained glass, and on caskets. If in modern times artists have largely lost interest in Thomas, the compelling story of his life and death inspired first Lord Tennyson and later T. S. Eliot, whose *Murder in the Cathedral* combines dramatic power with a degree of historical perception rarely found in writers of fiction.

Although Thomas's conduct mostly lacked the absolute sanctity which marked that of Anselm's, if we look below the surface there are clear signals that his fight against the king was very much more of a clash of principles than of pettiness or of personalities. His stay during his exile at the noble monastery of Pontigny may well have intensified in him that self-sacrifice which, as a schoolboy, he had observed amongst the Austin canons of Merton Priory, whose habit he wore and whose prior had been his confessor. Like all great Christian rebels down the ages, he opposed the State unflinchingly primarily because of his conviction that ultimately the powers of the secular government were subject to the immutable laws of God, not to the local regulations of politicians. If in the heat of combat he at times claimed more than was wise and did not always display that immense patience which dealings with the peppery Henry II demanded of a Christian, these were properly seen at the time to be minor defects in one who stood out so fearlessly against the head of the most powerful government in Western Europe and whose behaviour exhibited totalitarian tendencies incompatible with the inherent universalism of the Christian Church. To defy Henry consistently, as Becket came to do, demanded a conspicuous courage which only deep conviction could breed, and this defiance inevitably won the archbishop both admiration and gratitude, as the remarkable explosions of joy which greeted his return to Canterbury from exile so clearly demonstrated. That his opposition was very likely to culminate in his death was something which much less acute minds than Becket must have foreseen, and the incontestable crudity of his murderers merely underlined the current menace of royal power.

Of his age one of the shrewdest of Becket's multifarious bio-graphers long ago wrote, 'Merchants, lawyers, villeins, barons felt themselves in danger of being stifled by an overmastering central power, the power of an unrestrained and arbitrary king. Such a danger could only be averted by the struggle of each class in turn. And the Church alone could fight with any prospect of success, for it alone had solidarity in different lands and could invoke forces in its support which would prevent its isolation in no small quarter of the globe. If the barons tried to conquer, to rule men as they willed, they discovered that that was a game which the king also could play and generally play better. They could not resist him when they were alone. Still less could other classes, save only the estate of the Church. Thus it was that the poor looked to the Church for pro-tection; her ideals were utterly different from those of the other classes, and when she rose to them men found shelter against op-pression under the covering of her wings. Slowly by her action in defence of her own claims she made national liberty possible. So Stephen Langton, one of the heroes of English Liberty who gave to Magna Carta what it had of national beneficence found in Becket a predecessor of whom he delighted to honour' (W. H. Hutton).

PART THREE

The Age of Consolidation

c.1199 - c.1340

CHAPTER 6

CONSOLIDATION IN DIOCESE AND PARISH

THE thirteenth century in Western Europe was without doubt one of the most fruitful in its long history. Widespread and pertinacious developments of the previous century and a half came to fruition and produced enrichments of the highest importance, a substantial increase in wealth and population in most areas reinforcing their effectiveness. Particularly important were the developments in Italy, France, Flanders and England which, in the centuries with which this volume is concerned, contributed much more than their share to the efforts which built up the remarkable civilisation of Western Europe.

If in many regions town life made only minor progress, in Italy it flourished immensely, providing the sophisticated setting in which the Renaissance was ultimately to flourish, whilst in St Francis of Assisi (d. 1226), St Thomas Aquinas (d. 1274) and Dante (d. 1321) were produced the most remarkable trio ever born in one land in the space of a hundred years. At the same time, university life took on elaborate and progressive form, notably at the great centre of legal studies at Bologna, as it did in Paris where the spectacular Abelard (d. 1142) had done much to give it that pre-eminence in the study of the arts which it has never lost. North of the Alps, thanks mostly, but not entirely to France, there reared up the great Gothic cathedrals by which men are still entranced. In the influential sphere of monasticism the mendicant orders which now developed provided the Church with one of the most potent missionary weapons it has ever acquired, whose mode of life has been found as valid for modern as for medieval times. Much less spectacular but equally fundamental was the development of an ecclesiastical machinery of great efficiency in which the enforcement of a carefully thought out and complex canon law was taken very seriously by a hierarchy of officials who were mostly much more highly trained for their work than they had been a century before. In England, as elsewhere, a major factor was the vigorous and close co-operation between the sophisticated Roman curia and the local episcopate which, significantly in this age when the spirit of reform was so very potent, attained a very high standard.

THE EPISCOPATE

So far as England was concerned, the death of the untrustworthy John in 1216 occurred very opportunely from the reformer's angle, not only by removing to other spheres one who was almost totally lacking interest in ecclesiastical renewal, but because his successor, Henry III (1216–72), was a mere child of nine so that no overbearing royal intervention was on the cards for some time. Further, the regency which was now in control was very much on the side of the angels. Dominant influences at first were the papal legate and Archbishop Stephen Langton (d. 1228) who had been so prominent in the creation of Magna Carta and whom at least one authority has termed 'perhaps the greatest of our medieval archbishops'. Under such conditions top-level influence in the crucial matter of episcopal appointments was clearly in excellent hands and, as in such matters 'nothing succeeds like success', a tradition of high standards in this matter was steadily established which took some time to erode.

The king came of age in 1227 and though very pious with something of a penchant for pilgrimages, which he passed on to his son Edward I (1272–1307), had a mind of his own vitiated by poor judgment which led him from time to time to take a strong line over episcopal appointments, though by later medieval standards the cathedral chapters of his day had often a fair amount of elbow room. But, by and large, the English episcopate of the thirteenth century was both conscientious and industrious, not combining with their ecclesiastical responsibilities unnecessarily large secular ones with that resultant neglect of episcopal duties which had reached such scandalous proportions by the close of our period.

'It is to the three generations of bishops following the Lateran Council (of 1215)', writes Knowles, 'that the church of England chiefly owed its full development and organisation. It was, indeed, a remarkable century. In all the medieval centuries the group of bishops who came nearest to the pastoral ideal, it might well be the generation of which Robert Grosseteste (d. 1253) was the leader and spokesman. It contained two canonised saints, Edmund (Rich) of Canterbury and Richard of Chichester and half a dozen others noted both for ability and piety and venerated long after their death.' With this high estimate another expert opinion concurs: 'On the whole the English bishops in the thirteenth century were able and respectable. As leaders, administrators, visitors, builders and patrons of learning they have never been excelled' writes Powicke.

He goes on to point out that 'under the exacting conditions of a career which became more and more "professionalised", the election of monks as bishops was not encouraged.' In the period from 1216 to 1340 the total of monastic bishops in England reached the not very considerable figure of twenty-two of whom fifteen were Benedictines. With this we may compare the corresponding situation in the period from 1066 to 1215 when there were twenty-five monastic bishops of whom nineteen were Benedictines. It is worthy of note that in both cases almost all the Benedictine bishops held sees which had a Benedictine chapter. The contingent of thirteenth-century friars who were promoted in England is small but distinguished, two of the three becoming archbishops of Canterbury. No few bishops came from the now vigorous and highly trained men who held important posts under the Crown, of whom a useful fraction had some university training.

Non-monastic bishops cannot be forced into neat social pigeon-holes to placate the modern lust for computerisation: then, as now, they varied greatly. As Powicke shrewdly remarks, 'the really effective influences which gave coherence to the episcopal body were life in the schools, family connexions, patronage and licensed or legitimate pluralism', and the episcopate of these times, as always when fully effective, was drawn from various sectors of society. St Edmund Rich, archbishop of Canterbury from 1234 to 1240, was an Oxford don of undistinguished origin who, after protesting against royal and papal exactions, retired to the great Cistercian abbey of Pontigny where his tomb yet remains; he achieved canonisation with remarkable speed in 1247. St Richard of Chichester, one-time Chancellor of Oxford, was a protégé of his, also of unspectacular parentage, who showed immense pastoral concern for his diocese, but Thomas Cantilupe, bishop of Hereford (1275–82) and canonised in 1320, was of aristocratic origin.

These men lived as simply as they could, but there were now a certain number of bishops who lived in a style at which modern Holywood would not turn up its nose. Such a man was Antony Bek, elected bishop of Durham at royal behest in 1283, though it must be admitted that the fact that his see had enormous secular responsibilities attached to it, made it impossible for any holder of this office to live a simple spiritual life. He began well enough by turning down the request of the archbishop of York, made immediately after his consecration, that he open his episcopate by excommunicating the priors and monks of Durham Cathedral, though he later blotted his copybook by shutting them up in the church with a mere six loaves and sixteen herrings for sustenance. He was usually escorted by 140 knights to which were added twenty-six standard bearers when he faced the Scots, and by the time of his death (1310) for no very good reason he had become Patriarch of Jerusalem and King of Man. To succeed him, very speedily and wisely, the monks of Durham elected to the bishopric one of their brethren, the admirable Richard of Kelloe. However, he soon departed this life and scandalous wire-pulling at top level acquired the see for a relation of the queen, one Louis de Beaumont (1318–33). Weak and obstinate, he was so ignorant of Latin that despite special coaching he could not read his profession of obedience; floored by a complex word, after a pause he hurriedly remarked in French, 'Let it be taken as said'. Thus bishops of Durham, like those elsewhere at this time, were by no means cast in a single mould. However, there is no doubt that by the mid-fourteenth century, though passable prelates were yet to be found, the éclat which had characterised the English episcopate under Henry III and Edward I was now little in evidence.

Synod and Council

At the time of the death of King John a major priority was publication and enforcement of the reform programme contained in the recent Fourth Lateran Council and, as recent scholarship has shown, this was a task on which the English bishops worked with an assiduity of which beavers would have approved, taking with a seriousness of which there is very little sign in the twelfth century the work of keeping the faithful fully informed of their responsibilities (a task which contemporary social conditions made very far from easy) and reiterating major needs with no little frequency. In the thirteenth century English bishops now held diocesan synods with assiduity though provincial assemblies were fewer than officialdom rather optimistically enjoined, and came to be in certain ways eclipsed by the new clerical body which ultimately claimed the name of 'convocation' (page 237).

The diocesan synods included, at least in theory, all the clergy of the diocese along with heads of monasteries or their 'proctors', i.e. legal representatives, and met once or twice a year. Here, *inter alia*, the bishop's ordinances were read, partly to give them publicity but also to allow consideration of any difficulties herein. They became very comprehensive, covering especially the conduct of the clergy and laity, the care of church property and regulation of worship. Understandably, each church had need of a copy of these. The legal custom of these centuries left no notable gaps which allowed a bishop to become a law unto himself, so many diocesan statutes largely repeated provincial regulations, occasionally with some smallish variation. The synod also took cognisance of a variety of minor local matters which were not of immense import but could not be left to solve themselves.

Above the synod of the individual diocese was the council of the province, which contained all the bishops and a somewhat complicated selection of what are termed the 'inferior clergy'. Its president was the archbishop of the province, who could use it to promulgate a set of canons which seldom showed any sparkling originality. Very important was the council of the southern province held at Oxford in 1222 under the guidance of the admirable Archbishop Langton. Its sixty canons cover a wide range of matters in a workmanlike way, promulgating decrees of the Fourth Lateran Council along with supplementary ones. Another such council held at London in 1257 is remarkable for its elaborate 'Complaints of the clergy', tidily arranged under fifty heads. The total amount of English conciliar documents at this time is, by medieval standards, very considerable, and was made more complex by complications which followed the rise of Parliament (page 235). From the point of view of the clergy and the man in the street the enormous output of episcopal injunctions on every aspect of their ecclesiastical responsibilities was of very great value, even if for one reason or another these were by no means always adequately implemented.

Episcopal Functions

By the middle of the period covered by this volume the powers inherent in the office of a diocesan bishop had been developed in a very extensive way to cover an enormous number of matters which differed considerably in kind. As we have seen, major functions, which only he enjoyed, were to dispense the sacraments of confirmation and of holy orders. The former followed baptism and was principally conferred on children. In the thirteenth century episcopal statutes for Exeter and Winchester order confirmation to be received within three years of birth, if parents could find a bishop, and they were to fast on bread and water every Friday if this was not done. This is amongst the finest examples of that blithe optimism which marked so much medieval legislation, whether ecclesiastical or not. For, surprising as it looks amidst so much very efficient contemporary organisation, it seems to have been no one's job to organise confirmations so the rite was administered in a singularly haphazard fashion, being too often covered by hazy injunctions to the faithful to get their children confirmed whenever they happened to hear there was a bishop in the neighbourhood. Not surprisingly, confirmation was neglected to a remarkable extent. Archbishop Peckham found an 'infinite multitude' of unconfirmed children in the diocese of Coventry. Bishop Hethe was accused of leaving children unconfirmed by not travelling round his diocese and a provincial council of 1322 spoke of 'the prevalent neglect of confirmation'. This neglect was due primarily to two factors—firstly the slow travel of the times which tended to make contact between the bishop and the major part of his flock virtually impossible and, secondly, the immense pressure of work on a diocesan which made it tempting to accord a low priority to confirmation, which unlike ordination or Extreme Unction, was an auxiliary rite. But the result in medieval England is certain—'thousands upon thousands must have died unconfirmed' avers Knowles.

Much more fundamental for the life of the Church was that conferment of holy orders which was an episcopal prerogative, at least so far as major orders were concerned. The number of grades of holy orders was not the same throughout the medieval centuries in Western Christendom, nor was the official line between which were major and which were minor orders, the subdiaconate at first belonging to the latter but finally to the former. For ordinations certain special seasons of the year were detailed. The bishop could confer the four minor orders (of door-keeper, lector, exorcist, acolyte, and at first sub-deacon) on the same person on the same day. Gradually in the episcopal ordination lists, reference to all these minor orders except acolyte tended to fall into disuse, this title being the only one of them usually noted to accompany those of the higher orders of sub-deacon, deacon, priest and bishop. Eighteen was the minimum age for minor orders, nineteen for sub-deacon and deacon and twenty-four for priests. Theoretically ordination was to be preceded by each candidate undergoing an examination of their character and theological knowledge. One contemporary manual stresses that the tests were not to be too stiff and there is little sign that they were. A serf or one born out of wedlock could not be ordained without these disabilities being legally removed and all ordinands had to be in possession of a 'title' or means of financial support after ordination (page 271). If a diocesan was too busy to carry out an ordination he could get clergy ordained by another bishop whom he legally authorised to do this by what were termed 'letters dimissory'. Archbishops and bishops because of their extensive commitments made increasing use of this right and of assistant bishops to carry out ordinations on their behalf.

The total number of those ordained to one grade or another of the sacred ministry was considerable and came to include a very large number of un-beneficed clergy who found employment of one kind or another. In fifty ordinations between 1282 and 1302 no less than 5349 men were ordained by Bishop Gifford and in the Exeter diocese between 1308 and 1331 Bishop Stapleton ordained 770 sub-deacons, 822 deacons and 791 priests. It is interesting to compare these figures with the carefully analysed statistics of later ordinations in the diocese of Norwich. Here, between 1413 and 1486, 392 ordinations services were held for 4100 men. These took place with great regularity at the four 'Ember-tides' which tradition set aside for this purpose, seldom in the cathedral but usually wherever the bishop found it convenient to be. 530 men were ordained by letters dimissory for work in various other dioceses. The advance from sub-deacon to priest usually took less than a year.

Less important was the episcopal function of consecrating the major adjuncts of local worship—notably churches, churchyards and altars. The immense amount of rebuilding and extension in England in the late twelfth and thirteenth centuries made a good deal of this necessary. Cardinal Otho on his visit to England had found this much neglected and took appropriate action. (It is worth remembering that provided the altars had been consecrated, the fact that the church which contained them had not, was of no great practical importance.) This work, together with the allied tasks of reconciling churches or churchyards which had been polluted by bloodshed was clearly a rather minor chore which hard-pressed diocesans tended to hand on to the assistant bishops who were used with increasing frequency in the latter part of our period and sported exotic titles. Piers Plowman mentions picturesquely prelates

'That bere bishops names
Of Bethleem and Babiloigne
That huppe about in Engelond
To halwe mennes auteres
And crepe amonges curatours'.

TAXATION

The thirteenth century was a very notable one in the history of taxation, especially for ecclesiastics who now found themselves liable to be grievously ground between the upper and nether stones of Crown and papacy. Bishops were inevitably involved in drawing up the assessments which often led to heated controversy, and they might also find themselves undertaking the laborious and thankless task of collecting the revenue concerned. On top of this now, as for so long to come, the English episcopate was a major element in the House of Lords of the fully evolved Parliament, a fact which, together with various other calls of business in the capital, led them to acquire private hostels in London.

By the mid-fourteenth century the taxes were various. Peter's Pence dated from pre-Conquest times, but in the usual medieval way had paid little attention to price rises, so now was far from lucrative. At the top end of the scale were the taxes now sought with infuriating frequency by the English Crown and the papacy. But the labour involved here, though not negligible, was much less than that required to fulfil that supervision of spiritual life in his diocese which fell to the bishop as being its Father in God.

Amongst the various ecclesiastical activities which a diocesan had to supervise, that of visitation was high on the list. As we have seen, the Cluniac, Cistercian and mendicant orders and a very limited number of individual Augustinian and Benedictine houses were exempted from the jurisdiction of their diocesan bishop, but considerable numbers of monasteries were not in this position and to see to the good estate of these was episcopal obligation.

The bishop was equally responsible for ensuring the good estate of the parish clergy and laity of his diocese. This task was obviously far too large to be carried out without extensive delegation of his powers to various functionaries, of whom the archdeacon was much the most important. However, with a frequency which almost certainly varied extensively from place to place and is often not clear, the bishop would visit the parishes of his diocese—every three years coming to be the desirable norm, though being very far from generally observed.

Through sheer necessity created by social circumstances over which he had no control, a medieval bishop had to be accompanied by a large staff. The Third Lateran Council of 1179 strove to limit the expenses this involved (which were paid by those being officially visited) enacting *inter alia* that a bishop could not claim expenses for more than thirty horses, a decree notably violated when Bishop Giffard arrived at Worcester Cathedral with no less than 150 steeds of one kind or another. The fascinating accounts so obligingly provided for us by Bishop Swinfield of Hereford (1282–1317) shows that he usually had thirty-six horses—a number which was not un-reasonable—during the long and laborious visitations which he undertook. He sometimes changed his habitation far more often than a Victorian circus; he and his household moved no less than eighty-one times in the space of the 296 days covered by the roll, the most restless period being the fifty days after 10th April when he spent the night in no less than thirty-eight different places! There were three meals a day, all mostly consisting of beer or wine, with bread and meat which tended to be heavily spiced in a number of flavours. The amount of food consumed was clearly enormous even on fast days: on one Friday some forty or fifty people were provided with two whole salmon, one conger, over 300 eels, 900 herrings and seven hake, and Moorman reckons that on Easter Day there was ten pounds of meat provided per person, eked out by pigeons and eggs; perhaps some of this went to hangers-on and local poor.

But increasingly for many medieval bishops this time-consuming operation on what was mostly very routine work did not seem the best way of expending their limited time, so much so that in some cases it was accorded very low priority. To a limited degree such a view was defensible, since much of the work could be equally well done by the archdeacons. To them much of it was entrusted, though, of course, this development had the deplorable result of failing to establish those intimate, personal links between the bishop and his flock which are of the essence of Christian living and which the Church in Italy, with its cosy little dioceses, has perennially maintained.

APPROPRIATION

In England, as elsewhere in the West, amongst the major new developments in ecclesiastical organisation with which from the early thirteenth century bishops had to concern themselves extensively, was that officially termed 'appropriation'. This is the name given to the legal process by which the income of a parish church which was in the patronage of an ecclesiastical corporation was officially divided into two very sharply defined portions, one of which added to the income of the patron as rector, the rest being allotted as hitherto to the priest who served the parish, who would rank as a vicar. (There was not in medieval times any question of part of such income being assigned to a non-ecclesiastical person or corporation, a practice termed 'impropriation' and common in post-medieval times.)

The primary motive behind appropriation was to increase the revenues of the ecclesiastical corporation concerned where need for this had been established (the huge majority of the bodies to benefit by it being monasteries whose financial needs in the thirteenth century especially were very considerable) whilst also ensuring that the priest in charge of the parish had an adequate income and a secure legal position. Though the point cannot be proved, it is at least highly likely that at this time no small proportion of English monasteries at one stage or another were heavily in debt. Most of them were engaged in the very expensive task of erecting the complex set of buildings which their way of life required, on an elaborate scale and in the stone which was now rapidly replacing wood as the major building material. On top of this came the expenses for organising and developing the lands which now everywhere were passing extensively into monastic hands. The numbers of brethren were increasing and often the older monasteries rebuilt all or part of their conventual church in the new Gothic style, consigning to oblivion unfashionable Romanesque work. Constructing the permanent buildings of a new monastery in days when the number and wealth of English society were far from large was an enterprise that could often involve protracted financial strain, which was intensified by two external pressures.

Medieval England was no stranger to political disorders which had undesirable financial repercussions, this being notably so in the northern province which was never free from the menace of Scottish raids which had early established a tradition of very great ferocity; those of the early fourteenth century were particularly destructive, necessitating very considerable reductions in the assessment for taxation of some ecclesiastical institutions. But often very much the greatest and most persistent drain on monastic funds, so far as the outside world was concerned, was the maintenance of the venerable tradition of showing hospitality to travellers, expressed supremely in the *Rule of St Benedict*'s injunction 'let a guest be received as if he were Christ', an injunction which its followers cherished faithfully down the centuries. It is to be remembered that in medieval England bad roads and the very widespread lack of financial resources reduced travel to very minor proportions; there was not the slightest manifestation of an hotel industry and virtually no tourist trade. Though there were some hospitals which provided accommodation, their contribution to the travellers' needs was on a very small scale, and a very large share of this responsibility rested on the shoulders of the monasteries which were numerous, widely spread and generally had a good deal of spare space that could be used for this purpose—often a long room over stabling accommodation where the unfussy could sleep, and with less primitive accommodation for others.

Maintenance of beds and board for numbers which might be very large in frequented areas entailed non-stop expenditure, whilst delicate monastic tradition usually forbade use of a scale of fixed charges, and relied on a sense of moral obligation to pay according to their means, which their guests by no means always displayed in full measure. Almost certainly a good deal of cadging went on here, even pious kings of England by no means always paying the full costs of their court's sojourn at a monastic house—thus in 1306–7 King Edward I with a household of around 200 installed himself at Lanercost priory with disastrous results on the place's finances.

To fill such financial gaps, with great frequency petitions were made for the appropriation of parish churches by their monastic patrons, which very often cite the cost of maintaining hospitality as a major or the major cause of their financial need. Especially in the thinly populated north the only hospitality a traveller could expect was that of a religious house, though these were far from numerous. Bolton Priory, built in a beauteous but infertile region, stood near a route of some little importance with few neighbours for miles around so was inevitably greatly burdened in this way. In 1301, plagued by debt, it secured permission to obtain financial relief by appropriating its quite wealthy church of Long Preston. The archiepiscopal deed permitting this shows in detail the needs for some such step, 'perpending also how, by reason of the taxes and extortions that are in these days imposed and ordained, and of the barrenness of the land, which in your parts hardly produces half its former revenue and of your own neighbourhood, which, as it is said, suffers not a little from famine and in which you continually support almost the entire hospitality and maintenance of the poor, being situated almost on the king's highway, albeit your own re- sources are scarcely sufficient for this, in as much as hardly any lodging is to be found elsewhere for strangers or other persons travelling through these parts so that they are compelled to resort to you very often and almost as a matter of necessity' and adds that 'for these reasons you are oppressed by debt, so that unless God shall very rapidly lend you helping hands you will scarcely be able to breathe in order to live on your own goods, being lamentably poor.' As if this was not enough it was farther noted that 'a great part of your monastic buildings, being built of ash wood is already threatening to collapse and cannot be repaired without considerable expense.'

With this tale of woe may be compared the one rehearsed in the deed wherein the bishop of Worcester, in 1314, allowed the brethren of Great Malvern Priory situate in a very fertile area to appropriate the church of Powicke, a mile or two away down the Worcester road. Here, it was detailed that 'certain manors and churches ... without fraud, deceit or fault of the monks have been finally taken from them and lost in the commotions of wars and devastation of property in Wales and England' as a result of which the convent was unable to meet the costs of maintaining its complement of twenty-six monks, its thirty resident poor and the claims of hospitality, whilst constant demands from the popes and extortion by secular princes, had involved them in a burden of debt so that 'unless a speedy remedy is effected it will be necessary to diminish the number of monks and of the poor and thus curtail the service of God.' The bishop approved the request for appropriation, partly on these grounds, but partly also because of 'the burden of hospitality, which ... affects and harms their monastery more than others.'

The overall financial gain to be had from these appropriations of parish churches to their monastic patrons was potentially fairly considerable owing to the very large number of the former which passed to the latter. In the huge passion for monastic foundation which animated twelfth-century England it had been very common indeed for donations of the advowsons of parish churches to be included for three main reasons. In the first place contemporary opinion tended to disapprove of ecclesiastical appointments being in the hands of laymen since, as protracted experience showed, they so often appointed to them low-grade friends and relations. Secondly, a fair number of these livings had attached to them resources which were appreciably greater than a parish priest of the times might reasonably expect, leaving a surplus which might be utilised by their owners. Thirdly, contemporary opinion ranked gifts to further the monastic life as the most laudable and profitable forms of almsgiving.

In the course of the twelfth and thirteenth centuries Augustinian and Benedictine monasteries thus acquired the patronage of an enormous number of English parish churches which quickly ran into four figures and increased somewhat in later times (it is possible that the ultimate total was in the region of 3900). Not infrequently twelfth-century barons would give to monasteries which they had founded the patronage of all their parish churches. Lesser folk might give a single advowson, a gift which, of course, as cynics may observe, did not in practice cost them anything much, beyond the loss of right to nominate to it.

Very early began the utilisation of these advowson by monasteries to augment their finances. In the twelfth century it appears that the delicate task of deciding which benefices could be thus appropriated and the respective shares of the income be assigned to the patron and to the incumbent was often settled in a somewhat slapdash and unofficial manner, some monasteries showing a tendency to take action therein which it is difficult to distinguish from greed. As early as 1102 a council at Westminster ordered that 'monks do not accept churches without the consent of the bishop nor so rob of their revenues those which are given that the priests who serve want things necessary.' The problem was a general one in the West and met with regulation at the Third Lateran Council (1179) which ordered that monasteries were to pay adequately the incumbents of their churches and not to remove them or alter their stipends as they pleased. As so often in such cases, the decree was resented and by no means universally obeyed, but officialdom stood firm.

The remarkable Innocent III, amongst his great range of concerns, gave major attention to this problem with others allied to it, making provision which came to fruition at the Fourth Lateran Council of 1215. Canon 32 of this august assembly after noting that 'a vicious custom which must be eradicated has grown up where patrons of parish churches and certain other persons claiming the profits for themselves, leave to the priests deputed to serve them, such a scanty share that it is not adequate to sustain them', adds further, 'that in some regions a parish priest got only a minute part of the tithes' so that in those regions scarcely any parish priest could be found who was even moderately well-educated: and concludes by ordering that 'a sufficient portion be assigned for the priest.' The incumbent of the benefice (known as the rector) was to reside and officiate where possible but otherwise must take care 'to have a perpetual vicar canonically instituted who (as is aforesaid) should have a suitable share of the profits of the church.' This canon has been termed 'the Magna Carta of the parish priest. ... Often ignored, often over-ridden, often misinterpreted, it stood firm throughout the Middle Ages as the bedrock of the vicarage system' (Hartridge).

Henceforth if a benefice was appropriated it was to be served by a resident 'perpetual vicar' who, as his name suggests, had complete security of tenure, provided, of course, that he steered clear of major misdemeanour. He was entitled to a reasonable and clearly defined share of the revenues of the benefice concerned, whose details the Lateran decree could not possibly define in very detailed terms because of the huge variety in the value and nature of the revenues of Western parish churches, and the considerable variations of their currencies.

The necessary local follow-up of this decree in England was initiated by the noble Archbishop Langton, notably at a great council at Oxford in 1222 in a carefully worded canon. This opened with the reminder that 'very often the luxury of worldly goods shuts off and draws away some people from the office committed them, to the scandal of the people' but also 'poverty of these same things compels others to beg miserably to the shaming of our (clerical) order' and goes on to enjoin that a perpetual vicar receive a minimum revenue of five marks (i.e. 68s. 8d.) except in parts of Wales where poverty had made less than this customary. As to customary payments due from the church, the bishop was to decide how they were to be allocated *vis à vis* the rector and the vicar. Following this decision the English episcopate made no small efforts to ensure that their parish clergy were not underpaid, a notable lead being by Hugh de Welles, the good bishop of Lincoln (1209–35) who has left invaluable rolls recording the results of his vigorous work to settle with exactitude the extent and nature of the revenues to which incumbents of appropriated parishes in his diocese were entitled.

This was an infinitely more complex task than modern man might expect, owing partly to the very great variation in sizes of contemporary parish revenues in medieval England, but even more to the fact that much of the parish priest's emolument was paid not in cash but in kind—the tithes or tenth parts of the fruits of the earth (interpreted in the widest sense) which varied immensely in their nature. As a result it would be difficult to find two vicarages which were absolutely identical in the resources that they allotted to their vicar. Major tithes were usually wholly or largely reserved for the holder of the parish living, i.e. usually a monastery which ranked as its rector. But all or most of the lesser tithes might be allotted to the vicar and a very miscellaneous lot they might be. For example, in the case of the Worcestershire parish of Childs Wickham these covered wood, milk, calves, young pigs, geese, eggs, honey and bees, gardens, yards, lands dug with the spade, doves, mills of every kind, flax and hemp. (One of the fascinating minor problems unsolved by dons to date is the way in which such complex miscellanies of agricultural produce were utilised in practice by medieval vicars; what, for example, did these do when they received in due season what must have been small mountains of eggs?). Provision was also often made for a specified yearly payment in cash to the vicar and an important element in his receipts were 'offerings of all kinds at the altar' as they are sometimes termed. They correspond to modern church collections in so far as they were paid in cash mostly at religious services, but differ from them in that they were, in effect, compulsory and also because they were made not every Sunday but on a very limited number of specified occasions, which included Christmas, Easter and the patronal festival. Besides this, deeds of appropriation make careful arrangement for the vicar's place of residence which, then as now, usually consisted of a house near the church with a garden attached. Although the vicar was celibate his official abode was often fairly spacious, partly because he might have an assistant lodging with him, but also to enable him to provide that hospitality which medieval folk regarded as an indispensable element in Christian living.

The parish had certain other official obligations and deeds of appropriation make it clear which of these pertain to the vicar and which to the body holding the patronage of the living. There was a fair amount of variation in detail of these arrangements. At Childs Wickham, Bordesley Abbey, who held the rectory as was usual in such cases, had to 'repair, rebuild or re-roof the chancel' and provide it with certain books. But it was for the vicar to find 'linen, vestments and other ornaments necessary for divine service in the chancel', and also to provide a competent clerk. He had also to pay the procurations due from the parish (page 180). It is difficult to say how equitable by contemporary standards the terms of such appropriations were. These seem to have been reasonable enough, at least at first, though in some cases the share of financial obligations laid on the vicar looks excessive and in process of time the growing importance of ecclesiastical taxation almost certainly hit hard some of the poorer livings, whilst some benefices which avoided the net of appropriation might find themselves bound to pay an annual pension to their ecclesiastical patrons.

THE INCUMBENTS

To ensure that a vicar normally received a reasonable share of the revenues of the parish whose pastoral work he headed was a comparatively simple operation, though the actual payment of tithes might often cause friction. Immensely more difficult because it resulted from very widely spread and deeply rooted social and economic factors, was the problem of ensuring that the incumbents of the English parish churches in our period acquired a reasonably high level of true piety and sound learning. Here this problem posed major questions. Firstly, in view of the fact that private patronage was very important and most English diocesan bishops often far from untouched by contemporary social pressures, it was most difficult to ensure that nominees presented for institution to parish churches were people who were fit for the heavy responsibilities of a parish priest. As we have seen, economic forces were a major element in the undoubted fact that throughout our period some of those who held livings had little or no pastoral zeal. Again and again bishops and councils fulminate against clerks being promoted to benefices who not only had not received the priest's orders so essential if they were to do the work properly, but refused to proceed to them thereafter, and against other defects only explicable by similar causes, though the extent of this abuse is unknown.

The main reason for this was the fact that in an age when England was very far from having great riches and was dominated by an economy which allowed only a very limited choice of careers, an ecclesiastical benefice offered one of the very few ways of acquiring what was by contemporary standards an independent household and a reasonable standard of living. Because of this, country livings were often used by local lords and squires holding the patronage thereof to provide for relations, friends or servants of one kind or another and there is no doubt that in the latter part of our period benefices great and small (preferably the former) were treated by top people from the king and barons downwards as bits of property which might be utilised to support members of their now large staffs, provided the official duties of such posts were carried out by deputies paid at cut-rates. It is this which led to some worldliness among those who superficially look like clergy though close inspection shows them to be laity who were in theory (but not always in practice) in clerical clothing.

To our very sex-conscious generation it may seem clearly obvious that the insistence on celibacy of the clergy which triumphed conspicuously in England from the late twelfth century could be to some an insuperable bar to ordination to the higher grades of the sacred ministry. Again and again medieval men broke the laws of Church and State with a degree of impunity which often seems remarkable and in this matter it is not difficult to find individual cases of parish clergy who were married, though, as always in prohibited sectors of society, such folk were much more concerned to 'lay low and say nuffin' than to provide useful information on their numbers to gladden the heart of future historians. In no part of our period is the evidence adequate to enable us to make even a reasonable guess as to the exact proportion of the medieval English clergy who acquired spouses of one kind or another, though there is no doubt that if it had been more than a minute minority it would have left behind it far more considerable traces than now exist. Can it be that the sexual urge of contemporary society was far less strong than seems likely to the modern observer? Certainly in the case of the English bishops of the latter half of our period, no small part of whom owed their promotion to aristocratic connections or administrative skill, and whose lives are much better documented than those of most other sections of the English Church, there is very little indication of them seeking to combine their high ecclesiastical position with some form of marital relationship.

If positive social pressures tended to cumber English benefices with men whose interest in the spiritual responsibilities which long-established theory had attached to them was apt to be distinctly limited, it is arguable that this situation would have been considerably bettered had the medieval bishops of Western Christendom not largely abdicated their major responsibility of seeing that those called to the priesthood were adequately suited and trained. But to them this idea did not occur. The intellectual and spiritual state of the clergy, undesirably low as it seems to us, was clearly higher than that of the laity, and probably became increasingly more so. No action was taken since no strident demand for it was audible.

THE ARCHDEACON

By the end of the twelfth century the dioceses of England had all been given one or more archdeacons. Each of these was responsible for a wide range of business either in the whole diocese, if it was a small one, or over a fairly extensive area of it in other cases. In the thirteenth and fourteenth centuries these activities are well documented and their onerous nature very clear. Among the politer titles accorded to the archdeacon was that of 'the bishop's eyes'.

A perennial and time-consuming activity was the archdeacon's duty to inspect periodically (in theory every year) all the churches of his area. One aim of this was to ensure that the places possessed all necessary vestments, books, utensils and other ornaments and to see whether the list of these contained any additions or losses since the previous survey or their condition had seriously deteriorated. Each church was to be as well provided with these as their finances allowed. There is no doubt that throughout our period there were no few parish churches whose possessions of this kind were more restricted than was desirable. Sets of vestments might be small in number and not always in good condition and altar vessels made of inferior material, like the apparently considerable number of pyxes for the Reserved Sacrament which Henry VII in his will sought to replace (page 354).

But the invaluable record of a visitation of this kind carried out by the archdeacon of Norwich in 1368 shows us that by and large, in this admittedly fairly prosperous area the situation was satisfactory: 'the churches of Norwich and Norfolk in the fourteenth century were on the whole, well provided with sufficient and suitable ornaments and furnishings' concludes the editor. He goes on to show that no less than 94 per cent of the churches possessed the eight service books which archiepiscopal injunction required and at least 82.5 per cent of them had the ornaments enjoined.

Of obvious major importance also was the soundness of the building, notably walls, windows and roofs, and this the archdeacon would seek to check. He would inquire also whether the parish priests maintained the public worship by day and night as was their duty, chastising those who were defaulting in minor degree and referring to the bishop more serious matters such as cases of clergy who were non-resident or not in the requisite grade of holy orders, and grave neglect by the patron of the living. This visitation was clearly a detailed affair and to cover his costs the archdeacon was entitled to levy a tax that was known as 'procurations' on each parish church concerned. He also saw to the collection from almost every parish under his surveyance the amount of Peter's Pence due from it and 'synodals' payable in connection with twice-yearly synods. These sums were mostly quite small but varied considerably from place to place and it was useful to note them alongside the inventory of chattels of each church, as with the Norwich inventories. Thus we find such notes as 'the value of the same [church] is 100s., Michaelmas synodals 2d., Peter's Pence 2d., Easter synodals 2½d., Procurations 2s.,' after which comes the exact list of its various ornaments, etc.

The behaviour of the local congregation was equally his concern. The misbehaviour of medieval English laity mostly follows stock patterns. Violence in the churchyard and even in the church was far from unknown and, if it resulted in bloodshed, would demand 'reconciliation' of the area by a bishop. Dancing and sports in the churchyard occurred fairly frequently and improper songs roared out from time to time. Less common but not unknown was the habit of choosing foolish Christian names for children. The fact that bedroom space in medieval England tended to be strictly limited accounts for the archdeacon being expected to stress the not in-frequent conciliar degrees which ordered mothers when in bed to be careful not to overlay their children. He might also seek to ensure that the latter did not stray too near unguarded fires and wells. These duties produced no little business but were surpassed in spec-tacularity by sexual offences of the perennial types over which the archdeacon had jurisdiction.

Because of its concern with adultery and fornication the arch-deacon's court became known as 'the bawdy court'. Partly because of lay-rooted dislike of being hauled up to answer for such offences but partly also because of the corruption amongst its lesser officials, the archdeacon's court became intensely unpopular and had a reputation for unfairness which cannot have been totally undeserved, though very deficient evidence makes it imposssible to decide to what extent this reputation was deserved. It has recently been com-mented that 'the archdeacon's court came in for a good deal of abuse in the later Middle Ages, possibly because it was efficient . . .

Chaucer satirised, probably with some reason, its excessive pre-occupation with fines at the end of the fourteenth century' (Hill). A big part of the trouble may have lain in the fact that the procedure allowed too much arbitrary action (from which there seems to have been little easy way of appeal) by underlings who, as often, were by no means all patterns of moral rectitude and had far too easy opportunities to pick up money on the side. Chaucer's thumbnail sketch of the Summoner is unlikely to have been compounded from pure fantasy:

'He would allow—just for a quart of wine—
Any good lad to keep a concubine
A twelvemonth and dispense it altogether
. . .
And if he found some rascal with a maid
He would instruct him not to be afraid
In such a case of the Archdeacon's curse
(Unless the rascal's soul were in his purse)
For in his purse his punishment should be
"Purse is the Archdeacon's Hell" said he'

(tr. Coghill)

Elsewhere he extends the attack on the summoner who 'knew so much of bribery and blackmail, I should be two years telling you the tale'. In fairness it ought to be added that bribery in varying degrees was as common in contemporary England as in Hanoverian times and that the archdeacons and their staff worked to enforce rules which by and large may well have improved the quality of English church life.

On top of all these responsibilities the archdeacon was perennially liable to be faced with missives from his bishop ordering him to see to some matter or matters which at that juncture seemed to his lordship to require immediate attention. Parishioners must be at their mother church for the Pentecostal procession, not forgetting to fetch with them the traditional oblation. The archdeacon must see to the 'sequestration' (i.e. management during a vacancy of a particular church)—he was entitled to a third of its profits until this was ended. He must ensure that inmates who had fled from their monastery either return to resume their habit or be imprisoned. He would also see that laity knew the correct mode of baptising infants, in case they had to do this in an emergency. The archdeacon or rural dean must relay episcopal directives to local chapters of clergy, enforce clerical celibacy and be vigorous in defending ecclesiastical liberties. The flood was unending and must have meant that an archdeacon worked a very great deal harder than most of the clergy of the cathedral to which he was attached.

RECORD-KEEPING

From the point of view of the ecclesiastical historian few of the remarkable advances in English church life in the thirteenth century were more valuable than the stupendous and systematic attention to the keeping of records of contemporary ecclesiastical business which now developed and has been faithfully maintained ever since. This development was no isolated venture but part of a major tendency of the times. With the pontificate of Innocent III (1198–1216) begins the tremendous continuous series of papal registers—an invaluable source for English church history—as are in England the so-called 'Chancery Enrolments'; the Close, Patent and Charter Rolls, royal records whose origins belong to exactly the same period and whose contribution to our knowledge of our ecclesiastical history is equally fundamental. Such records may be regarded as the ancestor of the modern carbon copy (now in process of being out-dated) and sprang from the same cause—the obvious need for any large and competent business to keep copies or digests of material likely to be required for reference purposes in the future. As a result of this process an enormous amount of new light comes to be thrown on no few aspects of church history about which in earlier times we know little or nothing. Thus, for example, the Chancery Enrolments enable us to follow with a remarkable degree of precision the often protracted and complex process involved in the appointment of a new diocesan bishop.

The background of the very extensive areas of most medieval English dioceses and the fact that no few English bishops of the thirteenth century had previously been royal officials, make it very far from surprising that a similar movement towards the keeping of business records quickly developed in English episcopal circles. As is natural enough, this movement was not a highly organised and uniform one but proceeded in a somewhat piecemeal and haphazard fashion. A fairly rapid development was evident over the format of records. At first, rolls were often used to record the information preserved, made by sewing a series of skins end-to-end. But these were most inconvenient for later use owing to their often considerable length (an early roll concerning the archdeaconry of Lincoln, for example, is thirty feet long), so that steadily such things were replaced by quires of parchment which might later be sewn together to form a register. However, what material was preserved for future reference was a matter for the local authorities to decide for themselves, and there was no uniform choice, more and more miscellaneous matter being liable to be incorporated as time went on.

Details of appropriation of individual churches were obviously useful to have at hand in view of their utility, complexity and great variety. Amongst the earliest registers is 'the old book of ordinations of vicarages' compiled for the bishop of Lincoln, mostly in 1218, which records details of some 300 such things on eight rolls—one for each archdeaconry. Names of clergy duly appointed to benefices was another useful item, as were lists of those ordained to the various grades of the sacred ministry at the regular ordinations. But a great variety of other documents occur in episcopal registers, such as indulgences, wills, official enquiries of various kinds including monastic visitations, and records of various other episcopal acts (whether by the diocesan or bishops duly commissioned to perform them) such as consecration of churches and churchyards. In the course of time parliamentary and ecclesiastical taxation often added to the contents. The earliest surviving register of the archdiocese of York consists of two rolls drawn up for the great Archbishop Walter de Gray which begins in 1225 and throws enormously valuable side-lights on every part of the unwieldy area which he ruled. By the last decades of the thirteenth century English dioceses had begun a series of such episcopal registers which were henceforth faithfully maintained; these include Exeter (1257), Bath and Wells (1264), Worcester (1268), Hereford (1275) and Canterbury (1279). For one reason or another, here and there the run of volumes has been broken by time. By the end of the period covered by this book many types of documents have acquired a degree of verbosity and a good many records we would fain have had were not preserved. Nevertheless, enough remains to fill a great number of gaps in our knowledge, though unfortunately no English register systematically records such minor but useful information on transitory matters as the size of the monastic communities visited and the number of times a year their members went to confession, as are preserved in the magnificent Norman register of Odo Rigaldi, who became archbishop of Rouen in 1248.

A humbler but nevertheless very useful English ecclesiastical record whose obscure origins go back to the period here under consideration is that which has come to be known as the 'Church-wardens' Accounts'. The earliest surviving examples go back only to the middle years of the fourteenth century; the surviving total of those of pre-Reformation date is quite small, largely because of the very transitory nature of the business with which they deal. In the thirteenth century bishops, archdeacons and rural deans worked pertinaciously to make their diocesan machinery efficient and *inter alia* were much concerned to see that the parish churches were kept in good repair and provided with everything necessary for the right conduct of public worship. Though ecclesiastical officials had to see what was wrong and check that deficiencies were made good, the local chores in connection with this had clearly to be left to the laity of the local congregation. The form of machinery for this was finally established not by orders at top-level but through many local experiments, which in the thirteenth century took no uniform shape. But in the following century it became the norm that the various duties concerned with the maintenance of the fabric and fittings of the local parish church should be put in the hands of two of its trustworthy male members, who ultimately came to be termed churchwardens though, as in so much else, even here the uniformity was not total (as late as 1529 a Halifax will makes mention of 'the kirke wardens otherwyse called the kirke maisters'). Very usually these officials were elected for two years, but in successive years and not simultaneously. They kept careful records of all official income and expenditure and annually presented accounts for approval by the parishioners. The accounts are simple affairs but go into their business in very great detail, thereby providing invaluable information on matters theological and non-theological as well as being of immense value to the historian of the locality with which they are concerned. It is, however, to be noted that their terms of reference are very largely ecclesiastical, the considerable social responsibilities with which churchwardens ultimately came to be involved dating only from Tudor times.

Annual expenditure, of course, might vary considerably. Major repairs or extension of the church were usually paid for by raising money by the imposition of a 'church rate', in effect a tax levied on owners of property within the parish in proportion to its size. Repairs to roofs, walls and windows, as always, could be expensive, and the boundaries of the churchyard had to be kept in good order. Regular items of expenditure included the provision or repairs of such things as vestments, service books, the supply of incense, and bread and wine for the Mass. Bells seemed to have involved a good deal of expense, not least when, as apparently sometimes happened, a tradition developed that a retiring churchwarden could take a bell-rope as a perquisite. Clocks and pews were coming into not infrequent use by the end of the period here reviewed, but were not regarded as essentials.

How was the money for such maintenance raised? Most medieval parish churches had nothing that could accurately be termed endowment, mainly because of the poverty of the times. But, as wills show us luminously, occasionally smallish pieces of property were left them, often with some special purpose in view such as the maintenance of a light before a specially loved statue. Sometimes, though not frequently, flocks of sheep or swarms of bees were given, and hired out by the churchwardens. Very small sums came from the sale of the remains of torches, while a major source of revenue at longish intervals was the 'Church Ale' or 'King Ale', a species of village fair which lasted several days and during which were provided common meals and various kinds of simple entertainments including plays, minstrelsy, dancing and competitions. A notable fact, and one which illustrates the conditions of the period, is the almost total absence of those frequent collections of cash during public worship on which modern church maintenance depends.

It is most regrettable, though, under contemporary social conditions, very far from surprising, that the medieval English Church never perceived the value of recording baptisms, marriages and funerals (the precursors of modern registration of births, marriages and deaths), this innovation being introduced in the time of Henry VIII, offsetting to some small degree the quite unparalleled destruction of English historical and literary sources which characterised his reign.

Secular Cathedrals and Colleges

The fact that secular cathedrals and colleges of medieval England survived the Reformation and the monasteries did not, along with the still obvious architectural magnificence of the former, makes it tempting to over-estimate their importance in this period. As we have seen (page 77), the number of secular cathedrals fell short of double figures and the total number of secular colleges (most of which were minor institutions) was a very small fraction of that of the monasteries. Further, it is to be remembered that the rôle of the medieval cathedral in local church life was far less prominent than is now habitual, partly because of the over-large size of most dioceses and the poor communications, but also because of the great strength of local parish life. Many of the faithful who lived a relatively short distance from their cathedrals mostly saw their diocesan very rarely; indeed, in some areas he must have been normally invisible.

Most bishops lived outside their cathedral cities on one or other of their outlying estates, and as time went on found so much business which tended to call them to London that it was desirable to acquire a house there. The bishop of Winchester could happily lodge at Southwark where his diocese met the Thames, but the lordly bishop of Durham soon found himself a London house and most others followed suit in the course of the thirteenth century.

By this time the bishop and his cathedral chapter had become distinct financial and legal units, the latter developing the passion for legal privileges so rife in these times, being perennially ready to whittle away episcopal rights and oppose episcopal claims. The powerful chapter of York, for example, fought tenaciously and successfully to reduce to small dimensions the perfectly reasonable claim of their archbishop to carry out visitations to ensure that all was well. After no little friction, in 1280 the chapter magnanimously agreed that their father in God was entitled to do this every five years but was to be accompanied by no one but two of the canons themselves. Further, he was not entitled to put detailed questions in writing or examine individual members of the chapter against their will. Concurrent with this process in most cases was the division of the cathedral income between the bishop and the chapter, which was reasonable enough in view of the fact that by now there was not the slightest hope of their maintaining that full communal life which had been the norm in the early days of cathedral life.

It is typical of the priorities of medieval church life that however much bishop and chapter might engage in combat over legal privileges, when it came to ensuring that their cathedral was built or re-built in grandiose beauty, they were totally at one. It is interesting to note that in this field of the history of English secular cathedrals the thirteenth century was of incomparable importance. The Romanesque cathedral of York was early found inadequate and an elaborate re-building campaign inaugurated, whilst the new cathedral at Salisbury and the re-built ones at Lincoln and Lichfield belong to this epoch as does much of Wells.

By the end of the thirteenth century the major staff of the English secular cathedrals had largely assumed what was to be for centuries its classic shape. At the top of it were the four 'dignitaries' (page 87-8), but the major part of the higher clergy was constituted by holders of 'prebends' which had been created sporadically since the Conquest but went on to assume a static number which varied from cathedral to cathedral.

What was a prebend? The word (*prebenda*) had no classical ancestry and, like many medieval Latin terms, for long had no single technical meaning. It was, in effect, a specific endowment which supported a member of the clerical staff who was appointed by the diocesan bishop and was known as a prebendary. A number of these posts were created in the two centuries which followed the Norman Conquest and came to differ enormously in value. At the bottom of the scale were some so slight as scarcely to be worth tenure; at the other were prebends like the 'golden prebend' of Masham at York which in 1291 was assessed at £166 13s 4d at a time when few of the prebends of Hereford and Lichfield were rated at more than £20. Although the average value of the prebends of York was far higher than that of most other English secular cathedrals, London included, their income in 1291 varied considerably. Six were rated at £10 or less and another six did not top the £20 mark. The average value of the York prebends was about £48, some £8 more than those at Lincoln, no less than six of them being assessed at £100 or more. But elsewhere such sums were largely unknown.

It is to be noted that though this was by no means invariably the case, these prebends frequently included a benefice which might be served by the prebendary concerned or by an official deputy. An overall examination of medieval prebends is much desired and is the preliminary to any full understanding of the motivation behind their establishment. To modern eyes two of their features may seem surprising—firstly, the fact that major pastoral responsibilities were very seldom envisaged. If great lay magnates established small collegiate churches in their castles it was largely in order to provide themselves with a literate staff to carry out secretarial and administrative work for them. At the top of this group tower the great royal foundations like St George's, Windsor and St Stephen's, Westminster (page 264); at the bottom, rather pathetic little establishments like Bridgnorth.

The position of prebendaries of the great cathedral churches was, however, much more complex and created an almost unbroken series of ecclesiastical headaches. Here were a largish number of clerks legally attached to the cathedral but having often responsibilities which tended to direct them elsewhere. Prebendaries whose endowment came at least partly from a benefice might be drawn to reside there rather than face the considerable complexities of life in a medieval cathedral close, where the firm insistence on the provision of hospitality at all times was a constant drain on their resources. Had all the prebendaries of a cathedral or large college wished to reside permanently—a contingency that never arose—housing them all would have proved a major problem. Royal and episcopal officials, especially the former, might find what seemed to them at least to be reasonable cause for prolonged absence, but absenteeism in the case of the dean, chancellor and treasurer—the 'personnages' (*persone*) as they were sometimes called—whose primary responsibility clearly lay in the cathedral, created difficulties. As a result, the statutes of the secular cathedrals especially were repeatedly concerned with regulating the non-residence of their staffs, which could not possibly be totally forbidden but had to be controlled. Thus the statutes of Salisbury Cathedral of 1214 orders that one quarter of the canons be always in residence with the four 'personnages' who are bound to keep continuous residence, 'excepting those canons who are exempted by the king or the archbishop or bishop.' The custom was also developed of having a common fund from which resident canons' income could be augmented to meet the special expenses to which they were liable, amongst which the dispensing of hospitality was apt to be prominent. But contemporary social factors made this whole problem a very trying one to which no very satisfactory solution could be found. Almost inevitably, since prebendaries could not be in two places at once it early became usual for them each to have a vicar to deputise for them.

CHAPTER 7

MONASTIC CONSOLIDATION

The Older Orders

By the opening of the thirteenth century in England as on the Continent, the huge expansion of Benedictine and Augustinian monasteries which had long been so evident had for some time been slackening. The numbers of new foundations were now much fewer and they were mostly on a much smaller scale than many of those set up in the hundred years which immediately followed the Norman Conquest. This decline was in part due to an economic factor. The shrewd Henry I was only one of many who had been well aware of the undesirability of unduly straitening secular revenues by alienating very extensive parts of it to monastic use, so that, significantly, much of the endowment of the various monasteries which he established came from spiritualities not temporalities. This was the case with his foundations at Carlisle and Cirencester and the same was true of Henry II's foundation of Waltham. After this time the establishment of rich monasteries was very rare indeed, partly, though only partly, because so many of them were now founded by people from the squirearchy or upper middle class who had not at their disposal huge estates like those of early Norman barons. The rather imprecise evidence which is all that remains to us on this subject suffices to show clearly that establishment of new monasteries of the old orders certainly slowed and affected the orders to varying degrees.

In the period c. 1200 to c. 1340 the increase in the number of Cistercian houses was very small. They had accumulated fifty-one by 1154 and sixty-eight by 1215, but in the following century and a half acquired only another seven. The unaffiliated Benedictine houses had expanded mightily in Norman times, when the tide was running so strongly in their favour. They had about 200 houses of one kind or another by 1154 but had reached their peak of 228 by

1216. The Austin canons retained favour somewhat longer, albeit on a small scale. Independent houses of the order, if we exclude alien priories and hospitals, totalled about 179 by 1216 and 208 by 1350.

It would be as foolish to interpret this slackening of expansion as an indication that monasticism was losing its appeal as to hold that the very small number of new railway stations set up here in the inter-war period denoted a fall in the popularity of British railways. Just as in the last century the enthusiasm for building railways and canals went further than was sagacious, so now the enthusiasm for Augustinian and Benedictine monasticism was more than adequate for the needs of later days. We have various signs that these older monastic orders were by no means out of favour in the thirteenth and early fourteenth centuries, notably the steady flow of benefactions to them and the steady increase in their recruitment. Recent research suggests that the number of Austin canons and Benedictine monks in England which in 1154 was in the region of 5500 reached its medieval peak of about 9750 on the eve of the Black Death. The same impression of progress is given by contemporary architectural evidence which shows that at this time many religious houses were setting up domestic buildings on a large scale, which it would be foolish to regard as having been inspired by nothing but optimism. But the dominant concern of the older monastic orders in these times was certainly the very sensible one of consolidating the very strong position they had by now acquired.

CONSOLIDATION

From the economic angle consolidation was now very necessary, since for long English society had been lavishing on the monasteries hosts of benefactions often varying from huge estates given by mighty barons to very minor pieces of property given by others of no social account. Quite innocently these benefactors inevitably created some difficult problems, since their gifts were frequently scattered and in some cases so isolated as to be difficult to run on a profitable basis. To have refused them would have seemed discourteous but acceptance of them created many administrative headaches.

The history of monastic estate management has very little religious significance, largely falling within the domain of the local antiquarian and the economic historian, but cannot be totally ignored. In the efficient organisation of their estates the Cistercians were now great pioneers, as is understandable enough in view of their ethos. They gave new vigour to the establishing of what are termed 'granges'—large farm centres like the home farms of later days. These were mostly not very far from the abbey which owned them and for long were largely staffed by lay brothers. The original endowment of such places was often consolidated by the acquisition in one way or another of adjoining properties, so as to make it an easily workable whole and the resources of the estate systematically developed. This was an old and obvious practice long adopted to some degree by ancient wealthy Benedictine abbeys, but now became very much more extensive and intensive though, of course, hosts of minor houses never owned important estates of this kind. The term 'cell' is also given to some of these subordinate establishments used for agricultural purposes, though this is better (though by no means generally) reserved for small dependent communities which have either a parish church or a small monastic one as their centre, but the distinction between the two types is not to be pressed too far. In the Cistercian order granges were very common, and cells in the restricted sense almost non-existent. With Augustinians and Benedictines the reverse was often the case, even if the brethren concerned seem seldom to have fulfilled pastoral responsibilities where these existed. In such circumstances it was usual to hire a secular priest to undertake any attendant pastoral duties. The Austin canons could do this work, though the extent to which they did so at this time cannot be determined. Those in power sought to ensure that in such cases the canon did not live without the companionship of a few of his brethren, but the minimum total of three or four which they usually demanded was probably far from uniformly achieved. A good number of these cells seem to have been very thinly endowed and faded out in the course of time especially, it may well be, after the catastrophic fall in the monastic population which followed the Black Death.

GENERAL CHAPTERS

Very much more important for the student of monastic well-being was the provision of the safeguards needed for the maintenance of those high standards of life to which inmates of monasteries were called. This was entrusted to two different types of machinery— regular general chapters of the order concerned on a general or a local basis and the periodic visitation of individual houses by the bishop or archbishop of the diocese (page 198).

As has already been noted, the Cistercians got off to a very early start in this field, from their very early years running their order by what was in effect a parliament of its abbots held annually at Cîteaux, whose decisions were put into force where necessary by abbots of the locality concerned. These general chapters began in 1116 and their voluminous edicts cover a very wide range of action great and small with next to nothing left to local initiative. Those of the thirteenth century display immense activity characterised by great efficiency and a freedom from rigidity which compares very favourably with much ecclesiastical legislation in these and other times. A minimum of thirteen brethren for a new house of the order was demanded and also the site of a proposed new abbey was carefully inspected by local abbots to ensure that it was suitable; thus the abbots of Neath, Buildwas and Flaxley were sent to see the site offered for a new abbey by Prince Edward (1266) to check on its desirability. The abbot of Quarr was deposed for running up un- authorised debts (1269) and the abbot of Kirkstall threatened with suspension if he did not quickly pay up money which he owed a cardinal (1279). The abbot of Tintern whose absence from general chapters was said to be due to ill-health was to resign if he could not attend the forthcoming one. Similarly persistent and minute was control over liturgical matters, not least over the calendar for com- memoration of saints.

The considerable success of the Cistercian general chapters must have been a major factor in the decision taken at the Fourth Lateran Council of 1215, whereby all other monastic orders which had not already got them were to establish similar machinery, those prin- cipally involved, of course, being the very large numbers of houses of Benedictines and Austin canons which did not belong to some independent order like the Cluniacs or the Premonstratensians, which by now had their own machinery for this purpose. However, in England as elsewhere, this decree posed difficult problems since the numbers of monasteries concerned were very large and they were scattered far and wide over the country, whilst no few of them were far from affluent and might well view with distaste the often long, trying and expensive journeys which such general chapters would involve, even though these were set up on a regional basis which did not require them to leave the land of their birth. Thus with the English Austin canons having houses here as far north as Hexham and Brinkburn and as far south as Bodmin and Hartland it was going to be highly unlikely that anything approaching a high level of attendance would be normal. Even if, as came to pass for some time, general chapters were held separately for the northern and southern provinces this would still involve long and dreary journeys, as when the priors of Lanercost and Carlisle were summoned to such places as Bridlington and Guisborough.

A further disincentive was the long tradition of working as independent units current amongst Augustinian and Benedictine monasteries, which produced an individualist outlook curiously comparable to that produced by similar long lack of common action amongst Victorian Anglican clergy. This partly accounts for the impolite note on general chapters of his own order made by the Barnwell chronicler to the effect that their decrees were 'easily published and rejected with equal ease'! Similarly, as Knowles points out, English Benedictines tenaciously refused acceptance of a scheme of reform which was 'so practical and to all appearances so reasonable because it required uniformity at the expense of individual usage.' A further factor which almost certainly reinforced the disinclination of Austin canons and Benedictines to attend their local general chapters was the very limited scope of the work there. Those of the Cistercians concerned themselves not only with general problems but with a whole variety of particular matters which meant that there was often very considerable incentive for Cistercian abbots to attend, the more so since they were often employed as agents for the general chapters in a whole host of ways. In sharp contrast with this, in the case of unaffiliated Benedictines and Austin canons much of this sort of business, notably questions of discipline, was left by canon law in the hands of the diocesan bishop concerned. Few things are so soul-destroying for those seeking to be holy as that of making a trying journey to attend a committee where little of importance is likely to be done. Certainly attendance at local English general chapters seems often to have been far from impressive, though it was often palliated by the presence of official deputies. In the Benedictine general chapter of 1225 only fifteen of over sixty superiors came in person and at that of 1253 fifteen were present, twenty-three sent 'proctors', i.e. official representatives, and eleven were absent without excuse.

General Chapters of the English Austin Canons.

At Augustinian chapters absenteeism was swollen by unwise machinery. As Salter notes, 'it is easy to see why members were eager to escape these chapters. The president, diffinitors and visitors had something to do, but the rest of the members had no work but to hear three sermons and attend three masses.' Their history is not fully documented, though useful records of parts of it remain and have been printed. The first general chapter met in 1216 and included houses of both provinces but soon after, in 1223, it was decided to have separate assemblies for northern and southern provinces, an arrangement which lasted until 1340 when by papal initiative the two areas were again united. In 1265 began a commendable movement to seek to produce a uniform set of observances to replace the immense variety of practices then much too prevalent. This was ultimately done by the *Statuta de Parco* which for some time was of importance in the north, though later overshadowed by new constitutions drawn up for black canons in general by Benedict XII. As was so usual in the medieval church, new rules were not completely put into practice.

The Benedictine General Chapters

The Benedictine chapters were at first divided into northern and southern units, but the former was of very little value since the number of houses therein was very small indeed and several of them were already closely linked. The first meeting of the important southern province probably took place in the winter of 1218–19 and there steadily developed in its successors a profitable interest in sizeable common problems. The importance of their abbots integrating their daily life with that of their brethren and not maintaining something like the separate ménage which social pressures were tending to demand, and the equally real danger of heads of the greater houses living in settings of too much grandeur were amongst problems tackled, as was the perennial one of deciding how far tendencies towards a more luxuriant form of worship should be approved. The trying question of how often the brethren be allowed to have meat and whether they should be allowed some small private allowance was also considered. More novel was the decision, taken after a good deal of hesitation, to establish a communal house of study at Oxford, which finally came into being in 1291.

Its constitution was curious and reflected the lack of strong common feeling in the order. The place was set up on land held by Malmesbury Abbey, with some communal accommodation built at the cost of the general chapter and various premises owned by individual houses. Although some major matters of general interest were profitably considered the acts of the Benedictine general chapters, these mostly lack the vigorous and wide-ranging attention to detail which characterises those of the contemporary Cistercians. Given medieval social conditions, the opportunities which these local assemblies provided for renewing old friendships and building new ones may well have been amongst their greater advantages.

THE MONASTERY AND THE BISHOP

Down the centuries it has been the rule of the Church that the responsibility for overseeing the welfare of all institutions within a diocese is normally that of the bishop or archbishop who is at its head. So far as Western monasticism in our period was concerned however, there gradually built up certain major exceptions to this rule. At an early stage Cistercianism—very much a papal darling— obtained the privilege of exemption from such episcopal visitations as did also the Cluniacs and the orders of friars. This privilege was very far from unreasonable in view of the fact that all these orders had effective machinery of their own to supervise the life of their houses, a task for which a very limited proportion of contemporary bishops had much in the way of qualifications or much time to spare. A good deal more questionable was the granting of this privilege of exemption to individual monasteries, in England mostly large and wealthy Benedictine ones. It is difficult to resist the feeling that search for this privilege was inspired more from a desire for spiritual one-up-manship than a passion for spiritual progress.

The privileges which exemption conferred were various and mostly not of great significance, though this did not prevent them having a prestige value. The newly elected head of an exempt house might be free from the normal necessity of being blessed by the diocesan bishop in his cathedral and of professing canonical obedience to him, whilst he could invite any Catholic bishop to perform major episcopal acts such as consecrations and ordinations in his conventual church. An exempt house was free from excommunications imposed by the bishop and from general interdicts and its head was exempt from attending the local diocesan synod and from obligations connected with it. The bishop could not claim the right to hospitality for himself and his considerable retinue there when carrying out an official visitation of his diocese, nor celebrate Mass or perform ordinations in the church unless invited to do so. Most important of all, in many ways, was the fact that the local bishop could not carry out a disciplinary visitation of an exempt monastery on his own initiative, a privilege which rendered it very difficult to correct anything seriously amiss there without recourse to Rome.

By 1216 there were, however, only seven exempt English Benedictine abbeys—St Alban's, St Augustine's Canterbury, Bury St Edmund's, Evesham, Malmesbury and Westminster. As Knowles so properly stresses, this exemption was far from being an unadulterated blessing for the houses concerned, since on various matters it involved them in recourse to Rome which might be very expensive indeed in time and money and might even lead to shocks like the brethren having their nominee for a vacant abbacy replaced by a papal one if their election was held to be invalid—a thing on which it was not always difficult for the skilled staff of the curia to insist. In any case an expensive visit to Rome by the newly elected head was, at first, essential. In 1257 the abbot of Bury St Edmund's paid 2000 marks to avoid this. In 1302 the abbot of St Alban's, when at Rome, found it advisable to pay out no less than 3000 marks in *douceurs* to various officials. However, the huge majority of monastic houses in medieval England were liable to visitation by the bishop or archbishop who was in charge of the diocese in which they were situate. Probably this task was one which tended to be neglected by the English episcopate in the twelfth century, but after this time there is no doubt that it was taken seriously.

The procedure employed in such visitations was carefully formulated and usually the proceedings were far from brief. The visitation began with the official reception of the visitor by the community concerned at the entrance to their monastery and this was followed by a service at which a sermon was preached by the former who, as was usual in these times, often showed no little ingenuity in his choice of text—that of Bishop William Gainsborough at a visitation of Worcester Cathedral priory was 'I went down into the garden of nuts to see the green plants of the valley, to see whether the vine had budded and the pomegranates were in flower.' There followed a meticulous and separate examination of each member of the community which allowed them to draw attention to confidential matters requiring attention and enabled the visitor to get an overall view of the religious and financial situation of the house in question. After this very necessary but time-consuming investigation the visitor would decide whether or not it was a case of 'all is well' (*omnia bene*). If it were not, he would in due course issue a series of 'injunctions', clear cut instructions regarding matters which had to be amended. The elaborate nature of his investigation is a clear indication of the high importance attached by the authorities to the monastic life and contrasts starkly with the very minor investigations made at this time into the spiritual welfare of both the parish clergy and, much more, of the laity whose misdemeanours were almost certainly more liable to be lurid than those of monastic provenance. However, the inordinate size of the English dioceses made these visitations inevitably much less frequent than was desirable, notably in unwieldy York and Lincoln and densely populated Norwich.

From the mid-thirteenth century onwards throughout our period there have survived a fair number of reports of these episcopal visitations and injunctions, which are of immense value to the ecclesiastical historian. But those which survive represent only a fraction of the whole total of such visitations and are very unevenly distributed over both the dioceses and the centuries. The picture which they give of the monastic life at this time is far too complex to allow of any neat summary in the space available here, with the monasteries varying very greatly in size, wealth and morale. Obviously the dangers which faced one of the plutocratic Benedictine abbeys of England tended to differ greatly from those confronting small houses of nuns living precariously at the back of beyond or those of a fashionable house of friars in a flourishing town.

Both inside and outside the monasteries of medieval England life was apt to be very monotonous. There were few excitements and, in many areas, few very interesting visitors, on top of which, of course, the poor communications provided no easy way of keeping in regular touch with absent friends and relations living more than quite a small distance away, whilst the range of pastimes was very limited, hunting being almost the only one which could provide any considerable thrills, a fact which does much to account for its popularity. Under such circumstances it is not surprising that amongst houses of Benedictines and Austin canons one of the commonest faults revealed by episcopal visitations is that of brethren indulging in some recreation on which the powers-that-be frowned. They are not infrequently rebuked for unnecessarily going outside the monastery sometimes on hunting expeditions, though these may not always have involved much more than setting dogs to chase the local rabbits. Gossiping with secular folk in or near the monastery was another obvious way of breaking the tedium.

In houses standing on highways intimately linked with the Continent, like the two great Canterbury monasteries which, significantly, had exceptionally spacious accommodation for guests, the flow of visitors back and forth included a steady stream of very variegated visitors, but far more houses were situated in rural areas where traffic was light. In northern England tranquillity was periodically shattered by ferocious inroads perpetrated by the barbarous Scots, who burnt churches as well as sometimes massacring and enslaving inhabitants. (In 1215 the Scottish king and his men sacked the monastery of Holm Cultram even though the former's ancestor had founded the house and was buried therein.) In 1322, rather accidentally, the English king got involved in a major battle on the lonely land above Byland Abbey, but such colourful happenings as these were, of course, highly exceptional and literally hundreds of monasteries must have led existences as devoid of drama or disgrace as those of modern clergy houses. There is nothing to suggest that sexual lapses within the monasteries presented a major problem. Not uncommon, however, are indications of financial problems which, in the period before the Black Death, seem not infrequently to have been caused by lavish spending on building schemes, though always there were smallish houses which, through no fault of their own, found it difficult to make ends meet. Taken as a whole there is nothing to suggest that the standard of Augustinian and Benedictine life in these times was anything else but higher than that of the rest of contemporary society and there are plenty of indications that, by and large, the monastic life continued to inspire that considerable affection which had been so marked in England from early Anglo-Saxon times.

THE MENDICANT ORDERS

One of the most remarkable and profitable characteristics of the Western Church has been its repeated capacity to enlarge the scope of its monasticism so as to include various activities which primitive exponents of the ideal regarded as alien to it. At the Counter-Reformation and in recent times this profitable reassessment has been very evident, but what was in many ways the great turning point in this process came in the early thirteenth century with the establishment of what came to be called the 'mendicant orders'. (The word mendicant means 'begging' and was given to the new orders because they insisted on living on alms and not on endowments; members of the order came to be termed 'friars', meaning 'brothers'.) Their way of life very notably and very fruitfully complemented the work and witness of the Augustinian and Benedictine orders which had won a place in the affection of the faithful that was very valuable but left room for others.

The mendicants' programme of living was characterised by three features very novel in monastic history. In the first place their main occupation was pastoral work. With great skill and sophistication they sought to reinforce the often very amateurish efforts of the contemporary parish clergy who, being human like the rest of us, by no means universally enjoyed seeing their work done in more skilled fashion by men who were, in a sense, outsiders. In two major ways this pastoral work of the mendicants or friars was of especial value. Firstly, at a time when literacy amongst the rapidly growing bourgeoisie was expanding the friars provided carefully educated preachers who could intelligently expound the word of God, their efforts herein tending to be very much more effective than the sermons preached, not only always very frequently, by parish clergy of whom many had received little or no effective

training for this important side of their work. The friars not only
acquired what was, by contemporary standards, a very high degree
of education, but carefully studied the technique of preaching,
providing for example, collections of entertaining anecdotes to
leaven the content of their discourses—a move to be repeated long
after by certain Protestant clergy. In no small degree, as a result of
their persistent work, that invaluable asset the instructed layman
(or lay woman) was at last to be found by the end of our period in
numbers which were not negligible, though England, being so
rural, inevitably lagged somewhat in this respect and never produced
anyone to rival Catharine of Siena (d. 1380), a simple dyer's daughter
brought up under Dominican influence whose stupendous religious
insights led her to become quite unintentionally one of the major
religious influences of her day, consulted by folk of all kinds and
putting her in a position which allowed her to rebuke severely even
the pope himself—a facility of which she availed herself.

Also of immense importance in the development of a sound lay
piety was the invaluable influence of the mendicant orders in developing effective use of the Sacrament of Penance commonly known
as confession. How was a sinner who repented of major misbehaviour
to be treated by the Church? To this question the classic answer was
only very gradually evolved after centuries of experience. At first
authorities took the hard line over the very major sins such as
apostasy by refusing forgiveness for it, but this was soon seen to be
inconsistent with Christ's unbounded love for those who repented.
Later, some Christian reconciliation was governed by 'penitentials'
—codes listing offences with penalties therefor with the same
comprehensiveness and clarity as marked the lists formerly displayed
on English railway stations to show the general public the cost of
transport of everything from cellos to corpses. But such an approach,
however suited to business matters, was unsuited to spiritual ones,
wherein the gravity of offences might vary greatly according to the
persons involved and its attendant circumstances.

In the end, both Eastern and Western Churches independently
worked out a similar and much more flexible system for reconciling
the sinner to God and His Church. This required the wrongdoer to
confess his offences fully to a priest who might question him to
get a clear picture of the spiritual problems involved in his case
but who was very strictly forbidden to reveal to anyone at all

H

information given to him during confession without the previous consent of the person concerned. Provided the confessor was assured of the real sorrow for his offences of the person involved he would give him or her spiritual advice aimed at curing the particular deficiency or deficiencies and then enjoin an act of penance and pronounce the divine forgiveness which his ordination to the rank of priest or bishop enabled him to do, in a formula including the words 'by His [i.e. God's] authority I absolve thee from all thy sins in the name of the Father and the Son and the Holy Spirit,' to which was added the comforting words, 'Go in peace for the Lord has put away thy sin and pray for me a sinner too.'

This form of confession and reconciliation was first worked out in the monasteries where one might expect such spiritual experiments to take place, and spread steadily on its own merits, being, for example, extensively utilised by pious laity in Norman England like Henry I's Queen Maud. At the Lateran Council of 1215, in the hope that the move might assist the laity to cut down their pretty considerable output of wrong-doing, it was laid down that henceforth all the faithful should confess their sins to their parish priest in this way at least once a year. Like no little medieval legislation, both ecclesiastical and non-ecclesiastical, this order may be regarded as over-optimistic. Though confession once a year was not without its value, especially for those committing the cruder sins, it was scarcely adequate for great spiritual progress. In any case, whilst sophisticated folk amongst the townsfolk of the great cities of Italy might treat it with the circumspection desirable if it was to be effective, there must have been no few crude folk who treated it a good deal too casually to produce useful results. Further, at this time a major obstacle to full use of it was created by the certain fact that very many parish clergy received no adequate training to undertake what is the most difficult and delicate of all their responsibilities demanding, as it does, not only a total capacity to maintain that seal of secrecy which was fundamental to the system, but psychological and theological insight adequate to recognise the nature and cure of the spiritual problems involved. Such qualifications were undoubtedly very often in short supply amongst many parish clergy of the Western Church in the thirteenth century, yet on these canon law imposed the major part responsibility for hearing confessions. The very important pastoral gap thus created friars very deliberately and scientifically set out to fill. As a result they very quickly became much famed and desired for hearing confessions, in the process inspiring a jealousy in the breasts of contemporary parish clergy.

If this full-blooded participation in the parochial life of the church was one major novelty in the way of life of the mendicant orders, another equally startling and admirable to very many contemporaries was its novel and very radical conception of the nature of monastic poverty. As we have seen, the traditional monastic programme of the Benedictines and Augustinians involved total poverty of individual members of the community, but accepted without question the desirability of the monastery to which they belonged acquiring possessions such as lands, houses, farms and appropriated churches, with the result that much more by intention than by design, by the end of the twelfth century in England, as elsewhere in the West, there had evolved a situation in which no few monasteries had a very great deal more wealth than their needs demanded or looked likely to demand. Under the totally uncompromising leadership of St Francis the mendicant orders reacted with the greatest possible vigour against this conception of poverty, refusing in theory and very largely in practice any such permanent endowments, and insisting on living very largely on alms which they begged or were given. As a result they freed themselves totally from the sort of accusations of money grabbing which rightly or wrongly had come to be levied against some Cistercian houses and avoided the scandalous wealth of the largest Benedictine abbeys.

The third major revolutionary change in monastic thinking which characterised the mendicant orders, owing, in no small measure, to the pioneering work thereon of St Dominic, was a much more intensive realisation of the importance of theological studies. Clearly, for hermits living austerely at the back of beyond study of books was not a very high priority and the same, albeit to a lesser extent, was true of enclosed orders, though it was clearly undesirable that they should ignore the invaluable spiritual discoveries made by the great saints and mystics who had trod their way of life before them. But for any men who strove to undertake pastoral work in the increasingly lively and literate society of Western Europe in the thirteenth century, a solid basis of theological learning was essential if, for example, they were to expound the teaching of the Church accurately, refute the arguments against it now rampant in no few areas (though not in England) and to acquire certain insights essential for a good confessor. As a result, from a very early stage the mendicants established links with the growing universities of their times and built up their own educational machinery with remarkable competence.

On yet one more point the mendicant orders broke off with the deeply rooted traditions of monasticism. This was over what is technically termed 'stability'. In the earliest history of Christian monasticism a good deal too much responsibility had been left to individuals to decide on their vocation and this had led to some of them developing the irritating and unhelpful habit of drifting from one house to try out another. Amongst the very few passages in the *Rule of St Benedict* that displays any sign of indignation is that which attacks this religious dilettantism. The *Rule* insisted that a fully professed member of the monastery must remain therein until death, except under certain special circumstances such as being sent to a cell of the monastery or being elected a bishop. Such insistence obviously suited the way of life of traditional Benedictinism which, as we have seen, eschewed more than very minor direct contact between its members and the outside world, but was obviously incompatible with the vigorous and informed pastoral work which the members of the mendicant orders put at the forefront of their way of life. As a result these latter very properly developed a new view of stability which involved their members being bound not to a particular monastery but to the order as a whole so that it was perfectly feasible and very usual for them to be switched from one of their houses to others. Preliminary training might be given at one house, advanced instruction elsewhere, after which duty might send a man to some far distant friary, especially if he rose to high rank in its hierarchy.

It is probably true to say that in general most men are conservative unless they are vigorously pushed to become something else. It was almost certainly this conservatism, together with jealousy aroused by the undeniable fact that the mendicant order brilliantly remedied serious defects in the Western Church life, which accounts for much of the violent opposition which the lively and devoted medieval friars encountered in certain quarters, but it is a convincing proof of their permanent value that their way of life is in most ways as potentially fruitful under modern conditions as it was under medieval ones.

However, inevitably from their early years the mendicant orders clashed with the parish clergy whose work overlapped theirs so considerably. Although friars did not accept charge of existing parish churches they erected churches of their own, very largely in towns where sizeable potential congregations were ready to hand. Their early very deep and wide popularity inevitably led considerable numbers of laity to prefer to worship in these rather than in their own parish churches. Here they desired to go to Mass regularly, to make their confessions and quite often to be buried. Such inclinations greatly upset many parish clergy since such an exodus of their faithful wounded their egos, infringed their traditional legal rights to include in their congregation all those residents within the bounds of their parishes, and also tended to reduce their often not too princely incomes by depriving them of the traditional offerings made on such occasions. On the other hand the friars, being dependent on alms for their livelihood, could not be expected to forgo such offerings or to shut their doors in the face of those who found in their churches notably greater spiritual edification than in their parish churches. After no little controversy canon law gave real if not unlimited privileges in these matters to the mendicants, thus enabling their work to go forward despite some degree of surly hostility from the local secular clergy which never died away.

THE FRANCISCANS

The founder of the first of these mendicant orders, St Francis of Assisi, whom many account the most stupendous of all the saints of Christendom, was born in 1181–2 in the enchanting little Umbrian town from which his title derives. His father was a tough, well-to-do merchant engaged in the then very lucrative cloth trade, his mother a pious and sensitive native of the cultured land of Provence, with whose language and poetry she familiarised her son. Highly intelligent, generous and gay, with the aid of his father's cash Francis became a leader of smart society in the town, in whose life fine clothes and plenteous parties loomed large.

At first he aspired to that military career which the conventional opinion of the day rated so highly, but he had scarcely embarked on it before his sensitive soul found it totally unsatisfying, and he threw it over in his vigorous, uncompromising way. There followed a long and agonising spiritual crisis. Passionately he loved the beauteous world of nature he saw around him—the noble mountainous country behind the town, the lower slopes with their silver-grey olive groves and joyous galaxies of spring flowers, the delicate honey- and salmon-coloured stone with which the town was built. In his *Canticle of the Sun*, one of the first significant poems in Italian, he rapturised over the riches of nature: 'our sister Water, which is very humble, chaste and precious,' and brother Fire, 'gay, noble and beautiful, untamable and strong by which God illumines the night.'

But people mattered to him much more than material things and increasingly St Francis was agonised by the sight of that dire poverty which drove so many to fight and whine for alms in and around the town. By what right did he and his friends live in luxury with everything handsome about them, whilst so many others lived on or below the poverty line? The gospels which he heard so often through frequent attendance at the Masses he loved so profoundly gave no reason to believe that wealth was a great asset. Rather was its possession there stigmatised as a grave danger, which beckoned a man on to avarice or self-indulgence and away from assisting those neighbours to whom help was a top priority for seekers after Christ. Riches, after all, inevitably cut a man off from real unity with the indigent many. If the poor heard Christ 'gladly', as the Gospel said, it was partly because he lived a simple life devoid of luxury. Distaste of worldly possessions more and more dominated Francis, reaching a highly dramatic climax when, following dissension with his father over almsgiving, before the bishop and in public, Francis stripped off all his clothes and threw them back to his father exclaiming 'hereafter I shall not say Father Pietro di Bernadone but Our Father which art in heaven.'

Living only on such alms as locals gave him and praying in loneliness, Francis now, almost unintentionally, founded what was to become with electrifying rapidity one of the major monastic orders of Christendom. Its purpose was supernatural not social, not to 'do good' in the cheap modern sense or to preach a controversial social gospel, but to inspire men to that detachment from material things which is a fundamental characteristic of Christian life, more especially in regard to wealth. The first demand he made of those seeking to join his community was that they sell up their possessions and give the proceeds to the poor, and he was ever ready to see that they did not over-value money—when one of his followers proudly returned from begging alms with more money than might have been expected, Francis threw it on a nearby pile of rubbish, exclaiming 'Dirt! Dirt! Dirt!'

Preaching was to be the principal employment of the order, but they were not to seek great papal privileges and accepted aid mainly from local authorities. The necessary confirmation of their way of life by Rome had been procured in 1209 and for long thereafter the life-style of Francis and his followers fascinated popular mind to a degree difficult to parallel in Christian history.

However, to Francis this expansion brought in its wake very grave responsibilities and his health steadily deteriorated, partly through his not inconsiderable austerities—he tended to be over-hard on 'brother body', as he ultimately admitted. Running a vast ecclesiastical machine was not his métier and he retired to live for some time an eremitical life in a little hut on the top of the mountain of La Verna, given him for this purpose by an admirer, whence there lay before him as splendid a panorama of natural beauty as even Italy can display. Here one day in 1224, when rapt in prayer, his body became marked with the 'Stigmata', wounds corresponding in position to those which marked the body of the crucified Christ. Soon after, they took him back most gently to die. On the eve of departure from this mortal life (1226) he added to his *Canticle* a stanza blessing the Lord 'for our sister death of the Body'.

Hereafter, for very long his order flourished greatly numerically and expanded its way of life to pay notable attention to that great wave of interest in learning which was now giving the university life of Western Europe such remarkable éclat. Francis himself, though not hostile to higher study, saw accurately enough at this time that higher education could easily make a man conceited and cut him off from full-blooded unity with the man in the street, but for better and for worse the order got closely identified with the theological renaissance of the times. Two other problems came with progress. What about poverty now that things like houses of study and libraries of books were needed? Dispute over this ranged long and furiously before a *via media* was achieved. More trouble concerned Franciscan building. At first the utmost simplicity and cheapness was usual; the first chapel of the Franciscans at Cambridge was an austere wooden structure erected in very few days. But, as we shall see, popular opinion, profoundly visual minded as it was, would not stand for this sort of nonsense, desiring churches to mirror the bigness and beauty which were among God's characteristics. What sort of place should house the venerated body of St Francis? The strict line was quickly swept aside and men gave him a church in elegant Gothic, quickly adorned with a rich variety of artistic treasures.*

During the first century of its history the Franciscan order had various internal troubles, principally because of controversy within it over how it was to adapt for its work the very radical view of poverty held by its founder, experience quickly showing that the very special way of life to which St Francis himself had been called

---

* Although originally St Francis had no intention of establishing any order, ultimately he came to be regarded as the founder of three. Of these the First Order, much the largest and most famous, was for men, with pastoral work as its primary concern. The Second Order, very much smaller in size, consisted of houses of nuns, its original community being founded by St Clare, a young girl of well-to-do family in Assisi, who established profound spiritual unity with St Francis. Under contemporary social conditions engagement in the outside world was unlikely, and the form of life she developed was a very austere contemplative one with minimal contacts outside her cloister, which was attached to the little church of San Damiano, a kilometre down the hill from Assisi. Like St Francis, she was convinced by long travail that she was called to witness to the supreme importance of poverty, and insisted her house should have no regular income of any kind but maintain absolute freedom from material possessions. Understandably, the ecclesiastical authorities viewed this idea with some trepidation, since whereas members of the First Order could obtain the financial aid requisite for their simple needs by alms offered them for their pastoral work, notably preaching and hearing confessions, St Clare's had no such obvious source of income at all on which to rely. There followed one of the most attractive little combats in Christian history, with Clare, serene but unyielding, fighting top-level authority for the right of her community to live in absolute poverty, and high ecclesiastics fighting for a more conventional arrangement. As one of her biographers comments, no-one ever strove harder to acquire wealth than she did to be rid of it. One of the popes correctly noted that the Holy See had never received such a request and that it would not have been granted. But Clare's sanctity won the contest, and in her last days triumphantly she received the privilege of total poverty which meant everything to her. Her order spread steadily in Italy and certain other areas, but in England only three houses took permanent root, of which that at London—the Minories, begun in 1293-4—was the first.
The Third Order of St Francis was not a monastic order, but an organisation which linked together local communities of laity, both male and female, who desired to live a much stricter and more highly organised spiritual life than was at all usual at this time.

by God could not be taken over by his order without some degree of modification. Clearly, for example, money was needed if its student members were to have education for their work and a great town friary must acquire its own premises in fact if not in theory (sometimes we find Franciscan houses being legally the property of the local municipal authorities). But despite controversies the order's progress was immense and its life steadily became carefully organised, with its houses grouped together into smallish units called 'custodies' and larger ones termed 'provinces'. Although St Francis never wrote off the pastoral value of theological study, he was somewhat suspicious of theologians (as other of the greatest saints have been) fearing that they tended to cut themselves off from that all important person, the man in the street, and perceiving very accurately that in his day the rapid rise to fame of university studies tended to make dons think too highly of themselves and not appreciate the stupendous importance of humility in the Christian make-up. But very quickly indeed it was obvious that a preaching order as the Franciscans had quickly become could not possibly dispense with an efficient training in theology and for this provision was rapidly made, early links with the universities being firmly established, not least in England.

The arrival of Franciscanism in England came early and was carefully planned. Providentially an invaluable chronicle—the *De Adventu Fratrum Minorum* of Thomas of Eccleston—gives us a vivid picture of this early expansion. Colonisation opened in 1224 when a party of nine brethren landed at Dover. Given hospitality by kindly Benedictines at Canterbury, they quickly left a small colony there and then pushed on to found a second house in London (being herein helped by the Dominicans), albeit in a building which was in effect slum property. Soon after the third house was set up at Oxford, partly because of the town's reputation for learning but also because there were to be found many young men to whom the new way of life should be shown in case some found themselves called thereto. As we shall see (Chapter 13), the Franciscan contribution to the rise of university life in England was of immense importance.

Rapidly expansion continued. By 1240 there were at least twenty-nine Franciscan friaries in England, by 1255 there were forty-nine which, it is said, housed some 1242 friars. These friaries were grouped into four 'custodies' but the number of these soon rose to seven. This immense success of the order, and unlike that of the Cistercians, was not largely confined to a few decades. Men of every kind joined an early list, including even an abbot of Oseney. It was early said that the English friars were celebrated for three things— their bare feet, their coarse clothing and their refusal to touch money.

Patronage flooded in from every rank of society. Henry III and Edward I, both pious kings, gave them no little aid and there is no doubt that with the now influential bourgeoisie of England the Franciscans rapidly became very beloved. Much building was soon under way. At first there were those who sought to maintain the rather puritanical tradition in architecture, which regarded small and simple structures as being alone permissible. But this way of thought was contrary to medieval popular sentiment and by the end of the century the great naves of the friars' churches (the first ever built in England to satisfy the needs of preaching) differed in no main essential from those of major contemporary parish churches, though it is worth noting that their eastern limbs (which were usually reserved to be the chapel of the brethren) were nearly always small and simple, as were the belfry towers which in England separated them from the nave and normally were consisted of nothing more than a quite minor turret of the type we can still see at Richmond (Yorks.) and King's Lynn. Nothing witnesses more eloquently to the affection inspired by the Franciscans than the immense popularity of burial within the churches. An interesting list of the interments at the Grey Friars of Coventry has survived, but is eclipsed by another which records in fascinating detail the stupendous number of interments in the capacious London church of the order, where a spiritual 'house full' situation seems to have early prevailed.

THE DOMINICANS

Almost exactly contemporary with early Franciscanism and providentially complementary to it, was the second mendicant order founded by St Dominic (1170–1221), an aristocratic and sagacious Spaniard. He started his religious career as an Austin canon and early became involved in the immensely difficult task of combating the wild heretical ideas which in his day were causing immense strife in the south of France and elsewhere. Quickly he appreciated the great need to establish an order whose members had the mobility of movement which the older monastic orders lacked and also the theological training which enabled them to explain and defend with competence the teaching of the Church. From the first he saw his work as pastoral and his order took the title of the 'Order of Preachers' (*Ordo Predicatorum*). Profoundly as he differed in temperament from St Francis, the two men were so very far-seeing and humble that they entertained great mutual esteem. St Dominic, perceiving the pastoral value of missioners living a life of poverty in the Franciscan sense, adopted this for his order. Reserved and intellectual he lacked the stupendous panache of St Francis and, significantly, attracted very little interest from contemporary biographers, but his work was none the less important for this. With him, for the first time, a monastic order put theological education in the forefront of its programme, and at a very early stage the Dominicans established major links with various universities including that of Toulouse, which was put in their hands in 1229. A minor result of this reassessment was that manual labour, so long an essential part of the monastic way of life, very largely disappeared from the time-table. The order received from its founder a highly effective machinery of government 'complete in every detail and so perfectly devised that it has functioned with little change to the present day' (Knowles), which the Franciscans most certainly lacked originally, though soon they adopted a similar system. Starting from very different points, the Franciscan and Dominican orders quickly developed ways of religious life which overlapped considerably, even though each had its own ethos.

In 1221, the Dominican order first entered England, a small band of brethren now arriving in the distinguished company of the bishop of Winchester. They at once won the backing of the great archbishop, Stephen Langton, after their leader had preached an impressive sermon before him. Significantly they established their first house at the rising university of Oxford and their second at London. About 1260 there were some thirty-six Dominican houses here, to which eleven more had been added by 1273. Their final total of fifty-three was five less than that of the Franciscans. In both cases the huge proportion of these were set in cathedral cities or other places of importance. The English Dominican province held its first chapter in 1230; at that of 1250, 440 brethren are known to have been present. In 1263 their Oxford house was ranked as an international theological centre for the order.

If the Dominicans and Franciscans were the largest and most prestigious orders of friars in medieval times, it is important not to omit consideration of two others, which after unspectacular origins also played valuable roles in the medieval West.

THE CARMELITE FRIARS

The Carmelite friars, with a historical optimism impressive even by medieval standards, claimed as founder the prophet Elijah, with whom they did at least have a link through the fact that he had resided on Mount Carmel in Palestine some two thousand years before and where their order originated in the mid-twelfth century, being at first nothing more than an unclassifiable collection of hermits of a type which was common enough at the time. About 1210 the brethren adopted a rule of life involving little common life and great severity and isolation from human society. Soon after, the decay of Christian control of the Holy Land sent no few of the brethren to the West where they came under the influence of the mendicant way of life, both with regard to poverty and preaching. Understandably, opinion was divided as to the extent to which this new influence should be allowed to modify the old tradition, but under their General, the Englishman Simon Stock (d. 1265) the old eremitical programme of the Carmelites was largely abandoned for a common life in houses which usually were not isolated from society and Simon saw to it that firm links were established with both Oxford and Cambridge universities. Understandably the final solution was not achieved without friction, but by the end of the century the Carmelite friars had worked out a way of life which did not differ fundamentally from that of the other mendicant orders. Though the attraction of the eremitical life was never entirely forgotten by the Carmelites, the call of learning became much stronger and they made a valuable contribution to medieval theological studies.

Owing to those fortuitous, personal factors which so often influenced medieval Western life, some of the first Carmelite houses in the West were established in England. First was Hulne, on a superbly secluded site most appropriate for the contemplative life not far from Alnwick in far-off Northumberland, and founded in 1240–2. Soon after came into being friaries at Aylesford and Burnham Norton (both of which have left attractive remains) and Chesterton on the outskirts of Cambridge. The ultimate total of English houses was thirty-seven.

AUSTIN FRIARS

The fourth mendicant order was that of the Austin friars, so termed because, like the Austin canons, they followed the so-called *Rule of St Augustine*; their official title came to be Friars of the Order of Hermits of St Augustine. The thirteenth-century papacy had a commendable capacity for tidying up the luxuriant ecclesiastical growth of the times and in 1244 Innocent IV united various communities of hermits into a single effective whole, giving them the *Rule of St Augustine*, an arrangement which in 1256 Pope Alexander amplified. Though quickly influenced by the Dominican way of life, the order never entirely lost its affection for the eremitical life. Their first English house was that of Clare in Suffolk, set up in 1248–9. In less than a century they acquired a total of thirty-two houses which was not thereafter increased. One or two of their very early houses were set in spots greatly suited to the eremitical life, like that at Woodhouse, hidden away on a lonely hillside above the little village of Cleobury Mortimer. But very soon the order sought out mostly much more accessible sites, no few being in minor centres like Atherstone, Penrith and Orford, whilst important links with the universities of Oxford and Cambridge were early established.

The fact that the mendicant orders depended on alms for their existence made it essential that they should site their houses carefully so as to avoid over-competition for the far from unlimited alms likely to be available in many parts of medieval England. This, along with the obvious desirability of spreading their orders widely meant the total of some 180 houses of friars which existed in medieval England were very extensively dispersed over the face of the more populous parts of the land. In many of the smaller towns this financial factor led to there being established only one or, at the most, two houses of friars. Three orders had each a house in some of the fairly well-to-do towns with reasonably prosperous hinterlands, like the ports of Scarborough, Kingston-on-Hull, Yarmouth and Ipswich, as well as at Gloucester, Chester, Shrewsbury and the two lesser cathedral cities of Chester and Worcester. The cathedral towns of Durham, Ely and Rochester were in effect Benedictine preserves into which the mendicants found it prudent not to intrude. As might be expected, it was only in major places that we find houses of all the four orders of friars—the lordly cathedral cities of York, Lincoln, London and Winchester, the university towns of Oxford and Cambridge and major provincial centres like Bristol, Northampton, King's Lynn and Stamford.

There can be no doubt of the invaluable consolidation of English religious life which ensued from the establishment of the mendicant orders. In two very major ways they supplemented the existing forces. In the first place, as we have seen, they gave interest in theological training a very much needed boost, and there can be little doubt that as a result of this they were able to produce for the laity far more and far better sermons than those hitherto available in the parishes of both town and country. To this fact and to their expertise in hearing confessions we may attribute no small part of the high regard which the friars quickly acquired, though their very skill excited no small jealousy. The friars concentrated most of their efforts on urban areas where they could comparatively easily build up an effective congregation, though their houses were also used as bases for spiritual and financial foraging around the adjacent countryside. In view of the very limited contacts between monasteries of the older orders and urban communities this link had special value.

Integration into the church life of the thirteenth century of these vigorous mendicant orders inevitably posed some difficult problems both administrative and psychological which in England, as elsewhere, led to a good deal of controversy before a *modus vivendi* was worked out. Contacts between the friars and houses of Benedictines and Augustinians were mostly not of major importance since their fields of action often did not clash. It was with the parish clergy that major controversy was inevitable since the friars devoted themselves to that very pastoral work which for centuries had been almost entirely their monopoly. Had the parish clergy been in short

supply or had they been anywhere near as competent professionally
as were the highly-trained friars, clashes would not have been as
evident. But the circumstances of the time being what they were
inevitably brought controversy even though many parsons may have
been devoted pastors, like the one lauded by Chaucer.

The pastoral work of the friars posed both financial and psychological problems, as has been seen. As the friars were dependent on
alms for their very existence, it seemed reasonable enough that
they should draw financial support from the general public, especially
the far from negligible section of it which preferred to attend mendicant churches rather than the parish churches to which they were
traditionally bound. However, this attendance had financial repercussions of real practical import. Firstly it diverted to the friars
alms given at parish church services, principally, of course, at Mass,
but to a much lesser degree at confession and on minor occasions,
and also benefactions and legacies (which last were often linked
with a request for burial with friars' churches, a practice that rapidly
became immensely popular). This all clearly meant that the parish
clergy were liable to lose to the friars some part of their income
which, in many cases, was not very princely in any case. The more
popular the friars became the greater the financial loss which the
local clergy were likely to incur. On the other hand, as St Paul had
long ago pointed out in a similar situation, 'a workman is worthy
of his wages'—the parish clergy could not rightly expect the friars
to live on nothing, nor could they logically attack both monks
and regular canons for possessing wealth and the friars for not
possessing it as, at times, they give the impression of doing.

It may well be that the psychological problem created by the
immense pastoral success of the mendicant orders was even more
disruptive than the financial one. Clergy, like laity, being only
human, do not invariably welcome with open arms help from those
who can carry out their work better than they can themselves and
this, of course, was exactly what the friars were likely to do. There
can be little doubt that for most of our period much of the preaching
in many English parish churches was at best naive, at worst rank
bad, whereas that in the friars' churches was mostly the work of
men who were highly trained to preach. Similarly, the more the
value of confession was appreciated the more natural it was to
seek as confessors those who, like the friars, had received proper

training for this demanding task. Like so much of the trouble in the medieval Church, at the heart of this problem lay the chronic incapacity of the medieval episcopate to appreciate that the work of a priest demanded much more training than knowledge of how to conduct services and readiness to visit the faithful. The very complex and difficult problem of working out a *modus vivendi* between the mendicant orders and the parish clergy was not given a quick solution, but in 1300 the turning point came with the papal bull *Super Cathedram* which laid down a settlement allowing the friars to preach in their own churches except at certain times, and to preach elsewhere after due invitation. Friars specially selected for the purpose and authorised by the bishop so to do could hear confessions. The faithful could be buried in the churches and cemeteries belonging to friars but a quarter of the offerings were to go to the parish church of the deceased.

On the eve of the Black Death monastic life in England presented a very impressive picture. The total number of religious houses, excluding hospitals and the like, was in the neighbourhood of a thousand, of which just over a third belonged to Benedictines of one kind or another and slightly fewer to Austin canons of various sorts. Of the remainder about 180 were houses of friars and 146 houses of nuns. The monastic population had almost certainly risen steadily ever since the Norman Conquest, to reach a total in the region of 18 000 of which some 6000 were Benedictines, some 4000 Augustinians, 4500 friars and 3300 nuns.* But only very hazy conclusions on this matter can safely be drawn.

If by now monasteries were still few in remote areas of the north and west, so also was the population there. In most parts of England monastic life was now a well-established and much beloved element of contemporary society whose spread and scope had been notably augmented by the friars. It is arguable that at no period was the prestige of the monastic ideal here so considerable as in the first decades of the fourteenth century.

---

* The very fragmentary and uneven evidence on this question has been studied by J. Cox Russell whose conclusions are utilised by Knowles and Hadcook. The latter sometimes go rather dangerously beyond the evidence in their estimates of the original size of some houses.

CHAPTER 8

MONARCHY AND PAPACY

RICHARD I AND JOHN

HENRY II died on 6 July 1189 and was succeeded with ease and rapidity by his eldest surviving son Richard, the first English king of that name. The new sovereign had little interest in anything but matters military and was provided with a magnificent excuse to indulge in these at the expense of neglecting the government of his kingdom by the fact that the recent collapse of the Latin hold on the Holy Land—seen notably in the loss of Jerusalem (1185)—had led to vigorous Western preparations to launch a new crusade. After looking in briefly on his new realm, principally to collect money for this purpose, Richard disappeared from it in December. He was absent for four and a quarter years, not only accomplishing nothing at very great expense, but getting captured during his return journey and securing his liberation only by promise of a very large ransom. After another flying visit to England to collect more cash Richard disappeared to France where he died from wounds received in a minor and unnecessary engagement on 6 April 1199. Understandably, his gross inattention to English affairs, coupled with the almost inevitable breathing space which followed the mighty conflict between Henry II and Becket, meant that relations between Church and State in England during Richard's reign were largely unruffled.

The new king was Richard's younger brother John, whose claim to the throne was not irrefutable but was established without immense difficulty at the expense of his nephew Arthur (son of his deceased elder brother Geoffrey) whom he captured and went on to have murdered (1203). Undersized, like so many of most famous aggressives of history—he stood a bare five feet five inches—John did not lack intelligence or industry and often displayed an energy that was nothing short of feverish, though at times punctuated by curious fits of apathy. His very undisciplined nature could be paralleled in his Angevin ancestors and was not helped by the fact that he had the misfortune to have had parents neither of whom understood him. Of orderly Christian living he showed no sign, manifesting too often a disregard of its worship which profoundly shocked contemporaries. Soon after his accession he refused to take communion on Easter Day (traditionally the most important occasion for this) whilst, at his investiture as duke of Normandy, he showed no consciousness of the solemnity of the occasion, but joked with boon companions.

Although the matter is not one on which informed opinion is agreed, it is at least arguable that he was the victim of some fairly serious psychological disorder. This may have lain behind the very unpleasant streak of sadism in his character which led him to display a morbid passion for watching the duels by which in his day certain legal disputes were settled, and probably motivated certain ferocious acts, notably the murder of Arthur (in times when eliminating rivals in this way was not as usual as it is today) and his starving to death in a dungeon in Windsor Castle of the wife and children of a baron who had offended him. The intense restlessness which led him to have his court much more on the move than even contemporary conditions demanded may be another indication of abnormality, like his fits of inertia, notably that exhibited when the great duchy of Normandy was being wrenched from his domains by the king of France. Major indiscipline is seen in his failure to exhibit towards his baronage that minimum consideration which tradition and common sense expected. He worked with vigour and intelligence to extend the power of his governmental machinery but without any care to safeguard as far as possible that understanding between monarch and baronage which was one of essential foundations of feudal society. To his barons William the Conqueror may well have seemed to be, like a celebrated headmaster of later days, 'a brute but a just brute'; to an important section of his baronage John seemed just a brute. With such a man on the English throne friction with the ecclesiastical authorities was almost bound to come. When it did arrive it culminated in a collision between the monarchy and the papacy as spectacular as those connected with the names of Becket and Henry VIII.

The starting point of this celebrated confrontation was the question of the appointment of a successor to the archbishopric of

Canterbury rendered vacant by the death of Archbishop Hubert Walter (13 July 1205). On hearing of the vacancy, with his accustomed rapidity John moved to Canterbury, only to find the monastic chapter there involved in a dispute with the bishops of the southern province over the latter's hoary but unconvincing claim that they had the right to participate in the archiepiscopal election. The bishops played the card now usual in such situations—appeal to Rome. The monks, very accurately expecting to be pressurised by John to elect his nominee, sought, a little naively, to avoid this by hurriedly holding the election without awaiting the usual royal *congé d'élire*. They chose their subprior and quickly packed him off to Rome with some of his brethren to secure papal confirmation of his appointment. John furiously insisted on the chapter electing his nominee, John de Grey, then bishop of Norwich. The resultant tangle was one which could only be sorted out at Rome, and was given fullest and most intelligent consideration by the eminent lawyer, Pope Innocent III. Inevitably rejecting royal pressure, he proposed for election Stephen Langton, a thoroughly admirable man who had established a high reputation as a theologian at Paris, before becoming a member of the Roman curia. The delegation of Canterbury monks accepted this, so that in theory Stephen became archbishop. John never liked being beaten and inevitably refused to accept the decision, partly because Langton would not be amenable to him as would John de Grey (who seems to have lacked any kind of panache), but also for a much more telling reason—the fact that Langton had been chosen without any previous consultation with the Crown, a breach of ancient English custom which clearly might have very dangerous consequences for the future if it was allowed to go unchallenged, however right and proper it might seem to those who, like Innocent III, held very lofty but somewhat novel views of the nature of papal power.

Here was a clash created by two legal traditions, both of which could claim respectability. Innocent, acting from the highest motives and well within his rights as he saw them, offered a candidate whose qualifications for the high post were irreproachable. On the other hand in England it was axiomatic that archbishops would only be elected after the Crown had been fairly and squarely consulted over an appointment which was of major constitutional interest— 'the archbishop was far more than the primate of the English Church, he had by tradition an important place in the secular government of the realm and he held a great barony with almost palatine franchises. No English king could allow this great office to be filled without his approval' (Paynter). As we can now see from our historical arm-chairs, the situation would not have arisen had it not been for the profound distrust of John which very understandably existed in both ecclesiastical and non-ecclesiastical circles.

The undisciplined John, never one to appreciate the value of the *via media*, predictably reacted violently to this thwarting of his will. He took over the valuable revenues of the chapter of Canterbury Cathedral, and expelled their rightful owners from the country. Papal delegates were forbidden to hear cases in the country and he seized the English benefices held by Italians (which, however, cannot have been very considerable in aggregate). For good measure, for entirely different reasons, he quarrelled with the archbishop of York, his somewhat trying half-brother, who found it advisable to retire to the Continent. Meanwhile Langton, having been consecrated by the pope, took up residence in the noble abbey of Pontigny where Becket had found refuge forty years before.

After warning John had proved of no avail, in the summer of 1207 the pope sought to pressurise the king by one of the few major moves open to him, the imposition of an 'interdict', which came into force in March 1208. In theory at least, this meant the virtual suspension of most public worship save in special places and under special circumstances. Many monasteries had already obtained papal authority to continue their great daily round of worship, albeit 'with closed doors', but so far as the general public was concerned, facilities for worship were reduced to the barest minimum with no ecclesi-astical offices except 'the baptism of infants and confession for the dying'. Marriages were not solemnised in churches nor were ser-mons to be preached there. 'For the religiously minded life in these conditions can scarcely have been tolerable' comments Lane Poole and, of course, at this time the great mass of people were religiously minded. Although his subjects were ordered to disregard it, there can be no doubt that the interdict increased the unpopularity of the king. His image was further damaged when in November 1209 Innocent proceeded to declare him excommunicate. In effect this made him a spiritual leper, the faithful being in duty-bound to avoid contact with him. By this time several sees were vacant and

most of the existing bishops deserted John. Obviously, total observance of the excommunication was not to be expected, but it exerted
useful additional pressure.

Viciously and vigorously the king took counter-measures, skilfully using the situation to help satisfy his now very considerable
financial needs (caused notably by heavy military expenditure).
Not without its comic side was his tax on clergy who were married,
a move against which it was difficult for the supporters of the
canon law to protest. Much more oppressive were the very large
sums which he acquired in one way or another from the monasteries.
The Cistercians with their flourishing wool trade were an obvious
target. The chronicle of Meaux Abbey claims that the king now
extracted no less than 30 000 marks from the English houses of the
order, including 1000 from the abbey itself, a proceeding which led
some brethren to be forced to take refuge in houses of other orders.

However, steadily it became clear to the king who, with all his
defects, was no fool, that he would have to cut his losses. In 1203–4
he had suffered an enormous blow when the spacious and fertile
land of Normandy had been seized by the king of France, and he
inevitably incurred immense unpopularity from his obvious military
incapacity and the enormous taxes which he was imposing on a
public which had never experienced exactions of anything like
comparable magnitude, and saw no signs of getting value for money.
Negotiations with the papacy had never been written off but it
was clear that the stalemate here would persist without some totally
new initiative. The situation deteriorated further when, early in
1212, John found that the pope was considering taking the most
extreme step of declaring him deposed. Whether or not this sentence
was actually put into practice is disputed by modern historians, the
evidence hereon being confused. But the threat was very serious,
since the king of France was straining at the leash to extend his
influence spectacularly by invading England with papal blessing, as
William the Conqueror had done a century and a half earlier.

It was now apparent to the king that he must reduce the opposition
he had aroused and that peace with the Church was the least expensive way of so doing. In May 1213 came the settlement of his
dispute with Rome. John agreed to accept Stephen Langton as archbishop of Canterbury and to refund royal exactions from ecclesiastical bodies after these had been carefully assessed. On top of this,

by a colourful concession he formally surrendered his kingdom of England to the pope and received it back from him as a papal fief, thus becoming technically a vassal of the papacy. As a sign and symbol of this subordination there was to be paid to the pope an annual tribute of 1000 marks a year.

It has been urged with some degree of truth that under the feudal conventions of the age tenure of a kingdom in this way was not necessarily regarded as degrading and it can certainly be paralleled elsewhere, notably by the similar tenure in these times of the kingdom of Sicily by the German Emperor. The nature of immediate English reaction to this act of King John is difficult to assess and may well have been mixed. But after John's death, as we shall see, there steadily developed in England an anti-Roman feeling which we find clearly voiced in the much later chronicle of the so-called 'Matthew of Westminster': 'He (John) resigned his crown to pope Innocent and did homage to him, making a slave of a country of most perfect freedom so that the prince of many provinces became subject to tribute, drawing up a deed on the matter which was a mournful and hateful one to those that heard it.'

Whatever later ages thought, the immediate effect of it was something of a diplomatic triumph for the king—'a brilliant manoeuvre' a modern historian has termed it—for the act at once put John under Innocent's protection and thus knocked the bottom out of the French king's hope of papal backing. With his usual ingenuity and lack of scruple John proceeded to wriggle out of repayment of a large part of his ecclesiastical debts and now devoted his main energies to the climax of his efforts to regain Normandy and with it personal credibility. With optimistic words he launched an attack on the French down in Poitou, but his efforts petered out fruitlessly, leaving all to depend on the assault to be launched on King Philip Augustus by John's ally, Otto of Germany, and certain minor supporters. What stubbornly retains its reputation as one of the decisive battles in the history of the Middle Ages in general and France in particular, took place on 27 July 1214. On that day Philip, with banners unfurled and trumpets sounding, moved out from his base in the great city of Tournai and successfully lured his enemies to attack him near the bridge of Bouvines on the old Roman road to Arras, on ground which favoured him. The fighting which followed was ferocious and during it the king of France so narrowly avoided death that, as so often in history, the French must have been convinced that God was a Frenchman at heart. In the end John's allies were decisively defeated. Normandy was a total loss.

John had nothing to show for all the vast sums of money which he had exacted from his people so his reputation was in tatters. He had never appreciated the importance of conciliating baronial feeling and it is not surprising that there now developed the greatest crisis in English feudal history. In origin the revolt which broke out was very far from being the work of an extensive section of the English baronage, but steadily with the wise handling of Langton the opposition gathered strength and responsibility. There now built up rapidly the celebrated crisis in English history which culminated on 15 June 1215 in a meadow between Windsor and Staines, where King John formally accepted and sealed the Great Charter (*Magna Carta*), a document subsequently so significant that even the historical debunkers of modern times have shrunk from writing it off. This very complex document and factors which lay behind its production contain much which is non-ecclesiastical in nature and cannot be here studied in any detail, but certain comments on it are meet to be made.

To some degree it is now clear that the king's misfortunes were the product not of himself but of his times. It was unfortunate for John to come to the English throne at a time when the economic conditions and governmental problems made it so very difficult for the Crown to pay its way. It was also unfortunate for him that his reign extensively overlapped that of the ambitious and vigorous French king, Philip Augustus, who fought with shrewdness and success to dismember the Angevin Empire. On the other hand John had major defects which combined to create a wide and deep distrust of him never again inspired by any ruler of England. He had no capacity to fraternise with his barons in the traditional feudal fashion, but persistently played a lone hand, a fact which, together with his outbursts of cruelty (notably his murder of Prince Arthur which shocked contemporaries very greatly), inevitably ruined that baronial confidence in the monarchy which was then essential for social peace. It was quite impossible for keen churchmen, whether ecclesiastics or laity, to regard him with that deep respect which medieval tradition usually led them to accord to their king and which was enjoyed by the great mass of the sovereigns of medieval

England. Their dislike was based both on the king's heavy exactions which hit them so very hard, and on the harsh fact that his character lacked such fundamental traits as the piety and that self-discipline which his position demanded; his lack of scruple might have passed without comment in the financial world of modern London or New York, but in the more disciplined medieval West excited strong disapprobation. Further, in a feudal society which expects the monarch to be able to defend his realm in hour of need John was again out of place. He was devoid of the military skill which had given his brother Richard undeserved panache, nor did he possess the comparatively easily obtainable quality of firm determination to fight back, as he showed in the lack of effort which he displayed immediately after the disastrous loss of Normandy in 1203–4. It is of course indubitable that many of John's baronial critics, notably the youngish hot-heads prominent in the early stages of the crisis, were very far from being a band of idealists, no few of them displaying that habit of wearing social blinkers for which modern trades-union leaders have now become celebrated. But this does not alter the fact that the primary function of a monarch is to govern, and here John, for all his business competence, was singularly unsuccessful, being largely responsible for provoking what was much the greatest constitutional demonstration in medieval English history.

Very notable in the crisis of the Great Charter was the invaluable contribution made to the protest movement by Stephen Langton. Left-wing archbishops of Canterbury, like left-wing bishops of Rome, belong to a very rare ecclesiastical species, and it was providential that in this hour of immense crisis there came to the fore a shrewd and progressive primate who was capable of moulding the opposition into an effective whole and ensuring that its inevitably complex demands were as reasonable as the highly exceptional situation allowed them to be. Taken as a whole the barons were a brash lot, and it is doubtful whether anyone save Langton who, combined with his constitutional position as the first subject of the Crown, high intelligence, great courage and incontestable integrity, would have been capable of presiding over the genesis of the Great Charter.

Although in process of time the Great Charter became one of the most celebrated documents in English constitutional history, it is worth while noting that its permanence was by no means inevitable. It may well have seemed to some that its survival was as close run a thing as the Duke of Wellington asserted the battle of Waterloo to have been. At once the Charter came up against two major obstacles. The first of these was the firm condemnation of it by Pope Innocent III as a thing base, vile, illegal and unjust. Such a judgment coming from so shrewd and sensible a man seems at first sight to verge on the inexplicable. Here it must be appreciated that when the great English crisis came to a head Innocent, always one to work himself too hard, was stupendously busy in organising the Fourth Lateran Council of 1215 which, as we have seen, was the mightiest council which the Western Church of our period was to witness. Further, it is important to realise that in these times, as for long to come, it was virtually impossible for the popes in far distant Rome to appreciate all the subtleties of the local life of the English Church. Like the catastrophic 'deposition' of Elizabeth I by Pius V in 1570, this condemnation might not have been voiced had its originator been fully briefed on the complexities of the English scene, whilst to put legal fetters on the monarchy in these days seemed to many indefensible. As it was, Innocent, understandably but very inaccurately, regarded John's affray with his barons as merely one more example of that unreasonable behaviour to which medieval barons were so prone. He would have been wiser to have pondered very lengthily the significant fact that the shrewd and God-fearing Langton, whom he knew so well and of which he approved so highly, was the leader of this opposition to John. But Innocent was for all his intelligence and highmindedness, a lawyer, and as such in the last resort for him what settled the matter was precedent. For the Great Charter there was no precedent in the long centuries of Christian history.

The second major obstacle to acceptance of the Great Charter was the military opposition of King John who was now basking in the unusual position of being the papacy's blue-eyed boy and whose permanent acceptance of the Charter was always in question. Quickly he moved against his baronial foes and met with no small measure of early success. However, early in October 1216 John fell ill. Indulgence in his favourite compound of peaches and new cider led to serious deterioration in his health and on the 19th the movements of the restless king ceased for ever. He was interred, as he desired, near the burial place of St Wulfstan in Worcester Cathedral. With his death the whole political scene in England was transformed radically and rapidly, and the Great Charter survived what was destined to be the major threat to its perpetuation.

The terms of the Great Charter fall into two sections of very unequal size and significance. Of these much the smaller is the provision made at the end of the document for a committee of barons who were to ensure that its terms were duly observed by the king and were empowered to declare war on him to ensure this, if necessity so demanded. This provision was immensely revolutionary in ages drilled to display profound respect to monarchy as a thing sent by God for the good of man but, given the shiftiness of John, was clearly not only justifiable but imperative. With John's death justification no longer existed for such baronial watch-dogs, so this provision was omitted from re-issues of the Charter.

The rest of the document consists of sixty articles, precise and mostly quite short, almost all of which aim at remedying particular grievances put forward by the barons. As contemporary etiquette in such things demanded, the ecclesiastical took precedence over the non-ecclesiastical. The first article opens with the declaration that 'the English Church shall be free and have its rights undiminished and its privileges unimpaired' and goes on to confirm specifically the freedom of elections, 'which is considered most necessary for the English Church'. However, this latter promise was often disregarded by future sovereigns as blatantly as it had been by their predecessors, whilst the preliminary abstract promise of freedom was much too hazy to be likely to guarantee any worthwhile fruit. From the ecclesiastical angle in the narrower sense of the phrase, the Great Charter cannot be said to be of much interest or use, even if it became one of the great constitutional landmarks of history. 'The reign of John', suggests Tout, 'was the culmination of a long tendency in English history, most rapid since the accession of his father, towards the establishment of an absolutism in which the rights of all classes would disappear and the arbitrary will of the king be supreme. The story of his reign should reveal how very near that result was of accomplishment.' Although in post-medieval times Western Church leaders much too often sold themselves to the local monarchy, in medieval England there was often evident a refusal by leading churchmen to do this, of which Langton's part in the struggle with John is in many ways the most illustrious example.

FROM HENRY III TO EDWARD III

King John was succeeded by his nine-year-old son, Henry III, who assumed personal power in 1227. His reign, which ended only in 1272, was the longest of any English sovereign until that of Queen Victoria and roughly marks a major turning point in the complex history of the relations between the English Crown and the Roman see. In the three centuries which separate it from that of Henry VIII there was steadily built up a relationship between the English monarchy and the papacy in which major head-on collisions of any magnitude were largely absent, and ideological warfare of the type generated by the early Gregorian Reformers seldom obvious. Although the canon lawyers and the English secular lawyers seldom very aggressively paraded their claims, neither did they abandon them. Instead, to come to discrete understandings in practical terms came to be recognised by both sides as being largely the best way of doing business, with the result, as we shall see, that for long before the Reformation the popes and the English kings had reached gentlemen's agreements that reduced strife between them to small proportions, albeit not without disadvantage to lesser ranks of society.

In the great clashes periodically produced by the Gregorian Reform constitutional and financial issues were inextricably interwoven. Though the same was to some extent true in the latter part of our period, very largely now the constitutional wrangling of the past tended to be pushed into the background (it was, after all, very apt to be fruitless) and instead most clashes between kings and popes tended to come over financial matters, for the very good reason that by the late twelfth century the English monarchy and Roman papacy had both developed machineries of government which were very elaborate, highly expensive and were to become more so. The steady growth in population in these times, the increase in wealth and the growing inroads into feudal organisation of an economy in which money was playing an increasingly important part, all combined to produce important new thinking over modes of taxation which, as so often, had major constitutional repercussions.

THE ENGLISH MONARCHY AND FINANCE

Throughout the thirteenth century the English monarchy was anxiously seeking to enlarge its revenues, for several main reasons. One of these was the steady rise in prices which now persisted and which had an adverse effect on royal revenue since no little of this came from sources which could not be adequately increased to take account of it. Of major significance also was the steadily growing complexity of governmental machinery in England at this time which early gave it a high degree of efficiency difficult to parallel elsewhere in the West. The financial might of the Exchequer was early established and by the mid-thirteenth century the rapidly expanding Chancery was turning out huge masses of documents great and small; also there were growing up the great courts of law which were to dominate English justice until Victorian days. Economically unproductive was the military expenditure of thirteenth- and fourteenth-century England. Fighting was now much more costly than in Norman days through various advances in efficiency, notably the increasing use of mercenaries and the growing habit of erecting very sophisticated castles in stone. Like many medieval monarchs, kings of England were now very ready to engage in warfare, for combat on the grand scale now enjoyed the same high social prestige as hunting, shooting and fishing in later days. Both geography and history now provided particularly abundant opportunities for military action.

Termination of the long tradition of sporadic warfare on the Scottish border was almost impossible. Under Henry III there was something of a lull, but major fighting flared up ferociously under Edward I who developed a near pathological passion for the endless and profitless task of subduing the Scots, *inter alia* ordering that after his death his bones were not to be at once buried in Westminster Abbey but were to be carried into battle against them, a foolish provision which was disregarded. Warfare went stubbornly on under Edward II (1307–27) and northern England was subjected to great suffering; Wales, of course, was too small to be more than a minor military problem, and effective opposition here was now smashed for ever by Edward I, who inaugurated the erection of a string of massive castles in north Wales at enormous cost—the most spectacular white elephants in British military history.

But English expenditure on warfare in these areas was of minor overall significance when compared with that which was dispensed off and on for the next two-and-a-half centuries following the loss of Normandy by the English Crown (1203-4), which climaxed in the Hundred Years War between the two countries (1338-1453) wherein English attacks were mostly feckless and ultimately almost totally fruitless.

In view of all this, it is not surprising to find that throughout the thirteenth century and beyond the English monarchy had huge financial commitments which could not be met out of old arrangements; so developed the more efficient machinery for taxing the faithful, not least the clergy.

THE PAPACY AND FINANCE

If the financial needs of the English monarchy in the thirteenth and fourteenth centuries were very great, they appear relatively trivial when set against those of the contemporary papacy, which sprang from two main sources—the vast increase in the amount of business referred to Rome from all parts of the Western Church, and the threat to papal independence in Italy from certain major political figures.

In England, as elsewhere, from the twelfth century onwards there developed a widespread and deep-rooted tendency amongst ecclesiastics great and small to have recourse to Rome. Mighty men, such as lofty Benedictine abbots, might present their case in person or send a delegation of their subordinates to the Eternal City, but the great majority had to rely on written recourse. Already, by the time of Innocent III (1198-1216) the range of English matters referred to Rome was quite remarkable. At the top of the scale, of course, was the correspondence with the highest dignitaries from King John downwards over the very major problems like the interdict and the final royal submission to the papacy. But along with these were hosts of matters of quite minor importance. A canon of Norton Priory who at his profession had changed his Christian name from Henry to Augustine, consults Rome over his naive fears that news of his new nomenclature might not get through to the celestial regions, as a result of which he might lose the benefit of prayers offered for him under the original name. Equally devoid of major significance was correspondence over the nature of the privileges to be accorded to the precentor at St Paul's Cathedral caused by the prevalent, almost Anglican, haziness on the matter—'in English churches the customs vary and some of the cantors have a lesser rank and some a greater ... their ranks being varied or mutually inconsistent cannot be made uniform.'

Something like an unregulated passion for total uniformity on minor matters seems to have pervaded much of Western society and generated great quantities of papal correspondence. But behind all this lay a deep and wide growth in the importance accorded to the Roman see, which now attained a position which fell little short of a spiritual despotism. Of this development illustrations are very easy to find. To John, Innocent III writes 'over all He [Christ] has set one whom He has appointed as His Vicar on earth . . . so all men should obey His Vicar . . . all secular rulers for the sake of God so venerate this Vicar that unless they seek to serve Him devotedly they doubt if they are reigning properly.' Robert Grosseteste, the illustrious bishop of Lincoln (1235–53), though by no means totally subservient to papal demands, accepted a similar theoretical position, writing of 'the Lord Pope, in respect of whom all other prelates are moons and stars, receiving from him whatever power they have to illumine and fertilise the Church.'

Although we are here primarily concerned with the financial repercussions of this very demanding belief on contemporary Western society, certain allied observations on it may fruitfully here be made. In the first place the assignation to the papacy of what were virtually despotic powers was a considerable novelty. At no time had such an extremist view prevailed in the Christian Church of the early centuries, and it was totally incompatible with long and impressive theological tradition of Eastern Christendom. Secondly, it is to be noted that its dominance in these times owed much to pragmatic reasons, Rome providing legal uniformity and coherence at a time when the very luxuriant growth in a rather disorderly church life made such things highly desirable. Further it is note-worthy that in this period, whatever the canon lawyers might now say and think about papal power, the official voice of the Church expressed in contemporary General Councils made no attempt to extend or define officially the powers of the Vicar of Christ. It is no accident that fairly quickly this extremist view of papal power excited opposition which before the end of the fourteenth century had become very vociferous. However, major pleas for a more primitive conception of papal authority which were made at the Conciliar Movement and later by the Council of Trent, were fruitless and moderation triumphed only in our own days at the Second Vatican Council.

By the mid-thirteenth century credence in these very sweeping powers claimed by the papacy had become very extensive in the Western Church, but it is to be noted that this did not mean that every example of their employment by Rome was automatically accepted with ultra-montane meekness. Again and again we find strong opposition to particular Roman actions. Bishop Grosseteste, for example, though he wrote, 'I know and I truly know that the Lord Pope and the Holy Roman Church have this power that they can freely dispose of all ecclesiastical benefices', went on to oppose most vigorously certain exercises of this claim (page 241).

The second problem with major financial repercussions which faced the thirteenth-century popes was a major non-theological one —the chronic political instability of Italy, which persistently involved the medieval papacy in tides of troubles. In our period there was no kingdom of Italy, only a congerie of small states which never envisaged being of one mind, but mostly preferred rivalry to unity. Although Venice developed a remarkably effective machinery of government, other city states failed conspicuously here, and Roman municipal life in medieval days never looked like achieving stability.

For the papacy this local problem had various trying repercussions. At an early date the popes found it necessary to employ as a private fortress, San Angelo, originally an elaborate monument used for imperial burials, situate beside the Tiber a few hundred yards down the road from St Peter's, with which it was finally connected by a massive wall containing a passage which linked the two. But this bolt-hole, however august, was inadequate and repeatedly medieval popes had to quit the Eternal City to seek refuge elsewhere, sometimes very far afield indeed. Such absences entered a new phase, as we shall see, with the 'Babylonish captivity' of 1308–77, during which period the papal court resided at Avignon. Although some medieval papal absences were caused by purely local disorders, like those of the tenth century by which the papacy, through no fault of its own, was reduced to a most scandalous state, other major ones were due to invasions of Italy by lay rulers. With the rise of the controversial Gregorian Reform, emperors and popes on various occasions were at logger-heads, so that in the twelfth century papal absences from Rome were very frequent, refuge sometimes being sought as far afield as France. Particularly violent was the later conflict between the two forces in the period in and around the pontificate of Innocent IV (1243–54) when the highly ambitious Emperor Frederick II finally clashed most violently with the papacy, notably through his wish to unite the kingdom of Sicily which he had inherited with his German lands. This particular dilemma was far from new and, under the conditions of the time, from the papal point of view no happy solution was feasible. Either the papacy had to meet force with force as Innocent now did, hereby building up most trying financial and other problems, or else it must let the invader wreak his will. This might well have lead to the papacy being improperly subjugated to lay influence, as had already been seen notoriously in past days and was now to threaten again in the Avignon papacy. Because of his very violent clash with the Emperor, Innocent's financial demands were inevitably very considerable and caused much friction with local authorities, the more so since demands on this scale were much of a novelty.

THE RISE OF TAXATION OF THE CLERGY

From the point of view of the English clergy in the thirteenth century no new development can have been so unpleasant as the introduction of systematic and far from infrequent taxation of their incomes, a development which became increasingly evident as the decades slid away and one in which they were very liable to be trapped between the upper and nether millstones of the Roman see and the English monarchy.

It is to be noted that the latter never questioned this double status of the clergy. It left to the ecclesiastical authorities the tricky task of fixing the assessments of clerical wealth (page 233–4), but accepted the theoretical right of the papacy to tax the clergy of the land, though it kept a firm eye on the extent of this and might seek to get substantial shares of the proceeds. So far as England was concerned, the clergy were one of several elements of the community which was now taxed on a novel system. Instead of the rough-and-ready methods of Norman times, the late thirteenth century witnessed here the introduction of a system of taxing individuals on the basis of a percentage of their wealth.

This revolution in method began in the latter half of the twelfth century, and in origin was linked with the deep contemporary concern to make a massive effort to buttress up the Crusading movement which had recently suffered a serious setback, notably in the capture of Jerusalem by the great Moslem leader, Saladin, in 1187. Early the following year Henry II arranged to impose on his lay and ecclesiastical subjects what was known as the 'Saladin tithe' (being a tenth part of the income involved) which was destined to be 'a turning point in the development of non-feudal taxation'. In 1193 a similar levy of a fourth and a tenth was exacted to ransom that expensive luxury known as Richard I. From now on in England similar carefully assessed taxes were very extensively used, providing a major element in royal revenue.

By the end of the following century the clergy were being persistently pressed for money by the king and persistently tending to fight rearguard actions against his demands on grounds of varying credibility, but which were often reasonable, their consent often being linked with requests for the remedy of grievances against the Crown. This process, along with the contemporary innovation of taxation by the papacy, obviously posed two fundamental questions. How was the wealth of individual ecclesiastics and ecclesiastical corporations to be assessed and by what machinery was a grant to be made?

THE QUESTION OF ASSESSMENT

Human nature being what it is, the acquisition of knowledge of the exact income of a person or corporation is usually far from easy to obtain, and in thirteenth-century England this was certainly true. Under the conditions of the time it was inevitable that local ecclesiastical wealth should be assessed by ecclesiastical and not by lay officials. The first major attempt to do this comprehensively came in 1253-4, as a result of the pope having granted the king a tenth of English clerical incomes in return for his undertaking to go on a crusade. This 'valuation of Norwich' (so-called after the bishop of Norwich partly responsible for organising its compilation), was based on information taken by the rural dean and three or four incumbents of each rural deanery. Perhaps inevitably, its findings were much disputed, and the allegations that, in any case, royal officials proceeded to exact taxes at a higher rate added fuel to the flames of local indignation.

In 1291 Pope Nicholas IV ordered a completely new valuation of English ecclesiastical revenues. Headed by the bishops of Winchester and Lincoln there was now mounted a massive financial investigation of each diocese which produced a mighty survey known as 'the Taxation (*taxatio*) of pope Nicholas' and which was destined to be employed as the official yardstick for ecclesiastical taxation in England right down to the eve of the Reformation, when it was superseded by the *Valor Ecclesiasticus* of 1535. This document, unhappily still only available in a most inadequate edition, is replete with difficult technicalities and is not a total survey of English ecclesiastical resources (churches too poor to be taxed, for example, going unmentioned) but is of immense historical value, giving us our first systematic and detailed survey of the subject. Its appearance elicited from contemporary ecclesiastics no inconsiderable amount of understandable groaning—'three assessments have been made in turn for the oppression of Holy Church,' declares the chronicler of Barnwell Priory, 'the first called that of Walter bishop of Norwich, the second of Master Raymond of Nogeriis, the third of bishops John of Winchester and Oliver of Lincoln . . . The first was tolerable, the second wounded, the third pierced right through to the bone.'

This complaint was by no means groundless, for it is clear that various churches originally exempt from taxation through inadequate income later had their assessments increased to figures which brought them into the tax-gatherers' nets, whilst a number of wealthier churches had to pay at a much higher rate—the assessment of Reculver, for example, rose from 50 to 200 marks, and that of Wimbledon from 20 to 60. Fragmentary evidence shows very considerable if uneven rises in the total diocesan assessments: that of Durham increased from £3839 4s. 3d. to £8427 14s. 8¼d., Ely from £2635 8s. 10½d. to £6788 12s. 8½d., and Norwich from £14 487 15s. 9¾d. to £25 526 7s. 1¼d. Henceforth the clergy were taxed at the rate of a fraction of the sum at which their offices were rated in this *Taxation* of Pope Nicholas, the size of this fraction being varied and figures of a tenth and a fifteenth being common.

THE MACHINERY OF TAXATION

In what way was the taxation which king and pope so persistently demanded from the clergy to be granted? To this double question the answers were very different. So far as the papacy was concerned the huge authority with which recent canon law had now invested the Roman see meant that it had come to be taken for granted that its abstract right to demand taxation from local churches was not to be questioned, though it was perfectly legitimate to discuss and haggle over the amounts. In 1296 the over-active Pope Boniface VIII, in the bull *Clericis Laicos*, re-asserted an old claim that lay taxation of church wealth required papal authority, but this was very much a dead letter.

But what about royal demands for money? Here the question was complicated. From the time of Edward I (1272–1307) such demands were very frequent and the fact that they were made at irregular intervals meant that decisions would have to be made when provincial councils were not envisaged. For a while at least, equally trying from the clerical angle was the attempt by the Crown to have both higher and lower clergy make their grants alongside the representatives of the laity in the new-fangled institution which came to be known as Parliament; an institution which was rapidly assuming what came to be its classic form during Edward's reign and the half-century which followed it.

This body consisted of two major elements. First there was the body of ecclesiastical and lay dignitaries which by immemorial feudal custom the Crown was bound to consult on certain major matters, notably questions of peace or war. This consisted in England of the two archbishops, all the diocesan bishops (who ranked as barons), a rather arbitrary selection of heads of English monasteries, along with various great lay lords whose qualifications for this position in early times was not clear-cut. Well before the end of our period this element had solidified into that single body which we now know as the House of Lords.

The second element was new, only very slightly fore-shadowed before the time of Edward I, and was based on representation of the lower elements of society which were legally of free status, i.e. not villeins. The Crown sought to have it consist of three elements— representatives of the counties of England elected by its freemen;

representatives of a rather arbitrary selection of English towns, and representatives of the lower clergy. For some little time two questions over this were in doubt. Firstly, were the county members and the burgesses to meet together or separately? Fairly quickly, owing to the particular pattern of contemporary English society, it became established that they should form a single unit which became known as the House of Commons. Secondly, and much more important from the ecclesiastical viewpoint, was the question of whether the representatives of the lower clergy should join in this new institution or meet on their own.

Down the ages civil servants, both pious and impious, have tended to regard the local Church as essentially a department of their domain, and in the late thirteenth and early fourteenth century officialdom of the English Crown sought to have the lower clergy meeting in Parliament in tidy fashion. But this was not to be.

From the ecclesiastical angle such an arrangement was undesirable for it would render the clergy far more liable to being pressurised than if they debated royal demands on their own. They had their own interests to protect and, by and large, were much better qualified than town and county members to hold their own against insistent civil servants. Tradition down the ages had led them to insist that, in the last resort, they should not be under royal control. It is very significant that when in 1314 the archbishop of Canterbury strove to put into effect the order to 'cause to appear' (*venire faciatis*) in order to consider a royal demand, the clerical representatives to whom this demand was addressed made strong objections, since this was a phrase used in civil courts entailing severe penalties if disobeyed. It was held to be highly improper in this context, since the clergy of the province or kingdom should not be summoned by royal authority, but by the archbishop at the request of the king—a perfectly defensible objection. In similar vein when, in 1339, the king, without consulting the archbishop of Canterbury who was then abroad, ordered the bishops to summon a clerical assembly, they refused, pointing out that when the Crown desired a grant from the clergy of a diocese or province, laudable custom laid down that the letters hereon should be addressed to the archbishop or his vicar-general. This ensured that no reply be made to the king, especially on difficult questions, before full discussion and consent by clergy of the whole province. At an early stage the English clergy, in considering royal demands for grants, were prone to consider making their assent conditional on the remedying of some grievance or grievances, thus acting as a useful brake on royal power.

The clergy now developed a machine of their own which came to be known as 'convocation' and was to survive in the Anglican Church down to modern times. From an early stage it was automatically dissolved when Parliament was dissolved and the provinces of Canterbury and York each had their own assembly. This took the form of an upper and a lower house, each house consisting of the local archbishop, diocesan bishops of the province, and by the heads of some but by no means all of the monasteries of the area. So far as the lesser clergy was concerned as early as 1283 the archbishop of Canterbury called an ecclesiastical assembly which included not only the above-mentioned elements but the heads of cathedrals and collegiate chapters and representatives of the beneficed clergy of each diocese. These last were a complete innovation in such circumstances and were known as proctors (*procuratores*). These representatives of the lower clergy were summoned by the king to his so-called 'Model Parliament' of 1295, and quickly became an essential element of convocation. Unfortunately we have very little surviving statistical evidence to illustrate the composition of convocation, but there have survived one or two useful indications of the numbers of representatives in both convocations in the second quarter of the fifteenth century. Each province, of course, had one archbishop, but York had only two other dioceses against the thirteen English ones in the province of Canterbury. The former had some 50 monastic representatives against 296 in the latter and 20 proctors of clergy as against 32, with some 26 other dignitaries against 82 of the southern province, whose total was about four times the size of the northern one.

The functions of convocation, especially in relation to provincial councils, were not defined in our period and varied from time to time. At first, granting money was its major preoccupation, but understandably it was convenient at times for it to deliberate on other matters.

Although it is unfair on medieval sovereigns to compare their relatively benevolent rule with the malevolent régime of modern totalitarianism, there is no doubt that just as today the Christian Church has been the main major brake on the latter, so at this time its bodies provided invaluable curbs on the potentially dangerous power of the medieval English monarchy. The author of a detailed study of the origins of convocation has no doubt of the value of the considerable strength of its contribution to the formation of the great constitutional tradition of English government. She lists four main areas where this was evident: 'their adherence to the principle that in assemblies or congregations which concerned the whole body of clergy, there should be representatives from every degree of clerical status; their insistence that those who were to give money for a grant should take part in the deciding of the amount thereof and the terms on which it should be yielded; their maintenance of the practice that the conditions of a grant and the grievances to be redressed should be presented in writing with clarity and precision of statement; and finally their constant emphasis on the principle that redress of grievances should be the inevitable recompense for a grant' (Weske).

However this may be, there is no doubt at all that from the late thirteenth century the English Crown extracted a great deal of taxation from the English clergy. A small part of this was secured by diverting to the royal treasury useful parts of taxation levied by the pope, but much more came through direct action. Systematic survey of this turgid theme belongs to the sphere of the economic historian, but illustrations of its importance are worthy of note. Weske's valuable lists of ecclesiastical assemblies in the province of Canterbury in the period 1222–1399 show how important were the series of demands from the reign of Edward II (1307–27) onwards, and how sturdily excesses were resisted. With the commencement of the Hundred Years War came steadily increasing financial pressure. The register of Bishop Bransford of Worcester (1339–49) shows a triennial tenth levied in 1337 being followed by tenths in 1338, 1340 and 1342, a triennial tenth in 1344 and a biennial tenth in the same year. On top of these came royal demands on wool owned by clergy in 1338 and 1347. In 1342 the bishop was pressed for a personal 'loan' of 100 marks and for a further 200 marks four years later. Finally, in 1347 a feudal aid was levied on his temporal possessions. If, as seems likely, the pace of architectural progress notably slowed in the latter half of the fourteenth century this may well be due more to the heavy contemporary taxation than to the Black Death which has been suggested as the principal reason.

PAPAL PROVISIONS AND ENGLISH APPOINTMENTS

Although papal taxation of the English clergy was bound to be unwelcome it was comparatively limited in scope (unlike that levied on them by the English Crown) and it seems highly likely that it constituted a comparatively minor element in building up that English hostility to the Roman court which becomes increasingly obvious from the mid-thirteenth century onwards. Much more unpopular, to judge by the contemporary denunciations of it which appear, was Rome's growing use of 'provisions'—official acts by which benefices were filled directly by papal action in disregard of the rights of patrons or chapters. This form of intervention would seem at Rome to have a double justification. Theoretically (and this, for some time, was widely accepted) Rome was the source of all ecclesiastical jurisdiction and therefore was fully entitled to override the powers which the law traditionally allowed to patrons, whether they were ecclesiastical corporations, feudal dignitaries or lesser folk. As a decretal of Pope Clement IV (d. 1268) put it, 'the full disposal of churches, parsonages, dignities and other ecclesiastical benefices is known to belong to the Roman pontiff, so that he can not only confer these by right when they are vacant, but can also grant a right to those that shall become vacant'. Looked at from the practical angle the claim was by no means inevitably hostile to the interests of the Church as a whole. It could be, and sometimes was, utilised by the papacy to ensure that high appointments especially were given to suitable candidates, and not to unsuitable ones whose promotion was urged for purely secular reasons, whilst at the lower end of the scale provision to minor benefices could be used for such admittedly useful purposes as financing education of clergy at the universities in times when very little financial provision for this was available. With regard to the provision to English benefices of non-resident Italians it could be argued with some degree of reason that, since local churches in the West derived substantial benefits from their links with the Holy see, it was not unreasonable to expect them to help towards the huge expenses of maintaining its massive machine through allowing foreign dignitaries to hold a benefice whilst non-resident, which last habit, after all, was very far from unpractised by their opposite numbers in England.

It would not be surprising if such considerations led respectable curial officials at Rome to regard local opposition to papal provisions as inspired by greed and unreason, vices which English opinion at this time vigorously attributed to the Romans. Certainly there was another very important side to the question. In the first place, in an age wherein precedent counted for a very great deal, papal provisions stood condemned as indubitably unknown in past centuries, as was the allied papal habit of granting 'expectancies', the right of nomination to a benefice not yet vacant. Secondly, the practise of provision was utterly incompatible with English law, perennially threatening the centuries-old right of electors and patrons over appointments to benefices, an objection which was by no means solely an academic one, but had major social implications. The practice would not only prevent patrons, from the lordliest abbey to most minor squire, from appointing to posts in their patronage men for whom they had a high regard, but non-resident holders of benefices, notably, of course, foreigners, would almost certainly neglect that offering of hospitality which was so closely connected with clerical life. The fact that the papacy might try to stifle opposition to its provisions by excommunications or threats thereof only added fuel to the fire of local opposition—why should a man be punished for doing only what his fore-fathers had done for centuries with full ecclesiastical approval? In any case papal provisions were, in effect, another form of taxation, a thing to which contemporary folk were even more averse than modern ones, partly because they had been accustomed to so little of it.

Such considerations inevitably not only bred growing local indignation in England from the mid-thirteenth century onwards, but inspired very vigorous opposition at every major social level from the monarchy downwards. The pope might be the Vicar of Christ but that did not automatically prevent him from making mistakes in matters of government and when he did, the faithful had the right, nay even the duty, to resist him. This is seen very vividly in the later conduct of Robert Grosseteste (d. 1253) the most pious and learned English bishop of his day. As has just been noted, he accepted in their fullness the immense theoretical rights hereon which the papacy now claimed, but in process of time the somewhat idealistic vision of the Roman curia which he had understandably acquired was severely battered by obvious indications of the scandals prevalent there—'O money, money, how much you can effect especially in Roman curia' he commented, and in the latter stages of his life he steadfastly opposed certain papal demands, notably that for a canonry in his cathedral of Lincoln for a nephew of Innocent IV—'as an obedient son, I do not obey, I contradict, I rebel', he sturdily asserted. This capacity to combine obedience with rebellion is very evident in the history of England's relations with Rome after his time.

EPISCOPAL APPOINTMENTS

For a very large part of the thirteenth century provision was very little used as a mode of episcopal appointment, papal influence, where active, being manifested in more conservative form. After Langton's death Rome kept a very watchful eye on appointments to the see of Canterbury, only in the case of Boniface of Savoy (1241-70) finding pressure in favour of a royal nominee irresistible. Papal provision, however, was not used here until 1272, when the election of Adam of Chillenden was quashed and Robert Kilwardby, an able friar, was provided to the primatial see. When Robert was translated, in 1278, the election of the bishop of Bath as his successor was also quashed, and John Pecham, another distinguished mendicant, provided.

From now on, for no little time to come there developed a considerable tendency for English episcopal elections to cause clashes of varying magnitude between the local chapter, the Crown and the papacy. Elections in which the chapter was left entirely to its own devices were very rare, at least in the more opulent sees. Thus the only example of this at these times at the great see of Winchester (in which, incidently, a monk was elected—the first of his kind for very long) occurred at a juncture when the papacy was vacant. Normally, Crown influence on elections was very active, again and again successful royal servants or other nominees securing attractive appointments. But it is interesting to note that in securing appointment of its candidates the Crown increasingly found it useful to have them appointed by papal provision, which might either supersede an earlier election or be a substitute for it. Such appointments had the immense asset of being top-level ones which could not be challenged or overturned by a disgruntled party in one of the

often protracted and expensive lawsuits which were so common a feature of these times. This increased use was considerable. During the long reign of Henry III only six bishops were appointed by papal provision, but from the time of Clement VI (1342-50) this became stock procedure, Bishop Trilleck of Hereford (1344-60) being apparently the last medieval English bishop not appointed by papal provision. It is to be noted that the power of the English monarchy and the comparative weakness of the papacy, notably during the 'Babylonish Captivity', meant that in this period foreign bishops were a very great rarity in England. There had been one or two under Henry III, though even these owed their promotion to royal and not to papal influence, but there were only two more in the whole of the fourteenth century.

But the tensions between the interests and outlook of chapter, king and pope very understandably not infrequently led to quite protracted disputes. If the chapter elected its own candidate this might be quashed by the papal court, which might be under heavy lay pressure to appoint unsuitable candidates. Hamo of Hythe, a monk of Rochester, was elected to the little see of that name early in 1317, after pressure from the archbishop and from a local peeress to choose otherwise had been rejected, but before the requisite interval for archiepiscopal confirmation of his appointment had elapsed, it was announced that the pope had reserved the see and given it to the confessor of the queen of England. The archbishop now claimed that since the election had taken place before the pope's reservation the latter was invalid. There followed a major lawsuit which was referred for settlement to the Roman curia, then at Avignon, in January 1318. After immense complications, which made it necessary for Hamo to go out to Avignon in person, a decision in his favour was given and he was consecrated on 26 August 1319. He left Avignon a month later having contracted a mighty debt of 1440 florins, to pay the which he had to sell a wood at Bromley. Other delays followed and only on 13 January 1320 was he enthroned in his cathedral. That Hamo's troubles here were greater than those of most of his fellow bishops was largely due to the fact that he had not got Crown influence behind him, but lesser examples of such clashes are not rare.

No few appointments at this time were due to lay influence and were by no means always laudable. Thus, in 1320 the chapter of Lincoln elected their chancellor to be the new bishop, but much pressurising at the papal court by one Lord Badlesmere led to the appointment of the latter's nephew who had no spiritual qualifications for the post and was below the minimum age for a bishop envisaged by canon law. In 1330 the lucrative see of Salisbury was similarly given to one Robert Wyville through the influence of the queen whose secretary he had been. In 1345 the pope quashed an election to the vacant see of Ely made by the chapter there and provided to it a candidate of whom he thought that the king would approve. The appointment of Robert Stretton as bishop of Lichfield in 1356 was only approved by the pope after considerable pressure from the Black Prince, it being noted that Robert had three times failed reading tests, apparently because of eye trouble rather than stupidity. Even where long wrangles over episcopal appointments did not occur in the fourteenth century, it was far from uncommon for a man to be elected bishop only to be replaced by someone who had strong ties with top people.

Here we may take note of a newish development which, though not of major significance in contemporary ecclesiastical politics, was not devoid of importance—the usage of filling the vacancy in an episcopal see by the transference to it of one who was already a bishop elsewhere—a practice known as 'translation'. This was an innovation frowned upon as late as the closing decades of the thirteenth century—between 1272 and 1300 only one in forty episcopal vacancies in England were filled in this way. But thereafter use of it greatly expanded. In modern times this translation is commonly used in order to move a bishop who has displayed considerable effectiveness from one diocese to a more demanding one. But the very strong Crown influence over higher church appointments in medieval England meant that in these times it was principally employed to reward royal favourites on a more generous scale. A man might be first appointed to a Welsh see or one of the minor English ones but in process of time moved upwards to a wealthier one.

CATHEDRAL CHAPTERS

From the point of view of both monarchy and papacy much the most attractive genre of ecclesiastical appointments, from the point of view of relieving their strained finances, was the archdeaconries and major posts in English secular cathedrals, notably those of deans, treasurers, chancellors and precentors and the fairly numerous common or garden canonries or prebendaries. Seen from the worldly angle these posts had major assets. In the first place they were mostly better paid (in a number of cases much better paid) than the general run of incumbencies of parish churches; secondly, they usually ranked as benefices 'without charge of souls', so could be held with other appointments; thirdly, since secular cathedrals were grossly over-staffed these offices could mostly be held by non-residents without any great spiritual disadvantage provided adequate deputies were appointed. In effect, therefore, they could very easily be utilised merely as a means of augmenting the income of the nominee concerned. These posts in England were comparatively few owing to the unusually high proportion of cathedrals with monastic chapters, but the more lucrative of them were very well worth having and greatly sought by careerists, ecclesiastical or non-ecclesiastical.

Minor canonries of English cathedrals were those of London, Exeter, Wells and Hereford and in general these were not thought substantial enough to be allotted to aliens by papal provisions. In the fourteenth century there was apparently only one such appointment at Exeter and three at Hereford. Far different was the situation in the case of England's three major secular cathedrals—those of York, Lincoln and Salisbury. There the lucrative appointments were greatly prized by royal and papal nominees alike. Traditionally they were normally made by the bishop of the cathedral concerned, though the Crown claimed the right to fill any such vacancies which occurred when a bishopric was vacant.

As with papal provisions to bishoprics these were rare for most of the thirteenth century but thereafter increased markedly. Their incidence varied much from place to place. In the fourteenth century six of the eight deans of Salisbury were aliens, but such a high proportion was exceptional; at York in these times there were four out of thirteen, at Lincoln only two out of thirteen. Similarly, variation is seen amongst the papal provisions of aliens to archdeaconries. They numbered eighteen of the sixty-two archdeacons of York and seven out of forty-nine at Salisbury at this time.

So far as the much more numerous and less exalted canonries and prebendaries are concerned we find a similar state of things. The proportion of alien appointments is neither immense nor negligible, but substantial enough to aggravate local opinion.

PARISH CHURCHES

To what degree did papal provision of aliens affect appointments to the thousands of English parish churches? A great deal of research will be needed before a comprehensive answer to this question can be given. However, it is clear that several factors guaranteed that very large numbers of them were unaffected thereby. In the first place it was not usual for Rome to interfere with the rights of lay patrons of advowsons; secondly a very large number of English livings were so badly endowed that by the time the deputy had been paid there would be little or no balance to be used for other purposes like this and, thirdly, by the time provisions came into operation the Crown had long been accustomed to utilise wealthy benefices in ecclesiastical patronage for its own ends, a practice with which it would have been unwise for the papacy to interfere extensively. All the indications are that the proportion of parish churches affected by provisions was very small indeed. Pantin points out that 'even under the lavish Clement VI, the average number of provisions to parochial benefices per annum was forty-two to Englishmen and 1.8 to aliens'. What is, of course, equally interesting and important is to know the number and nature of papal provisions made in these times for the benefit of local people. There is no doubt that, here at least, critics may cease from carping since a useful number of these provided means for clergy to study at universities which would otherwise not have been available.

By the mid-fourteenth century papal provisions were attracting most violent criticism in England. These contemporary attacks were by no means invariably accurate over the scale of papal provisions which diverted to Roman needs only a very small fraction of English ecclesiastical wealth. As Pantin puts it, 'papal provisors and especially alien provisors did not exist in large numbers. They were not an invading "army of provisors" as contemporaries seemed to think, but rather . . . a general staff rather than an army, enjoying a comparatively small number of extremely lucrative benefices'. But to the inevitably ill-informed locals who after all were bereft in medieval times of any extensive statistical information, this was unknown, whilst it was very clear to them that appointments which for centuries had been held by Englishmen were being diverted to foreigners, in the process disregarding native law, elbowing out local candidates and diminishing that hospitality which custom expected from the clergy. But provisions were only one of several elements which would now have produced major anti-Roman headlines, had such things as newspapers existed, and included papal taxation and the fees and douceurs demanded from no few of those who had recourse to Rome.

Inevitably this papal intervention in what were traditionally local preserves sparked off a long series of hostile demonstrations. An early example of such things was to be seen in Yorkshire, when a young landowner who had been deprived of the right of appointing to a benefice in his charge by a provision, initiated a protest movement led by masked and armed men which, amongst other things, emptied barns and distributed grain belonging to alien incumbents. In 1238 came a picturesque interlude at Oxford when a mob attacked the household of the cardinal legate who had installed himself in Osney Abbey. His brother (who had been made master cook to ensure that the food which was served at table was unpoisoned), perhaps losing his nerve at signs of trouble, hurled a pot of scalding soup in the face of an Irishman who had gravitated into the kitchen in search of nourishment or trouble, an act which was followed by a serious riot which led the legate to seek refuge in the belfry of the abbey.

The major source of our information concerning early anti-Roman feeling is Matthew Paris, a monk of St Alban's Abbey who was an accomplished artist and a vigorous and voluminous chronicler. However, his attacks need to be taken with tablespoons of salt, for he combines the usual medieval habit of wildly exaggerating the extent of the practices which he attacks with other vices. The penetrating A. L. Smith found his chronicling varying 'from firsthand priceless testimony to the most extravagant and worthless gossip' and finds that 'his perfectly maddening confusedness as to dates' invites comparison with the musician of whom it was said 'as for any notion which he has of time, he might have been born and bred in eternity'. To Matthew, the papal curia was 'that court without courtesy or money which is manifestly threatened with the wrath of God'. His citations of scandalous cases of papal exactions includes the payment of 800 marks from the abbey of Bury St Edmund's in return for papal confirmation of their newly-elected abbot, certainly a huge sum though one very unlikely to have brought this plutocratic place to the verge of indigence.

The kings of England were put in an interesting position by these various outbursts of anti-Roman feeling. To some extent they sympathised with it as they certainly did not welcome fleecing of the public by any officials except their own. On the other hand they had no doubts about the unique spiritual power of the papacy and no wish at all for major quarrels with it. It steadily became frequent practice for the English Crown to turn a very ready ear to their subjects protests against Roman exactions, but to employ them only as useful cards in their own unending diplomatic game with the papacy.

Criticism
and
Complacency

c.1340 - c.1500

CHAPTER 9

DIOCESE AND PARISH

The Bishops and their Staffs

THE CROWN AND EPISCOPAL APPOINTMENTS

In the final phase of our period the process by which the English episcopate was chosen was a good deal more complex than it appears at first sight. As has been already noted, normally choice was settled by papal provision, but this by no means meant that those candidates ultimately chosen were largely papal nominees. Theoretically, of course, the papacy was in the strongest position since its legal right to command in this matter was undisputed. But in practice its authority was severely restricted by three factors. The first of these was the potency of royal power in England, caused partially by the powerful machinery of government which had early developed here. The second was the unobtrusive growth of something closely akin to a national feeling which now manifested itself very visibly in contemporary anti-papal protests. Thirdly, there was the considerable weakness of the papacy during most of the early part of the period, during which its prolonged and very costly absence from Italy (1309–77) was followed by a most perilous period when no one pope was generally accepted by the states of the West (page 311).

Although it is quite certain that in the last century and a half of our period papal influence over episcopal appointments was far from being considerable, its provision often rubber-stamping royal proposals, it is important not to oversimplify the situation. The immense variety in the size and revenues of English bishoprics, along with local factors such as those extensive powers which made far distant Durham a most potent prince bishop on the German model, and the proximity of wild Celts which made Carlisle no place for gentlemen to live in, makes it most unwise to make very wide generalisations about English episcopal history and not to trust overmuch the uncomprehending clutch of the computer.

When a vacancy in a see had occurred, very often it was quickly followed by a curious and often arduous three-cornered contest between the local chapter, the monarchy and the papacy, the result of which was by no means always predictable, but depended on varying factors. This curious process of selection has comparatively recently been unconvincingly lauded: 'Perhaps nothing did more to maintain the health of the church than the fact that its bishops were selected neither by pope nor king nor chapter alone, but by a series of unedifying compromises between the wishes of all three' (Mac-Farlane). As we shall see, however, the huge proportion of English bishops appointed in these times was very far from being animated by that high pastoral zeal which their office demands, no few of them spending far too much time in fulfilling secular responsibilities. Usually, prospects of the local chapter securing the election of some local personage were not great, though as it normally knew of the vacancy before the Crown or the pope, it could at least start manoeuvring early. In the remote and poorish see of Carlisle the chapter was successful in these times in electing as bishop several members of leading local families. Contemporary Hereford, also far from fashionable, had a number of bishops who were either of monastic origin or careerists who regarded this as a useful rung in the ladder of promotion.

Perhaps partly because of the huge financial pressures produced by England's asinine engagement in the Hundred Years War, from the mid-fourteenth century onwards it became very usual for political factors to dominate English episcopal selections. Thus the mighty office of Lord Chancellor tended to be held by a bishop, though this pluralism mostly came in fairly short bursts of a few years at a time and from 1344 onwards the Lord Privy Seal was frequently bishop of the well-to-do see of Durham. A recent study of the history of the medieval archbishops of York notes that the accession of Alexander Neville (1374) marks the opening of a new epoch in which the old habit of often electing a person previously on the staff of the minster largely disappears, almost all future archbishops being translated from other sees for secular reasons, concluding, 'the spiritual welfare of the diocese of York let alone that of its cathedral church was . . . a very minor consideration in the choice of a new archbishop between 1374 and 1500' (Dobson).

Knowles notes of the period between 1325 and 1425, 'the [episcopal] office was now used to reward servants of the Crown who continued to fill high offices of State and perform important duties which entailed frequent and prolonged absences from the diocese ... Papal provision ... had little or no influence on the character of the bench.' In his classic study of the English Church in the fifteenth century Hamilton Thompson avers, 'no appointment of a bishop, at any rate to the important sees, was made without respect to his possible services to the government.' Thomas Gascoigne, writing in the sixties of the fifteenth century had gone so far as to assert, 'There are three things today that make a bishop in England, the will of the king, the will of the pope or court of Rome and the money paid in large quantities to that court.' Not infrequently no little unedifying horse-trading over such appointments went on between Crown and papacy which sometimes was very prolonged and very expensive and which might ultimately leave stranded some luckless person who had been selected as bishop at an early stage by one of the three elements.

In the fifteenth century the possibilities for Crown manipulation of episcopal appointments were augmented by the ease with which it was now possible to 'translate' a bishop, i.e., move him from one see to another. It was a weapon which could be and now was used by the king to advance a favoured bishop from one see to another which was, in the worldly sense, more desirable, or occasionally to downgrade a bishop no longer in favour by moving him to a lesser sphere of influence.

As a result of this, episcopal appointments in fifteenth-century England were periodically liable to become the prey of manoeuvring by top people. A most striking example of this occurred in 1425 when several sees were vacant and the council of the young king divided the episcopal spoils. It decided to move to the archbishopric of York the bishop of London and not the bishop of Lincoln as the pope had planned, and also to translate the bishop of Worcester to Ely, or to Norwich if the pope wished to push a candidate for Ely. The dean of York should become bishop of London, the bishop of Chichester be translated to Worcester and his see go to an English official engaged at the Roman curia. A friar, whose existence was certain though his name was unknown, should have the thankless task of becoming bishop of Llandaff; similar manoeuvring on the same sort of scale had been seen in 1388. It is impossible not to recognise herein the virtual collapse of that freedom of election which was of one of the main planks of the Gregorian Reform. Lay control was slightly less flagrant than it appears at first sight, since the councillors who took this decision included in their number the archbishop of Canterbury and the bishops of Winchester, London, Durham, Bath and Wells and Worcester, though, of course, they themselves owed their selection to the same system.

Alongside this tendency in episcopal appointments in the latter part of our period understandably went the habit of extensively selecting bishops from the aristocratic levels of society. In the twelfth and thirteenth centuries social origins were not of decisive importance in this connection, but now the growth in power of the English nobility, or rather of a major section thereof, allied with other factors like the long reign of the feeble King Henry VI now played into the hands of the aristocracy. Thus the father of the Thomas Bourgchier, who held the see of Canterbury from 1454 to 1486, had married the heiress of the youngest son of Edward III. Bishop Nevill of Durham (d. 1437) was the uncle of Edward IV and Richard II, whilst Bishop Courtenay of Exeter had no little blue blood. Bishop Beaufort of Lincoln (1398–1404), the twenty-three-year-old son of John of Gaunt and Katharine Swynford was one of several whose conduct inspired presentation of a bill in Parliament seeking to compel bishops to reside in their dioceses and not at court.

But the diocesans were not necessarily devoid of solid virtues. Many of those who ruled in England in the century and a half which preceded the outbreak of the Reformation were intelligent men with no crude moral blemishes, some of quite humble origin, who saw to it that the administration for which they were responsible was effective. Their piety seems largely to have been more than superficial and was often happily conjoined with a sense of the importance of using no scanty part of their wealth to improve social amenities. Thus Bishop Beckington of Wells not only made useful additions to the episcopal palace (including tanks for breeding fish) but established 'a goodly schoole with the Schoole Master logging' and a noble gatehouse. He also refurbished the picturesque Vicars' Close and gave the market place its water supply along with 'troughs, pipes and other necessary engines above and below ground', in return for which the burgesses were to pay an annual visit to his grave and there pray for his soul 'and the souls of all the faithful deceased'.

Existing ecclesiastical apparatus such men used vigorously and well, leaving behind them in the process priceless business records which are the envy of continental medievalists. But their eyes were so firmly fixed on the machine that they had no attention to spare for remedying major outside problems. They never did more than tinker with the problem of removing the gross ignorance of the clergy and laity committed to their charge. Very few of them had any interest in the theological problems which Christianity perpetually generates and as a result they never gave any reasoned consideration to the admittedly extremist views of Wycliffism, but relentlessly drove the movement underground, whence it ultimately re-emerged in power as unconsidered protest movements are apt to do. Above all they mostly failed to appreciate that to be a diocesan bishop in the Church of God is to hold a pastoral office which cannot properly be regarded as anything less than full-time, and must not, as now so often happened, be treated as primarily a social and financial perquisite. 'I am the good shepherd and know my sheep and my own know me,' said Christ. Judged by this test of pastoral care the bishops of late medieval England mostly were dismal failures. Very obvious and reprehensible was the immense drain on episcopal time and thought which the pluralistic position of some of them made inevitable. It is not surprising that so many major ecclesiastical problems were allowed to pile up unchecked in these times, or that of all the English archbishops and bishops who lived in the two centuries before the Reformation, not a single one has captured any great interest from posterity.

THE EPISCOPAL STAFF

The massive burden of administration which confronted most English bishops was very obviously far too much for even strong and skilled shoulders to bear and, as we have seen, there steadily developed a large trained body of officials who were busily and competently engaged in it. New developments now were much more those of extent than of kind. Devolution of episcopal and archiepiscopal duties was extensive indeed and in some areas left the diocesan with very few responsibilities, notably here being the arch-deaconry of Richmond in the archdiocese of York, where by the end of the period almost all episcopal duties capable of delegation were being carried out by the archdeacon and much of the rest by a series of non-diocesan bishops.

Assistant bishops, long little used, came to be extensively employed in the latter part of our period, and were of more than one species. Curious to modern eyes is the fact that no few of them were Irish bishops who had strayed over from the Emerald Isle for reasons far better known to themselves than to the modern histori-ans. Knowles has produced a longish list of such men bred in Irish monasteries who exercised episcopal functions in England in the century after 1350. To these were added assistant bishops who often bore exotic foreign titles such as Selymbria and Chrysopolis, of whom a substantial majority were local members of the mendicant orders, though the older orders were also represented. Their primary concern was to carry out liturgical functions which only those in episcopal orders could perform, notably ordination to the sacred ministry, confirmation and the consecration and re-conciliation of churches and churchyards. The fact that many of them had taken monastic vows meant, of course, that their services might be had very cheaply.

The very heavy administrative duties of a medieval bishop con-tinued to be greatly lightened through delegation of authority to the archdeacons (page 179). By the latter part of our period other officials were active of whom nothing has yet been said. Of these the chief was the vicar-general who, in effect, ran the diocese when the bishop was absent from it, as he so often was by the late fifteenth century. His powers lapsed when his lord and master returned to his nominal habitat, but were resumed when he once more departed. The nature and range of a vicar-general's authority depended on the nature of the official commission he received but the duties tended to be numerous and routine, including collection of episcopal re-venues, supervision of elections of heads of monastic houses, arrange-ments for ordinations and the execution and return of royal writs. Less powerful but employed on business which was related to that of the vicar-general and sometimes overlapping it, was the dig-nitary known as the 'official' or 'official-principal'. His work was primarily judicial, involving the hearing of cases pertaining to the

Annunciation of St Mary in the Newarke at Leicester'. To some degree the place was intended to provide that prestigious place of burial for the founder and his family now fashionable amongst great aristocrats. Very close to his heart was Henry's veneration for the memory of his brother Thomas, earl of Lancaster, whose execution in 1322 had been followed by a quite vigorous cultivation of his memory as a saint of God. 'Such considerations and the uncertainty of his own life amid the tragedy which had overtaken his brother and two of his royal cousins may have prompted him to secure the safety of his own soul and establish a permanent memorial of his house' suggests Hamilton Thompson. At the head of the establishment were a warden and four chaplains who were to have a common frater and dorter. Their round of services were to be shared by two clerks. But to this was added provision for no less than fifty poor and infirm folk to be chosen 'purely and simply for the worship and honour of the Crucified and the glorious Virgin', with five serving women to tend them. In 1345 earl Henry died, to be succeeded by his son Henry, earl of Derby, an immensely celebrated military leader who in 1353 got permission to turn the hospital into a college, its new complement being defined the following year as a dean and twelve canons aided by thirteen vicars, six choristers and three clerks. With them was associated no less than one hundred poor men and women with ten women to look after them.

But the aims of secular colleges varied a good deal. Thus the smallish one set up at Battlefield, near Shrewsbury, in 1409 was primarily concerned with remembering the souls of those who fell in the combat that took place on its site. A small contingent destined to become notable was constituted by the academic secular colleges set up at Oxford and Cambridge in these later times, wherein remembrance of the faithful departed was inextricably combined with the propagation of learning. Of this the most obvious example is All Souls College, Oxford, begun in 1438 by Henry Chichele, archbishop of Canterbury, with the king as co-founder. This was to be not only a chantry for the good of the souls of Henry V, the duke of Clarence and soldiers killed in the French wars as well as for the founder, his relations and all departed Christians, but also a place of study for what were curiously termed 'unarmed clerical militia' who would aid Church and Commonwealth.

It is to be counted to them for righteousness that the English

K

bishops of the period were responsible for the foundation of no small proportion of the earliest colleges of our two ancient universities. At Oxford the colleges of Exeter (1314–15) and Lincoln (1427) both took their names from the diocese of the bishops who had founded them. New College (1369–79) and Magdalen (1448) were both founded by bishops of Winchester; Merton (1266) had been begun by a future bishop of Rochester, whilst the foundations of Brasenose, Christ Church and Corpus Christi, all set up in the first decades of the sixteenth century, owed all or much to episcopal aid. At Cambridge the oldest college was little Peterhouse founded by the bishop of Ely, whilst both Gonville and Trinity Hall venerate as founder William Bateman, bishop of Norwich. In such places is still maintained the medieval tradition of regular public remembrance of 'our founder and benefactors departed out of this present life'. It is worth noting in passing that these grand secular colleges, like the secular cathedrals, in certain major respects bore certain very close resemblances to the monasteries set up in early days. Their elaborate round of worship was fundamentally the same even if somewhat less exacting, those who led it were equally bound to celibacy and the setting displayed the same passion for visual splendour and elaborate chant. But the degree of common life in secular colleges was, of course, much less marked, since its members could mix fairly freely with the outside world, could own private property and could delegate much of their liturgical obligations to subordinates.

PLURALISM AND ABSENTEEISM

Pluralism, in the ecclesiastical as distinct from the philosophical sense, denotes the simultaneous tenure of more than one benefice by a cleric, such pluralists mostly being in priest's orders. Under certain modern conditions, such as a shortage of clergy or inadequate endowment of small parishes, pluralism is a legitimate usage, provided the benefices in question are near enough to each other to be served by the individual who holds them. But mostly medieval pluralism took a different shape, owing to the very different social circumstances. It was usually not pastoral necessity which dictated it, but those immense social pressures of the times which, as we have seen, diverted ecclesiastical revenues from the purpose for which they were primarily intended to various other needs of which by no means all were praiseworthy. Such pressures had early led to extensive appropriations of benefices to existing ecclesiastical institutions, the which, on the whole, can be justified by what was often real financial need of the latter and the fact that adequate provision was made for paying the clergy whose income was thus docked (page 174). But other pluralism was very often much more difficult to defend since it seemed to some degree to work on the principle that 'to him that hath shall be given', and largely benefited an arbitrary minority of seculars a proportion of whom took the income but paid inadequate attention to the spiritual responsibilities.

Western canon law very properly sought to forbid anyone holding simultaneously two benefices which involved the 'care of souls' (*cura animarum*), principally since it was expected that the holder of a benefice would live on the spot and carry out his official responsibilities. However, provided a man had the means to pay a suitable deputy to undertake his duties (and the services of such deputies were very easily to be had at cut rates in late medieval times, as in Hanoverian England) and was authorised to do this, it was at least arguable that this absenteeism whether by a pluralist or non-pluralist was not always reprehensible. For example, the lack of any effective system of grants for education at universities led ecclesiastical authorities from the thirteenth century onwards to dispense chosen clergy from residence in their benefice for a specified period so as to allow them to engage in study there, provided adequate arrangements were made for fulfilment of their pastoral duties. This door was also opened more widely by those with less laudable intentions—notably by diocesan officials and royal servants who now frequently acquired a number of benefices which, it seemed to them, natural and proper to utilise to augment their income. Understandably, but unfortunately, the Roman court became increasingly ready to grant necessary dispensation or legal exemption from the law to hold posts in plurality, with the result that those with the right connections might hold a whole series of ecclesiastical offices concurrently. Unsurprisingly therefore, pluralism became a very obvious target for criticism in the English Church in the latter part of our period and one which it was next to impossible to curb under contemporary circumstances. As has recently been remarked, 'once dispensations [for pluralism] were allowed at all, the way was open to all kinds of abuses, they might be used, as a gift of a benefice might be used, as a source of patronage, a means of making friends of "the mammon of unrighteousness". The problem of checking non-residence without forbidding all dispensations was almost insoluble.'

But interested parties sought to defend it. A fourteenth-century pluralist, commissary to the bishop of Hereford and holder of a rectory, five prebends and a portion, urged complacently that an industrious and educated person (a category in which he certainly included himself) could look after two or even ten churches better than some others look after a single one, so that it is better for a parish to have a good incumbent at a distance than a bad or indifferent one on the spot—a judgment which, of course, ignores the advantage of having a good one on the spot. A powerful social sentiment working to the same end was the deep-rooted feeling that top people had some right to subsidise their staff through appointments to benefices, which was widespread in our period. As has recently been pointed out, in 1529 an Act seeking to deal severely with pluralism and absenteeism was passed, but exempted from its operation chaplains of the king, of his councillors, of nobles and of prelates. Long before, this 'all men are equal but some are more equal than others' approach had led even the Roman court to make similar concessions.

The total picture of pluralism in our period will not be drawn until much more research thereon has been done, but we have a very revealing cross-section of the situation in England in 1366, though this does not include the dioceses of York, Durham and Carlisle. It is recorded that the total number of clergy who at this date held more than one benefice was 551. Of these, 450 held parochial benefices and it seems probable that about 245 were resident, the rest constituting, of course, a very minor proportion of the 9000 and more incumbents of the day; nearly all these pluralists were rectors, not vicars. In the return were twenty-six chantry priests of whom no less than seventeen were attached to St Paul's but held also local city rectories, an arrangement at which it is hard to cavil, since their total income was not great and the duties of this double employ were easily compatible. Much more important a group was the graduate pluralists whose total seems to have been 167. At the top of the tree was a small group of men whose financial problems were now nil, headed by the dean of Lincoln who had raked in a collection of emoluments totalling no less than £403 6s. 8d. He was followed by the Italian papal nuncio with just over £300 and William of Askeby, the Chancellor of the Exchequer. However, a very considerable proportion of this graduate group were quite ordinary clerics with quite ordinary incomes; in many cases they were not even strictly pluralists since they held 'expectatives' which gave no benefice at once but promised one in the vague future. As is to be expected, graduate pluralists were numerous in the regions of Oxford and Cambridge.

As to the rest, their income varied immensely, being headed by the greatest pluralist of the century, William of Wykeham, bishop of Winchester from 1367 to 1404, and for a time Lord Chancellor of England, who accumulated preferment to the staggering amount of £873 6s. 8d. with the archdeaconry of Lincoln worth £350 heading a dozen other appointments. Near to him was another civil servant whose income was drawn from twelve posts, with three other leading royal officials following him not far behind. The hard facts make it very clear that English pluralism at this time was very far from being rampant, affecting as it did only a small proportion of appointments. It is equally obvious that very little of it went to papal officials but a very great deal to major servants of the Crown, whose need for it can scarcely be regarded as desperate.

A form of disguised absenteeism is to be found in late medieval times behind the creation of a category of minor clergy who were appointed to deputise for the holders of cathedral and collegiate prebends. These came to be known as 'vicars choral' since their principal function was to sing services due to be taken by the canons of the church to each of whom one was allotted. By now in such places, and especially in the great secular cathedrals of York, Lincoln and Salisbury, all hopes of maintaining a full common life for the canons of the place had ship-wrecked, largely because the value of the appointments made them major prizes for royal nominees of various kinds who increasingly came to regard them as largely mere financial assets, whose revenues they pocketed but whose functions they did not fulfil in person. Thus at the end of the fifteenth century Lincoln Cathedral had fifty-eight canons each with a prebend, a seat in the chapter and a stall in the choir but there were seldom more than five in residence. Few of the vicars choral were likely to be idle, the more so since not infrequently a resident canon might be absent elsewhere for good and sufficient reason, such as chapter business or the care of his outside ecclesiastical duties connected with the prebend. In such places a major distinction came to be drawn between canons largely non-resident and those largely resident who were rightly rewarded with additional emoluments, which in some cases were very considerable indeed. It is arguable that the largest secular cathedrals of England, at least, were mostly heavily over-staffed and no few of their leading dignitaries grossly overpaid.

SECULAR CLERGY

As we have seen, the total number of parishes was in the region of 9500. A limited number of these were held in plurality which would decrease the total of their incumbents, but to this total must be added holders of benefices without care of souls, notably major cathedral appointments and prebends of lesser collegiate churches, though here pluralism was particularly evident. Such beneficed clergy were, however, certainly very greatly outnumbered by those without benefices, who may be divided into three main categories[*]:
(i) Clergy today termed *curates*, who gave full-time assistance to the parish priest in places that could afford their services. They must have been most rare in the many tiny parishes to be found in plenty in England and their total number is not ascertainable.
(ii) *Chantry priests* were appointed to serve a permanently endowed chantry, either alone or with a companion or companions. Though mostly they had not security of tenure in law, in practice they were likely to be retained unless their conduct was found unsatisfactory. The total of these is uncertain, but at the end of our period certainly ran well into four figures. Some might have tenure for life, others for a fixed period of time.
(iii) *Household chaplains* were a miscellaneous class, many of whose members were part of the households of the top strata of society—royalty, baronage and the squirearchy. Some at least probably had

---

[*] Contemporary documents often fail to distinguish clearly the various categories and their relative numbers are very far from clear.

little or no pastoral work but no little administration. To their numbers we must add the smallish number of priests who served as chaplains to houses of nuns.

(iv) There also existed what was probably a very large class of clergy in priests' order who took whatever paid employment they could find, the which was often of a very temporary nature. (It is tempting to call these clergy stipendiaries, though this is not the contemporary sense of this word.) Most lived largely by saying Masses for that considerable section of the deceased laity who could not or would not afford the endowment necessary to acquire a priest to celebrate for their souls in perpetuity, for there is no doubt that by the end of our period provision had been made for many thousands of these requiem Masses. The wills also make very clear that many of these clergy had a reputation which fell below standard. Frequently testators making provision for these memorials go out of their way to stress that executors shall choose respectable clergy, clearly implying that many of those available were not so. Thus random samples show insistence on this in such terms as 'a priest of good name and demeanour', 'an honest priste that canne synge both plane song and prik song', 'an honest prest of sade and honeste conversacion', 'weldisposed prestes of the most honeste and clene conversacion'. Similarly, in 1408 a noble provided for thousands of Masses 'to be said for my soul in all possible haste by the most honest preests that can be found.' Clearly bequests for such huge numbers of private Masses to be quickly said must have pre-supposed the existence of very large numbers of non-parochial clergy whose income might be uncertain but who were highly unlikely to collapse from overwork.

In this connection another curious fact is to be noted. Eminently sensible canon law provided that a bishop should not ordain anyone to the higher grades of the ministry without what was technically termed a 'title', a word which in this context denoted adequate financial provision for him after ordination. These titles came to be three main types, (i) nomination to a benefice, which, of course, carried with it an official income; (ii) private means or 'patrimony', by which the individual could, if need be, support himself financially; (iii) membership of a monastic house, either through profession as a member of the community or in some allied capacity such as chaplain. It has recently been pointed out that certain of our later lists often display a most remarkable number of ordinations officially made for minor establishments highly unlikely to require such extensive help for their personal use. Thus the minuscule priory of Chipley issued no less than thirty titles in the period 1413–37, and the minor Gilbertine house at Marmont, eleven between 1446 and 1471. But the prize is surely taken by the hospital of St Giles in Norwich, which provided no less than 770 titles for ordination between 1413 and 1486. It was largely poorish houses which were involved in this practice and there can be little doubt that with it were associated bargains which were designed to circumvent the canon law, such clergy mostly acquiring ordination not so as to serve the house which officially provided them with a title but to join the mighty pool of those we have termed stipendiaries.

THE NUMBER OF CLERGY

Important and interesting to note is the question of the numbers of English clergy in medieval times. What did they total and how many were there in each of the categories into which they divide? For the period before the formation of our episcopal registers there is almost no evidence on most aspects of this problem, and even later the statistical evidence is sporadic and very uneven.

One of the very few major facts of which we are sure is the proportion of beneficed clergy who perished in the Black Death— around 40 per cent in the mighty dioceses of York and Lincoln and almost 50 per cent in Winchester, Exeter, Ely and Norwich. Understandably it has been suggested that half the English clergy died in this unique catastrophe. The degree of recovery certainly varied considerably for several reasons and was set back by other outbreaks in 1361–2, 1369 and 1374. However, some hold that by 1380 there were approximately 30 000 clergy serving a population of almost 1½ million persons over the age of fourteen, as compared with a monastic population of about 10 000, just as it is equally clear that such losses were by no means uniform throughout the land. The catastrophic fall in the civilian population apparently ended a situation wherein very precarious conditions may well have driven men into holy orders as the best available way of making a living, with a resultant drop in the number of ordinations. So, to an unascertainable degree, may the unfriendly criticisms of writers such as Wycliffe, Chaucer and Langland. It is, however, interesting to note that when the tide of recovery set in, the religious orders seem to have benefited from it appreciably more than the collegiate and parish churches and certainly no simple generalisation applies to all areas of the English Church. London produced comparatively few vocations to the priesthood, as did Kent, which in the mid-fifteenth century had acquired a considerable reputation for anti-clericalism, whilst Exeter and Durham had often produced alarmingly few ordinands. On the other hand, in the great diocese of York, ordination figures rose cheerfully and steadily for at least half a century after the Black Death. However, it is not feasible, at least at present, to reconstruct any very elaborate picture of total clerical numbers in the period between the Black Death and the Reformation, or to get any clear idea of the proportion of them which were unbeneficed, though there is no doubt that this was considerable, partly because the passion for private Masses and other clerical responsibilities were so considerable.

THE PROBLEM OF CLERICAL EDUCATION

Few of the major strands of medieval English life are more difficult to unravel than its educational history, which was very uneven and ill-documented, and mostly progressed in ways which often verge on the imperceptible. As we have seen, in the earlier part of our period the English episcopate was certainly conscious of the shortcomings of many of their parish clergy. Their fulminations against them, however, were singularly unconstructive and social factors made any marked progress hard to achieve. Had late medieval England been adorned with the huge and fruitful towns that early studded France and Italy, the country might have made real educational advances, for it was only in towns that there existed that well-to-do and well-endowed bourgeoisie who were prepared to take education seriously. As it was, major obstacles stood in the way of those lads in rural England who might be called to the priesthood. In many areas, notably East Anglia, the multitudinous small villages lacked anyone competent to teach that elementary knowledge of Latin which a clerk must acquire. In our own day such an attainment can be easily self-taught with the aid of books, but in medieval England books were available to few and were inordinately expensive. Slow communication, too, might prevent a youth in a rural area acquiring daily education in his nearest town. As a result, theologically-instructed folk were virtually non-existent in most parts of England and very thin on the ground elsewhere.

But there is no doubt that the standard of education of the English clergy certainly rose during the fourteenth and fifteenth centuries even if, as was unavoidable, the process got much further in some areas than in others and was very limited. Two factors were major influences here—careful production of literature specially written to spell out to the parish clergy of the wide responsibilities of their work and indicate how these should be fulfilled, and the growing tendency of at least a useful minority of the clergy to spend some time at the university.

The importance of the provision of manuals on the work for parish priests had now become increasingly clear and, as Pantin points out, their authors are 'a miscellaneous lot, ranging from an archbishop, a university chancellor and a canonist at the Roman curia to a parish priest, an Augustinian canon and two Benedictine monks.' In the thirteenth century instruction on these matters had tended to be given somewhat curtly in official episcopal or archiepiscopal directives, the most influential of these being an elaborate document drawn up by Pecham, the friar archbishop of Canterbury, and approved by a provincial council at Lambeth in 1281, which became the standard work on the subject for the area and was utilised later in a similar pronouncement for the province of York. A notable feature of it was its insistence that four times a year there was to be expounded to the people in their native tongue the Creed, the Ten Commandments of the Old Testament and the Two Commandments of the New, the seven works of mercy, the seven virtues, the seven vices and the seven sacraments.

In the fourteenth century this approach to reform tended to take a less official form, consisting to some extent of episcopal circular letters on particular matters and very much more influential systematic manuals of instruction for parish clergy, largely of non-episcopal origin, which certainly supplied a 'long-felt want'. Amongst the chief of these were 'the priest's eye' (*Oculus Sacerdotis*) of the Yorkshireman, William of Pagula, who died *c*. 1332. Like so much similar literature it paid special attention to the hearing of confessions whose spiritual utility was now being appreciated, showing, for example, how to evaluate the degree and nature of culpability in a particular case: 'the priest ought to enquire of the penitent if he was drunk, why he got drunk, whether perchance because he did not know the power of wine, or because of guests, or because of an exceeding thirst coming upon him.' Special advice for expectant mothers is included, together with a long list of offences which entail excommunication and include, oddly to modern eyes, breaking the terms of Magna Carta. A great list of pastoral duties follow, involving elaborate inventories of forms of misbehaviour and followed by fairly detailed doctrinal matters and finally some discussion of the theoretical and practical problems in connection with each of the sacraments.

But the best-known writer in this field was John Mirk, an Austin canon of the lonely priory of Lilleshall (d. *c.* 1400). His 'Instructions for Parish Priests' is written in English verse and of its 1934 lines over half is concerned to give detailed advice on hearing confessions. Much more substantial was his 'Priest's Handbook' (*Manuale Sacerdotis*). Its five books give detailed consideration to the character a priest should have, his daily behaviour, his conduct of services, especially of the Mass, table manners and old age, concluding comprehensibly with advice on 'the priest's supper and bedtime', an allegorical discussion of the nightingale, and 'a meditation on Heaven and Hell'. To these Mirk added the 'Festiall', an elaborate array of sermons in English planned around the liturgical year. Various other writers of the period worked to the same end and there can be no doubt that by the end of our period for some time there had been circulating a considerable number of practical manuals which did a very great deal to raise the standards of life and work of the parish clergy, and were reinforced by a variety of other theological writings.

For the history of the connection between the universities and parish clergy seeking to better themselves there, useful material exists but a synthesis of this is not yet in print. From the thirteenth century we have signs of interest shown notably in efforts to provide the necessary cash for clerical sojourns in universities, but the amounts were in very short supply. We find bishops ordering clerks to receive the minor but useful emoluments and also allowing an incumbent leave of absence from his parish for a specified period in order to study at the university, provided adequate provision was made for his pastoral duties to be carried out by a deputy, a practice which would, of course, only be feasible where the benefice in question was fairly well provided. It is interesting to note that later at both Oxford and Cambridge there were those who sought to have studies supported by papal provisions to benefices which might not be princely but were much better than nothing, so that limitation of provisions was not universally welcomed by this section of society.

Though, as we shall see, the early colleges of Oxford and Cambridge had only very small communities, steadily economic progress in England amongst other factors made at least temporary residence there none too difficult and long before the end of our period graduate clergy in fairly large numbers were to be found, no small incentive towards acquiring such status being provided by the fact that it opened a major door to promotion in both Church and State. In this connection it is worth noting that canon and civil law had a much higher market value than theology and were therefore much more widely studied.

Steadily throughout the fifteenth century we find signs of private individuals providing financial support for university students, both during their lifetime and after it, in times when without doubt learning was steadily growing in prestige and the rewards it brought in its train being very real. Thus a graduate would now stand a very good chance indeed of being one of that happy minority of secular clergy who acquired a benefice and might even become a pluralist, whilst a man's chances of employment by the king or some other top person were considerably improved by graduate status. It is, however, to be noted that many graduate holders of preferment were not primarily engaged in pastoral work, such responsibilities being in varying degree passed on to hired clergy.

We have various signs of the way this wind was blowing. No less than a fifth of the clergy instituted to benefices in the diocese of Canterbury in the time of Archbishop Bourgchier (d. 1486) were graduates and almost the same proportion is found in the diocese of Norwich in the early decades of the sixteenth century. Almost two centuries earlier in distant Cleveland and East Riding 22 per cent of rectories and 11 per cent of vicarages were filled by graduates. In the diocese of Lincoln, most of which would not have any special charm for graduates, by the early sixteenth century they were presented to 11½ per cent of the livings, three times more than a hundred years before. In London where, as always, a man could meet so many of the right people, by 1522 of fifty-two incumbents no less than six held doctorates and thirty-three master's degrees, and even amongst the unbeneficed clergy one in six were graduates, a proportion which was very certainly far above the national average (at this time not a single one of the latter was to be found in the lovely but isolated archdeaconry of Richmond). However, it is to be remembered that very often these graduates did not reside, being well able to afford to instal a clerical deputy whilst they occupied themselves with royal or ecclesiastical administration. Besides the graduates with their master's degree or even doctorate, there were those on lower rungs of the academic ladder, including some who had only been able to spend at the university a small fraction of the time desirable, but who would none-the-less help to heighten the level of clerical and, indirectly, of lay education.

An allied sign of progress in the Church life of England in late medieval times is provided by the steady growth of sermon literature in the fourteenth and fifteenth centuries, whose interest and importance is a good deal greater than might appear at first sight, not least for students of contemporary social history. However, a good deal more study is needed before we can reconstruct with precision the extent to which preaching influenced the life of the man in the street. The steady if slow and uneven rise in the level of English literacy was clearly a major cause of this, and it is possible that the immense and unexpected theological conflagration started by Wycliffe gave it additional strength. Wycliffe had quoted with approval the good Bishop Grosseteste's dictum, 'the excellent and greatest Work of Mercy is the preaching of God's Word'. It is interesting to note that Alexander Carpenter, the author of the mighty *Destructorium Viciorum*, writing about 1450, notes incidentally that 'now, in many places there is greater abundance of preaching of the Word of God than was customary before our time.' But there is no doubt whatever that though the clergy were theologically certainly better educated than the laity, the standard of learning which most of them had reached at the end of our period was by modern standards grossly inadequate. Only with the advent of printing and the great theological controversy generated by the Reformation did the standard of clerical education rise markedly. However, for the clergy's pastoral work enthusiasm is more important than education and there is no reason to doubt the existence of this, though its extent is incapable of assessment.

CHAPTER 10

THE MONASTIC FINALE

THE MONASTIC POPULATION

ALMOST the only spectacular development in the history of the English monasteries in the two centuries which immediately preceded the outbreak of the Reformation was the dramatic decrease in their population. Of this, much the major cause was the celebrated Black Death, a most deadly outbreak of bubonic plague which swept westward through Europe devastating England in the years 1348–9 and was associated with a few lesser but not unimportant outbreaks, of which that of 1362–3 was the most baneful. Statistical information on their combined effects are by no means as full as is desirable, but there is good reason to believe that monasteries suffered particularly severely, partly because their tightly organised common life made the spread of infection so likely once it had arrived. Almost certainly, however, the mortality was uneven, Cistercian monasteries largely isolated from society being much less likely to suffer from it than busy houses of friars set in towns with whose inhabitants they were wont to freely mingle.

The monastic population of England on the eve of the arrival of the Black Death appears to have been in the region of 17 500, and it has recently been estimated that this number was almost halved by the plague, with the mendicants being the most heavily hit. Only in very few cases have we statistics to illustrate this decline, but those there are display its seriousness. At Meaux Abbey in 1249 there were sixty monks and ninety lay brethren; totals which by 1349 had fallen to forty-two and seven respectively. In 1380–1 there were as few as twenty-nine monks and five lay brethren and in 1393 twenty-eight monks but no lay brethren. (The slump at the end of the century was obviously chiefly due to the fall of the birthrate earlier, but economic factors may well have done much to eliminate lay brethren in the order.) Certainly the decrease was of proportions utterly unparalleled before or since. It is likely that because of it the English monastic population dropped to a figure somewhere in the region of a mere 8000, but had risen to about 9500 by the opening of the new century, and had attained a figure of about 12 000 a century later.

The effects of this mortality on monastic life obviously varied immensely. Thus a mighty Benedictine abbey with fifty or sixty members could lose half its personnel and still be capable of carrying on its elaborate routine of work and worship, but a minuscule house of Austin canons might be totally or almost totally wiped out by the death of a mere handful of brethren. We may note in passing the problem created by the extensive buildings possessed by a community greatly reduced in size. Inevitably under such circumstances there followed much architectural alteration. In no few Cistercian monasteries, as at Fountains and Furness, the mighty lay brothers' quarters seem to have been divided up and put to other uses, and at Coggeshall, as elsewhere, pious outsiders seem to have been accorded additional accommodation within the monastic precinct. In some cases, as at the little Augustinian abbey of Creake, the church was now found intolerably large and the brethren walled off part of it. The sight of a mere handful of brethren seated in a mighty choir must have been depressing and not uncommon in smaller houses by the end of our period.

Most important was the difficult question of recruitment which arose in the decade after the Black Death. To what extent, if at all, should one relax the entrance standards for new members in order to rebuild the numbers of the community? This question is a perennial one with voluntary organisations, as youth leaders of today know well, and we have very little factual information to show us how it was answered by the monastic authorities of the time, though it is worth remembering that, in those cases where the number of the community had sunk below its official minimum it must have been especially difficult to be strong-minded enough to proceed cautiously in the matter.

Later evidence suggests that the overall standard of the monastic intake here did sink appreciably, though for this change the monastic mortality was only one major factor. It is quite likely that the very deep-rooted admiration for the Augustinian and Benedictine way of life which had been so remarkably strong in the twelfth century was on the decline, and that there was now beginning to gather way the idea that most monasteries ought to be engaged actively in contemporary society, as the huge proportion of them in Western Christendom came to be from Tridentine times onwards. There possibly came into existence that horrid vicious circle wherein to some degree attractive folk shunned entrance to monastic life because it seemed unattractive but it could not cease to be unattractive until attractive folk did enter it.

THE DECREASED NUMBER OF MONASTIC HOUSES

A very novel feature of English religious history in the two centuries before the Dissolution was the process whereby a fairly considerable number of independent monastic foundations were either totally suppressed or down-graded to the rank of a mere cell of some greater establishment, a loss offset only to a very small degree by a small trickle of miscellaneous new monastic foundations. The latter half of the fourteenth century saw the establishment of the small Cistercian abbey of St Mary Graces in London (a very un-Cistercian location) and of one or two houses of Franciscan nuns, whilst unexpectedly there were sudden signs of interest in the Carthusian order with its very austere regime. This very small body lived an eremetical life with more private than common prayer, and was the only monastic order in England whose members from the first lived in separate cells (of which some evocative remains may yet be seen in their ruined priory of Mount Grace near Northallerton). The mother-house of the order was the Charter-house or Chartreuse, near Grenoble, founded as long ago as 1084. The first English house was that at Witham set up in 1178, which gained no little prestige through its most saintly third prior, the saintly Hugh who became bishop of Lincoln in 1186 and was canonised in 1220. No other house was established here in the next hundred years, but, for reasons hard to elucidate, no less than six came into existence between 1342 and 1414. Their very exacting way of life was never relaxed, so that the order could claim it was 'never reformed because never deformed'. The London Charter-house begun in 1371 by the great soldier Walter de Manny (whose body was discovered intact on the site after World War II) was much beloved in early Tudor times. However, the final total of new monastic foundations in England during the last part of our period was quite minute.

On the eve of the Black Death English monasteries numbered about 1000, a figure which had dropped to about 900 a century and a half later. It is noteworthy that the losses were very unevenly spread. The shrewd Cistercians having, from the first, insisted on having sizeable and carefully sited convents suffered not at all, nor did the houses of mendicants though certain of their new foundations did not take root because of local opposition to them. Much the major sufferers were minor houses of Benedictines and Austin canons. Inevitably such places lived much too dangerously. An isolated interval of misbehaviour or inefficiency might ruin a house's reputation or its finances, a visitation of plague carry off all or almost all of its brethren.

Because of such factors, some dozen and a half English houses of Austin canons faded out or became cells. They included Alnesbourne and Peterstone which had suffered seriously from both flooding and the plague, Spinney where life had been upset by 'pestilences, barrenness and negligence of the priors', Chipley where had come impecuniosity and ruined buildings, Selbourne which in 1484 was said to have a prior but no brethren, Creake where in 1506 it was reported that the abbot had died leaving no brethren, and Cold Norton (1507) where half a century earlier there had been but two brethren of whom one was prior and the other decrepit. Ten more houses of the order, including several of more substantial stature, were to be included in those which, with papal permission (1524), Wolsey was to sweep away to provide endowments for his new educational establishments at Ipswich and Oxford. It is worthy of note that until his project got under way, very strict official investigation normally preceded the suppression of any independent monastery. In this its spiritual and financial position was fully investigated, and if change was needed the place was often down-graded to become a cell of a larger and usually local house. Wolsey's mass suppression of houses without this safeguard and the transference of their wealth entirely to educational purposes constitutes a major novelty.

A similar but substantially larger monastic suppression in England occurred in these times for quite different reasons and involved the 'alien priories' which, as we have seen, were monastic establishments in England under the authority of foreign houses, almost all being, for very obvious reasons, Norman. Their variation in size and status was considerable, some being conventual though mostly not very large in size, but others nothing more than isolated estates which added something to the revenue of the mother-house and were often run by a single bailiff or an isolated member of the community. Many of these pertained to Benedictine houses which had no common organisation so that when problems arose, as they now did, they were inevitably solved in piecemeal fashion.

Their history for some time had been placid enough, but this now changed, primarily through the long intermittent hostilities between England and France which finally culminated in the mighty conflagration of the Hundred Years' War (1338–1453). This put the alien priories in a difficult position for two reasons. Firstly because, like the Cluniac houses, they normally sent to their mother-houses regular payments, a practice which was clearly now open to criticism as providing aid for the enemy. Secondly, the fact that some of the personnel of the priories were French inevitably posed something of a security problem which, likewise, without being massive at least looked undesirable in an England where national feeling was now intensifying.

Though the amount of money they sent to France was small and such French brethren as there were showed little interest in treasonable activities, the alien priories inevitably inspired crude hostility. In 1289 transmission of money abroad was forbidden, and soon they were put in charge of government officials and various restrictions were placed on their foreign inmates, measures later renewed. As we have seen, Cluny was the mightiest Benedictine house this side of the Alps. It had in England now no less than thirty-eight houses of which eleven were quite big, the rest being dependent priories or cells with what was the stock complement of three or four brethren. To avoid the problems now created, certain of the smaller Cluniac houses bound themselves to expensive financial tribute to the Crown, but larger ones found the simplest solution to the problem was to secure English legal status by obtaining a charter of denization which *inter alia* terminated their obligation to send money across the Channel. Between 1351 and 1407 all the eleven major Cluniac houses in England took this step. From 1419 to 1464 a local vicar-general was put in charge of a now largely independent Cluniac province and from 1490 onwards all the Cluniac houses in England, along with exempt Benedictine ones, were put under the visitatorial jurisdiction of the archbishop of Canterbury.

A rather bad second in importance to Cluny in the matter of possessions in England was the noble abbey of Bec which in Lanfranc and Anselm had given England two gifts of very great price. It had useful daughter-houses at Stoke-by-Clare and St Neot's as well as no less than forty manors, in several of which small communities of monks were installed. These possessions suffered severely from the Anglo-French wars in one way or another, and after the middle of the fifteenth century links with the mother abbey had effectively distintegrated.

The rest of England's alien priories were much fewer in number than used to be thought and now met variegated fates. By the end of the fourteenth century there were not more than forty such places maintaining a conventual life, of which almost half were of reasonable size. No few of the latter had the will and the means to obtain denization. Others, along with the various small properties where no conventual life was established, tended to go a different way, being rented out or sold to the highest bidder, payment to the French mother-house concerned being promised after the end of hostilities. In 1414 Parliament, hyper-sensitive over the enemy, got the king to agree that all foreign monks should be ejected and alien monastic estates hitherto held by the Crown be retained by it, with the farmers thereof having the right to purchase them. This was largely done, though conventual priories mostly escaped this net. The king now promised compensation to the owners and arranged to transfer this confiscated property for the endowment of monasteries, colleges and churches. The first undertaking never became operative, but after some delay most of the confiscated property largely passed to ecclesiastical or educational corporations. This switching of monastic endowment to the cause of literacy is the first major example of a new tendency which Wolsey was to follow and seemed natural and laudable enough in times when the import- ance of education was being increasingly realised. It is to be noted that there now occurred none of the massive spoliation of church wealth for grossly secular purposes which was to be seen in Western Europe at various later stages, so that comparison of these sup- pressions with the Dissolution of the Monasteries under Henry VIII is not rewarding.

The Older Orders

Although the total number of English monasteries shrank so markedly in the century and a half which followed the Black Death this cannot be regarded as a major catastrophe since so many of the establishments involved were very minor institutions whose loss was not very regrettable. What of those which remained? Everything goes to show that the huge majority of them pursued that undramatic tenor of life which is the norm in established Christian institutions, then as now seldom providing sensational news for the outside world.

THE BENEDICTINES

As we have seen, there were immense differences in the size and revenues of English Benedictine houses which were not paralleled in the other contemporary monastic orders and this makes it impossible to give a precise bird's eye view of their history in these times. The matter which was of most general interest to them was the question of the observances by which they were to regulate their way of life. For various reasons, including the lack of any despotic machinery such as that so early evolved by the Cistercians, this matter was perennially liable to attract attention. A new phase in its history had opened in 1336 when Pope Benedict XII promulgated new constitutions for the order. These, as was usual in such matters, utilised a good deal of older material and though far from useless were not very inspiring but had 'no dynamic ideas' (Knowles).

For England a single general chapter was now ordered to replace the separate ones for North and South. Certain concessions over eating meat were made despite the deep-rooted tradition in favour of 'abstinence' (i.e. abstaining from the use of flesh) and limited use permitted of separate cubicles for sleeping instead of the traditional common dormitory, both of which seemed rather shocking innovations to conservatives but have now long been accepted as perfectly respectable. These regulations like a good many other medieval ones were framed over-optimistically, so were less effective than was hoped, but were by no means without value. The new constitutions by now covered every matter in detail and on several occasions later English general chapters sought to consolidate and augment their work. The acts of these English general chapters are fairly considerable in bulk but contain a good deal of indecisive action and very little of major interest to those not monastically minded. Very forward-looking were the papal regulations which sought to link the order firmly with the universities, though this idea was not new and for financial and other reasons met with only partial success.

As early as 1286 Durham set up at Oxford a little house of studies —Durham College—which Bishop Hatfield reorganised almost a century later to serve eight student monks and eight seculars from the province of York. What was rather optimistically hoped would be a general house of study for the order in this university began in 1283 as Gloucester College and this was made the place of study for monks of the southern province in 1291. Various major houses acquired shares of it, including the abbeys of Winchcombe, St Alban's and Ramsey who sported their coats of arms on the wall near the entrance of what later became Worcester College, as may still be seen. In 1331 Christ Church Canterbury founded at Oxford a small place of study named Canterbury College, which was made secular in 1365 but became Benedictine again about 1369. At Cambridge mighty Ely set up a small house of studies in 1321. Another study centre there, Buckingham College, was established by the general chapter in 1428, but was never large.

THE AUSTIN CANONS

As we have seen, the Austin canons acquired more houses in medieval England than any other order, but very few of them were large and far too many of them were dangerously small. It is unfortunate that extant evidence on the size of the communities which served English monastic houses before the Black Death is very scrappy indeed, many statements thereon being conjectural, including no few of those given by Knowles and Hadcock. It is very likely that quite a high proportion of the houses of Austin canons were originally founded for the classic 'full convent' of a superior and twelve brethren and that for a time, at least, they expanded their numbers, though it may be doubted whether many of them doubled this size. Certainly no little variety prevailed. Very few houses of the order rivalled in size major Benedictine abbeys such as those at

Canterbury, where literally dozens of brethren were to be seen in choir. Amongst the largest houses of Austin canons only a few, including Cirencester, Leicester and Holy Trinity Aldgate are known to have had as many as forty brethren. At the other end of the scale, even in the flourishing years before the Black Death, some minuscule establishments were to be found. Latton and Charley each had only three canons, Wymondley and Breedon only five.

Comparatively few houses of the Austin canons stood in fashionable areas (Aldgate, Merton and Waltham being the major exceptions here) and most of the wealthy houses probably owed their financial prosperity largely to estates inherited from the secular foundations which they replaced. The houses were so very widely scattered that their general chapters could not hope to attract the presence of more than a fraction of those theoretically bound to attend. Houses like Hartland tucked away in North Devon or Lanercost standing remotely below the old wall left by the Romans, must normally have lived a life of very great isolation.

The best known house at the end of our period was certainly the house of Our Lady of Walsingham, whose shrine had now established a considerable repute which brought in considerable revenue (see page 371) though the community was never a very large one and its building operations in late medieval times far from spectacular, as witness its very simple gatehouse which contrasts very vividly with the magnificent structures still to be seen at St Osyth and Thornton. In the field of spirituality the order's major claim to fame at this time was the work of Walter Hilton (d. 1396), canon of the unpretentious house of Thurgarton deep in the Nottinghamshire countryside, whose mystical treatises have won permanent respect.

Although the question has not yet been systematically investigated, it seems clear that to the end of their days the medieval Austin canons never engaged in parish work on any substantial scale though it now became more common than before. The larger houses might send a brother or two to one of their livings but this was probably more for financial reasons than anything else, and possibly in some cases to give a particular person a break from monastic routine. But this work was apt to be soul-destroying if it was not brief, because of the intense isolation often involved, and diocesans did not encourage it for this reason. In theory, as we have seen, canons in such places were to have several companions with them, but there is little sign of this rule being greatly observed in practice and indeed no small proportion of the houses of the order lacked the personnel to implement it. In any case, more than a brief break with the full communal life of the monastery was undesirable, though some small financial gain resulted when a parish was served by one of the brethren instead of by a hired secular priest.

The acts of the general chapters of the English Austin canons have not all survived, but do not seem to have been voluminous. A major event already noted was the reception of the new constitutions for their order drawn up at Rome and issued by Pope Benedict XII in 1339. These were given attention at a meeting at Newstead by Stamford in 1341, as was a bill for two hundred florins whose transmission the Roman curia had not overlooked. The new regulations cover some fifty pages of printed text, and display the traditional Roman capacity for systematic coverage of practical problems, albeit without adding thereto any deep analysis of underlying spiritual problems. Medieval clerics being what they were it is not surprising that the problem of combining these constitutions with local observances was accorded a consideration which was dutiful but unhurried. There was little headline news, though in 1404 the general chapter rejoiced at the recent canonisation of Prior John of Bridlington and ordered observance of his feast on 10 October. Thirty years earlier there had been some curious fulmination in chapter against an innovation in the field of footwear, which was held to have affronted the injunction in the *Rule of St Augustine* that dress was not to be *notabilis*.

Pope Benedict's attempts to give a considerable and permanent impetus to the connection between the older monastic orders and universities was accorded only very slow and partial acceptance by the English Austin canons. Their resources of money and manpower were both limited, so that implementation of these imposed considerable strain on them. Further, the houses were mostly in rural areas, where even the supply of teachers of Latin was not always adequate whilst long absence of their brighter brethren at the university imposed a real strain on smallish houses.

Official efforts to get even fairly well-to-do houses of the order to send scholars to the university were met by strong passive resistance, and finding the necessary cash to establish the requisite house of studies was tardy even by medieval standards. The establishment at Oxford of a small college (of St Mary) was begun in 1436 and backed by the king in an epistle sent to the order the following year pointing out firmly that, whereas other orders 'have byen and byen in multitude units and congregat in one place as honesty and perfection requireth of religion' (i.e. monasticism) the Austin canons studying at Oxford were 'dispersid and dividid among seculere pepulle . . . in gret dishoneste and repreve of your sayd religion.' Although some progress was made, as late as 1506 the general chapter was still concerned with raising funds for the project. Lists of houses of the order in trouble for not sending a scholar to Oxford are longish but the fines for this were far too large to be realistic, £30 being a usual figure; when the prior of Newnham was found 'absent from Oxford but present at Cambridge' he was not held to have committed an indictable offence.

The English Premonstratensian houses are the only monastic group whose internal condition at the end of our period is very clearly known. This is because of the vigorous series of visitations of them made by the abbot of Prémontre's commissary in England, Richard Redman (d. 1505) who, after being abbot of Shap, became successively bishop of St Asaph, Exeter and Ely. Knowles points out that ten of the twenty-nine houses concerned he found to be 'entirely and continuously satisfactory', several winning the highest praise. Of the others 'a dozen oscillated between a state of disorder that fell short of disaster and a degree of well-being that failed to reach absolute excellence', whilst in the case of the rest things were unsatisfactory in varying degrees for varying periods. His general conclusion is that 'on the whole it must be said that the white canons, though providing a number of distressing cases of decadence, do not give that extremely painful impression of stagnation and sordid vice that the reader of contemporary black monk and black visitations receives only too frequently.' The Premonstratensians, though not abounding in numbers and animated by no extraordinary fervour, were, on the whole, 'a well-disciplined body of which the members with certain exceptions, lived a tolerably observant life.' Of a number of the houses of regular canons in England the same may well be largely true.

THE INTERNAL LIFE OF MONKS AND
REGULAR CANONS

Invaluable glimpses of the interior life of no few English houses of Benedictines and Austin canons during the later centuries of our period are preserved in the records of contemporary episcopal visitations. As we have seen, the high regard for the monastic life which Christian tradition in East and West had so long maintained imposed on the diocesan bishop the responsibility of periodically checking by official visitation the condition of all the monasteries in his area which were not specifically exempted from this, either through belonging to an exempt order, like those of Cluny, Cîteaux and the friars, or through acquisition of an individual papal privilege. The hopelessly over-large size of no few English dioceses and the manifold pre-occupations of no few bishops prevented such visitations being held with the frequency desirable, and only a fraction of those which were held have left adequate records. But these nevertheless provide a very substantial sample which vividly displays the state of things in various houses of men and women following the Benedictine and Augustinian way of life.

However, such documents require very disciplined interpretation. If much of their text concerns things which went wrong, this is because where things were right this could be and was reported tersely in a mere two words *Omnia bene*—'all is well'. It is further essential to bear in mind that it was not feasible in these times to carry out similarly detailed scrutiny of the lives of the parish clergy, far less of the multitudinous laity, and it is highly improper to assume that in the field of their behaviour 'no news is good news.' It is highly likely that far more clergy than monks infringed the law of celibacy and that the unruliness found occasionally in English cloisters was proportionately much less than that to be found amongst the contemporary laity, not least in northern England.

MONEY PROBLEMS

One fact that stands out very clearly is the existence in monastic England of too many houses, both of men and women, which were far too small to generate a very strong religious life. The complex religious and social obligations of the monastic life required convents with a far larger staff than a mere handful of brethren too often found herein and such small places usually lacked the financial resources needful for such things as that hospitality which was *de rigueur* in these days. Although some of these houses either disappeared or lost their independent status before the Reformation, many others, including no few priories of nuns, lingered on in this unhappy state down to the end.

If the powers that be let so many such minor Benedictine and Augustinian houses maintain their independent existence it was for two main reasons. Firstly, because that almost idolatrous respect for private property which, in later times, threatened such ferocious penalties for quite minor thefts was much alive in medieval times, albeit in more merciful form, and inspired very great unwillingness in later days to upset an existing religious establishment. Secondly, there was an even greater unwillingness of contemporaries to terminate the arrangements for those prayers for their souls to which the founders of the twelfth and thirteenth centuries attached such importance. The inevitable result of this was that down to the eve of the Dissolution many areas of the garden of English monasticism never acquired that well-pruned and well-weeded quality so necessary for great fertility but suffered from harmful overgrowth and under-nourishment.

However, the menace to monastic virility caused by poverty was in some ways less pernicious than that produced in those few dozen monasteries (mostly Benedictine) which, as already stated, from an early date acquired far more wealth than they were ever likely to require for their reasonable needs and had adopted a rather easy-going life. This was one of several major factors which accounted for the rise of the mendicant orders and in the latter part of our period was much too evident in a few dozen English houses of the order.

On the eve of its suppression, at a time when a parish priest lived on a few pounds a year, Westminster Abbey had an income of £3470 with a convent of only about forty monks. Even when we deduct its inevitably heavy running expenses it is clear that the outside world could not conceivably regard the place as an exhibiter of poverty in any reasonable sense, even if surplus revenues were partially used for social purposes, notably the provision of artistic treasures of various kinds, which contemporary opinion certainly much venerated. In 1394–1400 an elaborate silver reredos was made for Canterbury Cathedral at the truly stupendous cost of £3428 and though it is unlikely that contemporaries were shocked by this, it made it very clear that the house was not indigent. Its purchase of an inn in the town (presumably as an investment) for £867 14s. 4d. must have given the same impression, even though at times the cathedral was no stranger to debt.

There can be no doubt that financial arrangement of the affairs of a large Benedictine abbey was apt to be something of an accountant's nightmare, at times oscillating wildly between great indigence and great affluence. Prior Henry of Eastry found Canterbury Cathedral in debt to the tune of almost £6000 at the time of his accession (1284) but by the time of his death thirty-seven years later had cleared this off and spent £21 000 on the church. Abbot Langham (1349–62) found Westminster £2500 in debt at his accession and had to sell off some of its valuables to meet the expenses of his accession. It is impossible to read sympathetically the *Rites of Durham* without perceiving what an immense force for social and religious good was this great cathedral priory. But it is also difficult to avoid suspecting that living standards therein were a good deal higher than those of the local townsfolk. Thus at meals in the refectory the monks daily drank from 'the Grace Cup . . . largely and finely edged about with silver and double gilt with gold' and each monk had his own mazer of exactly the same type. Under such a régime the quiet delight to be had from a simple life-style which monasticism must proclaim if it is to be true to itself was not visible.

Associated with this superfluity of the things of this world was the tendency for individual members of the convent to have personal belongings. Against what it terms 'this most baneful vice' the *Rule of St Benedict* (read regularly in medieval houses of the order) fulminated with exceptional force—'very specially is this vice of private ownership to be cut off from the monastery by the roots . . . let not anyone presume . . . to have anything as his own, not anything at all, since indeed it is not permissible for them to keep either body or will in their own power.' But in several ways this obligation was breached. By the fifteenth century it had become quite common for bequests to be made to monastic inmates, even Cistercians. Very often these were very small sums of cash which are unlikely to have caused much trouble, but much more valuable gifts were made, perhaps chiefly to members of very wealthy houses who, after all,

were likely to have very wealthy friends. The will of John Baret
(1463) of Bury St Edmund's bequeathes a whole string of gifts to
monks of the venerable abbey there, including half a dozen to the
abbot (amongst which was a silver ring and a good purse containing
6s. 8d.), 'my best powder box of silver and a farthing of gold'
went to Dom John Woolpit, and ivory 'tables' with a comb and a
pair of silver gilt spectacles to Dom John Ixnyng, whilst he left 12d.
and a 'pittance' (extra food allowance) of a loaf and a quart of wine
to each monk. Similarly, in 1319 we have mention of 'a rosary of
coral and pearls' which the countess of Pembroke gave to a nun of
the venerable and fashionable house of Shaftesbury.

Very widespread in Western monasticism during the fourteenth
and fifteenth centuries was the custom of individual members of
religious houses being entitled to a private allowance (known as a
peculium). It is unreasonable to regard such things as totally wrong
in principle, but there is a world of difference between the *peculium*
to be found in some religious orders today, which is in effect a
minute sum of money available for very minor and often essential
things, and the very much larger sums common in pre-Reformation
times which in some cases amongst other things were to be used partly as a clothing allowance. Any extensive private possessions were
obviously totally incompatible with that full common life which is
of the essence of Christian monasticism.* Along with this went a
tendency for monastic inmates to have private cubicles, as already
noted, though later experience has shown the provision of such
privacy to be not undesirable. Meals were sometimes not taken in
the refectory as the *Rule* expected, though when one realises that this
last was an enormous room with a lofty roof and totally inadequate
heating arrangements, one can scarcely blame a community, often
much reduced in size, for seeking elementary comfort elsewhere.

ACTION AND CONTEMPLATION

If the problem of what to do about money is perennially a major

---

* Well-to-do testators frequently left a penny or two each to friars or, much
less rarely, to members of older orders who attended their funerals. It is not clear
to what extent this was regarded as personal property and it is to be regretted that
very little is known as to the use made of such cash in times when the range of trifles
available for purchase was very limited indeed.

concern for the sensitive Christian, whether in monasteries or outside them, that of what to do about the outside world is equally demanding. Experience down the centuries steadily made clear that to both of these questions there was no stock answer but a whole series of different responses from which the individual must seek out that one to which he is called. St Clare properly refused direct contact with society, the popes who venerated her equally properly lived in the midst of it.

In its relations with the outside world Western monasticism has repeatedly displayed a remarkable versatility quite unparalleled in Eastern Christendom. Always there has been present the 'contemplative' strain whose followers live apart from the world and seek to influence it by self-sacrifice and prayer, and the 'active' element whose members mix freely in contemporary society. But the relative importance accorded to them by the faithful has varied. Until the arrival of the mendicants the former largely had the field to itself, but today it is very much in the minority. However, it is highly probable that in the later Middle Ages there was slowly developing that change of emphasis which the Counter-Reformation powerfully developed and the nineteenth century further reinforced whereby a very large proportion of monasteries are active, not contemplative, i.e. have some sort of social occupation as a major activity. In the twelfth century admiration for the contemplative form of monasticism was enormous and went very nearly unchallenged. But by the end of our period there are various indications that this form of life was under fire, partly as not being socially valuable. Bishop Oldham (d. 1519), founder of Corpus Christi and a devotee of the new learning exclaimed vigorously, 'Shall we build houses and provide livelihoods for a company of bussing monks whose end and fall we may live to see? No, no, it is meet to provide for the increase of learning and for such as by learning shall do good to church and commonwealth.' To some degree this attitude may have been fostered by the growth of materialism of which there are signs in fifteenth-century England and very clear proofs under Henry VIII. At the time of the Conciliar Movement a Spanish prelate remarked gloomily that whereas his people went to war in the cause of religion the English did so to make money. The growth of economic prosperity in England in the latter part of our period may well have been a major cause of the virtual extinction of lay brethren as a significant element in English monastic life by providing new openings for paid labour.

This decline in the public image of the monastic life must have been to some extent fortified by wild accusations, such as those against the mendicants which we have noted and which thereby reduced the spiritual standards of recruits. This helps to account for the very widespread disregard of two major features of traditional monasticism which were very visible in England, as in most other parts of the West, by the fourteenth century—the strict maintenance of a complex round of worship and strict discipline regarding contacts with the outside world.

There can be no doubt that one of the well-meaning but unfortunate tendencies of Western monasticism in the Middle Ages was an ever-present passion to make its common worship far too unwieldy to be sage. At different stages various attempts were made to curb this process but their net result was not impressive, new accretions tending to replace the old. The main sufferer was the Night Office, with Mattins and Lauds as its core, whose very great length was increased by added elaboration in ritual and music. If attempts at reform were mostly ineffective and half-hearted it was because of the innate conservatism of the times—'those who wish to advance in goodness and monastic perfection ought always to fear transgression of custom', averred the *Observances* of Westminster Abbey. More trouble arose through changed timing of the Night Office, which came to be mostly fixed at midnight, 'thus decisively splitting the night's sleep'. Not having the modern liturgiologists' profound disrespect for past religious experience, the medieval West retained to the end this over-weighty programme, but some houses limited its impact to a degree not ascertainable by working a curious shift system of which there is clear evidence in the larger Benedictine houses of England, where for much of the liturgical year in turns one part of the brethren worked the full liturgical programme, the other a much less demanding one. In small houses things tended to be less organised and too many members of the community absented themselves from choir in irregular fashion.

From our modern vantage point it is at least arguable that this distaste for full attendance at daily worship was to an important extent caused by the over-heavy liturgical burden usual in these days. A modern Benedictine points out, 'medieval religious as a whole retained as the dominating centre of their lives the obligation on each community to perform the liturgy in choir. In sheer quantity of daily liturgy (and, commonly, quantity of it sung to note) the ordinary, even quite small, medieval religious house surpassed the standards of even the most liturgical of modern monasteries and far surpassed the great majority of modern religious houses' (Aveling). Perhaps a slashing of the lengthy liturgical timetable and an augmentation of the time allotted to other aspects of monastic life would have provided a better religious balance.

Another factor behind liturgical slackness was that very major temptation to which medieval monks and regular canons were prone which they termed *accidia* and we call spiritual sloth. Theoretically, members of houses of these orders would mostly be confined to the monastic precinct, only the limited few who had special responsibilities which so demanded it mixing to any degree with the outside world. With no newspapers, TV or radio and conversation with visitors forbidden for all except the strongest reasons the strain produced by this monotonous régime was in perennial danger of being found excessive, and down the centuries the English episcopal visitations produce plentiful examples of relief from this strain being sought in two ways—either by illegal absences from the monastic precinct or by illegal meetings with outsiders within it. Here again modern conditions and modern practice for all except a tiny minority of strict (enclosed) communities tends to be more merciful and temptation to *accidia* less severe.

Two other factors may here be noted. The first of these was the growing tendency in our period (largely due to contemporary social factors) for the head of a large monastery to become a magnate whose daily life was no longer intimately intertwined with that of the community concerned. The *Rule of St Benedict* had ordered, 'let the abbot's table always be with the guests and strangers', though when there were few guests he might 'invite whom he will from among the brethren.' Here it is assumed that the abbot's table was in the monastic refectory. But as time went on, perhaps principally because of the great increase in number of guests and the expansion of other responsibilities, it became increasingly common for the head of a large abbey or priory to have private apartments which adjoined that hall which was in effect a second refectory, the head of the house no longer normally joining in that common life of the community on which such stress had long been laid and from which such strength could be derived. In some few cases, notably at Westminster, the abbot might even reside on some estate belonging to his monastery but well away from it. Walter of Wenlock, abbot of Westminster 1283–1307, has recently been described as 'no more than occasional visitor to the monastery on the greatest feasts or other important occasions', a state of things of which a modern writer claims to be 'if not dictated, it was at least made very natural, by a number of administrative and economic reasons.'

Another trying problem for the monasteries of our period (also non-theological in nature) was the attention the brethren had to give to social obligations, especially those demanded by their patron. Here much the heaviest sufferers were the great abbeys, the most notable example being Westminster Abbey. Through no fault of its own this was separated by nothing more than a wall from the major palace of medieval England and lack of accommodation in the latter was the main reason for repeated invasions of the monastic precinct of which some were of scandalous proportions. Government meetings of various kinds were liable to take place in various parts of the monastery, including those where strict silence and enclosure should have been observed, and the position was made worse by certain parts of the abbey being used for storing Crown property.

At Canterbury Cathedral there were somewhat different problems, notably that which resulted from its steady flow of visitors, no few of whom were of high degree and had to be received with suitable respect whatever the financial repercussions. Stone's chronicle gives us some fascinating glimpses of this unavoidable duty, noting various arrivals of royalty and great magnates from both England and France. The highlight of this time was surely the arrival in 1466 of an assemblage which can safely be regarded as unique, consisting as it did of the patriarch of Antioch, accompanied 'in honour of the King and the kingdom' by four dromedaries and two camels. The chronicler credibly claims that 'this was never seen in England before'; it is to be hoped that the brethren were given full scope to utilise this remarkable opportunity to enlarge simultaneously their knowledge of things ecumenical and zoological which this remarkable equipage made feasible.

It is to be noted that the hospitality, so beloved by St Benedict, was apt to be costly. When the king and queen with their court visited Canterbury in 1333 royal offerings totalled £78 6s. 8d. but against this was to be set the very considerable cost of entertaining them and giving very expensive presents to the royal pair as well as jewels, silks and gloves to lesser members of the party. St Alban's Abbey on a main road and near the capital suffered similarly. Thus during the Christmas season of 1423 it had to put up with the duke and duchess of Gloucester and 300 attendants accommodated in and near the abbey. The lesser houses of course suffered less, but were far from exempt. The finances of the little priory of Lanercost suffered disastrously when for some months Edward I found it a convenient headquarter during his war with the Scots, and even very small houses might find it politic to make gifts to people of local importance.

THE MENDICANT ORDERS

The history of the mendicant orders in the later part of our period is a good deal less clear than that of the Benedictines and Augustinians. This is partly because the mendicant orders were not liable to episcopal visitation and partly because their lack of possessions inevitably meant that they very seldom got involved in lawsuits which so often throw useful side-lights on the history of the older monastic orders. The Austin friars are the only mendicant orders whose history in England has in the latter part of our period been systematically investigated. Very little work has been done on the Carmelites and the studies on the Franciscans and Dominicans, though considerable, are very uneven in their coverage, dealing much with their theological work and comparatively little with the general history of their orders at this time.

THE AUSTIN FRIARS

In 1300 there existed twenty-two houses of Austin friars in England but expansion was far from over, this total having risen to thirty-three two centuries later. Amongst the late arrivals were friaries at Bristol (1313), Boston (1317), Canterbury (1318) and Droitwich (1331). A very trying feature of this expansion was the not infrequent and often vigorous opposition to the foundation of new houses, much of which came from major monasteries (mostly

Benedictine) which had possessions in the area concerned. This opposition has led the order's historian to go so far as to speak of 'war with the great abbeys' in the period 1331–63, and it led to at least four new houses of the order failing to take root. It is hard to see any defensible motive behind this attack on the Austin friars; the most charitable way in which it can be regarded is as a primitive example of those 'who-does-what' disputes so rampant amongst our trades unions today since, as we have seen, the establishment of a new house of friars might well direct some proportion of the local faithful from attendance at local parish churches and compete for their alms. It is interesting to note that the greatest protector of the friars was the Crown.

The ordination lists preserved in our bishops' registers do not suffice to give a complete picture of the number of Austin friars in England at this time, but Roth estimates that this was at least 700 on the eve of the Black Death. Recovery was slow because of the large fall in the birth-rate in the decades immediately after the Black Death. By the mid-fifteenth century the total number of brethren was about 550 after which, for unexplained reasons, there was a certain decrease.

As always, the daily round of the pastoral work to which the friars were so deeply committed, has left little trace in contemporary records beyond persistent bequests to them by ordinary folk and occasional major aid by the monarchy. Equally badly documented are the incomes of the friars' houses at this time. As with the other mendicant orders the main elements were several, including payments for preaching and for aiding in parishes, collections in mendicants' churches, stipends for celebrating private Masses (e.g. in connection with chantries) and begging. This latter activity took place in carefully defined limits to prevent over-competition for the alms of the faithful, and led to friars who worked therein coming to be known as 'limitours'.

The Austin friars' connection with Oxford was very close for most, though not quite all, of our period. Use of their buildings was made by the university for things academic. In 1346 it passed a statute that every bachelor should dispute and respond there once a year, whence originated the phrase 'doing the Austins', a term that lasted until the last century. In the intense theological activity here in the fourteenth century Austin friars were prominent. At first they were on good terms with Wycliffe but his extremism drove them away and led one brother to alter the title he had given Wycliffe in one of his books from 'most worthy teacher' to 'execrable seducer'.

Inevitably the order came to cultivate a real interest in book-collecting as one or two of its surviving library catalogues show. Amongst its most prominent scholars was John Capgrave who it was noted 'clung to his books like a limpet to his rock', a saintly man and a very prolific writer on theology and history. His works include a *Chronicle of England* (the first of its kind to be written in the vernacular since the far distant days of the Old English Chronicle), and the *De illustribus Henricis*, a curious rag-bag concerning men called Henry.

The interesting and fruitful combination of active and contemplative which had characterised the Austin friars from the first still continued. Thus in 1431 brother John White was given permission to spend three years in the little friary of Woodhouse, hidden most peacefully away in the hills above Cleobury Mortimer, and then to join an Observant house in Italy. Before this the order in England had produced its most famous member of the period. This was William Flete, a remarkable person whose importance has only recently become apparent. Born about 1300, after getting within reach of great academic distinction he shook off such things to seek a life of solitude in the remote monastery of Lecceto in Italy where his great sanctity led to him becoming one of the inner circle of confidants of St Catharine of Siena, 'the greatest woman saint of the middle ages', whose friend he was and to whose remarkable qualities his writings include tribute. A valuable counter-poise to this tendency was that interest in social justice which Roth notes as one of the characteristics of the English Austin friars at this time. A remarkable instance of broad-minded interest in things secular was provided during the Wars of the Roses by a friar whose passionate devotion to the Yorkists led him to spend a memorable night firing off cannon in the direction of a Lancastrian camp to disguise the fact that his own side had decamped.

Very intense research has failed to produce more than a very blurred picture of the level of the religious life of the English Austin friars in late medieval times. Evidence of any sexual misdemeanours is next to nil and, as with the other mendicant orders, there are very few signs here of houses acquiring considerable wealth as they did in certain areas of the Continent. Like the Cluniacs at the close of our period, contacts with the Continental houses were very severely reduced (after 1465 there is no sign of effective English links with the general chapters of the order). Also at this stage in Western monastic history the full common life was threatened somewhat. Here, as with the older orders we find, not unjustifiably, cases of a common dormitory being replaced by private cubicles or cells. Much more serious was the practice which developed to an unknown extent of certain brethren retaining private resources with which they built or took over private quarters in the monastery. Though it seems clear that at the end of the period the life of the order had lost not a little of its primitive élan it would be incorrect to regard it as being very gravely deficient, even if it was in certain need of a powerful shot in the arm.

THE LATER FRIARS AND THEIR CRITICS

As we have seen, the mendicant orders were in a difficult position *vis-à-vis* both the parish clergy and the older monastic orders. Their pastoral work inevitably rivalled that of the former, whilst their monastic life, notably with regard to the question of poverty, could be and was easily construed as an attack on the way of life of the latter. Added to this was the fact that their very skilled pastoral work was apt to excite jealousy. Even in the thirteenth century these frictions (which were nobody's fault but 'just one of those things') had been very evident. Time did very little to remove them and by the late fourteenth century friars faced a veritable hurricane of hostile comment which, as is so often the case, produced a good deal more heat than light. In interpreting the sweeping and serious charges hurled at the friars it is important to bear in mind that men of these centuries very frequently tended to display in controversy a passion for most wild and exaggerated comment which far exceeds that of the modern press at its worst. This wild extremism was due in part to the fact that the very naive society of the age was inevitably liable to make very naive remarks but, also, to no small degree, to the fact that contemporary social conditions made it impossible to obtain accurate factual information on a large scale. As we have seen, wildest ideas prevailed, even in the best circles, on so major a matter as the total number of parishes in medieval England and it was virtually impossible for any individual to acquire accurate and comprehensive knowledge of more than a tiny section of any aspect of contemporary society whether monastic or non-monastic. For the extremist-minded ignorance was bliss, and in the late fourteenth century led to the friars especially being at the receiving end of no little unfair and vigorous attack.

The most famous and least equable of their critics was the Oxford don, John Wycliffe, whose very radical attacks on Catholic faith and practice provided a programme ultimately to be admired by certain Protestant extremists and whose early friendship with friars soured to a most vituperative dislike of them. His criticisms of them include that charge of sexual immorality which is part of the stock-in-trade of anti-clericals down the ages. Now, as so often, it was made in vague and unconvincing terms by one whose knowledge of English life as a whole was very limited and whose outlook was far from dispassionate. Unconvincing, also, is his charge (notably echoed by the humourless *Piers Plowman*) that the friars used alms to build magnificent churches with sumptuous decoration and to acquire comfortable living quarters. Here the hard facts of the surviving buildings show that:— (i) with a few obvious exceptions such as mendicant churches in London, friars' places of worship were not large by contemporary standards (the Franciscan church at Reading, for example, is only a little over a 100 feet long); (ii) the eastern part of the church which was used by the friars as their chapel is almost always of great simplicity, as we may see today at the remains of the Franciscan church at Chichester, whilst the larger naves of mendicant churches wherein the faithful laity met for worship generally do not differ notably in size or magnificence from the richer parish churches in the locality; (iii) in any case the largish size of the greater mendicant churches, such as that of the Dominicans at Norwich, was not, as in the case of major Benedictine abbeys, largely uncalled for by local pastoral needs, but was demanded by the great popularity of the mendicants' preaching and the very widespread desire for burial therein which, for example, ultimately led to the floor of the huge Franciscan church at London being largely paved with grave-stones; (iv) extant remains of the claustral buildings of friaries, such as those at Walsingham and Gloucester, equally give no support to the charge that mendicant architecture was by contemporary standards over-luxurious, an accusation which rests largely on prejudice.

It is, however, worthy of note that the latter half of the fourteenth century, when attacks on the friars' large building activities were so marked, coincides with the period in which the London Franciscans were engaged on the reconstruction of their conventual buildings on a very large scale for the very good reason that there were then very large numbers of brethren indeed requiring increased accommodation. Further, the London Austin friars acquired at this time a new church whose gigantic nave (longer and wider than that of Exeter Cathedral) which may well have been demanded, both by their popularity and by the exceptional size of a community that was often swollen by no few visitors. These two developments may have done much to inspire the wild contemporary generalisation about lavish mendicant building.

The mendicants were charged *ad nauseam* with beguiling widows and others into providing them with money, food and other commodities. To this it may be answered that:— (i) since the mendicants' orders had no endowments, begging was a fundamental element in their daily programme; (ii) if they conversed with their supporters and were given food and drink by them, these were perfectly defensible concomitants of their pastoral work (as of that of the parish clergy) and cannot be criticised unless indulgence in them was excessive, a most nebulous question on which Wycliffe and those critics who followed him were not likely to have had any worthwhile precisions.

Equally unconvincing is Wycliffe's accusation that the friars used improper means to attract the faithful to go to their churches rather than to those of the local parish clergy to hear Mass, and to receive in confession both absolution and spiritual advice. From the pragmatic angle (and the layman is a pragmatic animal) the individual counsel received at confession was of immense potential value and, unlike absolution which was given in a short standard form by any priest, could vary very greatly in value according to the spiritual perception of the confessor. One only needs to take half a glance at late medieval England to appreciate that in most areas the friar with his long and careful training in matters intellectual and spiritual was immensely more likely to help the penitent sinner in cases complex and commonplace than the local parish priest whose training for this was, as we have seen, often inadequate. It is hard to believe that improper means were necessary to secure penitents. If Wycliffe had employed that capacity which he so enjoyed, against this defect of the secular clergy to which he belonged, curbing his wild and immensely unsympathetic attacks on the monastic life, he would be less vulnerable to that charge of being out of touch with the facts of life of which so many dons down the ages have stood convicted.

More worthy of serious consideration is Wycliffe's charge that the friars pressurised very young folk to join their order, before they had realised the full implications of such a step. Here it is to be remembered that:— (i) life began early for medieval folk. Lads commonly went to the university in their early teens and might marry at an appreciably earlier age than is now usual; (ii) contemporary law, unwisely as experience ultimately showed, fell in with this tendency to believe in an early age of responsibility, allowing monasteries to receive novices of very tender years and also expecting them to take final, i.e. irrevocable vows at a far earlier age after a far shorter period of probation as a novice than is usual nowadays; (iii) whilst some major responsibility for no little unhappiness caused by individuals being professed too soon must rest with the community concerned and with the canonists, it is not to be forgotten that parental guidance or lack of it must also have been a factor in creating such situations; (iv) we have no evidence at all to give any clear idea of the number of friars or of members of other orders who suffered through being professed to the monastic life too early in their life, and it would be totally gratuitous to assume that it was largish.

Did the friars in late medieval England depart significantly from the very high degree of poverty as some of their Continental brethren very certainly did? It is not at all easy to give a complete answer to this question. There are certainly a few instances of this, but there is nothing to suggest that luxurious living was at all common. At the time of the Dissolution some most valuable evidence on this matter was preserved by detailed official valuations of the buildings of English friaries and their contents. Without exception these show no signs of luxurious living standards but make frequent mention of furnishings which were often aged and worth next to nothing. Nor was there at this time any sign of grandiose architecture, the very modest belfry towers athwart the church of English friaries contrasting vividly with the stupendous towers still to be seen at lordly Ely, St Alban's, Tewkesbury and the primatial cathedral of Canterbury.

To term friars 'drones' as Wycliffe does is to go very far towards using language which, in this context, is unpardonable. The whole way of life of the mendicants made inactivity virtually impossible, notably in the many areas where their houses stood in rural areas with the faithful most thinly scattered far and wide as in Wycliffe's native North Riding. Here the Franciscan friary at Richmond, whose elegant little tower still attracts the eye, very understandably included in its accommodation 'a certain apartment where the friars commonly wash themselves when they come to the house tired and weary'. Wyclif's wild remark that 'a good friar is as rare as a phoenix' must rank amongst the most foolish ever made by a Balliol man.

Other factors help to explain why the mendicants met with no little hostility. In the first place their intellectual interests inevitably meant that the friars were unavoidably implicated in the violent theological debates which characterised Oxford life in the later part of the fourteenth century and the crudish medieval mode of controversy inevitably meant that because of this they would be pelted with religious brickbats which they did not deserve. No-one who appreciates fully the conditions of the times will take very seriously the friars' unpopularity with the parish clergy. The latter, like the rest of mankind down the ages, did not take at all kindly to find their main work being done better by outsiders, and it is very arguable, if not provable, that no small part of their very over-vigorous criticism of the friars was due to that jealousy which Christian tradition so long insisted on placing amongst the Seven Deadly Sins.

As is well known, to the long intense literary activity of theologians in England was added in the late fourteenth century some literary productions worthy of consideration by the historian, headed by writings of the entertaining Chaucer and the heavy-going William Langland (next to whom at meals, it may be conjectured, few deliberately sat, save perhaps in the penitential seasons of Advent and Lent). To use their references to the friars and other contemporary ecclesiastics as a basis for historical conclusions is permissible only for the half-educated, and the same is even more true of usage of *Pierce the Plowmans Crede*, a shortish poem written by a Wycliffite. It is cast in the form of a search for 'byleve', by the writer who consults on this matter a member of each of the four orders of friars, all of whom make uncomplimentary remarks about each other and all of whom he finds repellent, the truth he so desires being finally acquired from a simple ploughman—the 'man-in-the-street' of the fourteenth century. Very pertinently our leading authority on mendicant history compares this 'popular literature in which the friar is invariably shown as a hypocrite' with 'comic plays of a later age in which the clergyman is always portrayed as sancti-monious' (Moorman).

On the credit side of the account considerable and indubitable evidence of popular affection for the mendicant orders is furnished by contemporary wills, notably those of the townsfolk who knew them well. Bequests to them are frequent in those of lordly York. It has been shown that in the time when friars were entrapped in bitter controversy in fourteenth-century Oxford, one third of all known wills of the city make bequests to the Franciscan house there and to that at Cambridge no few are known. Of the immense popularity of the London house of this order there can be no doubt. Such tokens of affection were primarily due to the steady and un-ostentatious pastoral work of the friars in dozens of houses carefully sited in major centres of population and manifested especially in that skilled preaching whose supreme importance St Dominic had stressed so long ago, and in the perceptive hearing of those individual confessions whose value the medieval laity came increasingly to appreciate.

A notable contribution to English church life made by the friars at this time is provided by their most important links with the universities. As we have seen, the number of parish clergy who could afford the time and money to study at places like Oxford and Cambridge was very limited and economic necessity tended to make their sojourns very brief. The links of the English Austin canons with such places were few and frail, as were those of a con-siderable majority of those of the Benedictine observance, a small coterie of the very well-to-do abbeys of the latter being prepared to shoulder the considerable financial and other burdens involved. In late medieval times English universities had for long a very high reputation for theology and this would most surely have been a very great deal smaller had it not been for the English mendicants who were quite ready to let suitable members spend in study the enormous period of twenty or so years required to acquire a doctorate in theology and who had alongside them no few of their brethren from abroad.

CONCLUSION

Surviving sources are quite adequate to portray the final condition of that English medieval monasticism which came to so abrupt and brutal an end under Henry VIII. As we have seen, a major part of the troubles which beset it came from matters financial. In the case of few dozen houses the enormous incomes they accumulated in the course of time involved them in maintaining all the paraphernalia of government which big business demands, and diverted far too much of the attentions of major officials to the care of things pertaining much more to Caesar than to God. Imperceptibly this most seriously eroded that full common life so essential to the monastic ideal, whilst great wealth also brought with it a high standard of living which made a mockery of the monastic obligation to show forth by their poverty the satisfaction to be had from 'plain living and high thinking'. There is no reason to believe that the life of the monks of plutocratic monasteries like Westminster and Durham in the latter part of our period was grossly materialistic or marred by major moral deficiencies, but it is difficult to believe that its easy-going routine and more than adequate standard of living would offer adequate challenge to society or attract the type of heroic novices who would demonstrate to the world the Kingdom of Christ is a kingdom 'not of this world', the manifestation of which is, at bottom, the principal social function of monasticism. Further, the grossly excessive wealth of this tiny minority of English religious houses inevitably played right into the hands of hostile critics who greatly exaggerated its extent and used it as an argument for the suppression of the monastic life.

An inevitable result of a monastery holding great possessions was the tendency to regard administrative capacity as one of the most important requisites of an abbot—a view which finds no support at all in the *Rule of St Benedict*. As we have seen, this was very evident in the twelfth century (see page 128) and led to unfortunate secular behaviour. The fact that Abbot Langham of Westminster (d. 1376) became Treasurer of the Exchequer is one of several indications that his heart was not in the monastic life, as is the conduct of his immediate successor Abbot Littlington who, having heard of the danger of a French invasion of England, sought to go into battle in armour, a move which death most properly vetoed.

However, this defect was of modest dimensions, being limited largely to those few dozen plutocratic Benedictine abbeys whose history we have seen to be in various major ways untypical. It must not be allowed to divert attention from the very much greater number of English monasteries whose life was gravely handicapped not by a super-abundance of cash but by a grave and persistent lack of it. Our leading authority hereon writes, 'the fundamental weakness of the system lies in the difficulty of making two ends meet . . . in the smaller monasteries whose financial depression was permanently acute, need produced a general carelessness of living' (A. Hamilton Thompson). It is unsurprising but unfortunate that strong legal tradition and persistent official inattention to this admittedly highly complex problem prevented a radical overhaul of the machinery of monasticism, in which a much reduced number of houses with communities of that substantial size which makes so much easier care-free existence would replace the multitudinous, often minute, priories scattered unprofitably over the face of England in late medieval times.

In very varying degree, in proportions which will never be ascertainable, some English monastic houses had abandoned that full communal life which is of the essence of its ideal. In the worst cases which (pace Knowles) seem to have been mostly the large Benedictine houses, the abbot had what was virtually a separate household and mixed but rarely with his brethren. In lesser ones, if the abandonment of common sleeping quarters cannot be regarded as reprehensible, the employment of private rooms for eating and other traditionally communal engagements was unfortunate, as was the shift system employed to maintain the Night Office in an indeterminate number of houses.

Although instances of sexual misbehaviour in the monasteries can be found, the overall total of these is by no means large and there is no good reason to believe that it compares unfavourably with that of other sections of the contemporary population. Very widespread indeed and very powerfully undermining the potency of English monastic life in late medieval times was the disregard of the traditional rules to prevent monastic inmates showing undue interest in the non-monastic world by mixing too freely with peoples and pursuits of the non-monastic society, either through absence from the monastic precinct or by giving seculars excessive access to it. Monks were traditionally termed 'the athletes of God' because like athletes they gave minute and unremitting attention to detail. Of this need to be meticulous, in late medieval times, English monasteries showed far too little awareness. In no few, to some degree or other, individual members were allowed to accept for personal use gifts of money and other things. In many, access to the outside world from the cloister and vice-versa were available very much too easily, sometimes with most deplorable results.

To some extent monastic decline was caused by over-strict rules, but this was only a minor factor. Almost certainly there was some fall in standard of the entrants to monastic life, due partially to the drastic drop in the size of the population caused by the Black Death and its attendant outbreaks of plague, partially also to a certain decline in popular esteem for the monastic ideal, at least in its more conservative form. Bad machinery for supervising the exacting programme of the monastic life reinforced the slump. The old tradition of immense respect for the abbot or prior who headed an Augustinian or Benedictine house meant that orders therefrom were to be treated 'as if divinely given' (to quote the *Rule* of the latter) and combined with the old custom of normally according them tenure of office for life (a practice then not observed by the mendicants and much less widespread nowadays) meant that too often the head of the house who was patently unsatisfactory was allowed to continue to hold office by over-optimistic visitors. The rareness of some monastic visitations by over-worked diocesans and their representatives and the ineffectiveness of others worked to the same unfortunate end.

However, it would be very unrealistic to conclude that on the eve of the Reformation English monastic life was damaged beyond repair. The number of their inmates, which was quite healthy if less spectacular than of old even though the climate for this expansion was appreciably less friendly than of yore, was an indubitable sign of vitality and there were still many manifestations of piety and good works. The absurd superstition that the monastic life was now effete is belied by the continued existence of almost all major medieval orders today, aided by vigorous re-flowering both at the time of the Counter-Reformation and reinforced during the last century and a half when Western monastic ideals have been the subject of much fertile re-thinking. Of medieval monasticism one of the most learned and least sentimental of its chroniclers has affirmed and re-affirmed his conviction that 'the Religious Orders have been among the main forces of European civilisation; at certain times and at certain places they may perhaps have been the greatest of all civilising forces' (G. C. Coulton).

CHAPTER II

THE QUESTION OF RE-FORMATION

In much of the last century and a half of the period with which this volume is concerned life was unusually disturbed in both Church and State. In the non-theological sphere English energies were now heavily strained by the long struggle with France known as the Hundred Years' War (1338–1453)—a foolish and fruitless venture which involved tremendous expense—and also, on a much smaller scale, by the Wars of the Roses (1455–85), one of the very few sizeable civil wars in English history.

In ecclesiastical history we find the same lack of placidity. From 1309 to 1377 the Roman papacy found it necessary to write off residence in the disorderly city of Rome and resided at Avignon. Such a move, albeit justifiable by the chronic disorders in the Eternal City, inevitably caused enormous problems. First there came the nasty problem of housing the huge papal bureaucracy on which efficient functioning of the Western Church had so long depended, which at first even led to cardinals camping out in local churchyards. Then there was the problem of safety, which was of major significance in an area where local disorders were made worse by wild mercenary forces from the Hundred Years' War occasionally taking a change of air. In the end the great gravity of this problem led the popes to construct at enormous expense not only a strong stone palace at Avignon but to surround the city with a huge circuit of massive stone walls, still to be seen. In some ways worst of all problems was the persistent pressuring of the papal curia by the English and French monarchies, which were now incomparably the strongest political forces in the West and whose antagonism was very deep-rooted. By what was a quite unparalleled development during the 'Babylonish Captivity' at Avignon a series of French popes were elected who, unsurprisingly, nominated no small number of French cardinals—a development bound to undermine the reputation of the papacy as the neutral, final court of appeal.

The return of the pope and his curia to Rome in 1377 was followed by the removal of the papal headquarters from the cathedral church of St John Lateran, where Constantine had placed it over a thousand years ago, to the mighty pilgrimage church of St Peter's on the far side of the Tiber, built by Constantine with its high altar placed over a shrine which modern excavation shows to have been intimately connected with St Peter. When in 1378 the new pope died another major disaster hit Western Christendom. The cardinals split into two irreconcilable factions, each electing a candidate which it claimed to be the rightful pope.

Faced by this situation the states of the Western world were not of one mind. On one side was a faction backed by France, Scotland, Naples, Hungary and Spanish kingdoms; the other was supported by much of Italy, Germany and Flanders and by England. This fragmentation, however, was not only influenced by political frontiers but had widespread local effects, chapters of cathedrals and monasteries being disastrously split over which candidate was the rightful pope. Nothing was so obviously absent as a spirit of compromise, with cliques electing successors to their candidates when a vacancy occurred. The resultant chaos and bitterness was very considerable and contemporary canon law provided no remedy for this most scandalous situation, which could not possibly be allowed to drag on indefinitely. Happily, the intellectual life of the West was now brimming over with vitality and had a strong sense of the value of history. With remarkable speed there was put forward a highly reasoned solution for the situation. With firm support from early Christian history it was now strongly and scientifically urged that the ultimate source of authority was not, as medieval canonists had long urged, the papacy, but 'general councils', i.e. assemblies representing the whole Church—though in practice, for obvious reasons, the Eastern Churches were scarcely included in this Western thinking.

Thus got under way the 'Conciliar Movement' which strove vigorously, albeit with limited success, to face up to reform. The peak of the movement came with the Council of Constance (1414–17) which did not shrink from decisive action, declaring in April 1415 that it was a 'general' council, held power 'directly from Christ' and that its enactments were to be obeyed by all, popes included. In October 1417 was passed the celebrated decree *Frequens* which ordered periodic meetings of general councils. The implicit challenge to that medieval papalism of the Gregorian type now so long and so widely accepted in the West is obvious enough, and led a brilliant historian to aver that 'probably the most revolutionary official document in the history of the world is the decree of the Council of Constance asserting its superiority to the Pope, and striving to turn into a tepid constitutionalism, the Divine authority of a thousand years' (Figgis). For a complex web of reasons, theological and non-theological, this revolutionary attack on traditional papalism quickly collapsed. Only with Vatican Council II, in a much milder and more reasonable context, did there come about a notable reassessment of the position of the Roman see vis-a-vis the episcopate.

So far as the domestic history of the English Church is concerned the period of the Avignon Papacy and the Conciliar Movement had several effects which concern us. The fact that for well over half a century for various reasons the papacy was in many ways fighting with its back to the wall, meant that for better or for worse (and the choice between these two is not easy to make) it was not capable of doing a great deal to limit the various selfish gestures made by the English monarchy. From the papal angle the very considerable financial strain imposed on it by its residence at Avignon, inevitably increased its demands for aid and thereby its unpopularity in England. But, as we have seen, papal share in high ecclesiastical appointments in England was small and its protests against the Acts of Parliament whose terms were incompatible with its canonical claims, went unredressed. Negatively, the fact that the Conciliar Movement accomplished very little indeed in the way of ecclesiastical reform left future faithful various things to criticise.

ENGLAND AND PAPAL DEMANDS

As we have already noted, from the early half of the thirteenth century financial demands made on England by the Roman curia was generating vigorous local resistance, which a century later was major enough to be utilised by the monarchy as a useful counter in its perennial skirmishing with the papacy over matters financial and legal. In 1343 came a notable milestone here in the form of a memorandum drawn up for submission to the pope of which the implications were none the less serious through being formulated in language which has been termed 'respectful, indeed almost servile'. This based its case, as was inevitable, on old precedent and not on theological argument or current canon law, being primarily concerned to stress how provisions and the like made impossible fulfilment of the intentions of former benefactors of the English Church. Such intentions were specified as having been designed to ensure that 'the divine services of God and the Christian faith might be honoured, extended and embellished, hospitalities and alms given and maintained, churches and buildings worthily preserved and kept, devout prayers in the same places offered up for founders, poor parishioners aided and comforted and, in confession and otherwise, fully instructed and indoctrinated in their mother tongue by those who had charge of souls'. This understandable and not indefensible opposition to a system which allowed the traditional rights of the laity over local appointments to be snatched from their grip was obviously intensified when Englishmen saw some part of their ecclesiastical assets diverted to the purses of inhabitants of that land of France which became firmly established as their Public Enemy No. 1.

Although by the time this letter was composed the English Parliament was steadily becoming more conscious of its potential power it had no great strength of itself, but was now used by the vigorous and competent English Crown largely as a useful extra weapon in its unending encounters with the papacy. Lay and clerical criticism of the way the Roman curia worked was now outspoken and fairly widespread, but in the last resort it was far from potent for the simple reason that the English Crown had not the slightest intention of engaging in a series of head-on clashes with the papacy but sought largely by diplomatic means to pressure it into handing over to the monarchy the major part of available spoils.

The English Parliament now passed two acts which, superficially at least, seemed to gravely menace papal power in England. The first of these was the *Statute of Provisors*, promulgated in 1351. This gave legal authority to already existing practices, ordering that local elections and presentations were to be free from papal pressure. Appointments made by papal provision were liable to be forfeited to the Crown and any provisor disturbing the lawful holder liable to be imprisoned and fined at the king's will. This statute at first sight looks very forbidding but in fact it quickly became apparent that the Crown largely used it as a warning light to the papacy not to seriously intervene in royal control over the higher English appointments. It soon became a dead-letter despite being re-enacted in 1365 and 1390. With this were associated the *Statutes of Praemunire*. The first of these, passed in 1353, laid down that anyone drawing the king's subjects out of the realm on pleas whose cognisance belonged to the royal courts, if he failed to answer his contempt should be liable to imprisonment and forfeiture of land and goods; though no names were mentioned it was, of course, aimed at the Roman curia. In 1393 was passed a more extreme version of it which asserted that because of the pope's usurpations the laws of the realm are 'defeated and avoided at his will, in perpetual destruction of the sovereignty of the king' and repeated previous threats of penalties against those who brought into the kingdom or executed papal bulls and allied documents like excommunications. This was not intended to be utilised on more than a small scale but had some effect in limiting legal traffic between England and Rome. In theory, however, its scope was very wide, and this made it potentially an invaluable weapon as, long after, Henry VIII perceived.

JOHN WYCLIFFE

In the closing decades of the fourteenth century there suddenly exploded at the busy and long illustrious university of Oxford, a theological crisis of great moment. It was largely due to the extremely radical views propagated by an eminent but irascible don, John Wycliffe, who ultimately developed views on Catholicism comparable to those of the most radical elements of later Protestantism.

Born about 1330 in the tough North Riding of Yorkshire he went up to Oxford where he was to spend the greater part of his working life and where he early made his mark as a vigorous and able scholar, studying as prodigiously as Mr Gladstone was later to do. He was briefly Master of Balliol, but for most of the time lived in hired rooms in Queen's, for which he paid out the proceeds of the wealthy living of Fillingham in Leicestershire of which he was the non-resident rector. The papal curia refused him provision to one of the delectable canonries and prebends of his native cathedral of York but, in 1362, allotted him a minor one in the little secular college of Westbury-on-Trym near Bristol. He neither resided there nor appointed a vicar (whose salary would have engrossed a large part of the income) whilst also neglecting his obligations in regard to keeping the chancel in repair, misdemeanours which, it is only fair to note, were common enough at this time, and which he may well have felt to be justified by his conviction that his vocation was to the academic life and only by such conduct could he finance it. Three years later Wycliffe was appointed to Canterbury College, a small, newly founded establishment, but by an evil chance soon after, in 1367, the new archbishop of Canterbury reinstated the monks (whom his predecessor had recently removed) and expelled the brethren, including Wycliffe. Furiously but foolishly the latter sought to regain his position but his legal proceedings ended in total failure. Back to lodge in Queen's he went, having suffered financial loss as well as a humiliation which, it has been suggested, did much to stoke up that dislike of the monastic way of life which this highly-strung, ambitious don was steadily to exhibit. He had now a considerable reputation as a philosophical theologian and was building up an enthusiastic band of disciples. In his intellectual ability, simplicity of living, high moral character and lack of humour he reminds us of Calvin. In uncompromising self assurance he contrasts starkly with the ever-hesitant Cranmer, whilst his distaste for the delights of art, music and literature recalls George Fox.

Like other unwary dons after him, he let himself be lured onto the slippery ground of politics, his entry therein being perhaps due to John of Gaunt, a son of the now fast-failing King Edward III. His first function for his distinguished employers was to provide respectable academic backing for financial demands which the English government was now making on the clergy. In 1374 he was sent as one of a major mission to a conference at Bruges with papal representatives on this matter, but his totally uncompromising nature very clearly made him a bad diplomat. Hereafter he was employed as a propagandist, a role in which he was much more at home and in which he displayed an extremism very attractive to his employers. Certain parts of his attacks were far from original and far from unreasonable, notably his condemnation of the great ecclesiastics who occupied themselves so extensively in matters non-ecclesiastical. What marked him out from other critics and was to lead him into a most perilous position was his energetic and most persistent attacks on the traditional financial and legal position of the clergy. This obviously exposed him to counter-attacks which were magnified by the fact that, as a protegé of John of Gaunt, he inevitably inspired hostility from the latter's very powerful rivals. Criticism from leading pro-papal ecclesiastics of England led in 1377 to Wycliffe being condemned by the papal court, though not as a heretic, the university authorities being ordered to hand over him and his followers for episcopal examination. No modern trades union is apt to fight more furiously than did a great medieval university like Oxford when it felt that its privileged position was threatened, and the chancellor now declared mildly that the views Wycliffe had propounded 'though they sounded ill to the ear, were all the same true', whilst Wycliffe's royal friends pressurised the bishops before whom he appeared for examination to pass the mild sentence that he should not reiterate these arguments so as to avoid dissensions which would scandalise the laity.

But Wycliffe had now reached a position at which he could not remain. Either he must go back and make his peace with the ecclesiastical authorities or go on to a rupture with them. Had he left a massive diary like Pepys or Queen Victoria we would be able to reconstruct with certainty the factors which led this highly-strung, complicated man to take the latter course. As it is, we are dependent on the precarious footholds of surmise. It has been convincingly suggested that he suffered from high blood-pressure which, by the period of his rupture with the authorities, may well have reached an advanced stage and which certainly breeds *inter alia*, that irritability and inflexibility which indubitably characterised him in these times. However this may be, what is certain is that from now on nothing but trouble for him lay ahead. The extremist views which he now so forthrightly propounded excited immense controversy amongst theologians and high ecclesiastical authorities, though Oxford university long strove to protect him from wrath to come. Now, as in the crisis under Henry VIII, the situation was not helped by the fact that the English bishops of the time, with whom so much authority rested, were mostly royal nominees with few theological interests.

Most notable was the extremism of his views and their wide range. Had Wycliffe confined his attack to one sector of contemporary belief, such as, for example, that of papal authority (against which various very violent attacks had long been launched) the opposition which he aroused might have been kept within moderate bounds. As it was, his sweeping assaults on so many Catholic fundamentals, delivered in those violent terms so beloved by medieval controversialists, aroused a degree of opposition and fury against which ultimately no form of local defence had the slightest hope of being effective. In 1381 Oxford university condemned his views on the Mass and, as we shall see, next year a council at London held by the archbishop of Canterbury condemned a wide range of his doctrines. Oxford could not now protect him and Wycliffe withdrew to the well-to-do living of Lutterworth which he had long held and where, recalcitrant and energetic to the last, he penned a string of writings to convince the unwise world how right he was. On 28 December 1384, whilst hearing Mass, he had a stroke from which he died three days later. Still unexcommunicated, he was given Catholic burial.

In 1415 the Council of Constance condemned a major series of his theological views. In 1428 the then bishop of Lincoln had what were thought to be Wycliffe's mortal remains dug up and burnt, the ashes thereof being thrown into a nearby beck. By this time vigorous persecution had been launched on those who, with varying degrees of accuracy, were regarded as Wycliffe's followers, to whom the contemporaries early gave a name of Lollards, an uncomplimentary title of Dutch origin meaning 'mumblers'.

WYCLIFFISM

By what authority do you do these things? This question which was put to the revolutionary Christ is the fundamental one for any reformer, since on the nature of his answer to it the whole validity of his message depends. Wycliffe's response to it was very novel and very far-reaching. He wrote off the accumulated experience of the Church down the centuries which the Catholic view held to be of fundamental significance in elucidating the Christian way of life, and appealed very largely to the text of the Holy Scripture. Like all other theologians of medieval and Reformation centuries he was inevitably unaware of the immense historical and theological complexities inherent in the books of the Bible, and he also rejected the old traditional symbolic interpretation of it. Instead he insisted on purely literal interpretation of a Bible whose simplicity and clarity seemed to him obvious, even though his own conclusions on it were shared by very few others. With supreme optimism he believed the Gospel teaching could be grasped by the simplest mind. The views which he derived from this approach, unsurprisingly, differed immensely from that of the medieval Western Church, which Wycliffe, being what he was, went on to condemn in a very 'root and branch' way.

A most controversial aspect of his thought, and one which for practical reasons became apparent very early, was his teaching regarding authority or 'lordship' (*dominium*). In 1377, not without a certain amount of reason, the government was concerned about the money being sent to Rome in a time of stress, and on being consulted, Wycliffe, as was expected, urged that natural reason and Gospel law allowed a nation to stop such export to foreign parts when its own defence demanded this. However shocking papalists might find it, such a view could not be written off as totally unreasonable. Wycliffe, however, reacted very violently against the traditional allotment of so much power to the clergy with the pope at the head. For him the lay ruler, like the pagan emperors of Rome, was entitled to complete obedience even if he behaved unjustly, and had the power, indeed the duty, to decide whether ecclesiastical officers and institutions were misusing their temporal possessions and could proceed to confiscate the latter if they were. The fact that most English bishoprics and some few abbeys in England at this time had far more wealth than their reasonable needs demanded gave some very small defensibility to such an idea, but as a general rule it had nothing to commend it. As we have seen, one of the perennial abuses from which the medieval Western Church suffered and which was arguably the principal one, was the ever-present diversion to purely personal and secular purposes of church wealth by laity in the position so to do, with the Crown the principal transgressor. To make a monarch judge in a matter in which he had such a strong personal interest, as Wycliffe did, was to make the king judge in his own cause and was contrary to natural justice. Even if the position was accepted as theoretically defensible, in practice it was clearly undesirable since there was no clear way of establishing at what point a man's unworthiness reached the proportions which justified confiscation.

Equally radical was Wycliffe's somewhat hazy conception of the Christian ministry. Popes, bishops and the various grades of lower clergy had no automatic claim to authority but could, if need be, be replaced by a society of laymen—a singularly extremist reaction against Catholic tradition of which even Calvin would not have approved. Defensible was his claim that clergy and members of monastic communities had no exclusive right to the title of 'the church', for membership of which venerable tradition made baptism the prime qualification, but immensely more controversial was Wycliffe's assertion that 'it is contrary to Holy Scripture that ecclesiastics should have possessions—such folk should live only on alms and tithes', a view which the past experience of the Church did nothing to support, and which Wycliffe himself, though a cleric, showed no inclination to implement.

To modern minds none of the major lapses of both Catholic and Protestant theologians in the Christian West down the centuries is so indefensible as the support which some of them have given to 'predestination'—the view that by divine decree only certain persons are guided to eternal salvation, others being excluded for unknown considerations. This idea, mooted by Augustine, had little appeal in the East but was held by Wycliffe and was clearly likely to come into conflict with the wider idea that salvation was to be won by persistent personal effort to acquire perfection by good works and good worship. In this connection it is significant that he attacked the sacrament of confession now so widely found fruitful as 'superfluous and useless'. This last was one of his propositions officially condemned at the Council of London, along with others which included an attack on current views on transubstantiation, a maintenance that any deacon or priest could preach with episcopal or papal authorisation, that 'he who gives alms to friars is by that fact excommunicated' and a sweeping condemnation of the monastic life whether mendicant or not.

By the time of the Council of Constance, Wycliffism had become a variegated movement with an ultra-extreme fringe which inevitably played right into the hands of the conservatives, some of its members apparently maintaining inter alia 'that all the orders of mendicants are heretics', 'that the Roman Church is the synagogue of Satan', 'that all oaths made to corroborate human contracts and civil business are unlawful'.

It will be obvious that if Wycliffe, let alone his extremist followers, had had his way the structure and belief of Western Christendom would have been changed out of all recognition. The prospect of this occurring was, however, never on the cards and was made even less so by the fact to a degree which it is not possible to estimate, his cause became gravely discredited through temporarily coming to be associated with social disorder.

At the London council he was accused of maintaining 'that the people can at their own will correct sinful lords'. The social conservatism of England in his day was as deep-rooted as it was in Hanoverian and Victorian times, so such a view was largely regarded as nothing less than horrifying and very quickly events seemed to confirm this. In 1381 the peace of England was rudely and very suddenly shattered by the Peasants' Revolt which led to violent disorders quite unparalleled. The complex and controversial causes of the movement being predominantly economic and social and not at all theological do not concern us directly, but it is to be noticed that before the revolt had collapsed an extremist left-wing therein had become very evident. Medieval preachers for long had been used to stress the scriptural thought that riches were not sacred but dangerous, and wall paintings in no few churches depicted God putting down the mighty from their seat and exalting the humble and meek. But now, principally through one John Ball, a leader of the revolt, this thought was expressed in political and social terms, not in purely spiritual ones. The gross inequalities of human society were violations of the divine plan, inacceptable to God. To the Christian Socialists of modern industrial society such an idea seems obvious enough, but in the fourteenth century it made the revolt seem utterly discreditable in the eyes of many, an impression strengthened by various excesses committed by the rebels, of which the most news-worthy was their capture of the archbishop of Canterbury and his subsequent execution amidst great hostility (1381). That Wycliffe's followers were intimately connected with the Peasants' Revolt is not at all likely, but it may very well be that the extremism of the movement helped to discredit the teaching of one who was above all an extremist. Certainly he had trodden heavily on so many theological toes that his teaching was bound to be very far from inspiring that widespread support which, with the aid of the printing press, the much more conservative revolt of

Luther was to acquire so quickly almost a century and a half later. What did the Lollards who came after him, believe?

LOLLARDRY

The most obvious characteristic of Lollardry was its total lack of anything remotely approaching theological homogeneity. As has recently been said, 'one cannot talk of a single Lollard creed . . . beliefs varied, not only from group to group, but even from individual to individual within the same group.' Though Wycliffe was widely regarded as their teacher *par excellence*, his high-brow theology was far above the heads of most of the Lollards and with his views were conjoined in some Lollard minds a curious assortment of ideas of very varied origin and respectability. Of these some were pagan, like the assertion of a certain Lollard butcher that the sun and the moon were the only gods; others had a crude magical ring like belief in spells and the view that the Lord's prayer should be said backwards, though it is to be noted that such crudities as these were no new thing and could be found before and after in the undergrowth of popular medieval religion. The Lollards' ban on organ music links them oddly with the Eastern Orthodox and their prohibition of oaths and church bells with the Quakers. Much more major negations cut them off utterly from Catholicism. An early digest of Lollard beliefs includes condemnations of holy orders in the traditional sense; 'the pretended miracle of the sacrament of bread', i.e. transubstantiation; exorcisms and blessings of people and blessings of objects ('the true performance of necromancy'); the holding of temporal offices by clergy, special prayers for the dead, pilgrimages, and offerings to 'blind crosses . . . and deaf images of wood or stone' (the customary image of the Holy Trinity being 'specially abominable'); auricular confession, excommunication and indulgences, 'all manner of manslaughter', vows of celibacy and 'unnecessary arts . . . it seems to us that goldsmiths and armourers and all kinds of art not necessary for a man, according to the apostle, should be destroyed for the increase of virtue'. Significantly there is no attack on monarchy.

Much Lollard belief was clearly very negative and because of this had very limited appeal to contemporary society which was highly conservative. In one major respect however, as we shall see, they were ahead of their time—their insistence on the whole Bible being available for reading by the laity in a vernacular version (page 328) and not as hitherto in Latin. It is very significant indeed that although the Lollard Bibles were quickly banned in England, what is remarkable under all the circumstances, is the large number of them that have survived, showing almost certainly that now as so often in the medieval West, faithful laity felt it proper to ignore an official ruling which seemed unprofitable.

REPRESSION

Just because, at a very early stage of its history, Lollardry was not only banned but vigorously persecuted by the ecclesiastical authorities of the day it is impossible to estimate the number of its supporters. But there seems little doubt that at no stage did it ever win the allegiance of more than a very small percentage of the contemporary population of England. The Crown and leading nobles were perfectly happy to use Wycliffe and his academic reputation as a tool wherewith to attack papal exactions, but once he opened his barrage of violent and incessant attacks on major elements of the current theological system they rapidly deserted him. The illustrious university of Oxford, or rather that section of it which had some sympathy with him, was ultimately not prepared to fight against the powerful official forces that gathered to oppose him. The huge mass of the lower levels of English society were illiterate country dwellers with no interest in theological debate, but entertained a very firm devotion to Catholic worship and all that this implied, and there is no reason to suspect that more than isolated groups and individuals of them gave their allegiance to Lollardry. Only in one section are there some signs of a break-away movement, albeit not of considerable proportions. For some time cloth-making from the good local wool had been flourishing in England, and evidence suggests that amongst its weavers Lollardry gained some little support.

Although for several years earlier Wycliffe's theological views had caused immense fury in academic circles, the starting point of major action against them was the synod of theologians which met at London in 1382 and which condemned as heretical and false twenty-four propositions from Wycliffe's writings. Soon after, the archbishop of Canterbury held a great council at Oxford and sternly broke up the new movement which it had been harbouring. Lollardry had now no great centre but sprouted precariously where local circumstances permitted. By this time there had grown up within it a body of 'priests' or 'poor clerks' who acted as itinerant evangelists for the new cause. They seem very largely to have been both unlearned and unorganised, but worked busily preaching radical views. A very notable feature of their way of life was their stress on reading the Bible in the English translation, which, as we shall see, was the major fruit of their movement.

The conservative-minded authorities were inevitably much alarmed by the Lollard teaching and after contacting the papal court on the matter, in 1395 asked Parliament to introduce the death penalty for heresy (see page 340). Circumstances bred inaction for a while, but in 1401 the statute *De heretico comburendo* ordered that unlicensed preachers be arrested and imprisoned until they abjured or, if they refused so to do, they should be handed over to local royal officials and publicly burnt. Just before the statute had been promulgated, William Sawtry, a Lollard leader who had resumed his unorthodox beliefs after disowning them in 1399, was arrested and soon after burnt at Smithfield, an event which was followed by a number of recantations. The campaign against them now launched under the highest ecclesiastical auspices and the extreme penalties which might be suffered inevitably meant that Lollards had the strongest reasons to avoid being caught in the searchlights of contemporary officialdom, so that the elaborate ecclesiastical records of the age do not afford more than very occasional glimpses of their activities.

Understandably there were dissidents who felt that only force could answer force, though with military resources and skill the Lollards were singularly ill-provided. The leader of the one and only Lollard revolt was Sir John Oldcastle, member of a Herefordshire family of some local importance who in 1409 was made a baron. He became a passionate devotee of the new movement. At first the king's regard for him held back official action. When he was finally imprisoned and brought to trial before the archbishop of Canterbury and the bishops of Winchester and St Paul's he was treated with moderation, but condemned himself by his extremism —the pope was the head of anti-Christ, the bishops were his limbs and the friars the tail, his judges would lead folk to hell. Excommunicated and given over to the secular power Oldcastle was accorded a respite through the king's favour but quickly escaped from his imprisonment in the Tower and sought to organise a rebellion. The main body of forces was to take the city of London whilst a small band was to capture the royal family, then at Eltham Palace (January 1414). The revolt flopped most dismally. Only a few hundred joined it, mostly men with no knowledge and little equipment. By no means all were Lollards and some even betrayed the plot to the Crown. With the greatest possible ease they were totally defeated, without any serious fighting or losses on the royal side. Quickly a few dozen captives were hung and intense search was made for suspects in various parts of England, but nothing like a blood-bath ensued. Oldcastle successfully went underground for a while but late in 1417 he was captured. Already condemned both as a traitor and an incorrigible heretic he was quickly put to death. This was the end of Lollardry as an effective protest movement. Its numbers, already minute, never became anything more and henceforth it was so discredited amongst the gentry that support therefrom was almost nil.

However, the Lollards had scared those in authority. For the rest of the century we find slight traces of their presence, mostly in documents transcribed in contemporary episcopal registers. Such records are few, and besides the Lollards who were caught and brought to trial there was an unascertainable number who successfully laid low.

THE LOLLARD BIBLE

What place did the Bible take in medieval English Church life? To regard it as having been that of a closed book is as untenable as the view that the city of Florence was named after a famous lady whose surname was Nightingale. No medieval ecclesiastical library was complete without a Bible along with commentaries thereon, whilst contemporary theological writings are thickly studded with texts from it, including curious ones from remote sections thereof little utilised today. If expense rendered it almost impossible for folk of moderate means to possess their own Bibles the wealthier clergy, especially if they were graduates, and the

wealthy laity could and did acquire copies. Thus in 1457 we find
John Edlington, rector of Kirkby Ravensworth, leaving to the abbey
of Vaudey 'a Bible covered with black which I bought from Master
Ralph Audeby', but if certain conditions herewith were not accepted by the monastery it was to go to 'the library of the parish
church of Boston'. However, such bequests were certainly rare;
Deanesly's search of 7578 medieval English wills produced mentions of a total of only 136 examples of which 110 were 'Vulgate'
Bibles, i.e. the version in Latin made by St Jerome (d. 420) which
had long been the normal one in the medieval West.

In the matter of Bible study we must draw a very clear-cut
distinction between use of the Bible by the learned and the non-
learned. The former were thoroughly conversant with the text of
the Bible and might cite it very frequently. To the latter the Bible
was not a closed book in the sense that they knew nothing about it.
But their knowledge of it was very uneven indeed. Since they
could mostly neither afford to buy it nor comprehend the Latin in
which it was written they had to rely very largely on knowledge
of it acquired in church services, notably from the sermons that
were preached with a frequency at which we can only guess,
mostly at the main Mass on Sundays and feast days in parish churches
and principally through the readings from the Epistles and Gospels
which were part of every Mass. By the end of our period (when
sermons were certainly much more frequent and much less naive
than they had been at its commencement) many medieval laity
certainly acquired no little fundamental knowledge of Christ. Much
of the Old Testament they would find unhelpful, though like
Sunday school children today, such stories as those of Noah and his
ark, and Daniel in the lion's den caught their imagination, as contemporary art witnesses. Windows and murals also often displayed
lordly figures of the Prophets, though their teaching, one suspects,
was apt to be well above the heads of many of the faithful and may
not have been greatly utilised. On a limited scale Biblical knowledge was imparted through the miracle plays performed on major
ecclesiastical occasions in major centres of population like York,
but the visual arts did much to popularise the major elements of
the Gospels (Chapter 14).

The man in the street at this time, however, cannot have had
any effective comprehension of the extreme complexity and very

varying value of the various books of the Bible. He was conversant with only those sections most relevant to his simple state of life and his picture of these was marred by two factors. Firstly, by the fact that so much of his knowledge came from short extracts. Not even that acme of religious experience enshrined in the four gospels, did he know as a whole, though he heard no small fraction of them read and expounded in church. Also most unfortunate was the fact that medieval churchgoers were well acquainted with a fair amount of apocryphal literature which must have greatly distorted their conception of early Christianity. Specially important here was the great collection of stories regarding the life and miracles of Our Lady. Her cult was very important indeed in late medieval times, as was the thirst for more knowledge about her than the very limited references to her in the New Testament could satisfy. From an early date, much more from affection than fraud, literature about her built up which included many stories which were often characterised by that same lack of contact with the hard facts of life which we find in the science fiction of today.

Three essentials were needed to produce a substantial Bible-reading public. Firstly, a dramatic fall in the price of books, which came only in the late fifteenth and early sixteenth centuries with the development in printing. Secondly, a very much wider appreciation of the value of learning to read than was prevalent in most of our period, a development which was very clearly but slowly under way in the century which preceded the outbreak of the Reformation and derived considerable impetus from the latter. Thirdly, and very important, was the necessity to break that hold over Western education held by the Latin tongue—as has been well said, 'the great vested interest of the Latin language was at once a guarantee of a clerical monopoly of learning and a steady brake on the progress of literacy in lay society' (Galbraith). This ascendancy of Latin was both unavoidable and fruitful in the centuries which followed the collapse of Roman rule in the West, but by the fourteenth century new social forces were at work in England producing and using a respectable vernacular, acquiring for it what has been termed 'a grudging recognition as a written language, adequate for business and education' (page 385-6). In view of this process it is not surprising that this period saw the effective beginnings of a movement to have a complete translation of the Bible in the mother tongue.

The history of the use of Scripture in the vernacular is immensely complex, varying from Church to Church, area to area and period to period. That of the English Bible in medieval times, for example, is not identical with that of the contemporary German Bible of which various editions had appeared before the outbreak of the Reformation.

Although in England, as throughout the West, the Vulgate was the norm, in medieval times before the Norman Conquest it was not unknown to translate into the vernacular various portions of the Bible, though this was far from common. From the mid-thirteenth century onward metrical versions of certain individual books of the Bible appeared, as did one or two versions of the Psalms. But the need was not felt to undertake the translation of the whole Bible into English until a small band of Wycliffe's followers produced the so-called 'Lollard Bible'. This came first in a very literal almost unreadable version which appeared about 1390. It was probably the work of one Nicholas of Hereford and was made from the Vulgate text. Soon after was produced a revised and more readable version probably by a team of scholars led by one John Purvy. At the Council of Oxford in 1407 the Lollard Bible was banned, but as with so much medieval regulation, this move was very far from being effective in practice. This ban opens with the statement, 'it is dangerous, as St Jerome witnesses to translate the text', but overlooks the fact that the saint was not deterred by the danger. It went on to order, 'no one shall in future translate on his own authority any text of Holy Scripture into the English language or any other tongue by way of book, booklet or treatise' and forbade reading the Wycliffite Bible and any other translations that might appear 'until that translation shall be recognised or approved by the diocesan of the place or if the matter demand it, by a provincial council.' It is to be noted that Western tradition at this time was by no means totally hostile on principle to vernacular translations. As Deanesly puts it, down to the late fourteenth century 'the attitude of the Church to biblical translations was determined by the attitude of the translator and the purpose of the translation; if this translation were made for some king or exalted personage, or by some solitary student, and remained a hallowed but practically unused volume in a royal or monastic library, no objection was taken to the translation as such; but if the translation was used to popularise a knowledge of the biblical text among lay people, prohibition immediately followed. From the end of the fourteenth century lay people of the upper classes could usually obtain license from their confessors to use translations of parts of the Bible . . . but, broadly speaking, those who desired to obtain such dispensations were few, since Bible reading was not recommended as an ordinary pious practice for the laity till quite the close of the middle ages'.

Why was late medieval official ecclesiastical opinion in England comparatively hostile to the vernacular Bible? To this question there was more than one answer provided in and after Wycliffe's day. Some opposition was due more to conservatism than anything else. This, perhaps, led Archbishop Arundel to declare that Wycliffe came to 'fill up the measure of his malice by devising a new translation of Scripture'. Unworthy of serious consideration was the contention now put forward by some that familiarity with the Bible text would lead to irreverence. Not much more convincing was the rather donnish argument that the linguistic problems involved in translating the Bible from Latin to English were so very great as to make the venture over-perilous.* This line of thought was emphasised by a Dominican contemporary of Wycliffe's: 'How therefore the properties of the language can be preserved in the English tongue, or any other barbarous tongue, which is by no means governed by rules or grammar, I fail to see. The English tongue is not only lacking in letters but even in words, for the best known and commonest Latin words have no corresponding names or words in English.' However, what is sauce for the goose is sauce for the gander and if doubt and dissension was an argument against pursuit of biblical learning, it was also very applicable to those massive doctrinal problems to which medieval friars applied themselves. But the fact that the friar pushes his argument too far must not blind us to the fact that, as the experience of Reformation theology soon made evident, the correct translation of the text of Scripture on many major matters was by no means obvious. Only

---

* It is to be noted that only with the scholars of the Renaissance came the realisation that since the Old Testament was originally written in Hebrew and the New Testament in Greek scholarship demanded that translations should be made from these original tongues and not from the Latin Vulgate which, incidentally, by the late Middle Ages was often preserved in somewhat corrupt texts.

in our own days has the progress of biblical linguistic scholarship made it feasible to produce vernacular versions of Scripture on whose accuracy both Catholic and non-Catholic agree.

Very much the major argument against universal Bible reading by the uninstructed laity (and be it remembered at this time a huge percentage of laity were almost totally illiterate) was the fear that this would lead to the propagation of unreasonable views totally incompatible with traditional Christian belief. This fear (which, of course, the fissiparous growth of Protestantism from the sixteenth century onwards showed to be far from foolish) was particularly important in the England of the Lollards, since the first complete English Bible was the product of a group whose radical theology was totally incompatible with medieval Catholic tradition and, incidentally, also with the more traditional theology of the Eastern Churches. The case of the English Bible would have received much more sympathetic treatment had a secular-minded local episcopate not left its advocacy to the theological extremists we call Wycliffe and the Lollards who were, it may be argued, the English Bible's worst enemies.

When the question of the English Bibles was hitting the headlines there, a Franciscan at Oxford wrote, 'since people are slow of understanding and the Holy Scripture is full of ambiguities or doubtful matters ... how, I ask, should their reading be a means of obtaining knowledge of the meaning of Holy Scripture?'. Such an argument, it may be thought, was half right and half wrong—right in so far as the medieval layman was utterly unqualified to make convincing comments on such tricky theological problems as the nature of the sacraments, of the sacred ministry and of papal authority, but wrong in so far as for a comprehension of the nature of the demands made by God on the individual soul, no special intellectual training is required. Christ revealed himself to 'little children' and it is significant that amongst the major saints few professors are to be found, but many who, like St Francis and St Thérèse, had very little formal education but were utterly dominated by the words of the Gospels.

It is certainly easy to oversimplify this question of Bible reading and doubtful if there is any easy and obvious answer even today when educational advances have narrowed the wide and confusing series of interpretations of the biblical text long current. The problem which verged on the insoluble was to find a way of affording access to the text of Scripture to the illiterate and uninformed which would not be followed by major theological differences of interpretation thereof which would shatter the unity of the Christian Church. Archbishop Arundel saw the value of the faithful study of the life of Christ but felt the faithful might misuse the Gospel text. The learned and ultra-pious Thomas More (d. 1535) pondered the matter in his thoughtful way. He recognised that down the centuries translations of the Bible had been regarded as permissible, but attacked the Lollard Bible, somewhat incorrectly, for having 'purposely corrupted the holy text', and thought that the answer was to allow devout and instructed members of society to read English Bibles after authorisation from their bishop though, as we have seen, the late medieval bishops had no great technical qualifications for such a task, nor in the literal sense, much time for such a duty.

At the root of the whole problem lay not so much the question of translation of particular words—though these in some cases might be very important—as the very complex problem of the exact nature of the authority contained in the Bible. The scholarship of the last century and a half has brought out very strongly two fundamental and inescapable facts: (i) that the Bible is not a single unit, but a series of units (the word Bible means 'the books', not 'the book') which, albeit united by the common purpose of displaying God's dealings with men vary immensely in nature, date, purpose and spiritual insight. Hence all extracts therefrom must be interpreted in very close relation to their context and not treated as isolated units of equivalent significance, like so many bricks in a child's box. (ii) that the Bible in general and the Gospel message in particular is dynamic as well as static. It is not a final message in the sense of saying all that is to be said about God but a revelation of the way to enlarged understanding. 'I have many things to say but you cannot hear them now,' said Christ, 'when He the Comforter shall come, He will guide you into all truth.' Thus, as the Church quickly perceived, her life was not only based fundamentally on happenings in Palestine in the time of Christ. When the ministry of deacons was instituted by the apostles it was not because Christ had specifically ordered it, but because to the Church with its built-in guidance of the Holy Spirit it was clearly desirable; 'it has seemed good to the Holy Spirit and to us' was the convincing argument. That the Church's spiritual efficacy demanded a certain capacity to evolve was a fundamental conviction of both Eastern and Western Christendom, though by late medieval times they were not at one on the nature and extent of this.

The major cause for the very strong condemnation of the teaching of Wycliffe and his Lollards by Catholic leaders both in England and outside it, and one which reinforced the drive against reading of the English Bible by the public in general, was the total rejection by the former of any major evolutionary element in Christianity—thus More wrote of the contemporary translator of the Bible, 'first he would make the people believe nothing but plain Scripture, in which point he teacheth a plain pestilent heresy.' Did the New Testament constitute only an end or was it also a beginning? Was ultimate authority to be given only to what the Bible declared in so many words, or was it also to be sought in the tradition drawn from it by the Church which Christ had founded and to which He had promised future guidance by the Holy Spirit? Here was the major problem of the Reformation, the problem of the nature of authority, of the relation of Scripture and Tradition. In very recent times progress in scholarship has shown that these two terms are by no means so hostile to each other as the sixteenth-century West believed, and that in some degree Scripture must be reinforced by Tradition. The Lollards, anticipating herein in extreme form the Protestants of later days, urged the total rejection of Tradition and thus created immense distrust in traditional Catholic circles. If the Lollards had not linked this most radical challenge to Catholic authority so closely with the importance of the general public freely reading the Bible in the vernacular, the considerable suspicion of the latter that they generated in England would not have been so strong.

As it was, as we have seen, a council at Oxford in 1407 forbade translation or use of any English translation of the Bible unless it had been approved by the diocesan of the area or, if need be, by a provincial council. In fact, however, as was not surprising considering the lack of spiritual calibre of the English bishops of the fifteenth century, the whole matter was evidently treated as a very hot potato and left untouched. It is possible that in process of time, some authorities at least turned a blind eye to the Lollard Bible which seems to have been appreciably more popular than those who gave it its title.

THE AFTERMATH

Any answer to the interesting and important question of the fate of Lollardry after it went underground depends fundamentally on how we define the term. It is doubtful if one can do other than employ it to cover all forms of major dissent from orthodox Catholicism, though Lollards themselves differed considerably on the nature and extent of their rejection of the current ecclesiastical set-up. For obvious reasons very little trace of it is preserved in official documents, though there is evidence of small-scale bubbles of dissent rippling the surface of English life down to the time of Henry VIII. The total number of known dissenters is very small and their beliefs far from unanimous.

Recent publication of the text of a trial of sixty alleged Lollards (fifty-one men and nine women) in the diocese of Norwich between 1428 and 1431 has thrown some interesting light on a section of the movement which may or may not be typical of the whole. Their major examination was concerning their beliefs regarding the use of images, confessions, the Mass, pilgrimages, tithes and mortuary fees, baptism, matrimony, consorting with heretics and invocation of saints. None were relapsed heretics and no death penalty was imposed. At least fourteen were found not guilty, most of the rest being punished by floggings, usually from three to six times. This was already a traditional punishment for certain other offences. The guilty person was publicly paraded in specified attire (often shirt and breeches) and carried a candle (which would be fairly expensive). He was flogged in the parish church or cemetery or market place, this publicity being perhaps the most unpopular part of the punishment. Of the later history of Lollardry an eminent historian wrote words which may still be true: 'That there continued a Wycliffite tradition without a break until the time of the Protestant Reformation need not be questioned, but it was so slight and attenuated that it exercised no appreciable influence upon our later history' (R. Lane Poole).

The mass of the lower orders were certainly conservative and were made more so by Lollard extremism so that any unusual ecclesiastical behaviour was liable to be condemned by them as Lollard. Margery Kempe (who died in the mid-fifteenth century) has left us the first English autobiography of a lay woman. She probably held no dangerous heretical views but was a rather curious person who developed a trying habit of restlessly wandering around holy places, lamenting and weeping loudly and copiously from high religious reasons, but in the process, greatly disturbing the faithful, especially when these outbursts occurred, as they often did, during public worship. What was to be done with this unusual person? The bishop of Lincoln having been informed by her that 'he dreadeth more the shames of the world than the perfect love of God', passed the spiritual buck, sending her to the archbishop of Canterbury along with 26s. 8d. 'to buy her clothes with and to pray for him'. The archbishop of York followed suit, finding it best to put her in charge of one of a number of volunteers for this curious employ saying to him, 'See, here is five shillings, and lead her fast out of this country'. The laity, predictably, were less patient. In London a woman in Smithfield told Margery, 'I would thou wert in Smithfield and I would bring a faggot to burn thee with'. At Hessle she was arrested as 'the greatest Lollard in all this country or about London either', and women came 'running out of their houses with their distaffs crying to the people "Burn this false heretic".' It is scenes such as this which vividly illustrate popular distaste of religious novelty at the time and which make it necessary to consider very seriously the recent view that the Reformation was a movement which Wycliffe 'did little or nothing to inspire and in effect everything possible to delay', and that he did 'more than any man in Catholic England—though admittedly that was not his intention—to discredit even moderate reform with the political class which alone had the power to carry it out' (MacFarlane).

However, such considerations must not be allowed to obscure the fact that various major problems to which Lollards offered unacceptable solutions, were very real ones which continued to engage the attention of at least some of the more thoughtful faithful, even if the contemporary episcopate showed no capacity at all to recognise the red light that they flashed. Much work has yet to be done on fifteenth-century literature before this concern can be fully appreciated, but a significant example of it is offered by 'the Destroyer of Vices' (*Destructorium Viciorum*) of Alexander Carpenter, an enormous and influential theological compendium finished in 1429, which illuminates vividly the life and thought of the times. The author does not voice Wycliffe's attacks on such fundamentals as the papacy and the sacraments, but makes lusty criticism of clergy of the time who go in for high-brow and lucrative studies 'to their damnation' whilst 'utterly despising Holy Scripture'. The laity, he urges, must be instructed laity, partly through hearing plenteous sermons (Alexander follows Wycliffe in citing Grosseteste's remark, 'the excellent and greatest Work of Mercy is the preaching of God's word'), but it was supremely necessary for them to know the Gospel message—'let infidels, heretics and enemies of the Christian faith blush with shame who say that the laity are not required to know, learn, understand or intermeddle with the Gospel ... the laity therefore are to be instructed by priests to hear Holy Scripture gladly, humbly learn it ...'.

Such criticisms hit the theological bull's-eye and other of his shafts are well on target, such as his condemnation of the luxurious life of great ecclesiastics who 'deserve to be called princes of provinces rather than pastors of souls' and of the 'pomp of temporal lordship with which the Church is polluted'.

However, the principal purpose of his tone was not so much to attack contemporary abuses as to provide a massive and very comprehensive theological handbook. Thus after consideration of Sin (whether Original, Mortal or Venial) comes elaborate treatment of the Seven Deadly Sins; Avarice, Gluttony, Lust, Sloth, Envy, Wrath and Pride—the first of which is considered under sixty-eight heads, the last under eighty with comment on a noble variety of subjects ranging from apostasy and magic to over-luxurious dress, horses and noble birth. Unfortunately his mass of good advice went largely unheeded and was, perhaps, also largely unread by those church leaders who alone had the power to put aright the things which were amiss in the English Church. But it would be very wrong to believe that at the end of the fifteenth century there was no serious criticism of contemporary church life in England—the shocking complacency so evident in much of the eighteenth century was not to be found even if in many areas the laity were content to tread the conservative path of their forefathers.

THE END OF THE CENTURY

The history of the final half century of the period which this volume seeks to cover is not an easy one to summarise, partly because it has not been a popular subject of study, partly because certain major sources, notably the chronicles and the Chancery enrolments are appreciably less informative than hitherto, partly also because much literary material and many of the episcopal registers of the period, like the massive tomes at York and Norwich, have been very little explored.

Although on the Continent major new currents of thought of immense importance were now running, there is little doubt that until the new century dawned there are few signs of them stirring the waters of English Christianity which now, as so often, was behind the theological times. The stupendous literary and artistic activities of the Renaissance spread rapidly in Italy from the late fourteenth century onwards, but made very little impact on England before the early sixteenth century. Much nearer home had been spreading in Holland, Germany, France and Italy a major religious movement which came to be entitled *Devotio Moderna*, whose most illustrious product was the *Imitation of Christ* of Thomas à Kempis, which gave an important impetus to individual study of the life and death of Christ, but had created no great stir in England by the end of our period. The little band of mystics which shone like great stars in fourteenth-century England had no successors and even the printing press, to grasp whose utility did not require great insight, arrived here late, the first printed book in England appearing in 1474, almost quarter of a century after its opposite number on the Continent. At the end of the period much in the English Church was largely running on local lines.

With the Roman see relations were unspectacular with no sign of major disharmony between king and pope largely because, as we have seen, the latter was now acquiring so much of the patronage and taxation he desired. Lay lawyers were maintaining their sharp-shooting over a legal no-man's-land that separated them from canon lawyers but the conflicts here cannot be regarded as of major import.

As has already been noted, the centralisation at the Roman curia of a truly enormous mass of church business, both major and minor, had long been under way and by the fifteenth century as the *Calendar of Papal Letters* shows most vividly the amount of English ecclesiastical matters which had to be referred to Rome for settlement was very considerable, including much that was of very trifling significance. Thus in 1402 the Austin canons of the little priory of

Haltemprice acquired papal license to wear shoes and not sandals as their ancient custom demanded and two years later a canon of Newburgh was given exemption by the curia from his obligation to celebrate a weekly Mass with music and in a loud voice because he had an impediment in his speech. Earlier, because of the poverty of his house, the abbot of Jervaulx was licensed to hold a benefice in the patronage of his monastery. When one remembers how many thousand ecclesiastical bodies and people great and small might now find it necessary to have recourse by Rome because of the very complex and very papalised common law which had developed in our period, one cannot fail to appreciate how top-heavy, expensive and often dilatory the machinery of the Western Church had become or fail to be surprised at the vigorous criticism which the curia had so long inspired. From the papal angle the vast expense of maintaining at Rome the massive administration inevitably required was a perennial problem of the first magnitude, demanding financial exactions from the faithful which were bound to breed unpopularity.

However, it is important not to over-simplify the problem and assume that all that was wanted to remedy it was an extensive transference of some of the wide-ranging powers monopolised at this time by the Roman curia to the local episcopates of the West. The centralisation of law under the Roman see produced an elaborate, uniform and highly rational ecclesiastical code whose claims to respect by the faithful were infinitely greater than anything which the local Western churches could have evolved on their own and gave the Church an invaluable uniformity of practice stretching over thousands of square miles of Europe. Further, as we have seen, the medieval papacy could, in very varying degree, act as a brake on that gross secularisation of church property and appointments to which the upper classes of medieval laity were perennially prone, and it would be naive to assume that the latter would not take advantage of the removal of the brake to increase their hold on ecclesiastical appointments in their locality. With obvious wisdom in ages when social life was crude, the law of the church forbade the ordination of a man of illegitimate birth unless he had obtained a special dispensation from this bar. To have done otherwise could clearly have opened wide an obviously improper mode of making financial provision for a bastard. If the power to grant this dispensation had been left to local bishops they were so very liable to local social and other pressures that they would almost certainly have granted them much more freely than was desirable, whereas the absence therefrom of local secular influences involved in an appeal at Rome probably far outweighed the disadvantage of bribery and corruption at the curia which prevailed there to an extent very difficult to determine. The fact of the matter is that the papacy at the end of our period, like the English government today, had quite innocently and almost accidentally reached a position wherein its powers had become so very sweeping that the very proper rights of the local community were in danger of being seriously undervalued. But then, as with government in England today, the problem of drawing the right line of demarcation between central and local authority was one of immense complexity with no facile or agreed solution to be had.

The popes of the period, though mostly by no means very scandalous, can be accused of getting priorities wrong. To demand vigorous support for a Crusade as did Pius II (1458–64) was to flog a horse that had been long dead, whilst the lavish patronage of Renaissance to art and letters dispensed by some popes of the period, however laudable posterity has found it, cannot have done anything to endear Rome to the men in England's village streets.

An obvious result of the dominance of this over-centralised papal machinery which had very long been evident and was next to impossible to remedy under contemporary conditions was the huge delay and high cost which often resulted from it. On top of this there was still that bribery perennially liable to appear in such circumstances, papal or non-papal, down the centuries. To what extent it would have been either feasible or desirable under existing social conditions to decentralise much ecclesiastical business, as has happened in the Roman Church since Vatican Council II, is a question very much open to debate. It is quite clear that, by and large, Roman use of English cash and appointments was very far from reaching major proportions. It is true that in 1497 the first of three non-resident Italians were nominated to the see of Worcester, but this was a highly exceptional situation and can be defended as one of those under-the-counter moves to aid papal finances in return for favours received, which had long been found useful on both sides. Peter's Pence now totalled a sum which can only be regarded as derisory, as can the idea that large sums of papal taxation were leaving the country. There are few signs of either major aggressive anti-papalism or of that romantic ultra-montanism of Victorian Roman Catholicism. As the reign of Henry VIII was to exhibit luminously the principal danger to the papacy came from the fact that it had gone so far to establish an *entente cordiale* with the English Crown that it had totally lost that éclat derived from being the protector of local rights against royal infringement which had made it so popular under Henry II. Public opinion drifted along, not seeking to be anti-papal but not universally feeling so strongly on the matter as to be aggressively pro-papal when the crunch came, a tendency much strengthened by the fact that their leaders, the bishops, were very largely king's men. It is significant that the most intelligent and pious opposition to Henry VIII came from one who was no great ecclesiastic—Thomas More.

No-one today can accept either the roseate picture of the late medieval English religion entertained rather than discovered by Belloc or the somewhat grimy one apt to be obtained from the pages of G. C. Coulton (who, however, was accustomed to aver that the condition of the English Church in these times was superior to those in many other areas of Western Europe). Under the social conditions of the time the dominant factor in determining to what extent if at all a community veered to the theological left at the Reformation was very likely to be settled not by popular opinion or minority pressure groups but by its ruler. Nowhere was this to be more obvious than in England.

For some time in the higher levels of theological study there has been growing appreciation of the value of the writings of the Christian mystics. In medieval England the first major figure in this field was Richard Rolle of Hampole (*c* 1300–1349) who after study at Oxford became a hermit and finally chaplain to the nuns of the small monastery from which his surname derives. His writings acquired very considerable renown in the sphere for which they were designed in late medieval times. At an unknown date later in the century an unknown person wrote *The Cloud of Unknowing*, which is now very highly thought of by those competent to judge it, as is the allied *Ladder of Perfection* whose author was Walter Hilton (d. 1396), an Austin canon of the little priory of Thurgarton. In the fifteenth century the mystical literature in England increased little, a major exception being *The Sixteen Revelations of Divine Love*, probably written at St Julian's church in Norwich, by an anchoress who was born about 1342 and who died about seventy years later.

NOTE:

Heresy and the Death Penalty. Heresy is the term applied to formal denial or doubt of a defined doctrine. In the first thousand years of Christian history it was not under any circumstances officially punished by the death penalty, nor has it ever been so in Eastern Christendom, but in the Western Church, by what is one of the very few major indefensible developments in its history, this practice prevailed for a while, originating in our period, persisting for some little time thereafter to be imitated on a smallish scale by some Protestant bodies.

Pope Innocent III (1198–1216) probably, if not indubitably, envisaged the possibility under certain circumstances of the punishment of heretics by death, and in 1231 Pope Gregory certainly approved this. The classic defence of this indefensible action was exposed by no less a person than Aquinas, relying much too heavily on logic and much too little on the Gospel. For him, to hold heretical views is to 'deserve to be shut off from the world by death, for it is a much more serious matter to corrupt faith through which comes the soul's life than to forge money'.* The Church should show mercy to the extent of admonishing the heretic, seeking to get him to abandon his error, and only condemn him if he refused to do so. Otherwise he was to be excommunicated, deprived of holy orders if he had them, and handed over to the local secular authorities 'to be exterminated from the world by death.' The great horror in which heresy was held led to death by burning being the form taken by this punishment.

In very partial extenuation of this revolting practice it may be noted:

(i) Death by burning was not confined to this offence but was used as a punishment for certain secular crimes, examples of this occurring in comparatively recent times. There is no doubt that for long,

---

* Forgery in this time was a capital offence.

popular sensitivity to physical suffering was a good deal less marked than it is in most areas today.

(ii) This final penalty was only imposed after efforts had been made to get the accused to return to orthodoxy, and usually after legal trials which seem usually to have been a good deal more painstaking than no few of those in our present times.

(iii) Even allowing for the small size of the medieval population, with a few notable exceptions, the number of people who suffered was totally insignificant by modern standards.

PART FIVE

Church and Society

CHAPTER 12

BEQUESTS AND HEALING

ALMSGIVING

ALTHOUGH the ancient Romans greatly benefited humanity by their insistence that society must be sustained by good order and a rigorously rational system of law, they cannot be said to have displayed any very considerable sensitivity to the major social problems raised by the perennial existence of poor and needy folk. Judaism took such matters much more seriously, but its narrow interpretation of the responsibilities of the Chosen People meant that their social solicitude was largely confined to folk of their own persuasion. In very vivid contrast to this is the constant concern for the corporal needs of men, irrespective of their race or religion, persistently displayed in various forms by Christianity.

In a memorable utterance recorded in the gospel of St Matthew, Christ has stressed with force and precision the immense spiritual value of giving practical assistance to those in need by specific deeds of mercy. To give food to the hungry, to give drink to the thirsty, to welcome the stranger, to clothe the naked, to visit the sick, to attend those in prison, was to engage in activities which would gain the divine reward—'Come, O blessed of my Father, inherit the kingdom prepared for you from the foundation of the world.' Elsewhere he urged in at least one context, 'sell everything you possess and give the money to the poor' and commanded all, 'lay up not treasure on earth where moth and rust corrupt and thieves break in and steal.' His followers supported this solicitude for the poor with enthusiasm. St Paul was asked by his fellow apostles 'that we should keep the poor in mind, which was the very thing I made it my business to do.' Very remarkable and immensely influential for posterity was the massive interest in poor relief shown by the first Christians at Jerusalem. Here 'not one of them claimed any possessions as his own but everything was common property to all' and a huge operation of poor relief seems to have been mounted. If care for the indigent was one inevitable good work, the dispensing of hospitality was another. To contemporary pagans this largely meant providing for the needs of travellers and it was presumably in this sense that the word was originally used in the New Testament. Thus the Epistle to the Romans *inter alia* urged the faithful to contribute alms and 'practice hospitality' whilst that to Titus numbered amongst the responsibilities of a bishop was that of being 'a lover of hospitality', a phrase which was to be cited in pontificals of later days, though the sense seems to have expanded.

Medieval man was fascinated by Christ's list of the deeds of mercy, picturing them repeatedly in his art, notably in stained glass windows and in manuscripts. But as he was quite sure that most of the best things went in sevens, he added to them a further injunction (from the book of Tobit) to bury the dead, which fitted nicely into place and covered what was a very real social need of the times. Contemporary regard for these actions in England was powerfully reinforced by official backing such as the influential canon of Archbishop Pecham which ordered the systematic rehearsal of these 'corporal acts of mercy' at public worship. To call almsgiving as an eminent medievalist once did 'the favourite pastime of the middle ages' is to sacrifice verity to a donnish phrase, for to the faithful of the times it was very much more than this, being a major and inevitable responsibility for all who took their religion seriously.

It is quite impossible to survey here the whole vast and complicated field of almsgiving in our period, especially that originating from people great and small in their lifetime. Of this we have very scanty documentary information. It is clear that major households were apt to find meals for a wide variety of visitors who had good reason to be in the vicinity. Thus the household accounts of Dame Alice de Bryene (1412–13) provide for a very steady flow of meals for guests which include wandering friars, local clergy, visiting workmen and a number of anonymous and unidentifiable people. Even the little house of chantry priests at Bridport seems to have entertained to meals quite large totals, for reasons which are not always clear—why did no less than four carpenters dine with them one Sunday?

But there can be little doubt that in much of rural England a man's almsgiving was limited by his small means until he had passed from this mortal life, when his will would make provision for alms to a variety of good causes often on a scale which by contemporary economic standards was very considerable. Though wills belonging to the first half of our period are not very common, in the latter half they profilerate and provide a spate of fascinating, very specific information. Besides this very potent source of good works, regular alms were dispensed firstly by various ecclesiastical institutions as an adjunct to their other activities, of which the monasteries were by far the most numerous and important, and also by 'hospitals', religious establishments where social work was a good deal wider in scope than that of the modern institutions of that name.

WILLS

It is important to appreciate that the scope of the will in the England of our period differed from the present one in various significant ways. Thus mostly, though not entirely, the bequests therein contained were confined to movable property, such things as lands and buildings being excluded. Further, it was compulsory to give to the incumbent of the testator's parish 'mortuary' or 'corpse present', which theoretically was his most valuable movable and due in recompense for unpaid tithes and offerings. In nature it varied somewhat according to local custom and the social position of the testator. For the great mass of country folk this obligation generally meant giving their best beast, though if there were less than three of the animals this was not due. Thus we have references to 'my best guds', 'my best beest', and in 1433 John Shakespeare, chapman, left 'my best animal as my mortuary'. In town the mortuary was usually paid in clothing. One will speaks of 'my best garment for my mortuarie after the custom of the citie of Yorke' and another testator there left as mortuary 'my best gowne with my hatt'. Higher up the social scale we have mention of 'my young gray hors to be my cors present' and Lord Scrope leaves 'my best horse, after the custom of the countre used with men like of mine honour'. Another will notes, 'bycause it is the good custome of the churche where the body liethe to have a corse present, therefore I will the place aforesaid to have my horse that I did ride oppon, saddle and bridle'. Not only was harness often added to the horse that was the mortuary, but those able to offer such things might also add the dead man's armour. Thus Sir Anthony St Quintin left his best horse with its saddle, bridle and equipment and 'my armour as is the custom'.

Generally a man who died leaving a wife and children had to leave a third of his chattels to each. So far as bishops were concerned, as Sheehan points out, in the early part of our period 'there was a fairly widespread opinion that it was not fitting for such folk to leave great wealth' and that 'surplus income from his see should be given in alms during life rather than after death.' This custom to some extent broke down later, for, as we shall see, some episcopal bequests were of enormous size.

Of major importance for our study is the fact that the primary purpose of the medieval English will was to be an instrument for almsgiving, a fact which, incidentally, does much to explain why parish priests were expected to ensure that the faithful did not die intestate and why probate became a matter for the ecclesiastical courts. Although bequests to relations and friends by testators are not absent, usually they are exceeded in number and importance by those made for charitable purposes whose range is very wide indeed and significantly never recognise the bogus distinction between religious and secular. Every bequest made for the glory of God and the betterment of His people was a pious gift and there was no fundamental difference between them. Thus the will of a Nottingham burgess, Thomas Thurland (1470), orders his executors to 'distribute and dispose for my saule and all Cristen saules in making of hegh weyes, synging of masses, relevying of pore and nedy peple and in other warkes of charite'. Similarly, another testator leaves the residue of his goods to 'charity and pious uses . . . such as relieving indigent monasteries, the marriages of poor maidens, succouring the poor and needy and . . . other works of piety'. Dame Joan Chamberleyn left money 'for the wele of my saule; that is to say to the exhibicion of pore chylder apt to lerne at scole, pore maydens well disposyd to mariages and to wayes or briges, broken or hurte to the neuance . . . of Crysten people amendynge and reparenge . . .'. Very often the will's opening clauses deal with the ecclesiastical steps taken to liberate the soul of the testator from purgatory with all convenient speed, which vary greatly in kind and in quantity, but these are inextricably bound up with arrangements for the testator's funeral which often combine no little liturgical complexity with social benefits.

FUNERALS AND ALMSGIVING

Again and again people of substance ordered that at the funeral the body should be attended by a contingent of poor folk clad in dress newly made for the occasion who carried torches and said prayers for the soul of the dead person. Such provision is made with more than usual detail in the will of Lord John le Scrope (1455) which provides that his sons and servants carry his body to the Scrope Chapel in York Minster preceded by 'twenty four poor men clothed in white gowns and hoods, each of them having a new set of wooden beads, walking before it'. These poor men were to stand, sit or kneel before the entrance to the chapel and pray that God grant his soul eternal rest, and each of them were to receive for his pains 6d. The total of such poor very often numbered thirteen in memory of Christ and the twelve apostles. Such a number was ordered for the funeral by Thomas White, a draper of Beverley. These were to have white gowns (black was a much more usual colour), hoods and shoes and were 'altogether on bended knee about my body on the day of the funeral [to] say the Psalter of the Virgin Mary'. Bishop Hatfield of Durham arranged for fifty such poor to stand round his body holding torches of wax and Lord Abergavenny provided for twenty-four. Lord William Bardolf ordered a body of forty-eight poor, half of them to be men dressed in black and the remainder women in white. In return for such services the poor concerned usually received not only the new set of clothes which they wore (which in the case of one male contingent was defined as shirt, belt, stockings, shoes, gown and hood) but a cash payment, usually of a few pence. Bequests to friars occur very frequently in late medieval wills and sometimes their presence at the funeral is requested. Thus a citizen of York left 5s. to each 'closter' of friars, willing 'that they come with thar crosses to my buriall before me'. Much less easy to parallel is the bequest to certain parsons of three gallons and to certain vicars five gallons of wine 'if they fetch me at my parish church'.*

* There are various indications of a cheerful approach to death. The testator just mentioned also left 10s. 'to Mastres Evers to drinke for my saulle with hir frendes and mine'. Anthony Middleton, merchant, provided 'to my neborows in the way of recreacion to make mery withall at ther pleasure 6s. 8d.', whilst a good lady who apparently ran a pub ordained 'I will that ther be a wholl brewing of ale given to my customers after the quantitie of thar tonnyng in a weke'.

Among the biggest items in the almsgiving which accompanied a funeral was the dole to the poor which was a major feature of many wills. A mere housewife of Easingwold leaves 20s. to the poor on the day of her burial and 40s. to the funeral dinner for her friends —quite considerable sums in her time. A chaplain gives the same but reverses the order of preference. But a York glover, with next to no stock and apparently little of value but a 'Sancte John Hede' and 'a byrde cage with a corde' could afford nothing, the more so since he owed money to 'the Wyf at the Bell at Doncaster', presumably for past potations. A York shopkeeper provided for ½d. each to be given to 'every poor man present at the church door', and one Thomas Findern (1525) to every man, woman and child coming to his burial a halfpenny loaf and 'a shiffer of cheese'. A Cornish squire left a penny dole to every man, woman and child at his funeral to pray for his soul.

Richard Pigot, sergeant-at-law, left twenty marks to the poor, 'for that I have been occupied in the worlde and taken men's money and not done so effectually for it as I ought to have done'. Sir Alexander Nevill bequeathed £10 in dole on the day of his interment for 'pure men, women and children', and Dame Alice Neville ordered ten marks 'to be distribute among pore folkes in money, mete and drink for me and and all my good doers'. The richer folk left considerable sums for the relief of the poor, as did Sir Ralph Bigod: £40 'to prestes, clerkys and other pore people coming to the church the day of my burial'. Sir Brian Stapleton arranged for his executors 'to deall penny doll' of 4d. to priests and 2d. to clerks. An archdeacon of Cleveland left £20 for the same purpose, Bishop Hatfield of Durham fifty silver marks, Bishop Strickland of Carlisle ten silver pounds. The noble Sir William Manney, buried in style in London, left to each of the poor at his funeral a penny 'to pray for me and for the remission of my sins', a provision which may well have amounted to a considerable sum. Roger, Lord de la Warr, ordered £100 to be distributed amongst the poor 'not by penny doll but that every person whom my executors may think fit shall have half a mark'. Unusual was the arrangement of William, earl of Salisbury, whereby there were to be distributions of 25s. to 300 poor men daily until his funeral. Elizabeth, countess of Salisbury, provided twenty-five marks to be distributed at 4d. a head amongst 1000 poor. Jane, Viscountess Lisle (1500), made a most elaborate will covering eighteen pages of printed text whose composition, one suspects, gave her no little innocent pleasure. In it she left £20 in alms 'among poor people the day of my burying or as shortly after as may be doon to every person, 1*d*.', thus implying a number of beneficiaries as high as 4800. To this one added a complex series of further gifts to the needy, including 300 'shirts and smokks for poure folke', half going to members of either sex 'where most nede shall be, to pray for my soule'. Cardinal Beaufort left the huge sum of 2000 marks to be distributed amongst an unspecified number of poor tenants. John of Gaunt provided that for 40 days after his death 50 silver marks to be given to the poor daily, with 300 more on the eve of his funeral and no less than 500 silver marks on the day of his burial. Archbishop Winchelsey of Canterbury left 40 marks for the poor of the diocese of Lincoln and 20 marks to each of the other dioceses of his province for the same purpose. For the good of his soul Archbishop Walter Reynolds left 1*d*. to each poor person on the day of his burial, providing that at least 100 marks be thus distributed, implying 16 000 recipients. But the ground record in this matter so far as the present writer has observed goes to Cardinal Morton, archbishop of Canterbury, who ordered the expenditure of no less than 1000 marks in connection with his decease, or more or less as his executors found fit, in gifts to the poor and needy and other appropriate good causes 'for the good of my soul', and to similar ends he left most of the residue of his estate. (It is, of course, to be remembered that the celibacy of the clergy had the useful effect of limiting to small proportions the amount of their legacies to relations.) Beside this sum, the £20 left by Archbishop Dene (1503) to 'the poor of both sexes converging on the said city and church of Canterbury to pray for my soul' seems unimpressive.

For clergy, a funeral also provided the chance of adding a small sum to their income, provided they attended the obsequies and prayed for the soul of the departed person, the bequests for this thus killing two birds with one stone. The scale of payment depended on the rank of the person, as we see in the will of Thomas Forme, sub-treasurer of York Minster. Of those present at his burial a canon was to receive 4*s*., a 'parson' 2*s*., a vicar the same, to each deacon and clerk and sexton 12*d*. and 8*d*. 'to every tribler and chorister'. Archdeacon Stephen Scrope made similar provision, with 6s. 8d. for a residentiary canon or the precentor, 2s. for parsons, 20d. for vicars, 12d. for deacons, subdeacons and thurifers, ending the list pleasingly with a small gift for the church cleaner. On top of this, as we have noted, were often payments to the friars. Clearly a major funeral would have a grandiose collection of mourners to match the grandiose setting.

Torches and tapers were *de rigueur* at least at the better class funerals, and were costly things whose use after the funeral wills often regulate in great detail—one lady left 'a torche to burne daily at the elevacion while he will endure'. The pall which covered the body at top social level might also be very expensive and so might be the hearse on which the body rested, whilst additional if minor expense was incurred by employment of bell-ringers and sometimes of that recently extinct personage, the bellman. On top of this was what might easily be a major item, provision of food for the mourners. Medieval English bishops seem to have successfully eliminated the meal on the eve of the funeral whereat the Irish tended to display unseemly exuberance, though occasionally we find trace of small repasts after the *Dirige* (which preceded the burial) like that ordered by the good Mrs Alison Clarke who ordered provision of 'comfettes, sugir plattes and suckittes' for her neighbours from Stonegate and Botham Bar. A meal after the burial was a very reasonable provision and seems often to be open to largish numbers on an occasion whereat it cannot have been easy to separate sheep from goats, so seems often to have been expensive.

Clearly the total cost of a medieval funeral with so much attendant almsgiving of one kind or another might often become very heavy indeed. William, Lord Willoughby, reckoned on expenses totalling £200 at his burial, 'in all charges viz. black gowns, the dole, dinner, the carriage of my body'. The same sum was allowed by William Beauchamp, earl of Warwick, but John, earl of Pembroke, estimated £300 or more. The curious will of Edmund, duke of York, 'of all sinners the most wicked' provided only £100. The accounts of the executors of Archbishop Savage happily survive and have been printed in *Testamenta Eboracensia* (iv pp. 308–33). Those concerned with his burial show in magnificent detail its various attendant expenses of which a major part went in alms of one kind or another. The main items were £38 3s. 4d. for over 2000 Masses, of which 300 were at Cawood, 571 at Beverley and 251 at York, the rest being widely scattered over several dozen churches. On 'cloth for liveray' £141 6s. 2d. was expended and on wax for torches and candles £21 7s. 11½d., on banners and pennants £8 2s. 2½d., to friars and others escorting the corpse £9 18s. 4d., to clergy high and low at the funeral £23 13s. 4d., alms to the poor at Cawood and on the road to York and on the day of the funeral £72 13s. 9d., 'for a souper and diner to all noble men, spirituall and temporall, and to other the commynaltie that wer at my lord's buriall' £66 17s. 9½d.

In view of this huge expenditure equivalent, of course, to the annual salaries of several dozen clergy (in the fifteenth century a few marks was a quite usual clerical stipend), it is not surprising to find from quite an early date various attempts made by testators to keep their funeral expenses within reasonable bounds. Already in 1359 Otto of Grandson orders in his will 'that no armed man or armed horse be allowed to go before my body on my burial day, or that my body be covered with any cloth painted or gilded or signed with my coat of arms but that it be only of white cloth marked with a red cross'. Humphrey de Bohun, earl of Hereford, ordered that he should be buried 'without great pomp and no great men to be invited to my funeral, which shall only be attended by one bishop and by common people'. A fellow earl ordered 'no men-at-arms, horses, hearse or other pompe'. The immensely wealthy Cardinal Beaufort enjoined somewhat hazily 'that my funeral be not celebrated in too pompous a manner', but very precisely Anne, duchess of Exeter, forbade her executors 'to make any great feast or to have a solemn hearse or any costly lights, or largesse of liveries according to the vain glory or vain pomp of the world at my funeral, but only to the worship of God after the discretion of Mr John Pinchebeke Doctor of Divinity.'

There can be no doubt that certain funerals of the English aristocracy in the latter half of our period already foreshadowed, albeit very modestly, the magnificent ones in seventeenth-century Poland which led one observer to write, 'one was under the impression of attending a triumph rather than assisting at a funeral'. Was not the meeting of a lord with the Lord of Lords a social occasion worthy of maximum expense?

THE NATURE OF CHARITABLE BEQUESTS

However elaborate and costly bequests in connection with a testator's funeral might be, obviously no small part of his alms went on other things. The fact that his wife and his children were each entitled to a third part of his movables explains why often there is limited reference to them in medieval wills. Instead these are usually dominated by a series of bequests of very varying value to a range of charitable purposes which is usually wide and which in the case of the wealthiest testators may involve many scores of items. To give more than a minute sketch of their nature is not here feasible.

As is only to be expected, bequests to parish churches are of all sizes and very frequent indeed. The Kent wills contain scores of very diverse and often very humble oblations. 'To the selying of the chaunsell my grettest oxe'; 'I will that a vestment be bought to the honor of Godd's divine service vii marks'; 'a basin to make a candle-sticke with'; 'to the high aulter my best kercher to make a corporas cloth'. More substantial was the legacy (in 1458) of John Younge of ten marks 'to make seats called puyinge'. Gifts for structural additions are comparatively rare. They mostly concern chapels and towers and are often made conditionally on the work in question being begun at an early date, though progress seems often to have been slow at least so far as the latter were concerned—the rebuilding of the belfry tower at Stoke (West Kent) mooted in 1479 got under way soon after but has not yet been completed. But those at the top of the social scale sometimes provided immense aid. Lord William Botreaux left £100 to succour the poor and also 'to buy books and vestements for such parish churches in my patronage as may have need of them'. The elaborate and generous will of King Henry VII records that 'we have often and many times to our in-ward regret and displeasure seen in . . . various and many churches of our realm the Holy Sacrament of the Altar kept in very simple and inhonest pixes, specially pixes of copper and timber' and goes on to order forthwith the manufacture of silver gilt pixes 'decorated with our arms and red roses and portcullises crowned, of the value of four pounds, to be provided for every house of friars and like-wise every parish church within this realm not adequately provided in this respect.'

So far as bequests to monastic institutions in the latter half our period is concerned it is not feasible to provide a clear-cut picture. It seems likely, however, that by this time substantial bequests to houses of the Augustinian and Benedictine orders were comparatively small in number, almost certainly not because these places had become in any way unpopular but because adequate provisions had long been made for their reasonable needs. It was, however, not uncommon for folk in the higher ranks of society to leave a vestment or piece of plate or some such thing to a monastery with which they had some special connection. Very much more frequent in the wills of the period are bequests to local houses of the mendicant orders which were mostly in the form of small sums of cash. Such things were essential since, as we have seen, friars relied largely on them for their livelihood. In towns it is very common to find well-to-do citizens leaving cash to each house of mendicant orders there. As the surveys of these houses made on the eve of their dissolution show us, to the very end in England the friaries largely retained that frugal form of existence which their founders had visualised. Hospitals of various kinds were mostly far from affluent and, in the large towns at least, seem to have attracted a steady trickle of mostly very small benefactions. Popular devotion to the Seven Corporal Acts of Mercy guaranteed that prisoners were often recipients of small bequests which mostly came from local townsfolk.

No few bequests were made in our period to good causes which rarely attract attention in modern wills. Medieval England never got around to making adequate provision for keeping in repair its roads and bridges, so bequests towards these, mostly small sums from local people, are a not uncommon feature of the wills of the period. An interesting and significant development clearly traceable as our period wears on is the smallish but growing tendency to bequeath money to provide for the education of a friend or relation or sometimes for a poor clerk. The very earliest examples of this can be found in the late thirteenth century, but progress here is very slow until about the mid-fifteenth century, after which time bequests for this purpose notably increase in number but are much more common in some regions than in others. From a very early period we find bequests made to provide marriage portions for poor maidens, the will of Henry II, for example, leaving largish sums for this purpose.

All these types of benefaction were regarded as being works of piety and occur repeatedly in very varying combinations, at least in the more affluent wills of the period. Thus that of John Scarle, Lord Chancellor of England, includes bequests to half-a-dozen monasteries of the older orders, besides others to the houses of friars of London, contributions towards the building funds and furnishings of a number of parish churches, doles to London prisoners, one to a scholar at Oxford, dowries for poor maidens and a very substantial gift to provide for the repair of chalices, corporases and manuals in poor parish churches. Such a testamentary miscellany occurs with very great frequency, albeit often on a smaller scale. As we shall see, everything points to the bequests of English testators being on a scale which, judged by the economic standing of the times, was nothing short of immense. Why was this?

The comparatively informal way in which medieval wills were drafted gives us various indications of the motives which prompted the very massive almsgiving of the times, and shows that, as was only to be expected, these did not follow a single pattern and that often more than one consideration was operative. Behind all of them was the realisation that a man's possessions were not his own but were given to him by God to be used for his purposes—significantly from time to time occur such phrases as 'the possessions which God has lent me'. Because of this a major motive of the bequests was to use things so as to display the divine glory. The early will of Prince Aethelstan opens, 'I have given my chattels and my possessions for the glory of God' and the codicil of the great Henry VII speaks of his bequests primarily as 'to the honour of God'. The same point is made in more detail in the will of one Nicholas Blackburn which prays God 'for myght and gracye so to dispos and ordeyn with the residue of the gifts that He has giffen me in this worlde that it may be pleasant and loving to him soveranly'. A rather different but allied viewpoint is found in another will which opens by quoting Christ's command, 'if you wish to be perfect go and sell all that you have and give to the poor' and proceeds to order that this be done.

The conviction which is stated in the texts more often than any other is the firm belief that almsgiving was good for the soul. As we have seen, this was a factor which had greatly aided the spread of monasticism in earlier days, and we significantly find in wills the same sort of phrase, 'for the good of my soul', the which we find occurring so very frequently in monastic foundation charters of the twelfth century. Thus the phrases just cited from the will of Aethelstan and Henry VII are immediately followed by 'and [for] the redemption of my soul' and 'the weale of our soul' respectively. Associated with this is often a reference to that divine judgment which lay at the root of so much medieval thought. Thus the will of Lady Joan Abergavenny begins, 'considering that the frail condition of this wretched and unstable life is full of perils and the conclusion is nought else but death, from which no person of none estate shall escape, and therefore purposing with the leave of God to dispose of such goods as He has lent me in such use as might be most to His plesauance and the profit of my souls and all them that I am bound to pray for . . .', whilst in the will of Sir John Neville we read, 'remembering the uncertente of this worlde and as it is ever due to dispose and ordeyne for the helth of ones soul'.

At the highest level Christian giving is inspired purely by a love which has no ulterior motive—as the hymn puts it, 'not for the sake of gaining Heaven or seeking a reward, but purely since Thou art my king and my beloved lord'. In the Middle Ages, as before and since, not all could rise to this exalted conception of their vocation and it is not surprising that there were many who looked at almsgiving as primarily something by which rewards were acquired. Thus the will of Margaret, countess of Richmond, refers to 'the great rewards of eternal life that every Christian creature in steadfast faith of Holy Church shall have for their good deeds done by them in this present life' and it would be very easy to quote other examples of this sort of sentiment in the wills of our period. But to work for a reward is not in itself improper and was an approach bound to be common in a society which had so very little theological instruction and tended to think in legal terms.

What is, of course, very open to attack is the view which regarded almsgiving as a way of automatically acquiring spiritual rewards, thus debasing what should be an act of Christian love into a crude commercial transaction. As we have seen, there is no doubt that a main concern of Western men in our period was to reduce to an absolute minimum the length of time they would have to spend in purgatory (page 16-17) and it was easy for crude minds to assume that more alms spent on good works the less this period would be. The will of an archdeacon of York asserts this barbaric view, making donations 'for the rather purchasing me of grace and the sooner obtaining of heavenly rest', but this is the unique example of such deplorable language found by the writer in extensive study of such documents, and it would be gratuitous to regard it as typical—after all, general opinion in the medieval England of our period seems to have had no doubt that archdeacons represented the lowest form of ecclesiastical life. Probably the great mass of people in these times took over the vigorous practical view implicit in the *Epistle of St James*, 'A man is justified before God by what he does as well as by what he believes . . . faith without action is as dead as a body without a soul'. What is beyond all doubt is that the motive force behind all the immense attention to almsgiving displayed by a society which, in England at least, was somewhat penurious, was inspired not by a hazy feeling of goodwill or primarily from a desire to remedy defects in the economy, but by spiritual factors—the wish to emulate Christ's deep concern for those in need and the attainment of that ultimate reward of the approval of Christ—'Well done thou good and faithful servant'.

Almost without exception the recipients of medieval alms were expected to pray for their donors, whether such recipients were the miscellaneous bevy of paupers and clergy at funerals, the priests who served chantries or the inmates of monasteries, colleges and hospitals (of this practice the present habit of Oxford and Cambridge colleges of holding a regular Commemoration of Benefactors is an attentuated survival). This explains why donors went to considerable pains to ensure that their memory and their need for prayers were kept alive in the ages to come. It is very significant that the stock inscription on most tombstones in our period opens with the name of the deceased person concerned and concludes, 'on whose soul may God have mercy'. Similarly, by no means infrequently when plate, vestments or other such things were given to a church, with them came instructions which ensure that the benefactor has prayer offered for him down the ages. Thus a dean of York leaves a set of vestments to the church of St Mary Redcliffe on conditions that his soul and that of his father be publicly commended to the prayers of the faithful on Sundays, and we find various gifts being inscribed with the name of the donor with this intent. It was to this end that small panels showing the donors and their spouses were often included in stained glass windows and the coats of arms of armigerous people were embroidered on vestments and inserted in windows and on tombs. Richard Rull, a vicar, provides for a tombstone bearing his name 'to move people to pray for my soul', William Norreys of Ash provided for a picture of his body with his coat of arms thereon 'for a special reminder for prayer' and Lady Anne Scrope a chalice with her name and that of her husband 'upon the fote for a remembrans to pray for us'.

A final point in connection with this deep medieval concern for intercession for those who had departed this life is not to be overlooked—the fact that it was the almost invariable practice for testators not to limit the prayer which they desired to their own individual needs. Usually the name of certain relations are explicitly included in their arrangements for these and almost without exception intercessions are also ordered to be offered for the good of 'all Christian souls'. Medieval almsgiving was not therefore a series of individual efforts to jump the queue for the exit from purgatory. If the wills do not mention non-Christian souls, this is not from religious bigotry but very largely because of the long-established fact that in these times almost the whole of Europe was Christian so that the welfare of the non-Christian was for most of the West, not least for England, something which did not enter the field of vision of the general public.

Complete analysis of the immensely numerous wills of medieval England will not be accomplished for very long to come, but the extensive pioneer work on it in recent years by Jordan and others shows very clearly two major points. Firstly, as is only to be expected of an age when most history was local history, the scope of almsgiving varied immensely from area to area. Wills of the City of London in the fifteenth and early sixteenth centuries show half the testators making bequests for chantries and some two-fifths leaving gifts to monasteries of which well over half went to houses of mendicants, whilst considerable sums were left towards church buildings. Doles to the poor and other bequests to them were very common, one being large enough to support eight poor men and five poor women throughout the year. Marriage portions were bequeathed in 10 per cent of the wills and doles to prisoners in 25 per cent, only 3.5 per cent to education but about 20 per cent to hospitals. Bequests to public work were few but biggish in size and included donations for enlarging the market place at Peterborough and repairing Cromer pier.

Different were the priorities which Jordan found in far-distant Lancashire in the period from 1480. This was a county of generous folk, its average charitable benefaction being 'considerably greater than that of any other non-urban county which we have examined'. Equally unusual is the fact that of its bequests almost 70 per cent was devoted to religious needs in the conventional sense as compared with 13 per cent to 28 per cent in other counties examined. Remarkable was the interest shown in education which received no less than 25 per cent of the bequests. Poor relief attracted far less than average support and next to nothing went to 'municipal betterment'. Such unusual statistics demand a much more intensive co-relation with local social history than has yet been attempted. Secondly, it is crystal clear that the total amount given to good causes of one kind or another was, by modern standards, nothing less than enormous. Thus it has been calculated that in the period 1480–1540 almost 30 per cent of the wealth bequeathed by the London merchant class was given to charitable purposes of one kind or another, a figure markedly higher than the corresponding one in the following hundred years. That this was so is undoubtedly due to the strong medieval sense of the importance of seeking to stand in right relationships with God by using wealth for the purposes urged in the Gospels.

MONASTIC HOSPITALITY

By the end of our period England was adorned with some thousand monasteries of one kind or another. Of these the houses of friars, totalling roughly a quarter of the whole, were totally dependent on alms for their own living so cannot have been in the position to dispense much to others. Amongst all the rest, from the first, hospitality of some kind and in some degree was a traditional part of their way of life. The great *Valor Ecclesiasticus* of 1535 gives us a huge and minute survey of the wealth of English ecclesiastical institutions on the eve of the dissolution of the monasteries, and study of it has shown that at this time some 3 per cent of English monastic income was devoted to charitable purposes, which represents, in effect, a very considerable sum which down the ages must have relieved large numbers of the indigent. Most of this monastic largesse was dispensed in two ways—support for the poor and provision for travellers.

THE POOR

For the poor which existed in medieval times contemporary monasteries made provision of various kinds. Sometimes from the first a house might be legally bound to provide for the maintenance of a specific number of poor, as at Cartmel Priory where its founder, William Marshall, ordered that there should be supported twelve poor men who were to pray for his soul down the ages. Sometimes the provision was for doles of food for folk who, presumably, emerged for it from nearby habitations of their own. Thus it was noted in 1535 that at Burton Abbey 8d. a day was spent on doles of bread, ale and meat and that £4 for twenty-four cloaks was distributed yearly on the anniversary of the founder's death. At little Tutbury, £2 was given to the poor every feast of Corpus Christi and £5 on the anniversary of the founder's death. But at plutocratic St Alban's twelve poor men were supported to pray daily for King Offa's soul. Like many major monasteries this abbey supported a hospital (in this case for lepers) as did the major monastic houses of London.

However, it is to be noted that the *Valor Ecclesiasticus* of 1535 does not picture more than partially monastic engagement in charitable fields. Like modern Inland Revenue authorities, the officials responsible were only prepared to accept as legitimate expenses those which could be justified by the strict letter of the law, though religious institutions tend to find such an approach inadequate. The *Observances of Barnwell Priory*, which picture in fascinating detail the daily life of a larger monastery, shows us that there the almoner (who was the principal dispenser of the house's alms) had a wide field of activity and certain unofficial sources of largesse including the 'left-overs' from meals, which in a large monastery may not have been inconsiderable—'To the almoner pertain the remains of the prior's apartment, the infirmary and the guest-house. He ought also to receive daily one whole loaf and one whole dish [of food] . . . for the soul of our Founder, and also the beer left over from collation' as well as certain other minor items. He was to see to major

N

distributions of food on Maundy Thursday and All Souls' Day and 'ordinary distribution of pease and beans twice or thrice weekly for part of the year.' Besides this five poor men were to be lodged and fed in the almonry and the almoner was also 'to make up every day for ever three plates [of food] for the use of poor men' from food left over. Recalling the 'corporal acts' of Christ the *Observances* notes, 'the almoner ought to be kind and gentle to the poor, for in them he is ministering to the Lord Jesus Christ. On this account he ought never or seldom, to be without a stock of socks, linen and woollen clothes and other necessaries of life; so that if by chance Christ Himself should at some time appear in the guise of a naked or a poor man, He need not go away empty without a gift.'

Though aid to the poor was a major preoccupation of the monasteries of medieval England it was at least equalled in importance by their concern for travellers. This interest was emphatically expressed in the *Rule of St Benedict* which ordered, 'let all guests who happen to come be received as Christ . . . and above all let care be scrupulously shown in receiving the poor and strangers: for in them especially is Christ received.' Obviously the amount thus dispensed varied according to the resources of the house and also according to its geographical situation. In areas like Lincolnshire and most of northern England, where population was very scanty and centres of population often very far apart, monastic hospitality to travellers played a very important role, and it was by no means unimportant elsewhere in times when anything that remotely resembled modern hotels were not to be found. Most towns of any size had at least one monastery dispensing hospitality within or just without its walls, and most of the great Benedictine abbeys stood on what, in their period, were major high-roads. The hospitality which they offered was particularly valuable for kings, barons, bishops and the like who normally travelled with a largish household for which adequate accommodation could not easily be found. Accommodation for guests in most monasteries was generally provided in or near its outer court. This kind of hospitality was very widely dispensed indeed by the various kinds of monks and regular canons. It is very significant that from the early stages in appropriation of parish churches in England by monasteries (page 170) much the most usual plea employed to obtain permission for this desired change was the assertion that the resources of the monastery concerned were suffer-

ing intolerably from the costs of entertaining large numbers of
travellers. Whilst it is true that occasionally this argument looks a
little thin there is no reason to doubt its substantial validity in most
cases.

HOSPITALS

The third major source of social aid in medieval England was that
furnished by the hospitals of the period, whose scope was a good
deal less specialised than that of modern institutions which bear
this name. As with the monasteries, their rise to significance in local
English life largely developed during the twelfth and thirteenth
centuries. At the time of the Norman Conquest their total number
was apparently not more than about twenty and for some little time
it was slow to increase. But gradually, aided by the growth in English
prosperity and population, from the mid-twelfth century onwards
their numbers rose fairly steadily. By 1216 these may have totalled
about 300, a figure which went on to reach its peak of about 650
in the mid-fourteenth century, though inadequate documentation
renders this point very obscure. For obvious social reasons the great
mass of them stood in or very close to centres of population. Probably partly because of the mediocre extent of urban development in
medieval England and partly because of the very considerable hold
over public affection which monasticism early established here, the
great majority of contemporary English hospitals were mostly
smallish and their buildings far from grandiose. Documentary and
architectural remains of their history is often little more than very
fragmentary.

London being the one town of lordly proportions in medieval
England, it was inevitable that only here were there to be found a
fairly considerable number of hospitals serving a widish range of
needs. What were to become two of the most illustrious of London
hospitals originated in our period as subsidiaries of two monasteries
—St Bartholomew's, Smithfield, pertaining to the priory of the
same name, and St Thomas', which originally belonged to the
priory of Southwark, another house of Austin canons. Both of
these had acquired a considerable income of over £300 by 1535, as
had King Stephen's foundation of St Katharine by the Tower,
which was subordinate to the priory of Holy Trinity, Aldgate. Also

important was the now vanished hospital of St Mary, that of St Thomas of Canterbury (St Thomas of Acon) and Elsing spital which was intended for 100 men and women, including blind beggars. Wealthiest of all were St Mary without Bishopgate, which in 1535 had no less than 180 beds and the Savoy Hospital set up by Henry VII to accommodate 100 men nightly. In London, lunatics were tended at the hospital of St Mary of Bethlehem (where their rowdy behaviour bred the name of Bedlam). For some time converted Jews were cared for in a special hospital and another smallish establishment looked after poor and infirm priests.

Nowhere else in England could such an array of hospitals be found, though at York there flourished the venerable and very rich hospital ultimately known as St Leonard's. Its complement came to consist of a master, thirteen chaplain brothers, four secular chaplains, eight nuns, thirty choristers (perhaps orphans by origin), two schoolmasters, several lay brothers and sisters and 206 poor sick people, with a sister and two good cows for the benefit of babies and delicate children. Daily alms were also dispensed to poor lepers and prisoners. The hospital of Newark at Leicester ultimately maintained 100 poor and infirm, but there is no doubt that the very great majority of English hospitals were very much smaller than such great establishments as these, many of them serving only one or two dozen folk or even fewer. The hospital at East Bridge, Canterbury in 1342 was staffed by a master, a chaplain and a lady help and maintained twelve beds for pilgrims. That of St Mary, Yarmouth was founded in 1278 for a warden, two chaplains, eight brethren and eight sisters, whilst that at Yarm served thirteen poor. The fact that most English hospitals were poorly endowed was probably a main reason for the fact that in the latter part of our period a number of them, at least temporarily, fell on evil days.

The constitutions of English hospitals varied considerably. The head of the institution was often known as the Master or Warden and he invariably had a number of chaplains to minister to the sick and maintain the customary elaborate round of services. As often other staff were celibate, medieval hospital life had a semi-monastic character. Hospital buildings in England were mostly on a very modest scale, and have left nothing which will bear comparison with certain mighty edifices on the Continent. The usual arrangement was to have a large rectangular hall running east and west, with a chapel at the eastern end and beds ranged round the walls on either side. The area between the beds formed a large open space which might be separated from the beds by screens or arcades. At Angers there still remains, very little altered, the huge hospital founded by Henry II across the river from the noble castle, but it is excelled in size by that at Tonnerre where the great hall is no less than 300 feet long and 60 feet wide. The old hospital at Beaune is much smaller but has the advantage of having an interior which still retains its traditional medieval layout. In England most of the hospitals have left very smallish buildings like those of St Mary, Chichester and the partially ruined St Mary Magdalene at Glastonbury. Well preserved are those at Wells and Sherborne and that which Archbishop Chichele built at Higham Ferrers. More pretentious but more altered is the Great Hospital at Norwich, and that of St Cross at Winchester.

Medieval hospitals served a wide range of unfortunates. In the early part of our period a novel and horrifying development was the wide spread of leprosy through Western Europe, this coming like so much else at this time, from the East. Amongst the first hospitals set up for lepers is that large one which Lanfranc founded at Harbledown near Canterbury about 1084. However, mercifully, albeit slowly, leprosy died away here and by the end of our period was hard to find. To the needs of those suffering from the various unspectacular complaints common in all ages a considerable fraction of medieval hospital accommodation was inevitably devoted, though too many of these were founded on a quite small scale.

The second major need for which medieval hospitals catered was the provision of accommodation for travellers. Substantial remains are yet visible of the great Maison Dieu which Hubert de Burgh established at Dover, the eternal main gateway to England from the Continent. Understandably, the great shrines at Canterbury and Walsingham attracted more than their share of traffic, and a certain number of hospitals came into being to help travellers visiting them. In scantily habited areas like the north and west hospitals were of very real value for travellers, even if they were not very large or numerous, for they provided almost the only shelter available. The long and desolate road from Yorkshire over to the Eden valley acquired a small hospital on Stainmore which linked up with another small one at Brough, but travellers from Kendal to Penrith must have had to rely on finding shelter at Shap Abbey.

The inmates of even smallish English medieval hospitals were not necessarily all of one type, and it was far from unknown for a hospital to change to some degree the purpose which it served, notably, of course, in the case of those founded for lepers. Some curious verses written on the eve of the Reformation about a large London hospital which, it has been suggested, was that of St Bartholomew, Smithfield, show an institution which was ready to accept a remarkably wide variety of people in need. It is declared that inmates included those 'that for their living can do no labour and have no frendes to do them succour', 'old people seke and impotent', 'poore women in childbed', 'weyke men sore wounded by great violence', 'sore men eaten with pockes and pestilence', 'honest folke fallen in great poverte, by mischaunce or other infirmite', 'wayfaring men and maimed souldyours . . . and all others which we seme good and playne have here lodging for a night or twayne, bedred folke and suche as cannot crave. In these places moost relief they have, and if they hap within our place to dye then are they buried well and honestly, but not every unseke stoborne [stubborn] knave for then we sholde ouer many have.'

Examples of similar diversity on a much smaller scale are easy to find. The hospital of St Thomas at Canterbury offered accommodation to poor, to people going to Rome, those coming to Canterbury and needing shelter and to pregnant women. The hospital of St Mary's, Ripon was founded for the care of lepers and blind priests and the giving of hospitality to pilgrims; St Giles Hexham was intended for poor labourers, lepers and infirm persons; St Mary Westgate, Newcastle-on-Tyne was founded for indigent clergy and pilgrims. However, there can be no doubt that very much the most important sections of those cared for by medieval hospitals were the poor, the sick and travellers. As time went on a fair number of English hospitals declined in revenues and numbers. Most of them never had much endowment and misfortune or incompetence could fatally undermine the financial position of the place, just as it could that of a chantry chapel.

The benefits conferred on the medieval English public by contemporary hospitals were clearly limited both in amount and in scope. Even the London hospitals could not cope with more than what must have been a smallish proportion of those who could have benefited by the amenities which they offered, and in outlying areas the available accommodation must often have been inadequate for local needs. Those who served the inmates were primarily motivated by spiritual considerations. They cannot have had more than very elementary knowledge of medicine in the modern sense, but they may well have had more than their share of that loving care and patience which means so much to the sick and aged. The dissolution of so many medieval hospitals at the Reformation meant *inter alia* that England quickly drifted into the dangerous situation of having virtually no nurses. (When, centuries later, the Crimean War brought urgent need for these the only trained ones to be found were some few Anglican and Roman Catholic nuns, so that Florence Nightingale virtually had to start from scratch to build up the modern nursing profession.)

HEALING AND PILGRIMAGE

Unlike so many Christian people in the eighteenth and nineteenth centuries, men of the medieval West cannot fairly be accused of showing little interest in that firm connection between the Christian life and healing which is so very evident in the New Testament. Fundamental to the ministry of Christ was 'healing every disease and every infirmity among the people', curing 'the lame, the maimed, the blind and the dumb' and to His apostles he gave powers to heal disease and conquer 'evil spirits'. The medieval Church, whilst praying for the sick in the traditional manner, also extensively sought healing through pilgrimage to the shrines of the saints. It is very significant that medieval *Lives* of the latter show very little interest in pedantic details like the dates of the various stages of their careers, and family background but stress heavily that the holiness of their heroes and heroines had the invaluable result of producing what they regarded as miracles. These might to some extent be found in the lifetime of the saint but the great mass of them often occurred after his or her death, their existence constituted one of the main arguments for canonising the person concerned. Again and again biographies of medieval saints have tacked on to them series of such stories and in similar fashion medieval stained glass windows devoted to them will usually have some panels which depict such things. The great majority of these were concerned with

healing of body or mind and it was these which, far more than anything else, gave pilgrimages to local saints and to shrines of Our
Lady their huge popularity. The cult of St Thomas Becket which
is very well documented owed its great fame to the large numbers
of cases of healing for which it was believed to be responsible and
which, *inter alia*, led to some of the pilgrim flasks from Canterbury
being proudly inscribed (in Latin) 'Thomas, the best healer of the
sick'. Although medieval pilgrimages were mostly very informal
ventures which have left very intermittent record of their existence
to enlighten the historian and were by no means solely concerned
with healing, there is no doubt of their considerable importance in
our period.

PLACES OF PILGRIMAGE

Centres of medieval pilgrimage fall into three categories—those
connected in one way or another with the earthly life of Christ;
those commemorating the Blessed Virgin Mary and those chiefly
honouring one or other of the multitudinous corps of saints of the
Church. But such centres often added to their own attractions by
acquiring other relics of one kind or another from a variety
of sources.

Shrines of Christ

From the first, obviously no centre of pilgrimage could vie in
lustre with that of Jerusalem and its neighbourhood which had witnessed the earthly life of Christ. Throughout the Middle Ages far
more of the faithful than modern man might expect made the long
and toilsome journey to and from it. Century after century, also,
men brought back to the West what they hoped and believed to be
relics of Christ, either directly from the Holy Land or from the By-
zantines of Eastern Europe who had moved in very early to secure
such things. Obviously most desired were what purported to be
relics of the Holy Cross on which Christ was crucified, and there
is no doubt that as time went on these proliferated to a degree
which must arouse the suspicions of all but the utterly credulous.
Their history had been the subject of a major French study but inevitably on the crucial question of authenticity or non-authenticity

of individual items usually very little can safely be said. In England the only such relic to attract any flow of medieval pilgrims was that preserved at the priory of Bromholm, though this was not of any major import. Another fragment of the Holy Cross was claimed by Waltham Abbey and gave the church there its dedication but does not seem to have won much outside interest.

Other souvenirs of the life of Christ, or what purported so to be, came to be sought out and venerated in many churches in Western Christendom. The only ones of these to be of really spectacular importance were mostly to be found at Rome, whose collection of relics of every kind was literally incomparable. Here the church of St Peter claimed to have the table used at the Last Supper, that of St John Lateran to possess some of the reed which smote Jesus' head and some of the sponge used at his Crucifixion whilst S. Croce claimed to have a large portion of the cross of the penitent thief. Canterbury was the Rome of England and various lists of its relics survive. Here, it was believed, was not only some of the wood of Christ's cross, but thorns from His crown and part of His seamless coat. However, these do not seem to have been more than auxiliary attractions for the faithful, whose major objective was beyond all doubt the shrine of St Thomas Becket. The objects which were the focal points of almost all English pilgrimages were either statues of Our Lady or remains of the bodies of saints. To them, lesser relics were mostly not more than useful adjuncts.

Shrines of Our Lady

In the first thousand years of Christian history very deep affection and respect for Our Lady, though by no means absent from Christian worship, as the liturgy of the Eastern Orthodox Church early displayed, was very much less in evidence than it later became in the West. Of her latter days, of her death and the place of her burial next to no authentic knowledge survives, she having slipped quietly out of history. But in the West from about the opening of the twelfth century, thanks above all to such preachers as St Bernard, devotion to her rapidly became much more pronounced and developed steadily and somewhat perilously through the rest of our period. Whereas in Anglo-Saxon England very few of our churches were dedicated to Our Lady but no few to St Peter (who, after all, held the keys of Heaven), almost all the Cistercian abbeys and a very large fraction of the houses of Austin canons in England took her as their patron, whilst her place in both public and private worship steadily grew larger in various ways. Although the Gospel references to her gave an added appeal to visits to the Holy Land, there was no special shrine of her there. Inevitably pilgrims avidly sought relics of things connected with her in some way and these were obligingly produced. Of them Rome inevitably had the lion's share. Here S. Maria Maggiore claimed to have her mantle in which the infant Christ rested in the manger, and St John Lateran some of her hair and clothing as well as a shirt which she made for Christ with her own hands.

When shrines of Our Lady became major centres of pilgrimage, as they did in the latter half of our period, it was usually a statue that provided the focus of devotion. There is no doubt that in later medieval times such places tended to displace in popular affection shrines devoted to the memory of lesser saints. Why and to what extent this was so is a complex question which cannot here be un-ravelled. To some extent, probably, it was due to the negative factor that a more educated popular opinion was getting much less impressed by the so-called relics of saints on whose authenticity Chaucer was by no means the only one to cast doubts. But more important was the subtle change in the psychological and religious atmosphere of the times which increasingly led to Our Lady being exalted to a degree of spiritual eminence which carried with it very grave dangers, even if it probably and profitably toned down the 'hell-fire' atmosphere of earlier popular religion.

Why one statue of Our Lady excited popular devotion and an-other did not is most obscure, but there can be no doubt that in medieval times quite an obscure place of worship might abruptly rise to at least local celebrity through an abrupt boost in the reputa-tion of its statue of Our Lady. In 1310, for example, for no very clear reason, the little Yorkshire chapel of Fraisthorpe witnessed an up-surge of devotion to a certain new image of the Virgin which 'arose suddenly and unexpectedly', but which in the long run does not seem to have been of any great importance.

Waterton's painstaking but somewhat peppery survey of medieval England's Marian shrines makes it clear that of them the only one which can be said to have reached much more than local importance was that of Our Lady of Walsingham. Somewhere about 1130 Richelde of Fervaques, a widow, erected at Little Walsingham a replica of the Holy House at Nazareth which may have contained a representation of the Annunciation (the announcement to Our Lady by an angel that she was to become the mother of Christ). Probably about 1153 her son, Geoffrey of Fervaques, established at this site a small priory of Austin canons which for long seems to have been of quite minor importance. However, in 1226 it was visited by the ultra-pious King Henry III, en route to venerate the relic of the Holy Cross at Bromholm Priory. He gave the priory the right to hold a fair and a market, and in the next thirty years he followed this up with a string of further benefactions including, in 1246, a gift of twenty marks to make a golden crown for the statue of Our Lady of Walsingham which would seem to have been modelled on that of Rocamadour and which rapidly became celebrated.

Henry's devotion to Our Lady of Walsingham was shared by his son, the future Edward I, who visited the shrine on no less than twelve occasions, despite the exceptionally busy life which he led. About this time some rebuilding of the priory took place. From now on English affection for the place steadily grew, so that by the late fifteenth century it had become quite rich and had been visited by every English sovereign of the period except one. On the eve of the Dissolution offerings at the shrine of Our Lady of Walsingham far exceeded those of at the shrine of St Thomas of Canterbury which for so long had enjoyed the biggest headlines. They totalled £250 1s. as compared with the mere £36 of the latter. In importance with Walsingham no other English shrine of Our Lady could compete, though those of Our Lady of Doncaster and Our Lady of Ipswich had some local following, whilst in Westminster Abbey an image known as Our Lady of the Pew attracted some little attention.

Local Saints

However venerated was the Holy Land and however beloved were the shrines of Our Lady in late medieval times, there is no doubt that then, as for very long before, the great majority of centres of pilgrimage in England were those where the focus of devotion was the burial place of one of the many score of local saints bred by the Church down the centuries. What in the technical sense of the word was a saint? The official answer to this question changed somewhat in process of time. He or she was a person of especial sanctity who was commemorated in the calendar of the Church and to whom churches might be dedicated and prayers addressed in public worship. But how was it decided whether a person had sufficient sanctity to reach this distinguished position? For a very long while the solution to this question was left very much to the local community. If, over the ages, a substantial and unbroken tradition of devotion to the individual concerned accumulated even over a rather restricted region, this sufficed. However, this was not an altogether satisfactory solution, since medieval clerics, like modern examiners, tended to vary in the standards they set. Thus early Devon and Cornwall produced a number of saints so large and so little known elsewhere as to raise the suspicion that the judgment of their locals on the subject was more notable for charity than spiritual perspicacity, and in various other parts of the West the same position arose.

Understandably, the reforming papacy decided to establish a more workmanlike procedure, wherein uniformity of standards was enforced. From about the close of the twelfth century it became the accepted rule in the West that the decision as to whether a particular person should rank as a saint, with his own office and name inserted in ecclesiastical calendars, should be taken by the Roman curia. Such a decision was made after examination and cross-examination of the facts of the case, undertaken with a scrupulous legal care of which the ancient Romans would have approved. Under this procedure in medieval England nine members of the faithful were thus canonised, i.e. had their names placed on the official list of the saints of the Western Church. They were St Gilbert of Sempringham (1202), St Wulfstan of Worcester (1203), St Hugh of Lincoln (1220), St William of York (1226), St Edmund of Abingdon (1246), St Richard of Chichester (1262), St Thomas of Hereford (1320), St John of Bridlington (1403) and St Osmund of Salisbury (1457). Though all were highly edifying people none had that immense spiritual éclat that would have made them famous on the Continent. The claims of ten others were officially pressed but not accepted. They were Robert Grosseteste (d. 1220), William de Marchia (d.

1302), Archbishop Robert de Winchelsea (d. 1295), Bishop Dalderby (d. 1320), Thomas of Lancaster (d. 1322), Edward II (d. 1327), Thomas de la Hale (d. 1295), Richard Rolle (d. 1349), Archbishop Richard le Scrope (d. 1405) and Henry VI (d. 1471).

However, the establishment of this process of selection in no way affected the status of those whom tradition had already ranked as saints nor, curious as it may seem to the ultramontane, did it prevent what can only be described as unofficial canonisation. A very un-expected example of this was revealed when the ruins of Rievaulx Abbey was excavated some fifty years ago, and there was found at the entrance to the chapterhouse the shrine of its first abbot, William, though of his cult no documentary mention of any kind is known to exist. In view of the extreme severity of the Cistercian rule regarding the admission of outsiders to its cloisters this act seems particularly lawless. Several later examples of similar un-official action occur. William of Bitton, bishop of Bath and Wells 1267-74, early renowned for his sanctity, was quickly acclaimed a saint and his tomb became a place of pilgrimage, especially for those suffering from toothache; when this tomb was opened in 1848 his own teeth were seen to be 'absolutely perfect in number, shape and order, and without a trace of decay, and hardly any discoloration'.

There are clear signs that there was in the late thirteenth century a strong popular movement to regard Simon de Montford as a saint, which was aided by some left-wing Franciscans. A little later, by what seems a very curious quirk of popular religion, there were not lacking those who greatly venerated Thomas of Lancaster, a baron who successfully concealed any signs of great spiritual éclat that he had, but led the opposition to the foolish Edward II and was executed therefor. Yorkshire wills give clear indications of real, if not widespread, devotion to Richard Le Scrope, archbishop of York from 1398 to 1405, a man of real piety who joined a northern rebellion against the government and was executed in his cathedral city when it failed. (It is a very curious and significant fact that in all these cases the individuals concerned were 'agin the government' in the best Irish way, as, indeed, were to some extent St Edmund Rich and St Richard of Chichester.)

By the end of our period an enormous number of saints were venerated in Western Christendom. Although the chief centre of devotion to a saint was the place where the person in question was buried, from a very early stage in Church history popular enthusiasm for tangible relics of such holy people led to it becoming quite common for some part of the saint's skeleton to be detached and acquired legally or sometimes illegally by faithful elsewhere. A very unedifying traffic in such things developed, notably satirised by Chaucer with his usual freedom from pedantic attention to accuracy. A number of great churches, notably those in pilgrimage centres, accumulated extensive collections of bits and pieces of what they, at least, believed to be holy people. An interesting guide book to Rome written about 1470 by William Brewyn, a priest of Canterbury, includes lists of relics at his own cathedral church, wherein major items were the bodies of no less than twenty-four saints albeit of very varying eminence, headed by that of St Thomas Becket and ending with the body of one Syburgis who is somewhat optimistically classed as 'very celebrated'. With these were associated arms of no less than nine saints, including those of such highly respectable figures as St Wulfstan, St Hugh of Lincoln, St Richard of Cirencester and St Osmund of Salisbury, as well as several heads and a few fingers and jawbones, some ascribed to very notable people like apostles, others to lesser figures like the virgin Austroberta whose name has never been a household word in Catholic circles.

It is unfortunate that we have only a very minute amount of evidence to show the extent of devotion to particular shrines in medieval England, so it is impossible to gain any clear-cut idea of their relative popularity or of the ebb and flow of their individual fortunes. However, it is indubitable that much the most popular English shrine for most though not all of our period, and the only one which tended to attract at least a trickle of pilgrims from abroad, was that of St Thomas Becket, in the cathedral church of Canterbury. Even in an age when 'battle, murder and sudden death' were not rarities the most brutal and spectacular murder of Thomas sent a shock of incomparable dimensions pulsing through Western Europe. The legal process of canonisation was completed by March 1173, but before this the general public had jumped the official gun and pilgrims were flooding into Canterbury in numbers which quickly swelled hugely. The visit in 1175 of the penitent King Henry II, in the course of which he was publicly scourged for his involvement in the murder, marks the start of a long series of visits by top people. It was quickly followed by one paid by the king of France who had aided Becket in his days of adversity; a papal legate and the king of Scotland came in 1180 and King Richard I in 1194. With no unworldly delay the monks of Canterbury developed the whole complex apparatus which medieval popular demand expected of a pilgrimage centre. In 1220 a new shrine for Becket's remains was set up and consecrated amidst much rejoicing, albeit following great expense which seems to have long crippled archiepiscopal finance. For generations to come the immense popularity of the shrine continued, fetching along with it a mighty pile of offerings, some of immense value like the great jewel offered by King Louis. Before the shrine Henry V prayed en route for his madcap venture which ended so successfully at Agincourt; near it Henry IV had been buried. However, in the latter part of our period there was certainly a slackening of popular interest in the shrine and at the Dissolution, as we have seen, offerings were not great.

In the thinly populated and somewhat penurious north of England no medieval shrine was of comparable importance to Canterbury. Much the most important one was that of St Cuthbert in the noble cathedral of Durham. Local affection for it was widespread at a very early date and seems to have long continued, though evidence on this in the rich archives of the cathedral has not yet been elaborately explored. Of the oldest English saints the only one belonging to pre-Saxon days was St Alban, whose body was preserved in the great abbey of that name. Unfortunately, history of the cult here is little known and it is not clear to what extent the immense wealth which the monastery acquired was due to its shrine. The major Benedictine abbey at Bury contained the relics of St Edmund, king of the East Angles, murdered by the Danes in 870 for refusing to abjure his faith. Here again the history of the devotion to it is obscure.

There can be no doubt that the life of the Anglo-Saxon Church had been characterised by very considerable piety whose exponents left behind memories of saints which, along with their earthly remains, were much cherished. St Werburgh of Chester, St Eadburg at Bicester, St Birinus at Dorchester-on-Thames, St Chad at Lichfield, St Milburg at Wenlock, St Elphege and St Dunstan at Canterbury, constitutes but a random selection from what was certainly a very numerous body of local saints, but their shrines acquired a repute that was mostly very local indeed.

In late Norman days the distinguished chronicler William of Malmesbury wrote enthusiastically of the repute of such folk: 'What shall I say of the multitude of bishops, hermits and abbots? Does not the whole island shine forth with such numerous relics of its natives that you can scarcely pass through a village of any importance without hearing the name of some new saint'. And he enquires pertinently, 'of how many have all notice been lost through lack of records?' Some three centuries later William of Worcester bears persistent witness to the existence of many lesser holy folk who have now long since been largely ignored. Such are the virgin St White buried at Whitchurch, St Wolfric in a church between Yeovil and Crewkerne and St Bradwell, a king's son and confessor in the church of Branston Axminster; St Sativola, a canonised virgin at Exeter, St Barnoc, a hermit at Bramton, St Matheriana who had worked miracles at Minster, near Camelford. He also notes the feast days of Bishop Hyldren and Bishop Mancus in the far West Country and the translation of the remains of St Keneth the hermit 'in Gowerland'. Near Penzance are venerated the martyrs St Mortan and St Just, and St Monnita, mother of St David in a church 'near Launceston where St David was born'. Mention is also made of the little-known hermits like St Mybbard, son of the king of Scotland and his companions St Mancus and St Wyllow, noting the days of their feasts, as well as St Elevetha, virgin and martyr at whose spring folk still drank and who was martyred by decapitation 'on a stone still to be seen'. But such shrines cannot be regarded as significant centres of pilgrimage.

THE PROCESS OF PILGRIMAGE

The very deserved fame of Chaucer's *Prologue* and his *Canterbury Tales* must not be allowed to obscure the fact that, like Trollope, he is a singularly dangerous guide to contemporary Church life, even if the latter's Mrs Proudy is a superb picture of a type to be found wherever non-celibate clergy proliferate.

Chaucer's pilgrims engaged in what was a very local pilgrimage, the distance from London to Canterbury being nothing spectacular. It demanded minor expenditure of time or money and very little inconvenience, the more so since some pilgrims could afford to make their way to Canterbury on horses rather than on the legs which

God had given them. Such local pilgrimages must, of course, have been common enough in most parts of medieval England, though we have no way of ascertaining what proportion of the whole they constituted. But they clearly differed immensely from those such far distant places as Compostella, Rocamadour, Rome and Jerusalem, which involved very substantial problems. Here the huge distances involved entailed very long absence from family and friends, with next to no chance of getting any news thereof until return. Even allowing for the generous amount of cheap hospitality to be expected, the cost might be considerable, whilst the exchange problems were extremely complex, as the elaborate section on them in William Brewyn's booklet makes clear. He details a very large number of different coins which the traveller might meet in the course of his journey and gives what must have been most useful hints on their relative value, a very tricky matter which must have given great scope for that cheating of the tourists which is as old as tourism. Further trouble might come from local potentates whose actions could not be effectively challenged. Thus William, in his outline of the route from Calais to Rome, at one stage provides an alternative road which 'with God's assistance' can be very well used by those who wish to avoid Cologne where the bishop (sic) was levying a tax on strangers. In some areas at least, notably, perhaps, in the mighty passes down to Italy, a man might fall prey to robbers. On the other hand most travellers were accustomed to the simplest accommodation and in many areas this was not difficult to find.

The Motives of Pilgrimage

The motives for going on pilgrimage, like the motives for founding monasteries varied in kind and in degree. Non-theological motives must sometimes have been operative, such as discontent with life at home, either because of marital trouble or some other personal factor, and the wish to explore the outside world.

However, this must not be allowed to obscure the fact that a pilgrimage was primarily a religious act to which other considerations were often secondary. Before undertaking his journey the pilgrim would make his confession to his priest and then seek divine blessing at a special service. At this he would lie prostrate before the altar whilst psalms and prayers for his safety were offered, after

which he rose and there followed the blessing of his scrip (a small
bag suspended by a cord over his shoulder and used to contain his
food and other minimum necessities) and staff and also, if he was
going to Jerusalem, of the cross worn on his habit. This latter was a
loose-fitting garment of strong material and might have a hood.
The pilgrim's hat seems usually to have been a large one with a
broad up-turned brim to which it early became usual to attach the
pilgrim badge or badges acquired during his journey. Celebration of
Mass and a few further prayers completed his act of preparation.

There were four main spiritual advantages sought after by
medieval pilgrims. Obviously attractive was the opportunity to see
and to pray in great and venerable churches wherein the faithful
down the ages have found prayer to come most easily. In other cases
what was probably not a large proportion of the whole went on
pilgrimage to fulfil a vow made for thanksgiving or as an act of
penance. Such pilgrimages are very seldom recorded but we found
one instance in the will of a certain Roger of Wansford which
ordains that his executors shall hire a man to go on pilgrimage to
the shrines at Bridlington and Beverley and thus implement the
'solemn vow which I made when gravely threatened and almost
suffocated by the waves of the sea between Ireland and Norway'.

A much more potent attraction to pilgrimage in these times was
furnished by the possibility it gave of acquiring the very considerable indulgences which were attached in one way or another to
the major pilgrimage centres of Western Christendom. The immense importance attached to these is implicit in Brewyn's handbook, where the writer rehearses in great detail those available
for visitors to the city of Rome. These had, of course, been built
up through the centuries by various popes to some extent, one may
guess, to encourage pilgrims to visit the Eternal City rather than
new-fangled medieval shrines. Certainly the number and complexity
of those available at Rome by his time can very safely be termed
beyond compare.

Of the great cathedral church of St John Lateran, which claimed
(somewhat unconvincingly) to be 'the head and mother of all
churches', he notes that 'there are granted here such great indulgences
that no-one can count them—they are known to God alone. These
pope Boniface (VIII) confirmed, declaring that if men knew how
great were the indulgences of the church of St John Lateran they

would not cross over to the Sepulchre of the Lord at Jerusalem nor to St James in Compostella'. At St Peter's were to be had certain indulgences of 3000 years to those who live near Rome and 9000 to those who live over the mountains and hills. At St Maria Maggiore there were indulgences of 1000 years available on all feasts of Our Lady. At S. Sebastiano 'there are every day a thousand years of indulgences . . . in the said church rest the bodies of xviii martyred popes each one of him giving his own indulgence, and many other indulgences there are in the aforesaid church because the bodies which rest there are countless'; it is noted later on that seven popes here 'granted each one separately seven thousand years of indulgences'.

Obviously no church or town elsewhere could begin to compete with this mighty stockpiling of indulgences though in the process of time the greater ones acquired quantities of them which were not to be sniffed at by those devoted to collecting such things. In his book William gives a list of the relics then possessed by Canterbury Cathedral and notes, 'the sume of the indulgences of the whole church is 37 053 years and 250 years in perpetuity.' It is extremely difficult to assess the appeal of indulgences to ecclesiastical men-in-the-street at the end of our period, but if Brewyn's interest therein is typical it must have been very considerable and have greatly enhanced the appeal of pilgrimage.

However, there can be no doubt that in many ways the most important and most interesting motive for going on pilgrimage to a medieval shrine was the hope of being cured of some malady. A recent work on which the following paragraphs are largely based has thrown invaluable light on this aspect of the subject. *

Although much of the original evidence regarding the healing activities of the shrines of medieval England has not survived (notably in the case of that of Our Lady of Walsingham which was so celebrated in the latter half of our period) enough remains to give us a very useful and convincing cross-section of what contemporaries regarded as miracles, though much modern opinion would find it preferable to think of them in terms of faith healing. There is no doubt that much of the medieval evidence is of high value if interpreted with discrimination, for, in their own interests, shrines did

---

* R. C. Finucane, *Miracles and Pilgrims: popular beliefs in medieval England* (1977)

not wish to claim cures which could be attacked as unfounded. It is worthy of note that in a high proportion of cases the medical details given are clear enough to allow a reasonably certain diagnosis: in the rest lack of precision is much more common than claims for utterly incredible cures.

Of the very large number of miracles at medieval shrines studied by Finucane, as many as nine-tenths are concerned with healing. In some cases the cures were not permanent, or were due to factors of an entirely unreligious nature such as remedying a condition due to a vitamin deficiency. But a number of others had behind them those psychological factors now so increasingly recognised as fundamental and which were curable by religious processes—cures of unquestionable authenticity being effected.

The miracles under consideration concerned a very wide range of maladies and, occurring as they did in a whole variety of settings, provide incidentally a whole series of invaluable sidelights on the contemporary social scene, half of the miracles examined having occurred in the home of the person concerned.

The healings are divided by Finucane into ten principal categories:—

(i) disabled and usually bedridden sufferers, with symptoms very vaguely described;

(ii) afflictions in specific areas of the body such as flux, dysentery, fever, toothache and insomnia;

(iii) impaired use of the limbs, ranging from arthritis to hysterical paralysis;

(iv) gout, dropsy and epilepsy;

(v) sores and localised swellings—tumours, ulcers, abscesses, and leprosy (which covered various conditions);

(vi) complications of pregnancy and childbirth;

(vii) blindness due to various causes which are not always specified, including debility and chronic dietary deficiencies;

(viii) mental afflication often erupting in violence, some of which was apparently due to eating rye affected by a certain fungus, but also to mental or physical trauma;

(ix) accidents such as drowning and suffocation of children through overlaying;

(x) deliberate violence of one kind or another, including suicide, murder, wounding, ordeal by battle, hanging.

Of the people involved in the miracles examined 61 per cent were men and 39 per cent women, the great mass of both belonging to the lower strata of society. The extent to which pilgrims were of local origin or came from afar varied considerably. For example, at an early stage in the history of Becket's shrine a third of the pilgrims in the sample studied came from abroad and the great majority of the rest from south-east England, including a quarter from Kent. On the other hand, the remote shrine of St Godric at Finchale never hit the headlines, its visitors being largely north-country, though at one stage with a higher percentage of women than usual—it is thought because its great rival shrine of St Cuthbert of Durham had a deep-rooted reputation for anti-feminism. It also seems clear that, at least in the case of the shrines of minor saints, the number of pilgrims decreased markedly in the latter part of our period though the process was by no means uniform.

CHAPTER 13

LITERACY AND LEARNING

THE PROBLEM OF LITERACY

DURING our period what proportion of the English population was literate, even in the limited sense of being able to read and write? Unhappily we have absolutely no useful statistics to show us the answer to this question but are inevitably driven to ill-informed and hazy guesswork. That on the eve of the Reformation the very great majority of the English population was still illiterate there can be no doubt, this being especially marked in the fair sex. The absence in England of that immensely flourishing commercial life which brought such wealth and sophistication to the great towns of contemporary Flanders and Italy meant also the absence of that substantial bourgeoisie which played so important a part in developing learning in those areas. The English population was overwhelmingly rural, mostly living in small and often scattered communities a simple agricultural life wherein there was no very great need for literacy and, in some areas at least, very few to cater for it; (East Anglia remained obstinately rural to the end of our period, and contemporary monastic visitations make it clear that there was then here a real shortage of teachers of that elementary Latin with which schooling began). In many parts of the north and west farms and hamlets were often so remote that provision of educational facilities was next to impossible and this, after all, was not of very much relevance to their pursuit of agriculture. In the towns this was not the case, but even here the series of small shops which largely looked after what was mostly very local trade can scarcely have required much in the way of learning. By and large the medieval English laity were obstinately illiterate because there did not seem to be any great need to be anything else, in a society which many centuries before had lost both that capitalism and firm belief in culture which marked the sophisticated society of ancient Greece and Rome.

A further factor which it is very easy to under-rate constituted a major obstacle to expansion of literacy and learning—the immense cost of book production. This was due to two main causes. Firstly, the fact that for almost all our period books had to be written by hand and secondly, that in these times the writing material employed was immensely costly. Amongst the series of invaluable inventions with which the remarkable people of China have endowed mankind few have been of such utility as that of paper. But use of this came very slowly to Western Europe. It was not employed to any great extent in France before the early part of the fifteenth century and another hundred years passed before there was a paper mill in England. Before this time the usual writing material was parchment or vellum, which was prohibitively expensive. This fact, together with the necessity of having books written out by hand, which involved enormous labour, meant that even at the end of our period books were both rare and costly luxuries; only a minute minority of the population had the means to purchase more than a very few. In these times a parish priest might expect a yearly salary of only a few pounds; a book could cost the same amount, or more*—so it is not surprising that monastic observances carefully enjoined that no-one should be allowed to borrow books without leaving adequate security for their return, or that books were occasionally chained as a precaution against theft. Contemporary wills show us that, as late as the fifteenth century, even quite well-to-do clergy and laity did not own more than a few volumes, most of which were usually connected with their work or worship. To market a great series of school or university texts or books of common prayer was quite out of the question.

THE-LANGUAGE PROBLEM

If the huge cost of reading matter was one stubborn obstacle to the spread of literacy amongst medieval Englishmen, another of comparable dimensions was caused by the fact that such people lived in a society wherein no less than three languages were in use, albeit to extents which varied considerably. Of these the most significant

---

* At this time even a very ordinary text might cost from £1 to £2; a missal from £2 to £10, and some service books up to £20, so that a book was an extraordinarily expensive object.

for most of the period, and by no means totally outmoded even at the end of it, was the Latin tongue which the old Romans had imposed so successfully on their mighty Empire as its official language, and which Western Christianity came to employ for the same purpose.

If the medieval Western Church continued this tradition of giving Latin the first place in its writing and speaking it was largely because of non-theological factors which made this seem the obvious thing to do. Besides having very deep-rooted social tradition behind it, Latin had a cosmopolitan quality which for long was not remotely challenged by any other tongue. Only in it could all the local Churches of the Western world communicate with each other, whilst at local level it provided a bond of unity within political units like the English kingdom wherein at the time there was nothing remotely approaching a national language. Further, Latin provided immensely superior means of communication to that of any of the various tongues of barbarian origin now current in the West, having a very extensive vocabulary, a very sophisticated grammar and immense adaptability to new requirements. Thus it effortlessly met the new demands which the great renaissance of the eleventh and twelfth centuries required. Very swiftly, for example, the English Exchequer produced its own very technical vocabulary, as did the theology and the canon law of this vigorous age. Inevitably, there-fore, for very long to come in England, as elsewhere in the civilised West, Latin was the language employed for all top-level official work, whether by kings, bishops or popes, and dominated also the realms of worship and learning. In it, for long, was written the great mass of correspondence and chronicles and other literary products of post-Conquest England. It was of enormous importance both from the social and theological angle that the public worship of England, like that of the rest of Western Christendom in these times, was conducted in Latin.

For long Latin met no major competition in England, a country linguistically naive and divided against itself. Down in the far West Country the Celtic tongue which the Romans had heard still flourished. In areas where Viking settlement had been dominant men used a heavily Scandinavian vocabulary and, in Cumbria at least, even employed the Runic alphabet down to the late twelfth century. If in the rest of England the Anglo-Saxon tongue was dominant there was as yet no uniform version of it, only several very localised dialects. Such a situation inevitably meant that in these times English had no serious qualification to be regarded as a national tongue. In the days before the Norman Conquest it had produced a limited amount of respectable writing, but for some time after it the currents of the time washed strongly against it, though the so-called *Old English Chronicle* in Norman England and the *Ancren Riwle* a century later showed that neglect of it was not complete. Obviously the Norman Conquest gave a considerable boost to the French tongue, which was much used by monarchy and aristocracy and infiltrated lower social levels in a version which we know as Anglo-Norman. For some time it was used quite extensively in law★ and literature, as well as spoken in high-class society but from the fourteenth century its importance declined as that of English steadily increased.

One major educational result of this situation was that for the whole of our period literacy and learning were dominated by the Latin tongue (significantly, when men now spoke of 'grammar' they meant that of Latin, not English, whilst a 'grammar school' was a place where one learnt Latin). Given the contemporary social conditions this linguistic complication inevitably imposed a very heavy burden on those who sought after literacy. The strain of this led, as we have seen, to the clergy often being inadequately versed in the tongue they employed in public worship, whilst increasingly as our period went on the laity grew somewhat restive at the dominance of this foreign tongue.

From roughly the later decades of the fourteenth century there are various signs that a truly national English literature is beginning to burgeon. If the works of Chaucer (d. 1400) are its most celebrated element, there are other less well-known ones, including some of the works of the English mystic, Richard Rolle (d. 1349), which built up very considerable popularity. In these later days literate laity very understandably found it only reasonable to write in English, notably the Paston family whose mighty fifteenth-century correspondence is one of the most famous and invaluable literary products of the times. Even wills to some small degree turn

---

★ To this day the official royal assent which transforms a bill into an Act of Parliament is given in French.

from Latin to English, like that of a noble lady wherein—in 1438—
she states firmly, 'I ordeyne and make my testament in English tonge
for my most profit, redyng and understanding'. However, so far
as major official documents—royal, episcopal and, of course, papal
—are concerned, Latin retained its supremacy to the end of our
period and beyond. It may be that for one reason or another interest
in learning Latin grammar was declining in the course of the
fifteenth century. The early statutes of God's House at Cambridge
assert in their preface that in many parts of the kingdom knowledge
of grammar, i.e. Latin, 'has fallen into great defect and decay for
lack of competent teachers', but this lack of supply may be due to
lack of demand. It is also interesting to note that statutes of Oxford
university composed before 1380 order teachers of Latin to use
French as well as English in their translations and explanations 'lest
the French language be altogether lost'.

In the following century, just when it looked as though the
language of Chaucer might have established an effective supremacy,
the advent of the reactionary influence of the great movement known
as the Italian Renaissance led perversely to the deification of ancient
tongues and opened the door to that neglect of modern foreign
languages in the English educational syllabus which today is of such
truly scandalous proportions.

Pre-University Schooling

Although useful modern work has greatly clarified and extended
our knowledge of the schooling prevalent in medieval England it is
very important to appreciate that this subject is one which is so
very thinly and unevenly documented that nothing approaching a
complete picture of it can ever be reconstructed. As Galbraith so very
properly has stressed, the documents of medieval England very
seldom pay any attention to individuals or institutions whose
existence does not in some degree have direct financial or legal
repercussions. Thus although monasteries as bodies with important
properties and privileges attract frequent mention, normally their
individual members do not, with the result that evidence on the
number of brethren in medieval English monasteries is immensely
rare, as is that of the names of their inmates (apart from that of the
head of the house) right down to the time of the Dissolution when

all were required to sign the deed of surrender of their establishment. Similarly, many of the establishments wherein the medieval school-children of England began to acquire the elements of literacy were very small and very informal, with little or no endowment, and as such had no attraction for enquiring officials. There cannot be the slightest doubt that there existed in medieval England very many more schools than will ever be known, albeit of a primitive type and sometimes not very long-lived.

Two examples of this important negative factor may here be given. In his will of 1558 a septuagenarian priest of Norwich left substantial alms to a house of nuns there 'bycause I have a great truste that thy wylle praye for me; and also bycause a verie goode devoute syster of the said howse ... was the fyrst creature that taughte me to know the lettres in my book'. Such a reference in an official legal document is immensely rare, but it would be unrealistic not to admit the virtual certainty that again and again in medieval England many kindly monastic inmates and clergy gave totally informal elementary instruction to children deserving of it. More important and almost equally elusive is detailed mention of small scholastic establishments having no endowment or legal existence. Such places must often have existed, at least temporarily, without leaving any written contemporary record of their existence. A very rare example of reference to such a school concerns the great Cistercian abbey of Furness and occurs in a lawsuit of 1582 between the new lord of the manor and the tenants of the former abbey lands. From this we learn, entirely incidentally, that before the Dissolution the abbey had maintained a school to which sons of the tenants of the abbey were admitted. The substantial pre-Reformation records of Furness make no mention of this school whatsoever and had it not been for the pertinacity of the later tenants in asserting their claims there would have survived no proof of it ever having existed. Clearly, such a text raises the considerable likelihood that other English monasteries may well have maintained similar institutions even though we have no surviving record thereof. Across the estuary from Furness was Cartmel Priory where we find a school being held in the church in 1584, which may well have a pre-Reformation origin though lack of evidence makes it impossible to settle the point.

It is therefore quite certain that, unlike the monasteries and parish churches of our period, but like its hermitages and anchorages, the schools of medieval England have a history so ill-documented that even elementary facts like their total number will never be ascertainable. The highly informal organisation of much elementary instruction must have meant that the number fluctuated considerably. This lack of precision is even greater in regard to the private tuition which took place in medieval England. That individual clergy and religious gave help to local lads is obviously something that happened, but it has left almost no trace and the same is true to a lesser degree even of that private tuition in higher social circles.

ELEMENTARY INSTRUCTION

The subjects in the primary education current in medieval England, as is normally the case, were largely dictated by the particular priorities of contemporary society, at a stage when these were very different indeed from those of today. As has been noted, the predominantly agricultural nature of the English economy meant that lay demands for literacy and all that stemmed from it were very restricted. On the other hand that immense preoccupation with religion which dominated the thoughts of contemporaries created very extensive needs for an ecclesiastical personnel that had to possess at least a modicum of literacy. The provision of the clergy to staff the thousands of parish churches of the time was one obvious example of such necessity, but was much more heavily reinforced than is always realised by the huge number of clergy who were involved, not in traditional pastoral activities, but in the offering of thousands of Masses for the good of the souls of the faithful departed. As we have seen, many of these were priests charged with the maintenance of chantries, but others of them held posts not intended to be maintained to the end of time by means of a permanent endowment, but were part of *ad hoc* arrangements, made for the saying of such Masses for the good of the souls of folk recently departed from this mortal life. The need for some modicum of elementary education which this concern for souls of those departed this mortal life involved was not limited to the priests who were to celebrate the Masses concerned but also concerned those laity who assisted the conduct of the Mass by acting as servers. At various points in the Mass come small parts which are to be said by the person or persons attending the service but not celebrating it, it being a very firm rule that a Mass could not be celebrated by the priest without at least one person to do this, save in circumstances which were very, very rare indeed. The bare minimum was assistance of a single server. There was no question of his office being open to women and this, along with the fact that often the great majority of Masses were said during the week when men would normally be at work, meant that most servers of chantry and allied Masses were boys. Such lads had clearly to have at least a working knowledge of the singing and reading, without which the service could not properly be conducted—though not more than a proportion of the Masses were sung. Though it was obviously desirable that they should also understand the meaning of the Latin which they were saying and they would in fact be likely to do, so far as certain fixed parts of the Mass were concerned, it was not necessary that they should do so from the public point of view—to choose and utter the words correctly would suffice.

As a result of this need there spread steadily over the England of our period what were for obvious reasons termed 'song schools' or 'reading schools'. (The high importance which industrial England was to accord to writing in elementary education was notably absent from medieval England for the very good reason that under contemporary social conditions there was very little call for it.) Although there is not the slightest doubt that instruction in Latin, singing and reading was very widespread in medieval England, for reasons already noted it is utterly impossible to get precise pictures of statistics relating to these subjects.

Such public schooling was mostly very informal indeed. It might be given by any duly authorised clerk in holy orders, not necessarily a priest, who had the time, knowledge and inclination. He might simply hold a class in part of the church, deriving his pay for this not from a fixed endowment but from offerings made by the parents of the pupils concerned. However, a fixed provision for this was obviously desirable if only to provide for a continuity which otherwise might be lacking. In secular cathedrals and the very limited number of well-to-do collegiate churches a very elaborate musical programme characterised the service for which it was clearly desirable to have specially trained choir boys. As a result of this from a very early date we find there 'choir schools' which put music very much in the forefront of their curriculum.

If reading and singing were the basic necessities for the conduct of medieval worship, some knowledge of Latin was obviously imperative if not for the server at least for those who celebrated the Masses and also for all who sought to go on to a higher education which might qualify them either to become priests, lawyers or government officials in royal and other households. Under the primitive conditions of the time, as we have already noted, the acquisition of a really sound knowledge of this tongue was no easy matter, though fairly considerable attempts were made to provide it at schools termed, as we have seen, 'grammar schools'. An invaluable survey of London in the twelfth century shows that already this highly exceptional city had three schools doing this with success, but often elsewhere such opportunities were not very easy to find. The knowledge of Latin imparted in a small village school may well often have given little more than a rough and ready apprehension of the sense of the Mass. But, as has been seen throughout our period, as the very abundant Latin literature of medieval England (both official and non-official) shows, there was always a small section of society which acquired considerable expertise in reading and writing it. From Norman times onwards we have great quantities of letters of all kinds in Latin, along with a goodly supply of chronicles for most if not quite all of the period, as well as floods of official documents both ecclesiastical and non-ecclesiastical.

It is only necessary to give cursory glances at the schools of medieval England to appreciate how very largely their operations were governed by ecclesiastical considerations. Nevertheless, there were already some slight signs of the commencement of that laicisation of education which is today so potent. The only highly educated class with members capable and often not unready to challenge ecclesiastical rights and privileges in late medieval England were the lawyers, whose work had attained considerable complexity by the end of our period and required not only a working knowledge of French but much technical knowledge, e.g. in conveyancing. For a while in Oxford were to be found facilities for studying such subjects, not officially unconnected with the University, but the growth of the legal profession in London steadily made its establishments there the best facilities for training budding lawyers. Here and there schools were founded with some provision for those not wishing to follow an ecclesiastical career, like that which Thomas Rotherham, archbishop of York (1480–1500), set up in the town whence he derived his surname, but such institutions form a very small element of the whole; almost all of them were founded late in our period.

In some ways the most hopeful sign of a broader basis of the scholastic syllabus in the future is to be found in the education increasingly used in the households of the monarchy and the great nobles. This started with the advantage of having far more adequate financial means than that available at the lower levels and the even greater asset that its pupils' education need not be dominated by what was, after all, for lesser folk the inevitable major factor—the necessity to qualify for some form of employment. Kings and barons were likely to possess adequate means to explore wider interests than pure utility demanded. The syllabus of instruction for young men (and even to a limited extent of young ladies) of high social position was only to reach its peak in the Renaissance of Italy, when for a while, folk like Vittorino da Feltri gave it a width of interest never again to be equalled. In our period if these heights were not scaled, real advance towards them was gradually achieved here.

For some time after the Norman Conquest the level of literacy in the families of kings and barons was nothing if not deplorable. In the twelfth century there was current in England the proverb that 'an illiterate king is a crowned ass', but it was only in the fourteenth century that we find eminent laity showing anything like a serious interest in literacy and its attendant assets. Edward II and Richard II were both book-lovers. The former is the first of our sovereigns to leave us ocular proof that he could write and it is with the latter that there begins the habit of English kings signing their official documents. By the fifteenth century there are unmistakable signs that the education in the royal household was being taken very seriously with extensive use of tutors and a far from contemptible range of subjects. The young Edward V is said to have been able to 'discourse elegantly, to understand fully and to declaim most excellently', whilst the young Henry VIII had an extensive education which made him 'perhaps more learned than any of his predecessors' (Orme).

Where kings lead, nobles tend to follow, and the fourteenth and fifteenth centuries in England saw a very pronounced increase in interest in literacy in such circles. We see the beginning of a small but significant trickle of well-bred young gentlemen going to the university and in the fifteenth century there are several examples of men belonging to the highest social levels collecting books and patronising writers. This literary interest was no esoteric thing but was combined with instruction in military matters (the precursor of later compulsory games), careful study of the art of good manners (nowadays excised from the educational syllabus) more especially regarding courtesy towards the fair sex which ran very deep, and training in cultural activities such as music and singing. Of this education religious practice was a fundamental part. A notable feature in fourteenth-century England, as elsewhere, was the effective rise of story-telling. Like so many things in the medieval West, Italy led the way, but with Geoffrey Chaucer who significantly had sharpened his wits by travel in France and Italy, we reach the first truly entertaining author of fiction in English history. Today his great good humour, sharp eye for pictorial detail and real interest in his fellows might have made him a film director of the calibre of Jean Renoir. If he has not got the latter's sympathetic interest in very lowly members of society it is because at this time literary circles were largely co-terminous with the aristocratic circles wherein he moved and in which he fitted so well and happily. If his writing has bred some misunderstanding about the contemporary English Church the fault is not his. But literary interest amongst the English laity, even in the higher social strata, was limited to a very small number indeed, which is primarily why the Renaissance took root so late.

THE QUESTION OF FINANCE

Although from the twelfth century onwards there was evident in many parts of the Western Church a growing realisation of the value of elementary education for clerks, the considerable lack of affluence of contemporary society at this time and for long to come rendered adequate financial provision for this far from easy to provide on more than a very limited scale, though contemporary devotion to almsgiving meant that real attempts were made to provide free schooling. The Lateran Council of 1215 ordered that free schools should be maintained by cathedrals and other large churches able to afford the expenses involved but this inevitably vague formula may not have been very successful in practice, even though English cathedrals and some of the greater churches had certainly had such institutions from an early date.

Latish in our period the rise of the chantries provided a body of men who had the necessary qualifications for elementary teaching and also a very great deal of spare time (page 260), so that it is not surprising that they played a useful part in the beginnings of primary education in England, even if their total efforts seem small to modern eyes. The inadequacies of our documentation, to which reference has been made, unhappily means that there survive only sporadic glimpses of these chantries. Although some chantry priests were legally bound by the terms of their appointment to instruct the young, others were not, but may have done so at least sporadically. It was after all easy to find space in the church or elsewhere for the school and to finance the tuition by a levy on the parents of at least some of the pupils. However it seems likely that though this contribution to elementary education was important it was not immense. The very well-documented surveys of Sussex show that chantries there were numerous at the time of their suppression, with some attached to the cathedral, but only four schools are mentioned in connection with them. In the very populous county of Essex it has been claimed, 'chantries were probably the main source of education . . . eighteen chantry priests, about one quarter of the whole, were employed in teaching' (Oxley). Whilst it is true that the very marked interest in the provision of elementary education which characterised the early sixteenth century may mean that a good proportion of the chantry schools mentioned in the mid-sixteenth century deeds were of comparatively recent foundation it would be unwise to take this for granted, and there may, of course, well have been chantry schools in earlier times which were on an informal basis and have disappeared as some of the chantries themselves certainly had. The same uncertainty befogs our knowledge of almonry schools maintained by monasteries like that at Furness already noted. Given the ample accommodation of most monasteries and the fact that many of them had secular clergy on the premises for chantry or other duty, some teaching facilities are likely but their exact extent is and ever will be indiscoverable.

By the latter part of the period in the more flourishing towns of

o

England there existed trade guilds of various kinds. Outside London few of these were very rich but it did not need great wealth to establish a school as some did. Of these the most famous was destined to be that at Stratford-on-Avon founded by the guild of St John the Baptist and the Holy Cross, which in 1426–7 built a new school and secured endowment for a teacher. A different set-up is found at the noble collegiate church of Ottery St Mary founded by Bishop Grandisson of Exeter in 1338 where the master, as well as teaching members of the place, enlarged his classes and his income by taking outsiders along with his other pupils.

Such ventures as these were not numerous and were completely put into the shade by two major educational foundations founded in the latter half of our period. The first of these was Winchester College set up in 1382 on the outskirts of his cathedral city by Bishop William of Wykeham to whose freedom from indigence attention has already been called (page 269). A century after the foundation of Winchester College came into being its prestigious rival, Eton College, near Windsor, founded in 1440 by the pious King Henry VI, whose final scheme provided for seventy scholars there, supported by a very lavish endowment. They could further their studies at King's College Cambridge, also established by their founder at very great expense. A third establishment on the same prestigious lines was initiated by Thomas Wolsey, son of an Ipswich butcher who became a cardinal and archbishop of York. He sought to establish a school in his own time which was to be linked with a new college at Oxford, but when he suddenly fell from power (1520) the latter was unfinished, though tradition asserts that good progress had been made with its kitchen.

The very defective evidence, very obvious indeed up to the opening of the fourteenth century, makes highly unwise anything but very guarded comment on the growth in the numbers of places of pre-university schooling in England during our period. Orme's findings—very properly cautious—do, however, make it quite clear that by the end of the thirteenth century a number of places of elementary education were in existence and that these were by no means confined to large towns and cathedrals but were widely spread over the land, some of them belonging to places of very minor importance like Cockermouth, Eccles, Malton and Plympton. But their number fell well short of three figures and even two

centuries later the grand total of such establishments whose existence
he finds to be beyond doubt was only 253.

The Rise of the Universities of Oxford and Cambridge

Few of the achievements of medieval Western Christendom have
proved to be of such far-reaching importance as its creation and
consolidation of a permanent university tradition—a thing which
China, Persia, Greece, Rome, Byzantium and the Moslem world
failed to achieve. The number of these early universities was not
large and their distribution was very uneven, being for long largely
confined to Italy, France and England, but their influence on human
development was immense.

The first foundations had only a very few of the characteristics
which were to become traditional. Pantin writes of 'the disembodied
character of the medieval university, which possessed practically no
endowments, no buildings, no visible plant ... The university was
in fact simply a collection of masters and scholars living and teaching
in hired houses or hired rooms.' These early places had no official
date of foundation but tended to drift into existence and in a few
cases even to drift out of it, for the considerable streak of disorderliness in medieval university life, often accentuated by bad relations
with the local townsfolk, led to various groups of masters and
students de-camping from one academic home to another—a move
made easy by their 'disembodied' life. In England at one time it
looked briefly as if a university was going to take root at Northampton, the favourite meeting place in medieval England, while one at
Stamford for a brief while rivalled Oxford. It is worthy of note
that although for a while higher learning flourished at the cathedrals
of Lincoln, Exeter, Hereford and York, progress was not maintained
and no English cathedral town ultimately housed a university in
medieval times. North of the Alps from the very earliest stages no
university could remotely compete in prestige with the university
of Paris, whose rapid rise to intellectual supremacy was achieved
in the first half of the twelfth century and has never since been
seriously rivalled so far as the arts are concerned. The beneficence of
geography to England in placing her so near Paris and of history
in giving her such strong political links with France in its crucial

early days of Western university development were amongst the major causes of England's two medieval universities of Oxford and Cambridge ranking amongst the oldest in Western Europe.

OXFORD UNIVERSITY

The history of medieval Oxford has been studied in immense depth by H. E. Salter who points out the very considerable advantages which geography had given it. Centrally placed in a rich and pleasing countryside, in the fifty years before the Conquest it had been often frequented by the kings of the period, and after it their successors had a favourite palace not far away at Woodstock where they housed England's earliest major zoo. Its communications both local and national were magnificent. Major imports could be had from Bristol, London and Southampton, and good roads linked it with Gloucester and South Wales. The route to Southern Ireland traversed it and useful local roads converged on it. Thus Oxford was a major commercial centre and was of substantial size. Given such conditions it was likely enough that in the course of the twelfth century Oxford would attract some of the now growing band of learned men, even if it was not inevitable that they should settle there permanently and thus initiate what was to become medieval England's premier university.

Quite early in the twelfth century there are signs of theological study at Oxford which must almost certainly be largely due to the initiative of local ecclesiastics, notably the early priors of St Frideswide's (the main church in the town), Walter, archdeacon of Oxford, who was provost of the little college of St George attached to Oxford Castle, and Master Wigod, the first abbot of Oseney. Before 1115 and after 1119 there taught at Oxford the French theologian, Theobald of Etampes, who is said to have had over a hundred pupils, and the equally eminent Robert Pullen was lecturing here in 1133. From an early stage it would seem that lawyers haunted the town seeking after their prey, and in 1149 Vicarius, an eminent Italian jurist, was also lecturing in Oxford. But such isolated interventions as these do not prove the existence of an organised body of teachers, and it has recently been argued with much force that only at the very end of the twelfth century was to be found there a body of teachers and students sufficiently organised to be entitled to be regarded as a university. By this time study of the arts, law and theology had taken firm root.

In 1210 we have mention of a 'master of the schools' (*magister scholarum*), a term implying a formalised body of students, and in 1221 there begins the long unbroken line of 'chancellors' who headed the medieval university. In 1229 some students deserted Paris for Oxford. But very much the most important factor in the process which the end of the thirteenth century had made Oxford a centre of theological studies that vied with the mighty Paris was the arrival of the friars, more particularly the Franciscans and Dominicans, both of which orders made a bee-line for the place, quickly establishing there, as Pantin notes, 'large self-contained communities living in their own buildings' that constituted 'such a startling phenomenon in thirteenth century Oxford.' The first Franciscans arrived in England late in 1224 and within a few weeks had sent a small band to Oxford where, as their chronicler notes, 'sweet Jesus sowed a grain of mustard seed that afterwards became greater than all herbs.' By 1233 they had some forty brethren there which had swelled to eighty-four in 1317 and 103 in 1377. The Dominicans, whose astounding capacity for efficient organisation of higher education on an international basis was unrivalled in the medieval West, as early as 1221 had set up in Oxford what was their first English house, and in 1261 elevated it to the position of a house of general study. Here were seventy friars in 1277 and ninety-six in 1305. The Carmelites, early noted for their learning, established themselves at Oxford in 1256 and had fifty-four there by 1305. Smaller in numbers but not unimportant were the Austin friars who arrived about 1266. Numerically the friars constituted a far from negligible part of the smallish population of the university in these times, and provided students who pursued a prolonged and disciplined academic life which contrasted markedly with the very comparatively brief sojourns which was all that many seculars could manage. Significantly, it was largely from the ranks of the friars that came most of the major theologians which gave medieval Oxford its intellectual panache. As we have seen, the part played here by Austin canons and various types of Benedictines was not considerable (page 289). The heads of Oxford and Cambridge universities had the well-worn title of chancellor, and at first were legally mere representatives of the local bishops (Lincoln and Ely), but inevitably they ultimately acquired an independent authority.

Halls and Colleges

Of the various marked differences between medieval and modern times at the universities of Oxford and Cambridge few are more notable than the very minor rôle which was played by colleges in the former age. Down to the fifteenth century the colleges, mostly poor and in number very few, housed 'only a tiny, privileged minority'. At first many students probably lived in individual lodgings, but steadily for social and disciplinary reasons there was a marked swing towards residence in 'halls', a practice made compulsory at Oxford in the early fifteenth century. These halls were in Salter's words 'nothing but ordinary houses which for long were hired out by locals to teachers and others.' Oxford had sixty-nine of them in 1444, fifty in 1469, and hereafter their number further diminished.

A college differed from a hall in three notable respects. It had its big premises, its own endowment and a firm common life laid down in special rules to be observed by members of the foundation. In these respects Oxford and Cambridge colleges resembled monasteries and cathedrals, as they did also in the fact that their members had firm obligations to remember regularly in their prayers their founders and benefactors (which they still do). Although members took no vow of poverty a number of them were chosen in part because of their indigence. In three major respects these early colleges differed from those of today—they were almost all very scantily endowed, had a very small number of members and of these a very high proportion were fellows, not students. Early significance was minor—'they were really external to the university—backwaters, not in the main-stream', writes Salter of the early Oxford colleges. The only major new fact about these collegiate foundations was that they illustrated the growing tendency to rank provision for study with the old-established 'good causes' for which almsgiving might laudably be devoted. It is worthy of note that of the twelve medieval Oxford colleges the great majority were founded by ecclesiastics. The only very grandiose establishment was New College, founded in 1379 by a bishop of Winchester who, as has been seen, was almost certainly amongst the greatest plutocrats in Western Europe. All the rest were of modest proportions. They were Balliol (1263–8), Merton (1274) University (*c.* 1280), Exeter (1314), Oriel (1324),

Queen's (1340), Lincoln (1427), All Souls (1438), Magdalen (1458), Brasenose (1509), Corpus Christi (1516), Christ Church (1525)*. This immensely strong ecclesiastical influence was partially due to the wealth of the medieval English episcopate but much more to the immense importance of the university as a place of theological and legal education.

CAMBRIDGE UNIVERSITY

That England's second university should have arisen at Cambridge is at first sight surprising. Here was a smallish town set in desolate fenland over which only journeying by water is attractive, with little but scattered, very minor villages in the vicinity and only the magnificent towers of Ely Cathedral to break the skyline. Well off the beaten track was Cambridge—'no pitched battle took place there, no councils of importance were held there and only one Parliament met there' notes Camm, to which one may add that its castle was third-rate and the town's churches largely unpretentious. Yet historical geography shows us that medieval Cambridge enjoyed real assets not now easily perceived.

Like most major medieval towns of any significance it stood at the junction of a major waterway with useful roads (at the one bridge in England which gives its name to a county). From it the waters of the Cam flowed sluggishly to reach the sea at what was in medieval times the major port of King's Lynn. North of the bridge one good road followed the high ground northward to Huntingdon and beyond, whilst another twisted round to go on to Ely. From the other bank serviceable if unprestigious roads led to useful places like London. Because of this position medieval Cambridge was 'a natural centre in economic and cultural affairs' and 'a clearing house for the agricultural produce of the surrounding countryside'. Unsurprisingly, therefore, on its outskirts, near the little Romanesque chapel of the hospital of Stourbridge still to be seen there, developed what a Tudor writer claimed as 'by far the largest and most famous fair of England' where very long before his day pushed and shoved

---

* As with monastic foundations, the establishment of a college was quite often a fairly protracted process, so that the dates of foundation which they claim must not be interpreted very strictly.

immense throngs from near and far. However, even more than in the case of Oxford, these geographical advantages did not ordain that the place would inevitably become a university town. That this came to be so must have been due in no small measure to fortuitous personal factors of which next to no record remains.

The first firm indication of higher education being dispensed here is found in 1209 when some Oxford students left their first place of study to find a second academic home at Cambridge, though why they chose this place we cannot now tell. Steadily from this time onwards came progress. The chancellor is mentioned as early as 1225, some students from Paris apparently arrived in 1229 and we have mention of a faculty of theology along with arts and canon law a generation later, to which civil law and medicine came to be added.

Here, perhaps even more than at Oxford, early university life was heavily indebted to the impetus provided by the arrival of mendicant orders. The Franciscans set up house here most austerely in or about 1226. They had fifty-eight friars in residence by 1277 and apparently seventy-five by 1289, a total complement which vies with those of the largest monasteries in contemporary England. The Dominicans had established themselves at Cambridge before 1237 a house intended for no less than seventy friars, which also had seventy-five in 1289. The number of inmates of these two houses far exceeded those of all the early colleges of the university.

First of these latter was a small house founded by the contemporary bishop of Ely in 1284 which came to be known as Peterhouse. But episcopal interest in Cambridge was not extensive. Of the following foundations, Clare (1306) and Pembroke (1346) were set up by pious but extremely formidable peeresses* and Corpus Christi (1350) by the guild in the town of that name. The interesting and much travelled Bishop Bateman of Norwich (d. 1355) founded Trinity Hall (1350) and aided the establishment of Gonville Hall (1349).

---

* The latter of these, Marie de St Pol, countess of Pembroke, established a possibly unique architectural precedent by providing herself with a very early example of a first-floor flat inside the conventual church of the abbey of Franciscan nuns which she founded at Denny, and a historical one by making a will which, at a time when the Hundred Years' War was under way, contained bequests to the kings of both England and France, the latter consisting of a sword without a point and a mysterious message.

All these were very minor establishments. After a gap of a century King Henry VI founded on a grand scale King's College (1441) though completion of the scheme took some time. It took over some earlier royal provision for students and was designed as a 'closed shop' for scholars of Eton College which the king had established down the road from Windsor Castle in 1440. Queen's College 'to laud and honneure of sexe feminine', even if inevitably for men only, was founded in 1448 and followed by St Catharine's (1473) and Jesus College, founded in 1497 by the then bishop of Ely by the novel expedient of dissolving a nunnery on the outskirts of the town and putting its site, buildings and revenue to collegiate use. In 1505 the little God's House which had been founded in 1442 was converted into Christ's College by the great blue-stocking of the age, Margaret Beaufort, countess of Richmond, for poor priests to study theology and *inter alia* worship in clean surplices. She also initiated the process which led to the hospital of St John in the town being converted into a college (1509–16). With the very major exception of King's none of these early foundations had originally more than very modest endowments, and the total of their academic personnel was not impressive.

THE SYLLABUS

To outline the wide and very complex history of English university life in the later Middle Ages is not within the scope of this work and would be unwise to attempt at a juncture when so much modern research on it is attaining the point of publication. But it is germane to our purpose is to discover the nature of the courses of study which there prevailed.

What is a university for? The most obvious of several likely responses to this question is that it exists to provide technical qualifications for major employment which as such are likely to command good salaries. As early as the mid-thirteenth century this dominance of practical needs was clear in English universities and protest was made that 'the lucrative arts such as law and medicine are now in vogue and only those things are pursued which have a cash value.' But, as the old Greeks had so firmly insisted, the supreme study of all studies was the problem of Man and the Universe. What was the purpose of life to which Man should direct his faculties? This primacy of seeking out the correct ideology, accepted by the great pagan thinkers of classical times, was given the same major significance by a great host of Christian theologians (known as 'scholastics') who had a prestigious part in the universities of the medieval West.

At the bottom of the syllabus scale was a somewhat elementary general course in what were termed the arts. Besides the all-essential grammar (i.e. Latin) it included some study of arithmetic, geometry, astronomy and the theory of music, but its principal concern was with rhetoric, logic and philosophy (natural, moral and meta-physical). Success in this course, which covered four years, made the candidate his Bachelor of Arts, a further three years being necessary for him to become a Master of Arts. Unsurprisingly, a large pro-portion of students did not stay this lengthy course. Many parish priests came up for a short time; some could not afford the expense of so long a sojourn, but idleness, vice and above all, probably, lack of aptitude also worked to the same ends—it would appear that in fifteenth-century Oxford about one third of those who began their studies acquired their B.A. and half that number their M.A.

However, this was by no means the end of academic possibilities, for some would go on to one of the higher faculties—theology, law (civil and canon) and medicine. Just as amongst the Greeks philosophy represented the peak of human enquiry, so in the medieval university theology was regarded as the queen of knowledge. From the early twelfth century interest in its various complex aspects of Christian belief had steadily increased and in the thirteenth century had be-come a veritable flood. The most celebrated of the first-class thinkers in the thirteenth century is St Thomas Aquinas (c. 1225–74), a Dominican bred in Italy though much engaged in teaching at Paris. His writings are enormous in bulk, filling no less than thirty volumes in a modern printed edition and are headed by his massive *Theo-logical Summary* (*Summa Theologica*) which until very recently occupied an unchallenged primacy in the Roman Catholic theo-logical circles. It consists of three parts. The first deals with God, the Sovereign Being, Source and Master of all things, ranging very widely to include such topics as the Trinity, Creation, Angels, the nature of Man. The second considers at length the nature of Man whose perfect happiness consists in vision of God, discussing *inter alia* the nature of law, of sin and virtue. The third part, which was left unfinished, concerns Jesus Christ, the Way whereby man returns to God and discusses principally the earthly life of Christ, the nature of the Sacraments and Judgment (Purgatory, Heaven, Hell, the Resurrection, the Last Judgment).

Though no English scholar attained quite the same degree of eminence as Aquinas, a remarkable number of them, mostly in the thirteenth century, attained considerable importance in the realm of philosophy and theology, far more than at any later stage in national history, most, though not all, being members of the mendicant orders, to which Oxford owed much of its fame. Here at a crucial early stage they were greatly aided by a secular priest, Robert Grosseteste who, from 1229-35, took charge of the Franciscan school at Oxford to which he gave immediate éclat. His successor here was a Franciscan, Adam Marsh, who had an immense reputation as a philosopher. Equally distinguished was the philosopher Alexander of Hales (d. 1246) who had gained high repute as a teacher at Paris when in 1236 he became a Franciscan.

The Cambridge house of the Franciscans was important in the early establishment of the theological faculty there. Here before he rose to fame at Oxford and Paris was Duns Scotus (c. 1265-1308) a Scot who acquired an enormous reputation, especially amongst medieval Franciscans, though through unsympathetic men of the Renaissance his first name was used to add the word 'dunce' to our language. But there is much to be said for the view that no scholar of our period was so remarkable as Roger Bacon (c. 1214-92) whose width of interest and modernity of outlook, as we shall see, were most remarkable.

Of the Dominicans it has properly been said, 'from the beginning the background of the order was fundamentally doctrinal and intellectual' and each priory had its teacher in theology, something of which the older monastic orders had not dreamed. As we have seen they early established houses at Oxford and Cambridge, but the early history of the order here was for some little time clouded by serious internal differences of opinion over the theology of their illustrious Aquinas. Of their various scholarly members Robert Kilwardby was of great eminence, lecturing at Paris for some time and later briefly archbishop of Canterbury (1273-8). His writings are varied and voluminous.

Theological faculties were rare in the universities of Western Europe in these times so it is a remarkable fact that they now came

into existence at both Oxford and Cambridge. Both went on to
produce a very highly sophisticated learning which drew hither
many students from foreign parts. However, the size of the sector
of English life which this theological renaissance (for it was nothing
less) greatly influenced must not be exaggerated. Indubitably its
main support came from the mendicant orders to whose work it
had so obvious a relevance. To the older monastic orders the appeal
was much less, though not negligible in the case of the greater
Benedictine houses. There were few intelligent laymen dabbling in
theology for obvious social reasons, and no great chances of plum
ecclesiastical appointments for theologians. Inevitably the theological
approach of these times was ultimately destined to lose some of its
appeal, but not before it had done much to enrich Christian life.

From what we have already seen, it is apparent that the somewhat
backward social conditions of medieval England meant that there
were very limited spheres wherein a trained graduate could expect
to find the well-paid posts which he naturally desired. Primary
education was primitive and far from universal; secondary education
in the modern sense very largely non-existent; there were no complex industrial concerns and only very scanty local government
posts of any rank. Very much the best hope for getting a well-paid
position lay in becoming an official either of the Crown or for some
great magnate, ecclesiastical or non-ecclesiastical. As we have early
in our period seen, both royal and ecclesiastical machinery had become very complex, being regulated largely by very sophisticated
legal rules. Papal and episcopal business especially, bristled with
legal technicalities, neglect of which might have very serious
consequences—at worst the failure of one's initiative, at best delays
and disputes unduly delaying a settlement and entailing additional
expense. The English government was smaller and simpler, but by
the second half of the century had become very sophisticated, its
legal machinery being also highly specialised and the forms of document used therein highly technical. Major officials on the staff of
one of the diocesan bishops of England would have to be versed
in both canon and civil law and so also would royal officials.

Because of such factors as these, canon and civil law from the
first were leading subjects for study in the rising universities of
Western Europe. The earliest major centre for them was Bologna,
strategically placed at the centre of a great network of roads that

connected her with prosperous towns of northern and central Italy, where the tradition of Roman urban life and memories of the majestic Roman legal heritage were still alive. Rome itself, rather curiously, like London, did not become a major centre of learning in medieval times. From the mid-eleventh century the study of canon law was led by Italians, firstly through individual compilers of which Gratian (d. before 1160) was the most influential, but later by official digests of subsequent official legislation. Because of its obvious practical importance under contemporary social conditions legal studies on a fairly large scale had begun before the theological activities of the twelfth and thirteenth centuries had attained great momentum. From an early stage flourishing law schools existed at both Oxford and Cambridge.

One does not need to have any extensive knowledge of the history of education to realise that almost always the scheme in vogue is in one way or another ill-balanced. The Victorian public school, for example, laid commendable stress on social behaviour and the stimulus to be had from studying ancient Greece and Rome, but wrote off almost totally the heritage of medieval Catholicism, the study of modern languages and, above all, the acquisition of that capacity for informed scepticism which French tradition has so faithfully preserved. Similarly, medieval university education had clearly major defects, the chief of which many would regard as being its disregard of most branches of science. Medicine, it is true, could be studied in medieval Oxford and Cambridge, but it was only in small demand and cannot be said to have made any very major progress in our period.

Interest in the other sciences in the great revival of the twelfth-century renaissance was perhaps wider than our present knowledge of it suggests but was certainly not enormous, though by the thirteenth century there was in England some thirst for knowledge of it and one English scholar at least showed in this respect a remarkable combination of wide interest and deep understanding. This was Roger Bacon (c. 1214–92) who comparatively late in life—about 1267—joined the Franciscan order. A most industrious writer, of him it has been said, 'the vast range of his knowledge and interests makes it difficult for any individual in this age of specialisation to give an adequate appreciation of him.' Modern research has been unwilling to accord him great originality, but it is clear that his wide-ranging mind and ceaseless search for truth of various types gave him a gigantic intellectual stature and made him a major pioneer in Western thought, albeit one too far ahead of traditional outlooks to acquire the contemporary support he so greatly merited.

Theology he by no means neglected, but to the historian what makes him so remarkable is his approach to it. In the first place, rising superior to long Western tradition he showed a remarkable sense of the importance of studying the language of the Bible scientifically as the prelude to correct understanding of it. Although not alone in this, he pointed out with great vigour the immense corruption of many of the Latin vulgate Bibles current in his age which, he observed, led to a situation wherein 'every lecturer makes changes in the text out of his head'. Errors must be scientifically corrected by preferring ancient readings to modern, common ones to rare ones. Above all, the original languages in which the Scriptures were written, the Hebrew of the Old Testament and the Greek of the New, must be grasped. So convinced was he of the importance of this approach to the all-important text of the Bible that he produced students' grammars in both these languages (that in Greek being apparently unique in the long and rich history of medieval Western learning) and insisted that the task of textual revision must be undertaken by an authoritative commission of scholars appointed by the pope, to whom he wrote, 'I cry to you against this corruption of the Text, for you alone can remedy the evil'. History vindicated completely his remarkable insight here, but unhappily medieval Western opinion utterly failed to see how right he was, and these developments for which he pressed came largely only in the nineteenth century. Had they come much earlier Catholic relations with the Eastern Churches before the Reformation and with Protestant Churches during it might well have been less acid.

Equally ahead of his time was Bacon's stress on the importance of scientific studying of the natural world though significantly he urged this not from a hazy belief in learning for learning's sake, but for a fundamentally religious reason: 'it is by knowledge of created things that we arrive at the knowledge of the Creator'. Again, in terms singularly acceptable to modern men and more than a little dubious to medieval ones, he insisted that the natural world was governed by fixed scientific laws, not by sporadic supernatural ones. Of what he termed 'the wonderful actions of nature which are done every day' he wrote, 'we think that they are done either by special divine operation or by angels or devils or chance*. But this is not so, except in so far as every operation of the creation is in some sort from God. But this does not prevent operations being done according to natural laws or reason; for nature is the instrument of God's handiwork.' Here again is an eminently modern viewpoint which by and large the medieval Western world was unable to stomach, to its very great loss. It inevitably led the ultra-active Bacon to explore scientifically the realms of nature, not least that of physics. He acquired to aid him here *inter alia* at very great expense a lens, and insisted on that accuracy of measurement of natural phenomena for which mathematics are all-important, and to which he accorded very great significance. His stupendous range of study included exploration and he sent the pope a map of the world in which he marked what he believed to be the latitude and longitude of various places.

Unhappily the profound and wide-ranging interest in experimental science which Bacon exhibited was a long way ahead of his times. Although it would not be true to say that study of it stood still after his time, its progress was very limited and here, as elsewhere in the West, major advance effectively begins only in the late seventeenth century. However, it is important not to blame the medieval West over-much for this and to remember that their achievement in the sphere of learning was very great when seen against the conditions of the times.

One of the major achievements of the Western Church, whether from the pagan or religious viewpoint, was the painstaking way in which it had kept alive the flame of learning in the five centuries before the era of the Gregorian Reform, in times when it had burnt very low and at times seemed likely to flicker out. This precarious situation was now substantially ameliorated by the rise of the universities in Western Europe which with remarkable rapidity took very firm root and became a potent and deeply respected element in Western society from which ultimately the great founts of modern learning largely derive. As was inevitable, their syllabus and priorities were heavily influenced by contemporary social conditions

---

* It is impossible to read medieval chronicles or biographies without appreciating the total accuracy of this charge.

very different from our own, and now have a rather antiquarian look, but informed observers do not now hurl at the universities of the medieval West the wild accusations too common in the past. It is today recognised that they grappled daringly and skilfully with the major problems of philosophy and theology even if their methods were sometimes dissimilar from our own, and that their controversies were characterised by considerable freedom of thought—'the more one reads about medieval universities the less one can believe in that sedulous regard for authority which is often denounced as their gravest defect . . . the anxious interference of papal and episcopal superiors, intermittent as it was bound to be, was quite ineffective as a check upon the speculative license permitted in the schools' writes Macfarlane.

If the range of study was narrower than it ought to have been, that is perenially true of university studies (the habit of modern universities of regarding as largely irrelevant the eternal problem of Man, God and the Universe would stagger both classical and medieval thinkers). Of permanent importance, as is now increasingly realised, was the hammering out of scientific method, i.e. the systematic collection, classification and consideration of evidence which largely began in the twelfth century and quickly became an essential ingredient in the university study. This development was an essential preliminary to the rise of modern science as well as to modern theology. 'To the historian of science medieval times are the seed-bed of modern growth . . . the interest for us of medieval thought in Europe is that of tracing the changing attitude of the human mind as it passes through states where science would have been impossible to a condition in which its rise follows naturally from the philosophic environment. The exponents of Scholasticism took the attitude of interpreters; original experimental investigation would have been foreign to their ideas. Yet their rational intellectualism kept alive, indeed intensified, the spirit of logical analysis, while their assumption that God and the world are understandable by men implanted in the best minds of Western Europe the invaluable if unconscious belief in the regularity and uniformity of nature, without which scientific research would never be attempted' (W. C. D. Dampier-Whetham, *A History of Science*).

The majestic civilisations of the previous epoch, amongst all their excellencies, were not able to establish a permanent machinery to cultivate the search for the higher forms of knowledge. Where they failed, the Western Church succeeded remarkably, and the prodigies of modern discovery are the fruits of a tree whose roots grew here. Trying though the history of Oxford and Cambridge has often been, their immense contribution to English learning is as beyond cavil as is the profound importance of religion in their establishment —as one expert on the subject has written—'the main motive underlying the private munificence of college founders in the middle ages was the priority enjoyed by them in the daily prayers and celebrations of such institutions'.

CHAPTER 14

THE CHURCH AND THE VISUAL ARTS

EDUCATION shares with religion the built-in disadvantage of having a huge potential which is seldom more than partially exploited by its leaders. In the Italian Renaissance top-ranking education was characterised by a magnificently wide-ranging series of activities the like of which has never been seen since, partly, it must be admitted, because its provision was so expensive. On the other hand, the public school ethos produced a lop-sided semi-barbaric educational tradition, which not only wrote off the desirability of being able to converse comprehensibly with men living on the mainland of Europe, but steadfastly minimised the value of that appreciation of the visual arts which has given such immense delight to truly civilised societies down the ages. Significantly, when in 1847 a superb series of fifteenth-century paintings were uncovered on the walls of Eton College chapel, their destruction was threatened on the irrelevant grounds that 'their subjects were derived from superstitious legends'. The Provost, considering them unfit to be seen in a building dedicated to the use of the Church of England, insisted that they should once more be covered over though, to his eternal credit, Prince Albert entreated in vain that 'by some mechanical contrivance it might still be possible for lovers of art to examine the paintings at will.' The Etonian authorities were, of course, highly literate, albeit within narrow limits, but failed utterly to recognise that appreciation of the visual arts was an integral part of a full education.

In medieval England education was equally lop-sided, though in an entirely different and more excusable way. Here, as we have seen, for powerful social reasons literacy had become the preserve of a tiny minority of the population and although it had increased in favour somewhat in the course of time, when the Tudor monarchy took charge of England the arts of reading and writing were practised by only a very small section. But the vacuum thus created was to some extent filled by the intense and wide-spread appreciation of the visual arts which characterised every level of society in the medieval West—just as it does today in modern Italy where, almost alone in Europe, affection for them still permeates the mass of the population. If the face of England is adorned with thousands of parish churches of indubitable charm, it is because the society by which they were built was one in which affection for the visual arts was far wider and deeper than it has ever been since. Conversely, if very few modern buildings in Britain attract any considerable attention through their inherent excellence it is partly because until recently study of the visual arts was pushed into the background of the educational syllabus.

ARCHITECTURE

SECULAR BUILDING

Of the various major differences between the architecture of medieval and modern England none is more obvious than the fact that whereas in the latter the huge majority of large buildings serve non-ecclesiastical uses, in the former a very high proportion of the major structures pertain to ecclesiastical activities of one kind or another. Medieval England had no massive government offices, no lordly business headquarters, no multiple stores or cinemas. Instead, because the first priority of contemporary society was the pursuit of the supernatural, parish churches, cathedrals and monasteries provided the great mass of major buildings of the times.

In some few areas of the West, notably in Italy, the ancient Roman tradition of grandiose civic architecture had never collapsed, and in the twelfth and thirteenth centuries took on new life, with small towns like Gubbio as well as lordly ones like Lucca providing themselves with piazzas bordered by dignified civic building. But in medieval England life remained obstinately rural. Towns here were few, mostly having small populations and no ambitious architectural ideas. Even in London the desire for finely planned squares with dignified attendant buildings scarcely caught on before quite modern times. If the guildhall here was a sizeable place, like the smaller one at York, it stood on an unspectacular site, whilst the halls maintained by merchant guilds in both these places were not architecturally very impressive. Inside many medieval English

towns no small fraction of the space belonged to ecclesiastical uses
of one kind or another, much of the rest being a tangle of often
narrow streets with unspectacular dwellings huddled along them.

The contribution of the baronage of medieval England to secular
architecture was decidedly modest. In contemporary France, on the
other hand, mighty aristocrats with huge resources were very
evident, like the dukes of Anjou who have left us a splendid castle
and a magnificent tapestry at Angers and, above all, the great dukes
of Burgundy who, in the fourteenth and fifteenth centuries, dispensed most costly patronage of arts and letters and lived in luxurious
Hollywood style (at one of their magnificent banquets was served
a huge pie which turned out to contain a tasteful mélange of live
musicians).

In England, partly because of the high degree of power steadily
maintained by the English monarchy and partly because the land
was so much less affluent than France, there were very few great
nobles with large sums to spend on such frivolities or on elaborate
architectural enterprises. There were, of course, some great baronial
castles but the total of such places was not very considerable. Most
major castles were royal castles, like the mighty twins at London
and Colchester constructed soon after the Conquest and massive
keeps such as those at Newcastle and Carlisle, built rather later in
the turbulent lands north of the Humber. But the total amount of
major military architecture in England was quite modest, the
standard Victorian work on existing medieval castles listing only a
mere fifty. In any case, by the latter half of our period the great
days of English military architecture were over. The amount of new
building in the fourteenth and fifteenth centuries was small, and
when, under Henry VIII, John Leland (the one and only holder of
the office of 'King's antiquary') pertinaciously toured much of
England, he found many castles derelict or semi-derelict, men
having long been understandably loath to spend cash on the maintenance of buildings most of which, under contemporary conditions,
were very far from being of constant importance for the safety of
the realm.

In England, major unfortified buildings like palaces were luxuries
which few but the king could afford. The great hall which Rufus
had built cheek by jowl with the abbey of Westminster was steadily
engrossed by royal officials who spent little on architectural inno-

vations, though next to it, admittedly, the English monarchy built and long maintained what seems to have been a highly desirable residence, on much of whose site the Houses of Parliament has intruded. Windsor, always a favourite royal residence, in late medieval times got so cluttered up by its noble chapel and lesser structures that it was just as well it was never in any danger of being involved in military operations. Attractive too was the royal palace at Clarendon, now utterly destroyed. But looked at mathematically, the total amount of major architectural effort absorbed by such places was minute. This was much more the case with the collegiate architecture of Oxford and Cambridge. By the end of our period the number of places of any architectural merit there was a bare half-dozen, including notably the Divinity School, New College at Oxford and King's and Queens' Colleges at Cambridge, but very little else; in any case the colleges of these days were at least semi-ecclesiastical. It is thus indubitable that the total of major buildings intended for secular use in England in medieval centuries constituted a very small proportion of the whole, looking most puny against that of contemporary ecclesiastical buildings which came to comprise something like ten thousand parish churches, a thousand monasteries and hundreds of minor establishments such as hospitals and chapels of various kinds. The immense glories of medieval English architecture were very largely the result of efforts which were not social or economic but religious in inspiration.

ECCLESIASTICAL ARCHITECTURE

The Rise of Grandiosity

Although in major ways the progress of English architecture throughout medieval times was mostly one of steady evolution, in one major respect the Norman Conquest roughly coincided with the start of a striking and very novel development—the growth of a passion for building on a scale far more lavish than either past precedent or present convenience demanded. Although building and re-building of churches in late Anglo-Saxon times were far from important, what was done was almost always on a very modest scale. The cathedral erected at North Elmham for the wealthy and populous folk of East Anglia in pre-Conquest days was not greatly over a hundred feet long, whilst when the plutocratic monasteries of Glastonbury and St Augustine's, Canterbury, indulged in some little church extension this was effected unspectacularly by tacking on far from pretentious additions to existing work.

Suddenly, utterly out of the blue, came an abrupt attack on this tradition of architectural modesty. This was the work of Edward the Confessor, in the very last days of Anglo-Saxon England. In emulation of lordly churches across the Channel he constructed a new abbey church at Westminster on a stupendous scale. The final structure (consecrated in 1065) was over three hundred feet in length, being thus longer than any known Norman church of the period and far larger than any practical considerations demanded. The enormous nave of twelve bays can seldom have been more than very sparsely peopled by the faithful whilst the massive arcades crowned by triforium and clerestorey had majesty and beauty but no very great utility. The passion for grandiose building in England which this place was principally responsible for generating, coincided with a very similar impulse elsewhere in Western Europe though, as Harvey has interestingly pointed out, there its forms of expression were different—'Whereas in England the greater churches impress by their sheer length, and in France by sheer height, it is the amount of ground that is covered that is striking in Spain.'

Certainly, very quickly indeed after the Norman Conquest most of the great English establishments in a position so to do, in what was certainly an age of very real financial stress, started to rebuild their churches on a scale hitherto quite without parallel. These were mostly existing cathedrals and the small group of very rich Benedictine abbeys. Of the former, Canterbury started building first (1070–1) followed with rapidity by Lincoln (1072–3), Old Sarum (1075–8), Rochester (c. 1078), Winchester (1079), Worcester (1084), St Paul's (c. 1090), Durham (1093), Chichester (c. 1095), Norwich (1096). Pioneers amongst the abbeys were Battle (1070), St Augustine's, Canterbury (c. 1071), St Alban's (1077), Ely (c. 1083), St Mark's, York (1089), Gloucester (1089) and Tewkesbury (after 1087).

As we have seen, monastic expansion in England proceeded apace from the early decades of the twelfth century onwards for very long to come, and archaeological evidence shows very clearly that in these times even quite small monasteries came to regard it as self-evident that they should provide themselves with a conventual church which was very much more elaborate than the mere number of their brethren or the size of their income would suggest. Thus no few houses of Austin canons having a mere one- or two-dozen brethren sought after and ultimately acquired an elaborate cruciform church over two hundred feet long, complete with triforium and clerestorey and with bold but largely unnecessary transepts projecting to north and south. Such enterprises as these demanded a very prolonged building campaign and made it common for such communities to have to wait fifty years for their complete church and a century or so might pass before their main conventual buildings took permanent form. We can well believe the correctness of the comment made by the well-informed contemporary chronicler, William of Malmesbury, that in his days many churches were seeking to emulate the grandiose architectural plans of Westminster and were running into financial trouble as a consequence.

This grandiosity was accompanied by increasing fondness for elaborate decoration which gave late Romanesque a much richer look than that of earlier times. About it St Bernard, as we have seen, made surly remarks, and in the early thirteenth century the Franciscans, or rather an extremist section of them, waged a campaign in favour of very simple church architecture. But this sort of thing left the medieval man in the street utterly unmoved, for he was nothing if not intensely visual-minded. By the end of the thirteenth century England was adorned with a great 'white robe of churches', whose number, grace and complexity would have staggered the men of Anglo-Saxon England as it was to stagger thousands more down the centuries.

What of the English parish churches and this search for grandiosity? Any answer to this sort of question must for two good reasons be guarded. In the first place, until we engage in England in that substantial excavation of medieval church interiors which has produced such fascinating results in Denmark, we shall remain in a great state of ignorance regarding the nature and frequency of their reconstruction and of the chronology. Secondly, the substantial lack of clear-cut statistics regarding the population of medieval England, especially in the period before the mid-fourteenth century, means that it is often difficult to decide whether the rebuilding of a particular church was due to the need to provide more accommodation or to the search for grandiosity. There is, however, no doubt that an enormous amount of re-building of English parish churches took place of which no written record has survived. Thus recent investigations of the venerable church of Deerhurst has shown there indications of work of ten different periods, whilst at Winchester excavation has shown, *inter alia*, that the church of St Mary, Tanner Street, was modified on at least twelve occasions between about 1250 and 1470.

It is likely enough that many English congregations imitated on a small scale the lavish building campaigns launched by cathedrals and monasteries, albeit mostly not before the mid-twelfth century. It is clear that as the Middle Ages wore on, in certain areas of England wealth became very much more considerable than it had been before, and here we find re-building of parish churches on a lavish scale. Very notable were the great 'wool churches' of the Cotswolds and East Anglia where, by the fifteenth century, had grown up a small but very well-to-do middle class which provided much for such widespread and wholesale reconstruction. Here it is almost as difficult to find a Romanesque church there as it is to find a Gothic one in Rome; the intolerance with which this movement destroyed earlier work has led to it figuring in a recent history of vandalism.

The Question of Style

In the period with which we are concerned architecture was almost totally dominated by a progressive attitude towards architectural style which contrasts refreshingly with the obscurantist Renaissance belief that there was only one true style, and that one which had already been fully exposed in ancient days. Much more subconsciously than consciously, medieval builders for most of our period worked out a style which was steadily, albeit gently, in almost constant evolution, ultimately producing the style, or rather series of styles, called Gothic. It must not be thought that this came to dominate the West. In Italy and southern France admiration for ancient Rome remained deep-rooted and Gothic had limited appeal. But in England and in northern France, the new style swept almost everything before it.

The details of this architectural evolution cannot be here explored, but must not be totally ignored. The style prevalent in England before the Conquest used to be termed 'Anglo-Saxon', but this is somewhat insular and unconvincing, since in all essentials it was largely paralleled on the Continent. In some ways it is preferable to term it 'early Romanesque' and employ 'late Romanesque' to denote the style current here between the Norman Conquest and the rise of Gothic a century later.

The most obvious features of Romanesque buildings were thick walls with shallow buttresses and smallish doors and windows, most of which had semi-circular heads. Roofing consisted mostly of wooden ceilings covered by tiles or thatch, but limited use was made of what are termed 'groined' vaults of stone, a number of which are found below ground covering crypts. Decoration was for long not extensive, but had developed a very widespread popularity and luxuriance by the latter half of the twelfth century, by which time doors and windows had for some time tended to be larger than before.

Gradually this Romanesque was transformed into a striking new style to which in very much later times the intolerant men of Renaissance Italy accorded the uncomplimentary title of 'Gothic', i.e. barbarian. This style was produced, not because of devotion to the absurd idea of 'art for art's sake' but principally to solve a major practical problem—that of finding a way of roofing permanently in stone churches which, as documents show very clearly, were very much more frequently destroyed or badly damaged by fire than is now the case.

The answer to this problem was much sought after by builders in England and France from the late eleventh century onwards. As the remarkable work of Bilson demonstrated, the first church to exhibit the correct answer in all its fullness was the cathedral of Durham, begun in about 1093—'here for the first time outside Lombardy was produced a great church designed from the first to be roofed with a system of ribbed vaults' (Clapham). This discovery opened wide the door for the development of the Gothic style which now rapidly evolved. (The fact that this major cultural advance was not made in their own country was long regarded as unbelievable by French scholars, but has gradually come to be accepted by them, albeit as a *faux pas* which Providence ought not to have permitted.)

To make this structural progress three main elements combined.

The first of them was the 'ribbed vault', i.e. one which had the junctions of its intersecting surfaces reinforced by a framework of stone ribs which knitted together the whole bay which it covered and guarded against that distortion or collapse under its own weight to which simple groined vaults were prone. These ribbed vaults took the major thrust of the roofing and concentrated it at the points where they themselves joined the side wall or arcade, as the case might be. To counteract the great pressure on the outer walls at these points it was necessary to greatly strengthen the buttresses there which, accordingly, instead of being shallow as of yore, became more and more substantial as time wore on. These two elements sufficed to vault effectively the side aisles of a church but not the great central vault. This was made feasible by the invention of the 'flying buttress'—a long stone pier, often with a curved under-side which linked the point at which this vaulting rib of the main aisle met the wall with the corresponding buttress of the outer wall, in the process bridging the area over the side aisle or aisles.

Perhaps because of its very remote situation the work at Durham seems to have had little immediate influence, but the new style was quickly and widely employed by the French with such vigour, skill and daring that it became deservedly known as 'the French art'. Amongst the loftiest peaks of its achievement are the great cathedrals of Beauvais, Amiens, Rheims and Chartres and Paris with others, like the cathedrals of Rouen, and Le Mans and the great abbey church of Pontigny, not far behind. From the late twelfth century the new style became all the rage in England and many building plans were scrapped or altered because of it. In the grand naves of Selby Abbey and Worksop Priory, for example, we can still see the steady change in style from Romanesque to Gothic made by the builders as they worked steadily westwards, leaving the former style behind them in more senses than one. In other cases came expensive reconstruction, as at Barnwell Priory where, as the chronicler notes, Prior Robert (1175–1208) 'totally demolished the church of great size and massive workmanship and completed and had dedicated another more becoming one.'

Once the new style had taken root here it continued to evolve throughout almost the whole of our period. Though there did not now follow any very major constructional novelty there were plenty of new looks. Thus steadily from the late twelfth century onwards doors, windows and arcades tended to use pointed arches instead of semi-circular ones, though the proportions of these altered as time wore on, and there were added other forms like 'ogee' and 'four-pointed' arches. The capitals and mouldings also steadily altered their forms, so much so that experts with local knowledge can often date buildings containing them to within quite a short period on the stylistic evidence alone. Vaults waxed in complexity, acquiring more ribs and complex patterns whose appearance was enriched by the use at the points of intersection of the ribs of 'bosses'— circular knobs of stone which were often intricately and gracefully carved with a whole variety of subjects, whose beauties have only become fully appreciated through the advances of modern photography. The grand climax of English vaulting, unlike earlier work in this field, had no effective parallel in France. This was the immensely graceful fan vaulting of which Henry VII's chapel at Westminster Abbey, the chapel of King's College, Cambridge and the Divinity School at Oxford provide most celebrated examples.

The discovery of ribbed vaulting rendered the space between the vaulting shafts of no major constructional importance, and the passion for stained glass windows, which developed so strongly in later medieval England must certainly have been a main factor in leading to virtually all of this often being devoted to these. The Sainte Chapelle at Paris (1242–7) had been one of the first examples of this, consisting of little but a series of huge stained glass windows set under a vault and by the fifteenth century this arrangement had become the norm in many English churches.

The forms of the tracery which filled the heads of the often very large Gothic windows also evolved steadily. At first this often followed very simple geometric patterns but in the early fourteenth century developed into 'bar tracery' which came to writhe and curve in shapes which are often of very great grace. Steadily hereafter, however, this was often replaced by a very stereotyped design, almost all the lights being substantially rectangular in shape, even if their heads might be cusped. This gave the windows a very mass-produced look—something rare in medieval art—and a certain resemblance to gridirons which an eminent Victorian understandably stressed. The reason for this standardisation was almost certainly the fact that such design was eminently suited for the stained glass which had come to be so beloved, accommodating easily, as it did, human figures of one size or another, in contrast to some of the earlier curvilinear tracery which assumed shapes in which no human or heavenly personage could be fitted without discomfort, except possibly an angel engaged in censing in a particularly complex way.

It is worthy of note that in England, as in France, there existed in our period effective monarchies which enthusiastically patronised Gothic art in all its forms. This made the style a great deal more popular than it might otherwise have been and helped to give most of the cathedrals here a strong family likeness. By contrast in Italy, where there was no monarchy but a very strong classical tradition (notably displayed in Rome, the Eternal City), Gothic architecture was given a very partial welcome. In Spain, where local life flourished so magnificently throughout our period, there was very little architectural uniformity and only limited obeisance to Gothic. Its art has been termed 'the most complicated in Europe . . . composed of elements from two different cultures, the Christian North and the Moslem South and profoundly affected by influences from Italy, France, Africa, the Near East and the Teutonic North.' (In architecture and, very much more, in the minor arts like pottery and textiles, there is no doubt that medieval England's achievement would have been appreciably more entertaining had not hundreds of miles effectively cut it off from significant contact with the fascinating culture built up by medieval Islam in Spain.)

It will never be feasible to paint in anything like fullness the total, most complex picture of architectural change in medieval English churches, though it is quite certain that in many of them it came frequently, at least on a small scale. In the monastic and other larger churches the extent of re-building or extension varied very greatly, being dependent on various local factors. It was by no means uncommon for Romanesque and early Gothic naves to be retained, though re-building of the east end was not infrequent.* But the poorer establishments, like some houses of Austin canons, and the austerer ones, like the Cistercians, quite often added little to their churches in the fourteenth and fifteenth centuries except new doors,

---

* It is interesting to note that post-medieval England retained an interest in Gothic largely lost in the continental West where classical and baroque art so often swept the board. It has been claimed, and probably with reason, that until the architectural chaos of recent times no decade in post-Reformation England passed without the construction of a church in the Gothic style.

more fashionable windows and a chapel or two. But throughout our period the amount of ecclesiastical architecture created was incomparably greater than that produced of non-ecclesiastical purposes.

OTHER VISUAL ARTS

SCULPTURE

If in medieval England architecture was overwhelmingly inspired by religious considerations, the same is at least equally true of sculpture. The virtual absence here of that civic life so dominant in Roman and Victorian times meant that the medieval public was not liable to be confronted by statues of local citizens in togas, or in morning dress, solemnly surveying public places of one kind or another. In medieval England figure sculpture was almost exclusively used for two purposes, both of which were ecclesiastical.

The first of these was to leave for posterity in churches, memorial effigies of members of families able and willing to afford the fairly considerable cost of providing for them. These figures, which were mostly life-size or thereabouts, were mostly placed over the place of burial of those concerned, which in many cases was in a chantry chapel founded by the person commemorated. The founder might have an effigy of his wife next to his own, or one on either side, if he was a widower who had re-married. The mortal remains of the person thus commemorated were often laid in a stone chest on top of which the effigy was placed. In a chantry this chest was at the west end of the chapel, the figures on it facing the little altar at the eastern end, and sometimes having uplifted hands holding a heart, in a very literal obedience to the injunction in the Mass, 'lift up your hearts'. The effigy was usually shown clad in the dress appropriate to the person concerned—whether merchant, noble, knight, cleric or housewife—and was usually painted.

So far as the clergy were concerned expense and possibly also more modest tastes tended to rule out such elaborate memorials, save in the case of a small coterie of great dignitaries. Effigies of medieval English bishops are common enough. Some of these are mass-produced ones made long after the death of most of those concerned, like those in the cathedral of Carlisle, but others are connected with

individual chantries. A notable example of these is the effigy of
Bishop Beckington of Wells, which he had made along with the
chantry chapel to which it pertains, some years before his death—
a common medieval usage. Below his statue is a luxury item not
very commonly found—a full-size representation of a decaying
corpse with lugubrious décor in attendance and known as a 'cad-
aver'. This was intended as a reminder of the very transitory nature
of this mortal life, and was not, as a short-sighted American tourist
opined, as a representation of the bishop's (non-existent) wife.

Effigies associated with chantries usually had around them a good
deal of other carving. At the corners of the structure might be
small statues of the saints, along with foliage and in the case of the
nobility, almost inevitably also shields with their coats of arms.
Sometimes along the base of the tomb in later medieval times were
to be seen a series of small ecclesiastical figures engaged in singing
what were presumably requiems, like those along the Harrington
tomb at Cartmel Priory where one of them, clearly the precentor,
is beating time with uplifted hand.

However, the amount of medieval statuary used for this funeral
purpose was vastly inferior to that used to portray for the faithful
those holy people called the saints, by whose life and prayers they
might hope for redemption. There is no doubt that by the eve of
the Reformation the total number of such things in English churches
ran into thousands. In French Gothic, great screens of such imagery
were sometimes externally displayed, notably on the facades of the
majestic cathedrals of Amiens, Rheims and Paris, but supremely at
that of Chartres, where the exterior is adorned to an unparalleled
degree with statues of very varying sizes, whose total runs well into
four figures. In England, perhaps because of the inferior weather
conditions of the land, cathedrals seldom had much statuary on their
exteriors, the major example of this being the great west front of
Wells Cathedral which, as far as is known, was not emulated by
any of the monasteries of medieval England.

In the interiors of English churches of every sort and size, however, statues of the great figures of the Christian Church down the
centuries were found in plenty, following the usual Western
practice, the which was based on two theological factors. The first
of these was the profound contemporary devotion to 'invocation' of
the saints (i.e. seeking the aid of their prayers), the second the fact

that, after duly considering the pros and cons of the matter, Western authorities refused to follow the custom of Jews, Moslems and Eastern Orthodox by banning the use of such things in their places of worship, but welcomed them as greatly strengthening personal devotion. As has been noted, every English parish church was legally bound to have in its chancel a statue of the saint to whom it was dedicated, and this was likely to be joined by various others in the nave and in side chapels as time went on, mostly put in by private individuals.

Incomparably the chief object of devotion was Our Lady, whose cult waxed greatly in the West from the twelfth century onwards, and who was depicted in pictures and statues with great frequency. It is unlikely that any parish church lacked some representation of her and many had several. At first she was often shown as the gracious mother, bearing the child Jesus in her arms or on her knees, but in later medieval times additional devotion seems to have been inspired by representations of her as 'Our Lady of Pity', which showed her seated, stiff with agony, the corpse of Christ slumped across her knees.

Below her were venerated hundreds of other saints, from whom each congregation would make its own selection so far as statues were concerned. Before the images and pictures of Christ and His saints it was very usual to burn candles which, as has been noted, were very expensive commodities in these days. The very numerous bequests of money for such illumination recorded in local wills of every kind incidentally give invaluable information on contemporary cults. Unfortunately, the wills do not always make it clear whether a particular light burns before a statue or a picture, each of which might stand alone or might pertain to an altar or chapel dedicated to the personage involved. The great popularity of these things at least in some areas is vividly displayed in very informative wills of late medieval Kent which are largely of fourteenth- and fifteenth-century date.

Thus Sittingbourne parish church had bequests for lights to burn before the great Rood (i.e. that of the rood screen) and the rather mysterious trio, Pete Cross, the Brown Rood and the Rood of Fortune, and for statues or other representations of St Mary, Our Lady of Pity, All Saints, St Anne, St Anthony, St Christopher, St Clement, St Erasmus, St James, St John the Baptist, St Michael, St

Nicholas and a picture of the Resurrection. Similarly, bequests to the church of Our Lady at Faversham mention altars or chapels or representations of the Trinity, Jesus, St Agnes, St Anne, St Anthony, St Barbara, St Christopher, St Clement, St Crispin and St Crispinian, St Erasmus, St James, St John the Baptist, St Katharine, St Margaret, St Michael, St Nicholas, St Peter, and St Thomas of Canterbury, as well as lights of the Rood, Corpus Christi, St George, St Giles, St Gregory, St John the Baptist, St Leonard, St Mary Magdalene, St Thomas the Apostle and St Edmund. Here occur also two unusual items—the 'bachelors light' whatever that may have been, and the light 'burning before Master John Shorne' (a local uncanonised luminary). Secular statues inside medieval churches were few but not always absent. With that curious habit of mixing what some would regard as things secular with things religious a few places, notably the metropolitan cathedrals of Canterbury and York, inserted in their great chancel screens a line of statues of the kings of England.

CARVING

Besides sculpture, carving figured largely in medieval churches. Their exteriors provided limited scope for this, though the corbel tables on which some roofs rested and the gargoyles from which rain water was spewed clear of the wall to the ground below offered some small facilities which were frequently taken. Inside, an object much loved by the carver was the font, whether it was of the square or tub-shaped type usual in Romanesque times, or the later, more elegant, polygonal type whose sides (often eight in number) offered him attractive facilities. Subjects found hereon vary much and include representations of the Seven Sacraments of the Church as well as no little heraldry.

Most of the medieval church carving was done in wood, a commodity in which much of contemporary England abounded, and flourished mightily in those parts of it, like East Anglia and the West Country, where good stone was rare. Specially notable were the great wooden roofs of late medieval churches which developed elaborate beauty and were supported by impressive complex series of carved beams, some of which might be adorned with vigorously wrought saints and angels. Now also immense skill was lavished on the covers which fonts were legally bound to have. Very notable are a number in East Anglia, one well-placed to judge awarding the palm to that at the church of Ufford in Suffolk, a miracle of delicate carving which rises no less than eighteen feet above its font and which he terms 'the most beautiful cover in the world' (Munro Cautley). Most medieval churches had screen work, notably that surrounding the choir stalls, and wealthy ones by late medieval times had misericords (page 448) which, like the canopies above them, gave the wood-carver magnificent opportunities. Much more often than might be expected statuary and carving were coloured, sometimes very elaborately, this being of course usual in the case of the heraldic coats of arms which were so extensively employed in medieval church art. The interior faces of church walls were sometimes whitewashed, which made for less murky light, but in some places at least decoration in colour was here added. In 1896 restoration of the nave at Gloucester Cathedral revealed that its vault had been elaborately decorated in red, green, blue and yellow, and in 1936 part of St Benedict's chapel in Westminster Abbey was found to have been given much colourful adornment which included fleur-de-lys and green leaves with red berries.

WALL PAINTING

If the old Romans had visited medieval England they would have found next to nothing in the way of mosaic decoration in which they were so expert, but no little of the wall painting to which they had been accustomed. Almost certainly, however, very little of it was to be found in the dwellings of the medieval English laity, though that this was not utterly absent is shown by the interesting remains thereof discovered after World War II at Longthorpe Tower, which in medieval days had been the residence of the steward of the nearby lordly abbey of Peterborough. Here, surprisingly well preserved, were found a fascinating mélange of subjects of the kind so typical in medieval art. A vivacious series of portraits of birds mixes happily with apostles, a hermit, a young man with a dog, a group of musicians, King David, the wheel of the Five Senses, the Apostles' Creed and the inevitable heraldic display. However, the presence of this was probably largely the result of the exceptional fact that the tower was so closely connected with one of the great Benedictine abbeys of England wherein patronage of the visual arts flourished.

In sharp contrast to this is the fact that, despite enormous damage to them at various times for a variety of reasons, enough wall-paintings of medieval times have survived in our churches to show that they were originally a very common feature there, at least from Norman times onwards, even if very few places have retained more than a small fraction of their original series. They were not exorbitantly expensive, and for this reason can be found in quite small parish churches, and were also much used in great monasteries.

In parish churches wall paintings of two subjects were very common. The first of these was the Day of Judgment which showed, often on quite a large scale, the judgment of the world by Christ at the Last Day. More cheerful and equally popular in late medieval times was, as noted, a very big representation of St Christopher, 'the Christ bearer'. He is usually depicted crossing a river and carrying the boy Christ. The picture of him was usually placed on the north wall of the nave opposite its main entrance, so was almost bound to be seen by the great mass of those entering the church. This position was dictated by the curious popular belief in these times that anyone who set eyes on St Christopher would be neither sick nor sorry nor die that day. But it was biblical scenes, especially those of the life and death of Christ, and the lives and miracles of the saints, which were the most popular subjects and had, of course, considerable didactic value in this situation. As was only natural, the repertoire did not differ significantly from that of the contemporary makers of stained glass.

STAINED GLASS

The considerable difference in local conditions and traditions meant that most major regions of the medieval West had their own artistic priorities. In that of medieval England very high in popular esteem was stained glass, a form of visual art in which the medieval Italians showed very little interest. Although a few fragments of pre-Conquest coloured glass have recently been found, effectively, like so much else in medieval art, the history of stained glass here begins in the twelfth century, with some English remains of this early period still to be seen at the cathedrals of Canterbury and York.

For long there existed the unsolved technical problem of how to avoid the obvious inconvenience of having a separate piece of glass for each colour and so getting rid of the considerable disadvantage of requiring a great deal of lead. This problem was partially solved in the early fourteenth century by the discovery of 'silver stain' which made it feasible to add a yellowish tinge to glass of other colours or to vary considerably the shade of yellow on a single piece of glass. As time went on the glass became clearer. Partly because the lead holding it requires regular replacement which it by no means always received, the considerable amount of medieval English stained glass which survives is very largely no earlier in date than the end of the thirteenth century, to which period belong the little coloured panels in the chapel of Merton College at Oxford (much the best city in England in which to study the evolution of English stained glass) and one or two others in the church of St Michael Northgate in the same city.

Stained glass windows steadily became very popular indeed in England, with various local centres for their manufacture coming into being notably at London, York and Norwich. (It is interesting to note that just when the early Gothic architects were producing larger and larger windows which could easily have provided a good deal of that bright light in the church interior which modern man expects, his medieval predecessor, visual-minded as ever, readily sacrificed this to acquire the beauty of whole windows full of coloured glass.) By the end of the fourteenth century this enthusiasm for it led to the production of some truly enormous windows filled therewith. The east window of Gloucester Cathedral (made about 1350) measures no less than 78 by 38 feet and is only slightly larger than that of York Minster, which also retains much of its original glass.

The subjects favoured for the hosts of windows of stained glass at this period varied very greatly. The long lights into which Gothic windows were divided gave very convenient homes for human figures, and very frequently contained selections of those leaders who had inspired and expanded the Church down the centuries, beginning with the Old Testament prophets and going on through the apostles to the 'doctors' (i.e. teachers) and martyrs of the Early Church and to the huge train of canonised people saints which came down to contemporary times so that, for example, recent arrivals on the saintly scene like St John of Bridlington (d. 1379) appear. Very common was it to devote a whole window to displaying scenes from the life and miracles of a particularly beloved saint. At York Minster we can still see windows devoted in this way to the two northern saints, St Cuthbert and the lesser St William of York, whilst the parish church of Ludlow devoted a large window to its patron, St Lawrence. (These subjects were, of course, much in evidence in other forms of contemporary art. Thus on the back of the stalls of Carlisle Cathedral are similar series of scenes from the life and miracles of St Augustine and St Cuthbert, the latter having been copied from pictures in a manuscript belonging to Durham Cathedral.)

But much the most popular source of subjects for stained glass windows were scenes from the Old and New Testaments with which might be conflated subjects from apocryphal biblical literature. At King's College, Cambridge is a magnificent series of twenty-five windows which providentially survived the menace of the most infamous of all English iconoclasts, William Dowsing. They unroll an elaborate series of New Testament scenes above each of which are what were optimistically thought to be an appropriate Old Testament one foreshadowing it, e.g. Jonah cast up by the whale is linked with the Resurrection of Christ. There are also here scenes from the *Acts of the Apostles* which understandably was not a very frequent source. The seven sacraments the, seven corporal acts of mercy and even the Ten Commandments are occasionally illustrated and provided useful visual instruction for the faithful. No few of the benefactors who paid for medieval glass were armigerous, and it was usual for them to be commemorated, sometimes merely by their coats of arms but often as small kneeling figures with their family coat indicated on their garb. This was almost certainly done to remind beholders thereof to pray for them particularly, and inscriptions giving their names were frequently added to make this doubly sure. This can be exactly paralleled with donors of vestments and plate, some of whom stipulate that their gift should bear their name with this end in view (page 359–60).

Almost the only priory church which has retained a very considerable amount of its original stained glass is that of Great Malvern, and this has happily been the subject of an elaborate study. The church was rebuilt in the mid-fifteenth century, its new windows acquiring their stained glass over a period of about sixty years—from about 1440 to 1500. Their subject matter was very systematically planned. In the great east window and two adjoining it were pictured the 'two fundamental events of the Christian faith, the Incarnation and the Passion'. In the north aisle windows showed 'a sort of catechism . . . the Creed, the Sacraments, the Decalogue, Lord's Prayer, etc.' Elsewhere, in the nave and aisles are 'the religious history of the world from the Creation, its beginnings to the end of all things'. Included in all this were dozens of saints from the apostles onwards, reinforced by a variety of other celestial figures now little known to the Christian public, like the Order of Dominations and the Nine Orders of Angels. Of very special interest here are the panels showing donors, which include representations of King Henry VII and Arthur, Prince of Wales. The stained glass of English cathedrals suffered immensely from iconoclasm but at York Minster a noble Puritan put his local pride before his theology, with the result that there is now preserved therein a very sizeable fraction of the extant stained glass of medieval England, which has recently been accorded the very intensive study which it merits.

EMBROIDERY AND TAPESTRY

Of the various minor arts which embellished the medieval church in England understandably few have left such scanty relics as tapestry and embroidery, a fact which is all the more to be regretted since the former (known at this time as *opus Anglicanum*) built up a tremendous reputation which made it eagerly sought by ecclesiastics of all ranks from the pope downwards. Its principal use was for the vestments used in church services, notably for copes (large semicircular garments worn over the shoulders like a cloak and kept in position there by a single very large button, termed a morse, which fastened across the breast of the wearer and was itself often a thing of very great beauty). Copes were worn not only by all members of the community on liturgical occasions but on major social ones, such as the visit of a king or queen to a great church. It was necessary to have at least two sets of them, one for ordinary use, the other for very special occasions, which meant that large and fashionable establishments like Canterbury Cathedral had to be well supplied with them—an inventory of 1315 shows that they had at that time no less than sixty-two 'common copes', as well as others. In such places vestments might be made of very luxurious materials, none more so than some copes and chasubles which Lanfranc gave to his cathedral, which when worn out, were burnt so that their gold might be recovered. It was not unusual for the grander vestments to be adorned with gems and pearls.

Of such major things only a microscopic number remain in England—the Victoria and Albert Museum displays several fine specimens. On the Continent one magnificent cope of *opus anglicanum* is to be seen in the Vatican Museum and another at Ascoli Piceno. Other vestments such as chasubles and stoles were similarly made, as were, in a very limited number of cases, the frontal or covering attached to the altar to veil its western face. None of these latter are likely to have been more luxurious than that which the pious and artistic Henry III had made for his new chancel at Westminster Abbey. It was of gold cloth enriched with pearls, garnets and enamels, and took the three ladies who worked on it almost four years to complete. Such things as this were, of course, far beyond the means of more than a tiny few establishments and ordinary English parish churches had often difficulty in maintaining even a complete minimum set of vestments which, in any case, were mostly made from comparatively modest materials—we find pious bourgeois bequeathing their best gowns to their local church to be made into vestments. A curious, invaluable and unique example of medieval embroidery is the so-called 'Bayeux Tapestry' which displays in strip-cartoon fashion the story of the Norman Conquest and is the nearest that medieval England ever got to producing a newsreel. Probably of English workmanship, it was commissioned by the Conqueror's half-brother Odo, bishop of Bayeux, for his cathedral church about 1077. It is worked in woollen thread on coarse linen and is 70.34 metres long by 50 centimetres broad.

Tapestry, being intricately woven from fine material finely dyed, was inevitably one of the great artistic luxuries of the times and understandably seems to have been much less common in England than in flourishing France. It was used both to adorn walls and furniture. Not much of it was made here and very little remains. It was used as a prestigious form of hanging for walls and was much in vogue amongst the wealthiest levels of English society. Less well-to-do houses, like less well-to-do churches, were sometimes content with 'stained clothes', but this particular form of adornment was one of the few whereof ecclesiastical patronage was not considerable.

METAL WORK

Of all the artistic products of medieval times none has left such scanty remains as the objects of precious metal, yet originally these were numerous. Cups, bowls and spoons which adorned the tables of many households, and in ages when banking facilities were scanty, could be pawned or melted down if financial hardship so demanded. But this has had the almost inevitable result that the amount of such household plate left by medieval England over the centuries has so small a number of pieces that they would not adequately fill even a smallish exhibition hall. Even the Oxford and Cambridge colleges have lost all but a small number of such treasures. At Oxford some individual items escaped, like the magnificent crozier of Bishop William of Wykeham at New College, but most went to give very fruitless aid to the war effort of Charles I. At the same time also disappeared almost all England's medieval coronation plate. A rare and most magnificent survival is the superb fourteenth-century gold cup now in the British Museum made for a French prince and richly set with jewels and enamels. The English aristocracy were certainly well provided with plate, though our bourgeois had comparatively little of it.

So far as ecclesiastical plate was concerned it had early been laid down that the chalice and paten used at Mass should be of precious or at least semi-precious metal. Very few of such things remain, almost all of them having been confiscated or in Elizabethan times melted down into what were thought to be less objectionable shapes, whilst next to nothing is left of medieval cathedral plate. Most substantial was the loss of the plate belonging to the English monasteries which has vanished almost utterly.

This varied greatly in extent and value from house to house. Houses of friars and nunneries mostly had very little of it and the same was true of small colleges like that at Burton, where a survey at the Dissolution notes six chalices (a not unreasonable number) two censers, an incense boat and the 'garnysshyng' of a gospel book and a cross. Very different indeed was the position of Fountains Abbey, the richest house of the Cistercian order in England at the time of the

Dissolution. Here a detailed inventory of its plate shows clearly that the brethren had been influenced by social pressures to a degree of which their founders would not have approved. The total value of its plate was estimated at just over £700, in days when a parish priest lived on a few pounds a year. Amongst the major items were a golden cross with a relic of the Holy Cross (£30), a silver cross set with stones (£26), a silver-gilt image of Our Lady (£22), two silver candlesticks for the high altar (£12) and 'one table for the high altar on principal days, with silver, gold and stones' valued at no less than £90. Not all will find such magnificence unreasonable, but it is more difficult to defend the very large amount of secular plate 'in the custody of the lord abbot', presumably used when entertaining (as was unavoidable) grandees of one kind or another. This included two silver basins and ewers and eight standing cups, the total value under this heading coming to just over £147. The total amount of monastic plate confiscated under Henry VIII was clearly enormous and the portion of it still extant is microscopic.

The Question of Finance

Where did the money come from to pay for all this immense patronage of the visual arts in the interest of ecclesiastical establishments? To this significant and interesting question no very neat answer can ever be given, as, with the exception of royal expenditure, such matters are very scantily and unevenly recorded in surviving documents and practice varied considerably. But certain major facts are clear.

PARISH CHURCHES

In the case of parish churches the matter was comparatively simple. Canon law insisted that local community keep in good repair the place of public worship which it was bound to attend, enlarging it when necessary and providing it with all the necessities for the due conduct of worship. Steps by the local ecclesiastical authorities to enforce these requirements seem, in general, to have worked well in practice. However, anything in the way of luxuries, such as unnecessary rebuilding in the latest architectural idiom or the replacement of an antiquated font by one with a modern look was an optional matter which it was up to local initiative to provide.

Inevitably, therefore, the extensive re-building of late medieval churches in an age in which, it is to be remembered, the population was always notably smaller than it had been before the time of the Black Death, was only likely to occur in areas where prosperity was marked. It is not surprising to find citizens of the wealthy Bristol area re-building magnificently their superb church of St Mary Redcliffe in the fifteenth century or, in humbler strain, to find a vast but sober parish church erected in the same period at Kendal, where the cloth industry had been doing well for the locals. Most notable of all are the famous 'wool churches' of East Anglia, such as Lavenham and Long Melford, lavishly rebuilt at the same epoch on a scale astonishing to find in places in this area which were little more than largish villages. Unhappily, very seldom indeed do we get detailed information on how such building was financed, though here and there we can still see attractive little notes regarding medieval donors. In the great parish church of St Mary at Beverley, down the road from the ancient minster there, are various obliging inscriptions—'Xlay (Crosslay) and hys wyffe made these to pyllors and a halfe', 'Thes to pyllors made gud wyffys God reward thaym', 'Thys pyllor made the meynstyrls.'

Normally, of course, it is completely impossible to be certain why a church was rebuilt. Was it poverty or conservatism or was it delight in their beauty which preserved noble Romanesque edifices like Adel, Iffley and Kilpeck? We do not know. Was it a stern episcopal mandate or a growing population or a wish to keep up with some local ecclesiastical Jones' which led so many fifteenth-century folk to rebuild their parish churches? Again almost always we do not know and never will. Normally, local resources would suffice to keep the building in a usable state but, as contemporary wills show us, major tasks such as rebuilding the tower might take long to accomplish—significantly, bequests for this sort of purpose quite often stipulate that work on the project must be begun within a specified fairly brief period, on penalty of forfeiture.

THE GREATER CHURCHES

The financing of the construction or reconstruction of great cathedral, monastic and secular churches constituted a very considerable problem and one which is in need of much systematic historical investigation. In most of such places there would not normally appear to have been any great funds available to help with such eventualities as this, and there can be no doubt that the costs had often to be raised in a series of very different ways over a period which was often lengthy. Documentation on this matter is very scanty before the fourteenth and fifteenth centuries and in the case of many establishments is largely or totally lacking, so that dating of the new work has mostly to be left in the hands of archaeologists.

There is no doubt that from soon after the Conquest a frequent method of aiding building funds was the granting of indulgences generally by diocesan bishops or, in exceptional cases, by the pope. These varied greatly in number and value. The impoverished little hospital abbey of Creake early acquired one of these—from the archbishop of York—but the great abbey of Furness acquired a considerable string of them in the late twelfth and thirteenth centuries from various diocesans. Some such things were very lucrative, like that granting his faithful the right to consume butter during the Lenten season, issued by the archbishop of Rouen whose profits, it is said, financed the erection of the great tower at the west end of his cathedral known as 'the Butter Tower'.

The founder of a new monastery seems to have been under a moral obligation to assist with the consequent building expenses, but mostly we have very little knowledge of how extensive this aid was. As the process of erecting the main permanent buildings might take the best part of a century, in most cases they can only have made very limited progress during the founder's life-time, and there was often no easy legal way for him to make great bequests for this, though it seems to have been feasible for him to cancel by will debts owed to him by the house. The Pipe Rolls of the Exchequer mostly refer all too little to church building, though *inter alia* make it clear that Henry II spent enormous sums on the rebuilding of the church at Waltham Abbey. Similarly generous was Henry III in the reconstruction of the eastern limb of Westminster Abbey in the latest French style, a task on which at one time over 400 workmen were engaged. Records show a few other similarly massive church building schemes financed by royalty, notably the chapels of King's College, Cambridge and Eton College, largely due to Henry VI, and the chapels added by Henry VII to Westminster Abbey and

Windsor Castle. But such auspicious beginnings as these were often very slow in attaining completion. Reconstruction of the nave of Westminster Abbey was not undertaken for a full century after Henry III had died and only ended when the west front was completed in the mid-eighteenth century. As the great French cathedrals of Le Mans and Beauvais show, in some cases the old Romanesque nave was never rebuilt to match a new Gothic east end.

Besides engagement in huge architectural ventures the English sovereigns were certainly often ready to give small-scale aid to minor churches in time of need, especially if they were patrons of them. Thus gifts of oak-trees from the plenteous royal forests not infrequently were sent to help with some new roofing, or sums of cash. An account book of Richard III shows that 'moved by pite' he sent to Creake Abbey the very generous gift of £46 after a disastrous fire there and that he made a smaller donation to aid the rebuilding of Windermere parish church after it had suffered the same affliction.

But there is no doubt that the kings of England, well-disposed as they largely were, could not possibly provide more than a very small fraction of the huge building costs in which the churches of medieval England were involved for one reason or another. Although documentation on this matter is defective it is highly probable that in most cases much of the money needed for a large-scale rebuilding campaign came from the local aristocracy who, after all, now, as in Victorian times, were the only section of the population with extensive resources to spare for this purpose. Thus, on the small scale, Sir John Harrington gave Cartmel Priory a much needed chapel for the parishioners in which his chantry was placed, and one of his descendants financed considerable rebuilding of the little priory of Conishead. To provide the great stained glass windows of the period local aristocracy repeatedly put their hands in their pockets and in return for this were often commemorated either by the insertion in a window of their coat of arms or, better still, by little portraits of them piously kneeling with their garments displaying their coat of arms to give the public that gazed on them in later times the clear social indication of who they were in order to acquire their 'pryeres'; very frequently underneath runs some such inscription as 'pray for the souls of Sir XY and Z his wife who had this window made'. The windows of Great Malvern offer attractive examples of this spiritual *quid pro quo*, in panels showing besides Henry VII, Sir Reginald Bray and Sir Thomas Lovell piously kneeling and having beneath them inscriptions asking for prayers for their souls. The great east window of Gloucester Cathedral is well provided with coats of arms of benefactors whilst the *Scrope-Grosvenor Roll* (a voluminous and fascinating report on the dispute between these two great families for the right to a particular coat of arms) shows us incidentally how much heraldry was to be found in the windows of churches and conventual buildings.

Town churches were, of course, apt to be in a somewhat better position over financing their building operations, being able to draw on a variety of local benefactors. By very great good fortune very full evidence has survived to show us how the funds for building at the large and very popular Franciscan friary in London was provided. Here, of course, were brethren who, on principle, owned no property but lived on alms so could make no financial contribution to the scheme. Founded in 1224 and soon acquiring modest temporary buildings, the house's campaign to provide very necessary permanent and more extensive quarters got under way in the last decades of the century. A mayor of London and the earl of Richmond were mostly responsible for the costs of erecting the capacious nave which the famed preaching of the friars demanded. The great new choir (very necessary for a convent whose members often numbered almost a hundred) was begun by Queen Margaret and completed by her niece, Isabella of Valois, at a total cost of over two thousand pounds. The thirty-six windows were provided by a variety of donors, mostly great London citizens or members of the aristocracy. (The same Register which so kindly provides us with these invaluable details gives us also another almost unique item—a very full and precise list of the names of those interred in the church and the exact site of their burial place. Behind the high altar was buried the heart of Archbishop Pecham, himself a Franciscan, and in front of it the body of Queen Margaret, with scores of lesser personages squeezed in elsewhere.)

An auxiliary source of revenue affording financial aid which might, directly or indirectly, swell the building fund of a very limited number of the greater churches, was that resulting from the donations of pilgrims to places which were fortunate enough to possess a venerated shrine. These were not very plentiful in England, though in the case of a select few were lucrative at least for a while. At Canterbury Cathedral, in its jubilee year of the death of St Thomas Becket (1220), the enormous sum of over £1000 was collected. Two centuries later the figure was just over half that sum and by the time of the Dissolution much smaller. At this late date the shrine of Our Lady of Walsingham which had long been slow in acquiring any great wealth had for some time been financially flourishing, income from its chapel, on the eve of its destruction, being estimated at £259 yearly.

In many parts of the West it is immensely difficult to visualise today the splendid artistic richness prevalent in medieval times. This was very heavily concentrated in its churches, but here the bigotries of Renaissance and Baroque art, the Reformation and the French Revolution, aided by the inevitable wear and tear of time have blotted out enormous parts of it so that only in limited areas like much of Italy and Austria can its abundance and complexity be easily seen. So far as England is concerned there is no easier way of appreciating the artistic wealth of its great medieval churches than study of the fascinating *Rites of Durham*, a remarkable account of the cathedral of Durham written by a former inmate of the house soon after the suppression of monastic life therein. To do so inevitably urges the thoughtful reader to ask what motivated this loving, continuous accumulation of artistic treasures of so many kinds. No answer to this question can be given with that absolute certainty beloved by scientists and mathematicians, and it is not to be assumed that only one kind of force was behind it. Human nature being what it is, a wish for ostentation and a determination not to be out-classed by a neighbour no doubt were at times operative, as was certainly that local pride which flourished so strongly. But it would be unrealistic to refuse to admit that incomparably the most powerful cause was that profound conviction that the bigness and beauty of God must be mirrored in His place of worship, which has characterised all the Eastern Christian and the great mass of Western thought on the matter continuously from early centuries.

CHAPTER 15

WORSHIP

THE PLACE OF WORSHIP

PUBLIC worship in medieval England took place in more than one type of institution. Semi-private were the chapels in the castles of the king and his barons and in the houses of the minor aristocracy. To such places access for regular worship was limited, and those of the faithful who were qualified to attend were mostly not exempted from important obligations to the incumbent of their local parish whose income, as we have seen, might have been seriously diminished if his parishioners were free to go where they liked for public worship. A small fraction of medieval Englishmen fulfilled their religious obligations at collegiate churches or at cathedrals or monasteries which had a parish altar pertaining to them, situate either within the church itself or in a separate building near it. But the huge majority of the faithful were legally obliged to attend worship at one of the thousands of parish churches round which so much local life was focused or, much more rarely, at one of the parochial chapels dependent on them. When some exception to this rule was desired, as, for example, to go to an outside priest for confession or to be interred in another church or churchyard, special permission for this had normally to be acquired. The multitudinous parish churches varied greatly in size and splendour but were uniform in a number of major ways.

THE CHURCHYARD

A medieval parish church invariably had attached to it a churchyard which usually surrounded it on every side. Church and churchyard had to be solemnly consecrated by a bishop and derived herefrom a special status which included the right of affording sanctuary (the churchyard is sometimes termed *sanctuarium*). For people and property alike, in time of trouble church and churchyard offered limited but valuable protection. The criminal fleeing from justice could find temporary refuge there even if, in due course, he might have to give himself up and quit the country. In times of strife, common enough in Norman England, the locals might seek safety herein for themselves and their goods. Thus, when in 1139 warfare surged around the city of Worcester, as a local chronicle records: 'anyone there might have seen the whole furniture of all the citizens carried into the (cathedral) church. . . . Behold the mother church of the diocese converted into an inn and a council chamber of the citizens. Because of the number of chests and sacks but little space remained to the servants of God in such a hostelry. Within chanted the monk, without was to be heard the sobbing of the infant.' Human nature being what it is, this privilege was not invariably respected, notably during the troublous reign of Stephen, and seems not to have been highly regarded by the wild Scots. On the other hand it was far from worthless, as is hinted by the decree of the Council of Clarendon which provided that chattels legally forfeited to the king were not to be detained in the church or churchyard, and by certain episcopal decrees of the following century which show that Jews thought it worthwhile to try and obtain protection for their property therein.

The principal purpose of the churchyard was to provide a place of burial for the parishioners, interments within the church itself for long being rare save in some town churches and houses of the mendicant orders (whose great popularity probably boosted this practice). It was thus clearly necessary to keep the churchyard as free as possible from obstacles to burials, such as trees, but medieval folk were ever ready to make exceptions in special cases, and in 1287 the bishop of the windswept diocese of Exeter ordered that, as trees were planted in local churchyards to prevent the church being injured by storms, the incumbents concerned were on no account to fell them. Although the local faithful departed were very conscientiously and regularly prayed for at public worship in medieval times, there was now no false sentimentality concerning the treatment of their mortal remains. In the larger parish churches at least, often a charnel-house was built to which, after a decent interval, bones of ancient burials were transferred, in order to make room for new interments.

Medieval graves do not seem to have had the low mounds which

are now usual, so that the churchyard of these times often presented
an attractive flattish area which again and again a faithful laity
found highly suitable for such non-theological activities as dancing
and football, a practice against which various bishops unsportingly
fulminated. For shopping, churchyards were equally attractive;
what could be more convenient than buying one's Sunday meat
from a barrow or stall sitting in the churchyard? Of this also the
ecclesiastical powers-that-be disapproved strongly and repeatedly.

For reasons which are not clear, the main entrance both to the
churchyard and the church was usually on the south; tradition seems
to have regarded the north as undesirable and burial on this side of
the church seems often to have long been avoided. In most churchyards the only object which broke the even line of the sward was
the churchyard cross, which was usually placed some little way
south of the south door of the church. Its main purpose is recalled
by an order of the bishop of Worcester in 1229 that all parish
churches in his diocese should have a churchyard cross to which
the faithful should go in solemn procession on Palm Sunday. These
crosses were often large and handsome, standing on a wide base
which sometimes contained a small niche, believed to have been
used in the Palm Sunday rites. To an extent which is unascertainable
the crosses' steps were used as a place from which to deliver sermons.
Of this the most famous example is the mighty cross in the churchyard of St Paul's, London, which came to incorporate a pulpit that
was greatly employed for harangues theological and non-theological, both before and after the Reformation.

In general, the church was the only building to be seen in a
medieval English churchyard, though we have occasional reference
to what must have been very small chapels therein. Before the
Conquest in certain areas detached belfry towers were to be found
there, but they were very rare after it and the old Continental habit
of having a baptistery separate from the church was almost if not
totally unknown in England. The charnel-house, where there was
one, seems normally to have been built against a wall of the church,
as were anchorages, though these seem to have been fairly rare. As
early as c. 1240 the bishop of Salisbury ordered that no anchorages
were to be erected in churchyards and any of those already in existence which lacked either adequate endowment or episcopal authorisation were to be destroyed.

Usually there were not more than one or two entrances to the churchyard, the main one being usually at least roughly in line with the south door of the church. Access here was generally by a lych gate (*lych* means corpse) which often consisted of a small roofed passage usually of rectangular plan, with its main axis running north-south. It served *inter alia* as a waiting place for the funeral procession, and because of this provided not only shelter but space for the coffin and occasionally a slab on which to put it down, and sometimes also benches on either side for its attendants. In times when clocks were rare and watches unknown there may well have existed here a somewhat Mediterranean attitude towards punctuality which would make such provision welcome.

THE CHURCH

A medieval parish church, whilst appearing to be a single whole, in fact consisted of two units which were distinct legally and usually architecturally as well. Of these, one was generally much larger than the other and adjoined its western side. It was termed the 'nave', apparently because its tall, surging outline was not unlike that of a ship (*navis*). Its companion on the east was termed the 'chancel' from the screens (*cancelli*) which separated it from the nave and which, if it had aisles, also closed in the choir-stalls. The wall between chancel and nave marked a major legal boundary and for that reason was scarcely ever moved, though it might be altered.

English medieval churches varied greatly in size. The largest abbeys and cathedrals might reach a length in the region of four or even five hundred feet, but many lesser ones were not much over half that figure. The smallest parish churches might be only about a hundred feet long though very many others were double that size or more. The rage for founding parish churches in the larger medieval towns like Norwich and York meant that often they tended to be small and over-numerous; some of them had become redundant before the arrival of the Reformation. By the fifteenth century a good deal of money was being spent on church-building resulting in some very large parish churches. At the other end of the scale, mostly in the lonesome north and west, were simple Anglo-Saxon structures like Escombe (Durham) and Brixworth which have come down to us with very limited post-Conquest alteration.

The plans of parish churches were very variegated. The simplest and often the oldest might have nothing more than a small aisleless nave and a small aisleless chancel. But from the late twelfth century onwards the habit of adding or extending aisles in the nave grew apace. By the fourteenth and fifteenth century this process was very evident in all but the poorest areas. One reason for it was the multiplication of chantries, another the increase in England's population. But the importance of the latter factor must not be exaggerated, for many such additions were made after population losses caused by the Black Death and its attendant epidemics: the growing desire for more spacious accommodation, so evident in domestic architecture in late medieval England, must not be forgotten. Some chantries were tacked on the existing structure in very untidy fashion, but very often they were accommodated in an aisle. In monastic churches in England, though not much in France, the cruciform plan for churches was greatly beloved, but in our parish churches this was rare, perhaps partly because of its more difficult construction, and the absence of the need for the additional space which its transepts supplied. By the end of the fifteenth century increasing expansion had often produced large aisled parish churches completely rectangular in plan.

The Tower and its Bells

Possession of at least one bell with somewhere to mount it was an essential feature of any medieval parish church. Poorish places might have only a single bell or a couple thereof, which were sometimes perched in a little bellcote which topped the western gable of the church. But very many more churches, as time went on, were much better supplied, the English for centuries having shown considerable affection for bell-ringing. Where there were several bells these were often large and had to be housed in a substantial belfry.* This was normally the upper storey of the tower, the bell-ropes running conveniently down to the ringers who stood on the

---

* A curious note in the *Life* of St Wulfstan suggests such belfries were still rare in his day, at least in some areas. The writer relates that the bishop 'was designing a building above the roof of the church for the bells to hang in; what is the correct name for such a structure I cannot at present remember'.

lower floor. In most parish churches the tower stood at the west end of the church and had its own entrance—a door in the west wall. In some of the larger churches the belfry was centrally placed between the nave and the chancel. It seems highly likely that before the Conquest in certain areas, including East Anglia, some of the towers were built as detached structures and were also employed as places of defence in time of trouble, locals being summoned thereto by the bell or bells sounding the alarm, but in later times such towers were tacked on to their church. In parts of the extreme north of England the perennial danger of Scottish raids throughout our period made necessary very solid towers capable of defensive use and with the minimum of decoration, which gave them a some-what military air, but in orderly and fruitful areas church towers were often rebuilt in late medieval times to become things of great beauty, as in Somerset where the superb local stone was then fashioned by very sensitive builders.

To church bells the medieval public accorded that semi-human status which sailors accord to ships. A bell was very frequently linked with the name of a saint. Of the hundreds of medieval bells which survive in England easily the most common dedication is that to Our Lady (of which no less than 960 examples are known), second place went to the two St Johns whose bells totalled 260 and third place to St Katharine, a very popular medieval figure, with 167. The inscriptions frequently found on them vary greatly. A Cornish bell has one which runs: 'The name of the bell is peace to souls, Virgin of Virgins pray for those who are being punished in purgatory that they may soon be delivered by the mercy of God'. The qualities with which they were credited included protection against storms, lightning and thunder and, according to some, even pacification of the enraged. Their main use, however, was to call the faithful to attendance at the services of the church and to participate in those which they could not attend by saying brief prayers on their own, notably the *Hail Mary*.* But bells came in useful in various other ways, notably at funerals, on festive occasions and to mark for all,

---

* The medieval form of this consisted only of two texts from St Luke's Gospel, 'Hail Mary full of grace the Lord with thee', and 'blessed art thou amongst women and blessed is the fruit of thy womb Jesus'. In the course of the sixteenth century came general use of the addition, 'Holy Mary, Mother of God, pray for us sinners now and in the hour of our death'.

both inside church and outside it, the solemn moment of the Mass when the bread and wine was consecrated to become in a non-physical sense the Body and Blood of Christ.

The Interior of the Church

The Rood Screen.

The interior of a late medieval church in England had the boundary between its nave and the chancel firmly marked by a massive structure which ran right across it from north to south, and was known as the 'rood screen', an enlarged type of it found in cathedrals and many monasteries coming to be termed the *pulpitum* (page 118). The rood screen was not one of the furnishings of a church which was legally necessary, and only reached its final form towards the end of our period, by a process which deserves much more study than it has received. By the fifteenth century, as contemporary wills show us conspicuously, it had become an object of very great affection. In its final form it had three elements:—

(i) *The screen* which ran across the west end of the chancel, including its aisles where such existed, and which *inter alia* often provided a back for the ends of the two rows of the choir stalls, which were turned to face the altar.

(ii) *The rood loft*, an often quite narrow loft which ran across the broad top of the rood screen. In many cases it was entered by a small circular stair set in one of the piers which supported the chancel arch. As Munro Cautley very properly points out, most of the lofts were very much too cramped to be of much practical value, though they gave useful access to the rood figures and the line of lights which often flickered delicately along the top of the western parapet of the loft. In cathedrals and many monasteries the loft was substantial enough to house an organ. The extent to which this loft was used for liturgical purposes is not clear.

(iii) *The rood*, which was a very large cross bearing a figure of the crucified Christ and having on either side of it standing figures of Our Lady and St John. It might be suspended from the roof over the screen, this part of the ceiling often being richly decorated, or, with its attendant figures, stand on a beam which ran along a parapet of the loft. It was sometimes termed 'the high cross'.

The Chancel

East of the rood screen ran the chancel, set on an east-west axis and generally rectangular in plan, though in Norman times a certain number were built with east ends that terminated in apses. In very many English parish churches the chancel had no aisles, though these were by no means unknown. The main function of the chancel was to provide a setting for the main altar of the church (known as the high altar) which dominated its eastern end, and seating for the clergy which was placed facing it. The latter consisted of two L-shaped blocks of seats or, more often in the larger churches, of stalls. These blocks had their longer sides running east and west and their shorter ones north and south, the latter abutting on the choir screen and being separated from each other by a large entrance which gave access to the nave.

To ensure that the chancel of a parish church was kept in repair was normally the responsibility of the rector. In Norman times this was a matter which seems to have been often neglected, but later the authorities became much alive to its importance and their insistence led to very considerable rebuilding of the chancels in the thirteenth century, perhaps due not only to past neglect but to an increase in the number of secular clergy and to the desire to build in the new Gothic style.

The east end of the chancel was dominated by the high altar. This stood close to its eastern wall which usually contained a large window or a group of smaller ones which provided invaluable light, especially in the morning—the time at which most of the daily round of public worship took place. The altars of this period were rectangular structures made of masonry and by no means always as large as many of their modern successors. Each was topped by a large stone slab whose upper surface bore five engraved crosses (one in each corner and one in the centre), reminiscent of the five wounds of the crucified Christ. Beneath the slab was sometimes enclosed a small capsule containing relics. Behind the altar might be a 'reredos', a panel or panels of either rich material or carving in wood, stone or alabaster which might be painted and gilded. Of the altar itself little might be visible. Its top and ends were draped by long cloths and the side facing the congregation by a frontal made of material (which might be embroidered or woven) or of wood or metal.

Contrary to modern practice, the altar had little or no permanent furnishings. No cross or crucifix stood there permanently, nor often during much of our period, any candlesticks. In the West as in the East, it had long been the custom to 'reserve' (i.e. store away) a portion of the elements consecrated in the Mass, principally for the use of the sick and dying, but also partly because prayer before this Reserved Sacrament was steadily found to be a very useful aid to private devotion. Late in our period this Reserved Sacrament was sometimes kept in a tabernacle behind or on the altar, but in England it was much more usual at this time to use for this purpose a pyx or small box of precious metal (sometimes in the form of a dove) which was draped with a cloth and suspended over the altar on a chain.

Immediately west of the high altar was a large space which was left open to allow for the movements of clergy during the services. On its southern side was a row of seats (usually three in number) set in or against the wall and known as the *sedilia*, for use at certain points in a high Mass by those officiating thereat. In the wall immediately to the east of it was a small niche with a drain in its base, used for washing the altar vessels in use at Mass and known as a *piscina*. In the wall between the sedilia and the choir stalls was usually a small door traditionally and very correctly called 'the priest's door'. It was a convenient entrance to the chancel, likely to be used much in the course of the maintenance of the complex round of daily offices to which the clergy were bound. The medieval English sanctuary was happily devoid of the infuriating set of steps usable only by those with microscopic feet, on the insertion of which Victorian architects were so often hell-bent. Sometimes in the chancel wall, though also found in other parts of the church, was a smallish window which has come to be termed a 'lowside window' whose purpose or purposes have been much discussed.

Lowside Windows

This name is given to a category of windows found in post-Conquest parish churches. They vary considerably in both shape and size though they are usually quite small and often rectangular. A distinctive feature of most of them is the fact that all or part was not glazed but had a shutter or shutters opening inwards. As with far too much ecclesiastical archaeology they have not received the systematical historical and architectural analysis which modern scholarship demands, though those in the county of Shropshire have been admirably classified.* Including three high-side windows the total is thirty-six, of which thirty are to be found in the chancel of the church concerned. The total number of surviving medieval chancels is about 130, so that the feature is far from being a usual one. Only six had more than one light and in eighteen cases the window had a shutter which in all but one case opened inwards. Though the fact may not be significant, seventeen out of the twenty-four examples which were roughly datable were 'Decorated' in style, i.e. of fourteenth-century date.

The purpose of these windows has been much discussed and there can be little doubt that, as Cranage urges, it was by no means uniform. The antique idea that they were for the use of lepers is picturesque but ludicrous. It has also been urged that the little windows were for the exhibition of lights wherewith to dispel evil spirits. It is quite likely that in a number of cases the shutters were opened to ring the sanctus bell at the consecration of the host at Mass for the benefit of the faithful who, from necessity or preference, were milling around in the churchyard outside; in certain cases there are small seats below or near the shutters which might have been used by the server.

Two further possibilities seem to the present writer worthy of consideration. Firstly, that the main purpose of the shutters in some cases was simply to provide ventilation in chancels which were often quite small, and on major occasions at least may well have been crowded. The fact that medieval stained glass windows could not be opened, that incense might be freely used, and that the medieval faithful had few facilities for extensive washing, may well have made some form of ventilation highly desirable. In this connection it has to be remembered that medieval bishops on ceremonial occasions were clad in a series of superimposed garments which must have tended to produce intolerable stuffiness, the more so since the outer vestment, be it cope or chasuble, was often very heavy.

A second possibility, which excavation might ultimately prove or disprove, is that in certain cases the shuttered window may have been

* D. H. S. Cranage, *An Architectural Account of the Churches of Shropshire* pp. 1075–1103.

the sole visible remains of an anchorage, for such habitations were usually built against the wall of a church and had an opening to allow for limited conversation with the outside world and reception of communion and confession. The outer walls of these fell largely into disrepair or were destroyed before and after the Reformation.

The Choir Stalls

Since the clergy would expect to spend quite a sizeable amount of time in daily worship in the chancel, adequate seating here was very necessary. In places of size this came to consist not of mere benches but of stalls in front of which ran desks. The head of the community, whether monastic or clerical, would have the stall adjoining the entrance on its south side, the second in command the corresponding one on the north side, with the rest placed in due seniority from west to east.

In places which could afford it, it was usual for each stall to have not only a separate seat but an elaborate canopy soaring overhead. These seats were usually constructed so as to be capable of being turned up and rested against the back of their stalls. On their under face was a bracket which was known as a 'misericord' and which was usually elaborately carved with one of a very wide selection of subjects. Some of these showed simply foliage, or one of the grotesque human faces which medieval men seem to have found entertaining, but many were much more interesting. Birds and animals both real and unreal were very commonly portrayed, hounds, eagles and elephants mixing happily with griffins, dragons and phoenixes. Very often contemporaries saw a moral lesson in nature where we would see none. Thus the popular pelican was believed to feed her young from the flesh and blood of her breast, and is shown so doing, thus typifying Christ feeding His Church through His Body and Blood. Though the point is not easily proved, it would seem that the purpose of having these seats which could be turned up was to furnish some little support during the longish parts of the services during which kneeling or sitting was forbidden. In front of the stalls ran solid wooden desks which often terminated in bench-ends which were topped by elaborately carved finials. In large churches at least, the amount of seating accommodation provided in the chancel seems often to have been appreciably greater than the size of the community which it served would require, presumably so as to allow for reception of favoured visitors and local devotees.

The Nave

If the chancel was the liturgical habitat of the clergy, the nave served a similar purpose for the laity, and because the latter were so much more numerous than the former, was always much the bigger of the two units. It was also much more frequently enlarged, either because, for one reason or another, the parishioners wanted this or because the diocesan bishop judged it to be necessary. In 1309 the bishop of Exeter, finding the church of Ilfracombe too small for its parishioners, ordered them to lengthen the nave by at least twenty-four feet and add two aisles within two years, under penalty of £40 fine if they failed to do so. The parishioners were responsible in law for the maintenance of the nave in good condition and for the provision of all the adjuncts necessary for the conduct of public worship. In the thirteenth century the efficient authorities of the times spelt out these responsibilities in detail. For the northern province the matter was settled by an ordinance of Walter Gray, archbishop of York (d. 1258).

This made it incumbent upon the parishioners of each parish to see that their church was provided with the following items: a chalice, a missal and a main set of eucharistic vestments (comprising chasuble, alb, amice, stole, maniple and girdle); three altar cloths, corporals and vestments for deacon and subdeacon as far as their resources permitted; a principal cope of silk for use on major festivals and two others for those who led the singing at these; a processional cross, a small cross for use at funerals, a bier for the dead and a bucket for holy water; a pax, a candlestick for the Paschal candle, a censer, a lantern and a handbell; a Lenten veil and two candlesticks for processional use; the following service books—a legend, an antiphonal, a gradual, a psalter, a troper, an ordinal, a missal and a manual; a frontal for the high altar, three surplices and a suitable pyx for the Host; bells with their ropes, a font with a lock and a chrismatory; statues including a main statue in the chancel of the saint to whom the church was dedicated; the repair of books and vestments when necessary; lights in the church; the repair of the nave with any building necessary, the repair of the tower inside and out, and of windows and the boundary of the churchyard. To rectors or vicars, according to local arrangement, belonged responsibility for the upkeep of the chancel with its walls, roof, glass windows, desks and benches.

The principal and occasionally the only entrance to the nave of the church was usually placed towards the western end of its south wall. Its doorway was large and from the late twelfth century onwards usually ornate. By the end of our period it had long been usual to place a porch around, which would be particularly convenient for those involved in the early part of the marriage service which took place here. The door itself was sturdily made and, in Gothic times, often had blind tracery. Immediately inside it in the adjacent wall might be a stoup containing holy water and not far away a box for alms which seems often to have been constructed out of a piece of tree trunk (*cf.* the present French term *tronc*, for an alms box).

At the west end of the nave, usually in the main aisle of the church, was the font wherein children were baptised. The water which it contained for this purpose was solemnly blest, and seems to have been kept longer than is now usual, the bowl being surmounted by a cover which contemporary regulations insisted on being locked. Both the font and its cover received major artistic attention. Early in our period the former was very often large, heavy, and tub-shaped, apparently to allow for total immersion of the child, but later on this was not thought necessary and fonts became smaller and more elegant, often having polygonal bowls. Frequently, the font stood on a small platform.

Often there was no door in the north wall of the nave, but by the end of the period the inner face of this wall had often acquired a very large painting of St Christopher carrying the Christ child on his shoulder across a river. Frequently in many English parish churches by the end of our period the space between the western side of the rood screen and the roof above it was occupied by a large painting of the Last Judgment. In the centre was Christ come to separate the good from the bad, and below, the dead rising from their graves to hear their fate. On the right of the Lord were those whose goodness had won them a place in Heaven being welcomed by the angels; on the left, those who had refused to be Christ-like are shown being forced into the mouth of Hell by horrific demons often armed with pitchforks and other pertinent instruments.

Although by the end of our period windows in many parish churches had engrossed much of the available space, wall paintings were now commonly and widely used. As the windows themselves were now adorned with brightly coloured stained glass, and screens and arcades often painted, the interior of the nave had a very colourful appearance which was further enhanced by statues and pictures, sometimes with lights flickering before them which were to be found in varying degree (e.g. much more in Kent than in Yorkshire) and were probably dotted around in the homely fashion of which strait-laced vergers disapprove. The very regimented air given to the naves of modern churches by the presence of large numbers of mass-produced pews was almost if not quite unknown at this time. For most of the period, little provision was made for the seating of the faithful, though it is clear that in the fifteenth century provisions of pews was not unknown, though on what scale we do not know.

By the time of the Reformation, as we have noted, a considerable number of English parish churches contained at least one or two chantry chapels. Some of these could be accommodated in the space beneath an arch, but others were spacious structures set in an aisle and guarded by screens. All had at their eastern end an altar at which Mass was to be perennially celebrated for the good of the soul of the founder and often for his relations, as well as was also often ordained, for 'all Christian souls'. As already noted, at the west end of some chantries which had had private founders (as distinct from those established by guilds) might be seen the effigy of the founder, with his wife if he had one or his two wives if he had re-married. Such tombs looked something like large beds, and this likeness was increased by the fact that they often had overhead a painted ceiling or tester.

Although by the fifteenth century preaching in England had become much commoner than in early medieval days, it is doubtful whether more than a proportion of the churches regarded a pulpit as a necessary feature, though some of this period do remain and are mostly attractively carved and painted. As Owst has shown, preaching in the churchyard was no uncommon thing; there seem also to have been movable pulpits.

Lighting and Heating

Extensive lighting in a medieval church was much less important than it is today owing to the fact that the huge mass of the congregation neither possessed anything so expensive as books nor had the capacity to read them. All modern means of illumination being unavailable, reliance had to be largely placed on candles of one kind or another or 'cressets' (stones with a series of holes scooped out in which could be put oil and a floating wick). By contemporary standards, candles were very expensive indeed, so their use had to be very carefully regulated as medieval wills repeatedly demonstrate. Gifts of them, of one kind or another, occur very frequently indeed, both for use at the testator's funeral rites and on later occasions. Their number, size and weight is often carefully detailed; even the time they should burn on various occasions and sometimes what should be done with the candle ends. It is difficult to reconstruct the reasons for the considerable medieval interest in candles, but it was probably due to something more than purely utilitarian considerations. However, for most of the time the interiors of medieval English churches must have been very dark by modern standards, not only because of inadequate facilities for artificial lighting but also because of the great passion for the use of stained glass windows which England, unlike Italy, developed mightily in our period. Though as time went on the small, dark windows of Norman and early Gothic days tended to be replaced by much larger ones, and developments in the technique of stained glass made it exclude much less light, the very wide use of stained glass and the frequent lack of bright sun often left the interior of our churches with a light which was in truth 'dim and religious'.

A most popular place for endowed lights by late medieval times was along the western side of the rood loft, but a simple light or lights might burn before one or other of the various statues, pictures or crucifixes which any sizeable church did not lack. In the majority of churches the only really sizeable light ever seen was that of the so-called 'Paschal candle'. This was set in a large and carefully decorated candlestick and, after use in the Easter ceremonies, burned until Ascension-tide as a reminder of the Christ who was 'the Light of the World'. In a handful of the most opulent churches of medieval England this candlestick was of huge dimensions, like

that described in *The Rites of Durham* which 'in latitude did containe
almost the bredth of the Quire, in longitude that did extend to the
height of the vault. . . . In conclusion the Pascall was estimated to
be one of the rarest monuments in England.' Because of the exor-
bitant expense of any form of artificial lighting, both in the monastery and outside it, the working day tended to be largely confined
to daylight hours, so that for example, the monastic time-table in
summer was much longer than it was in winter.

In medieval England heating was at least as much of a problem
as lighting, with no large supplies of fuel easily obtainable at
reasonable cost in most places. Warm clothing must have been of
great importance, though perhaps medieval people were less sensitive
to cold than people today. In church some use was made of braziers,
though these were clearly apt to be dangerous in such cluttered-up
places and perhaps accounted for a good share of those fires which
seem to have been frequent in medieval ecclesiastical buildings.
Those taking the services sometimes had available round metal
balls with hollow interiors filled with hot water to help to keep their
hands warm.

The Nature of Public Worship

LANGUAGE AND VISUAL AIDS

Although the worship of the Church has preserved down the
centuries a substantial common core of features, there has also often
been present various local and temporary differences, due in some
degree to changing environmental factors. As we have seen, in the
medieval West very strong social pressures directed the use of Latin
in the public worship of the Church. In medieval England use of
the vernacular in worship was not utterly unknown. It might be
used, for example, in the bidding prayer at Mass and in the prelimin-
aries of the marriage service, but otherwise it was largely ignored
and there is very little sign of any intensified use of it in public
worship in the century which immediately preceded the Reformation.

In defence of this devotion to Latin in worship it may be argued
that aesthetically it has much to commend it, for few tongues display
so forcibly the dignity of worship, whilst it is only necessary to

have slight experience of the august Liturgy of the Eastern Churches to appreciate that one can gain much from public worship in an unknown language, provided one knows the general outline of its structure. (The universality of the Latin tongue cannot be regarded as a powerful argument in favour of Latin worship at this time, since so few folk travelled very far from home and the prevalence of very strong local accents in the West must often have tended to bewilder at least some visitors from afar.) But the fact that such major portions of the Mass as the Epistle and Gospel would be incomprehensible to the mass of the congregation unless there happened to be a sermon and the preacher made some mention of one or both of them is of course to be deplored, as is the lack of interest in a fuller participation of the laity in the Mass. It is worth noting that, down to this day, the faithful of the Eastern Churches have not had the passion of their Western counterparts to lift up their voices in public worship with maximum frequency.

It is important to appreciate that the meaning of the Mass—the service *par excellence* of these times—was very much more apparent to medieval congregations than it might appear to have been at first sight today, owing to the very skilful and extensive use made therein of what the moderns call 'visual aids'. This process steadily gathered way down the centuries ultimately achieving results which, if they were by no means rigidly uniform, were certainly of very great utility to the uninformed faithful.

Thus, to take a minor example, when a man entered a late medieval church whilst Mass was in progress he would at once get some idea, if not always a very precise one, of its particular nature merely by observing the dominant colour of the vestments which the priest was wearing. This was principally visible on the chasuble (a large garment shaped like a cape which was worn on top of other vestments) though its stole and maniple would be of the same hue. All of these would be one of several colours, to each of which, in process of time, a symbolic meaning became attached. Thus a London pontifical of the early fifteenth century notes that 'white is amongst all colours the first, the purest, the most simple and most festal' so has to be employed *inter alia* for Christmas, Easter, feasts at Whitsuntide and for feasts of apostles, evangelists and martyrs; purple, 'dark and obscure of vision is indicative of penance and despising the world' so is suited for the penitential seasons of Lent and Advent; green, 'lively and pleasant and comforting to the sight' should be employed on the very numerous occasions when there was no special person or season to be observed. But in this matter more than most, divergencies were very marked indeed, with some remarkable local usages such as that which led Evesham Abbey to employ their great black chasuble at high Mass on Christmas Day, perhaps because of its magnificence.

It is equally important not to interpret the injunctions of the London pontifical with modern rigidity. After all, symbolic meanings of colours were not all obvious so that, unlike today, in medieval England the best colour for use during Lent was widely thought to be white, whilst, in any case, the incorrigible localism of the times often prevented such rules being put into practice uniformly. Furthermore, the non-theological factor called poverty deprived many small English parish churches of ownership of sets of vestments in the full range of colours desirable, or from invariably replacing them when they started to show evident signs of wear and tear.

Similar utilisation of visual aids lay behind the series of gestures which gradually came to be used by the celebrant of a Mass. If to the uninitiated at first perhaps they seemed baffling very little experience was needed to show their purpose, and it was advantageous for a newcomer to recognise very quickly what stage in the Mass had been reached, even when the words of the celebrant were inaudible or incomprehensible. Thus the reading of the Gospel which marked the culmination of the first part of the service had its importance accentuated by the Gospel Book being carried solemnly in procession and by the fact that, where this could be afforded, the Gospel Book had covers of precious or semi-precious metal set with precious or semi-precious stones. When the priest called on the faithful to 'Lift up your hearts' he lifted up his hands as a sign thereof. For the Western Church the grand climax of the Mass came when the bread and wine had been consecrated to become in a spiritual sense the Body and Blood of Christ. The Elements were then solemnly elevated by the celebrant and adored by all present, whilst a bell or bells rang out in triumph and a gently clinking censer sent clouds of smoke sliding heavenwards and lights in candlesticks were elevated in homage.

Such a stress on the visual element in worship obviously had very special utility under contemporary social conditions and was reinforced by others. Thus each of the major orders of the clergy had their distinctive garb, bishops wearing items of the outer clothing of those lower orders which they conferred on others, as well as special episcopal ones. At certain junctures, notably during processions and when giving the blessing, the bishop held in one hand a pastoral staff or 'crosier', the outward and visible sign of his place as pastor of the flock of Christ *par excellence*, a similar one being allotted to abbots and abbesses for the same reasons. As we have seen, the English archbishops ranked as primates and so on official occasions had carried before them a 'primatial cross' (which had two cross bars instead of one, which sufficed for lesser dignitaries). This, together with the pallium which they wore around their necks on major ecclesiastical occasions made archbishops very recognisable figures, whether they were depicted in stained glass windows or were standing on *terra firma*.

Great use was made of emblems to distinguish the large number of saints whose help was sought by medieval man. In process of time each of the apostles, for example, acquired a special one. St Peter carried the keys of Heaven promised to him by Christ in the Gospels, Not scriptural was the convention of displaying St James dressed as a pilgrim complete with cockle shell in his hat, his alleged shrine at Compostella being for long the greatest centre of pilgrimage in the lands north of the Alps. St John the Baptist who called men to 'behold the lamb of God which takes away the sins of the world' was depicted holding a lamb. A number of post-apostolic saints came to be adopted as the patron saints of certain sections of medieval society, like St Anthony of Egypt who is shown with a boar at his side, he having become the patron saint of swineherds, since he was said to have lived in the desert for twenty years with a tame boar for company. However, by the end of the Middle Ages there were already far too many saints chasing far too few emblems, so that identification was not always easy. As a further aid, the name of the saint was often added to figures in stained glass windows, a benefit to those who could read. But no system could be all-embracing. There were, for example, a host of canonised archbishops who inevitably looked much the same. However, such use of the visual factor gave much colour to public worship and much more comprehensibility to it.

THE QUESTION OF COMPLEXITY

Public Christian worship is perennially faced by the difficult task of maintaining a delicate balance between two tendencies which are both proper but which, to some extent, are apt to conflict with each other. It is very arguable that because God is big and beautiful, public, as distinct from private worship, should mirror this bigness and beauty, as the great liturgies of Eastern and Western Christendom have tended to do from very early centuries. But in public worship not only is God shown forth to Man but Man offers himself to God, and in so doing he may desire not only to hear and witness liturgical splendour but to participate in it in simple and comprehensible fashion, even though simplicity and comprehensibility are not characteristics of the deity.

In practise, only too often Christian worship has tended to concentrate heavily on one or other of these two options at the expense of the other, so that, for example, we have on the one hand the total informality and simplicity of the Quakers and the Pentecostalists and on the other the complexity and splendour of the Eastern Orthodox Liturgy and the Western high Mass. Today, obvious social pressures have stampeded many a liturgiologist into jettisoning the complex and the beautiful in order to fall down and worship the banal and the simple, in the hope of placating 'the common man' in whose existence he pathetically believes, having failed to appreciate that (in words which Marx used of Feuerbach) 'the abstract individual whom he analyses belongs in reality to a particular form of society'. In medieval England men tended towards the other extreme, delighting in a public worship which combined an enthusiastic love of visual beauty expressed in a rich variety of ways with a great textual complexity.

The elaborate round of Western public worship current in our period was based on two independent cycles of commemorations which were very liable to clash, principally, though not wholly, because one of them had fixed dates, the other variable ones. Both had the common aim of methodically focusing and uniting the devotion of the faithful all over Christendom on the various inexhaustible spiritual riches which had been laid down in the life and teaching of Christ and elucidated and re-affirmed by great spiritual leaders down the ages.

The earlier and the shorter of these two cycles was the smallish one which reached its peak in the commemoration of that climax of Christ's life when on the first Easter Day He rose again from the dead. The actual dates of this and other events in the life of Jesus had long been forgotten by the time the Church got around to establishing its calendars of worship and were not in themselves of any great import. What was unfortunate was that the Early Church decided to allot to commemoration of the key fixture of Easter Day, not a fixed day of the year (such as Christmas quickly came to acquire), but a variable one based on that trying object known as 'the Paschal Full Moon', which had long been influential in the Jewish liturgical tradition out of which early Christian worship evolved. Infuriatingly this erratic object was liable to appear as early as 21 March and as late as 25 April and never arrived on the same date twice running. As a result the date of the Christian Easter oscillated markedly. This would not have mattered so much had it not been decided to make dependent on the date of Easter that of certain other major commemorations. Thus, to Whitsunday was allotted the seventh Sunday after Easter and to the feast of the Ascension the Thursday which immediately preceded this, whilst the long penitential season of Lent was fixed to terminate on the Saturday before Easter Day.

The dates of such fixtures inevitably tended to clash in varying degree with those in the second cycle of Christian commemorations, the dates of which were static. This was the Calendar of the saints— people whose especial holiness had led the Church to commemorate their life and work by allotting a special day for this purpose, usually that on which the person in question had migrated to the after life. The total number of people whom the Western Church thus 'canonised' (i.e. officially gave the rank of saint), increased steadily century after century and their commemorations became very popular so that, for example, the medieval rite of Sarum (Salisbury) which was very influential in medieval England, came to allot no less than 259 days of the year to them.

In our period it was obviously impossible for any church to commemorate more than a small fraction of the saints. Which saints were chosen for insertion in the yearly calendar that regulated this question depended on various factors. It went without saying that all churches would give a place of honour to the five-star figures of

Christian history, such as the apostles, the chief martyrs and such obviously major luminaries as St Bernard of Clairvaux and St Francis of Assisi. But, as always in the medieval West, a healthy localism was much in evidence. Thus the calendars of English ecclesiastical establishments would naturally include venerated fellow-countrymen of past ages, some of whom were little known on the Continent whilst, equally naturally, everywhere monasteries would commemorate major members of the order to which they belonged.

The varying series of clashes of one kind or another which this situation inevitably engendered were made even more complicated by other factors, notably the fact that top-ranking festivals like Christmas and Easter were celebrated not merely for one day but during a period of eight days (known as an 'octave'). The fact that Sunday had always to be a feast day and that certain days were preceded by 'vigils' (days which were fasts) caused further headaches. The chances of collisions in the liturgical programme of medieval Western worship were thus enormous and might create highly undesirable complications. Thus the most important and joyous feast of the Annunciation of Our Lady, which commemorated the divine call to her to become the earthly mother of Christ, might clash with Good Friday, the most sorrowful day in the Christian calendar, when men's thoughts were focused on Christ crucified on the cross, His disciples having forsaken Him and fled. It was clearly out of the question to commemorate both such things simultaneously. Which was to be transferred and to what date? Such a question had real practical importance, for without a clear answer to it the faithful would not be of one mind, the sacristan would not know what vestments to put out, the choir what music to sing.

The complexity thus caused was greatly augmented by the fact that the medieval Western Church had steadily developed what was ultimately little less than a consuming passion for variants in the text of certain main services (notably in Mattins and in the Mass) which sought to highlight the special message of the commemoration in question. Hence for very many days of the year forms of daily worship were varied by the use of special passages known as 'propers', which became very numerous. They were mostly short and taken from Old and New Testaments, which were ransacked with great assiduity and even greater ingenuity, to provide what looked like passages appropriate for the occasion, whether it be some aspect of the life of Christ or the memory of some notable figure such as an apostle, a bishop, a martyr or an abbess. For the major office of Mattins it was also found appropriate and fruitful to provide a series of readings or 'lessons'.

The principle of making variations in the text of the service fit the occasion was a very ancient one—from the first, at Mass varying portions of the Epistles and Gospels were read for obviously desirable reasons. But by late medieval times these additions—it is unfair to write them off as accretions—had become too numerous, greatly complicating the flow of most of the services which they involved, though they were by no means totally indefensible. For example, the attention to the lives of the saints which they gave prevented the growth of the indefensible idea that saints stopped appearing once the New Testament was written, and saved the text of the Bible from being put on an unrealistic and unprofitable pedestal. The programme had been long and laboriously worked out, very largely in monasteries whose members were mostly little involved in the extensive pastoral and educational activities with which they since became so heavily connected, and for their needs in many ways it provided admirably, as its long life therein has demonstrated, furnishing a rich flow of worship which was never monotonous and always colourful, and imparting in the process no little knowledge of the Bible and of church history.

On the other hand it is very arguable that, even for the monasteries, had the régime been simplified it would have been healthier. The complexity of the task of sorting out year after year, day by day, the correct variants in the services must have plunged many sacristans, male and female, into profound despondency and alarm, and certainly produced forms of worship whose course the outsider would find it quite impossible to follow closely. Although it is true that as time went on handbooks were drawn up to help those concerned to thread their ways through the liturgical labyrinths, the comprehension of these was by no means an easy task. Of one of them (which delighted in the name of Pie) Archbishop Cranmer was later to write, 'there was more business to find out what should be read than to read it when it was found out', a comment which was very far from being unjustifiable.

There is much to be said for the view that the major problem was not so much the liturgical programme itself, which in a less florid form had much to commend it, but the social force which made it the general norm of Western public worship. The immense admiration for the monastic life in medieval days made it natural but unfortunate to conclude that what was good for monks was good for parish clergy and even for laity. For these latter, something shorter and simpler with opportunity for informal acts of worship might have been notably more fruitful. But it was not the first or the last time that the Church had over-simplified the very complex task of delineating its public worship. The liturgiologists of our day who seek so fanatically to make public worship as brief and as inglorious as possible in edifices with exteriors as banal as those of boy-scout huts and interiors with little more internal decoration than the average fives court exhibit the same degree of narrowness albeit in a different form.

THE SERVICE BOOKS

The exacting Anglican who believes in having the text of all the public services of his Church enclosed in a single volume and the tidy-minded Roman Catholic who expects his Church to exhibit rigorous liturgical uniformity from Tadcaster to Timbuctoo, must both regard with reprehension the marked localism and untidiness which coloured the liturgical life of the medieval West.

Although there certainly then existed a large measure of similarity in the text of the various services, there was also abundance of local variation on points of detail, mostly fostered by local tradition and visible even in the Mass, whose importance was incomparably greater than that of any other element of worship. Thus the venerable Church of Milan had its own rite, traditionally connected with its illustrious Archbishop Ambrose, as had Toledo from a much later date. In England the rites of the secular cathedrals of York, Lincoln and Sarum (Salisbury) were of major import, all having distinctive traits and attracting numerous adherents in various parts of the country.

Of the service books in use in the medieval West there was no uniform list and no uniform set of titles. Significantly in this pragmatic age, the contents of a particular book were frequently based on some practical factors. It is to be remembered that some of the

services were very long, that book production was very expensive
and writing had to be largish in days when spectacles were little
known.* It was therefore totally out of the question for all the
services of the medieval English Church to be contained in a single
volume of portable dimensions. As it was, the rites were divided
into separate collections in typically pragmatic fashion so that, for
example, all those pertaining to a bishop tended to be put together
as did those needed by a parish priest in his pastoral work. One
effect of this was the dispersal of texts of those most important rites
which qualify for the title of 'sacraments'. This word, of secular
origin, was slow to acquire a very clear-cut theological meaning
and even in the early part of our period the exact number of those
rites which could be ranked as sacraments was still debated. But
from the late twelfth century onwards, by a line of argument now
not always found fully satisfying, it came to be established in the
West that the total number of sacraments was Seven, a figure for
which medieval Western theologians had such a curious veneration.
These were Baptism, Confirmation, Confession or Penance, Mass,
Marriage, Holy Orders and Extreme Unction. Of the service books
of our period four were of major importance—the Breviary, the
Manual, the Pontifical and the Missal.

THE BREVIARY

The breviary was a book of worship expected to be employed
daily by monks, nuns and clergy of every degree, and contained the
texts of the office of Mattins and what are known as the Day Hours.
Mattins was the first service of the day and was said at a very early
hour of the morning in monasteries and somewhat later in cathedrals and parish churches. The Day Hours, which followed it at
intervals throughout the day, were six in number and mostly
acquired titles derived from the 'hour' at which, at least at some
stage, they were normally said. The first of them was Lauds (which
often immediately followed Mattins) after which came at intervals
Prime, Terce, Sext, None and Compline with which the day concluded. The times at which they were said varied a good deal, being

---

* Spectacles seem to have infiltrated into England in the course of the fifteenth
century. A pair of them bestride the nose of one of the apostles in Henry VII's chapel
in Westminster and a grander pair is mentioned in a contemporary York will.

less extended, for example, in parish churches than in monasteries; in the latter the services might be protracted by the music, which could be very elaborate. Mattins was much longer than the rest of these offices, partly because it included a series of readings or lessons, but all had a similar look through being compiled from the same sorts of materials.

Amongst these sources of fundamental importance was the Book of Psalms of the Old Testament, whose deep religious feeling and fine poetic quality gave it a very high place in medieval devotion (learning it by heart was one of the first tasks to be undertaken by those aspiring to lead the monastic life). The psalms were used either whole or in parts, which might be quite small, and were re-inforced by 'canticles', a minute number of similar effusions of which all but one was drawn from the New Testament. Hymns were very sparingly used in these times and prayers, albeit very numerous, were mostly curt, unlike some of those of the Eastern Church which tended to floridity. With these elements were associated 'antiphons' (brief Scriptural sentences) which might immediately precede or follow a psalm, 'versicles' uttered by the leader of the service and answered by 'responses' made by the congregation.

THE MANUAL

The responsibilities of the parish priest demanded a special set of services which came to be put together in a volume called the *Manual* or sometimes also the *Rituale* and, commonly amongst the English, the *Porthus*, a word which, like so many others in these times, appears in a huge range of variant spellings.

Herein no rite was no more important than that of baptism, by which the individual was made an official member of the Church. By a curious inhibition which characterised Western but not Eastern theology it was long believed that an infant dying unbaptised would be at a serious disadvantage in the after life, with the result that baptism very soon after birth was rigorously ordered in medieval England; adult baptism at this time was thus very rare. Water in the font was first blessed then utilised to baptise the child with appropriate prayer. The infant was also anointed with 'chrism'— an oil specially blessed for thus purpose by the bishop—and was robed for a few days in a 'chrism robe'.

Equally important for the parish priest were the rites for the dying. He was not allowed to quit his parish without making adequate arrangements for the administration of these during his absence. When death seemed imminent he would go to the house concerned, accompanied if possible by a server carrying a lantern, if it was dark, and a small bell which was rung periodically to warn the public that the priest behind him was carrying the Reserved Sacrament for the fortification of the dying person. The sick person would be urged to take the sensible step of making a will if this had not already been done and, after making confession and receiving absolution would receive both from the Reserved Sacrament and the sacrament of Extreme Unction—an anointing with the special chrism blessed by the bishop for this purpose and accompanied by special prayer. As we have seen, medieval English funerals were apt to be very elaborate affairs both religiously and socially, and were mostly followed by a series of private Masses and other services said especially for the good of the soul of the departed person but often enough also of 'all Christian souls'.

The third major rite in the *Manual* was that of marriage. In our period, as today, it had been preceded by announcements of it in church which aimed at ensuring as far as possible that there was no 'cause or just impediment' to the two persons concerned being united in matrimony. A preliminary part of the church service took place in the porch. Then inside the church came a brief rite making the couple man and wife, followed by a nuptial Mass for their benefit. Besides these major items the *Manual* included lesser ones including various forms of blessing, such as those for a person about to go on a pilgrimage, for the staff and wallet which was essential equipment for the journey, as well as blessings of various kinds of foodstuffs and, somewhat oddly, for the arms about to be used in the combat by battle known as the ordeal, which for some time was utilised medieval law—(the appeal of pacifism to medieval man was nil).

THE PONTIFICAL

To the bishop was allotted a substantial and most important range of rites which were largely or wholly assembled in the *Pontifical*. Amongst the most important was conferring of Holy Orders on the various grades of the sacred ministry by 'ordination'.

As we have seen, these had to be received separately, starting at the bottom end of their scale, but it was often usual to confer more than one grade of the minor orders on the same occasion. The principal element of ordination was the laying of the bishop's hands on the head of the candidate concerned, along with appropriate prayer that made clear which grade was involved, and also anointing with chrism. A new bishop had to be 'consecrated' by at least three bishops acting simultaneously. To the bishop pertained the consecration of churches and churchyards and their 'reconciliation' if they had been polluted by bloodshed or other grave misdemeanour; the consecration of altars and the small portable altar slabs much used in these times, as well as of chalices and patens (the vessels used at Mass). Amongst lesser responsibilities were the blessing of bells, of newly elected abbots and statues, and the installation of new abbesses, and of those retiring to hermitages and anchorages. An unpleasant duty which was necessary from time to time was the solemn excommunication by the bishop of serious and persistent offenders against some major law of the church; this had to be done in the correct legal terms, which *Pontificals* might provide though their contents were not uniform.

THE MISSAL

In the medieval West, as always before and mostly afterwards, the unchallenged focus of Christian worship was the Mass which came to be very widely celebrated with a great frequency never usual in the East. The texts required for it were largely or completely to be found in the *Missal*, which might make the volume a very bulky one. As well as an extensive series of collects, epistles and gospels, there were other numerous 'propers' for the great variety of special occasions with which Western calendars came to be stocked. The key point of the first part of the service was the solemn reading of the gospel which was often read from a separate book, and the same was true to lesser extent of the epistles. The *Missal* made provision not only for the two cycles of commemoration which formed the main part of the church calendar but also for other occasions such as prayers for fine weather or for rain and, much the most common, the form of Mass for the good of the souls of the faithful departed.

THE PROCESSIONAL AND THE PRIMER

Besides these major service books there were others of much less importance, such as the *Processional*, which contained the texts of litanies and prayers used in the various processions used on a variety of occasions in the medieval West. Clearly it was useful to have this as a small independent item which could easily be carried around. Of special interest is the *Primer* or *Book of Hours*, the prayer-book of the lay people. This has been claimed by one authority as 'of all the books of the middle ages . . . the most common and best known'. However, it must be admitted that we have no idea what proportion of the population at any one time in our period were in a position to acquire what was a very expensive item, though this proportion was very small if the rareness of mentions of it in contemporary wills is any guide. *Primers* became increasingly common from the thirteenth century onwards. Their contents were simple and short, but might include pictures which in some cases are of very great beauty. Though mostly in Latin a substantial minority are in English, and in some other cases both languages are employed. A main feature was the so-called 'Hours of the Blessed Virgin', an office in honour of her divided into seven short sections. Also present were the Seven Penitential Psalms and the Fifteen Gradual Psalms (both selected from the Book of Psalms) and forms of Evensong and Mattins in commemoration of the dead, termed respectively *Placebo* and *Dirige*, along with a Litany or series of Intercessions.

Although down the centuries the eucharistic worship of the Church has been at the centre of its being and has not altered in its essentials, its social setting has varied very greatly in the course of history. It requires a good deal of historical imagination to appreciate the dominating rôle played by the English parish church in the social life of our period. The churchyard was not merely a place of burial, but a haven of sanctuary in time of war and sometimes at least a place for shopping and sporting. On Sundays and feast days in times which knew little of village halls or social centres it was the venue for exchanging news and greetings. The church bells not only tolled when one of the faithful had passed from this mortal life, and when services were under way or about to begin, but rang merrily for joyous events or menacingly if some disorder threatened, as well as fulfilling in some small degree the functions of a village clock (which we only find coming on the scene in a few areas towards the end of the period). In days before art galleries and museums existed the late-medieval parish church stored within its walls artistic work of some quantity and often of considerable quality, as well as ecclesiastical antiquities. Although by the end of our period the English countryside was graced with a number of manor houses, they seldom competed in magnificence with the church, whose lofty roof-line and spacious windows contrasted vividly with the small and simple houses which clustered around it. This, men held, was as it ought to be, for God is so much greater than man, and the church was 'none other than the house of God'. Here perennially God joined Himself to man, notably in the Mass, where most mysteriously bread and wine was consecrated to become His Body and Blood. Here the faithful could steadily build up the capacity to love God and the things which He loved, Beauty and Truth and one's Neighbour who was made in God's image and of whose needs, material and spiritual, medieval folk were so acutely aware.

BIBLIOGRAPHY

Abbreviations:

AJ	Archaeological Journal
EHR	English Historical Review
JEH	Journal of Ecclesiastical History
TRHS	Transactions of the Royal Historical Society
CUP	Cambridge University Press
OUP	Oxford University Press

Some entries include (b) to signify background reading.
Pamphlets are indicated by (p).
Place of publication is London unless otherwise stated.

BACKGROUND

The Oxford Dictionary of the Christian Church, ed. F.L. Cross and E. Livingstone (OUP 2nd edn 1974) is an invaluable handbook with a wide range of articles that have extensive and up-to-date bibliographies. For general introduction the Oxford History of England vols 2, 3, 4, 5 and 6 and the Cambridge Economic History passim are most useful; the Cambridge Medieval History, stupendously dull and based on a plan long effete is of dubious value. There is no adequate general history of the Church in English: L'Histoire Générale de L'Eglise, ed. A. Fliche and V. Martin (Paris) fills this gap, vols 8, 9, 10, 11, 13, 14 and 15 covering the period of the present book.

Amongst studies of the English Church before the Norman Conquest are C. J. Godfrey, The Church in Anglo-Saxon England (CUP 1962) and M. Deanesly, The Pre-Conquest Church in England (2nd edn 1963). For the final phase see F. Barlow, The English Church 1000-1066 (1962).

ORIGINAL SOURCES★

No textbook, however sensitive, can reproduce the bouquet of medieval times sufficiently fully to render unnecessary some acquaintance with the original documents which they engendered. The great majority of these were written in Latin, but a significant fraction of those concerning England have been published in or with English translations or abstracts. The most important in many ways are those of the central government which, along with the publications of multitudinous historical societies, are listed in E. L. C. Mullins, Texts and Calendars; an analytical guide to local publications (RHS 1958). Of the major official records for the period the chief are the Calendar of Letters Patent (E), Calendar of Letters Close (E) and the Calendar of Papal Letters (E).

Episcopal registers are invaluable and are catalogued in R. Smith, A Guide to

---

(E) after an entry denotes that it is published wholly or largely in an English translation or abstract; (LE) that both Latin and English are employed; (L) that only the Latin text is given.

Bishops' Registers in England and Wales to 1640 (*RHS:* in the press); a goodly fraction of them have been printed, notably by the Canterbury and York Society and the Surtees Society. A useful list of printed collections of wills made before 1526 is given in M. Deanesly, *The Lollard Bible* (CUP repr. 1966, 391-8). A number of local archaeological societies have printed the early wills of their area, sometimes in translation or abstract. Most of the major chronicles of medieval England are in print, notably *Chronicles and Memorials of Great Britain and Ireland* (HMSO) and are largely in Latin; J. Stevenson, *The Church Historians of England* (5 vols 1853-8) is a useful collection of English translations of a number of them.

The original texts suggested for further reading in the following sections constitute only a very minute fraction of those available.

GENERAL

R. BRENTANO *Two Churches—England and Italy in the Thirteenth Century* Princeton 1968

A. HAMILTON THOMPSON *The English Clergy and their Organisation in the late Middle Ages* Oxford 1947

D. KNOWLES and R. NEVILLE HADCOCK *Medieval Religious Houses; England and Wales* rev. edn 1971—lists monastic and secular institutions with their dates of foundation, size etc.

J. R. H. MOORMAN *Church Life in England in the Thirteenth Century* Cambridge 1946

W. A. PANTIN *The English Church in the Fourteenth Century* CUP 1955

Texts

J. H. HARVEY (ed.) *William Worcestre, Itineraries* (LE) OUP 1969—contains an enormous amount of miscellaneous historical and architectural notes made by an indefatigable fifteenth-century traveller.

MONASTERIES AND ALLIED INSTITUTIONS

H. M. COLVIN *The White Canons in England* 1951

A. M. COOKE 'The Settlement of the Cistercians in England' *EHR* viii (1893) 625-76

J. C. DICKINSON *Monastic Life in Medieval England* (reprinting)
   The Origins of the Austin Canons and their Introduction into England 1950
   'Early Suppressions of English Houses of Austin Canons' in *Medieval Studies presented to Rose Graham* OUP 1950

R. A. DONKIN 'Cistercian bibliography' in *Documentation Cistercienne* ii (1969) 1-104 (very full on English Cistercians)

R. GRAHAM *St Gilbert of Sempringham and the Gilbertines* 1903

D. KNOWLES *The Monastic Order in England* CUP 1940
   The Religious Orders in England 3 vols CUP 1948-59

J. R. H. MOORMAN *The Franciscan Orders* Oxford 1968 (a general history)
   The Greyfriars in Cambridge Cambridge 1952

E. M. THOMPSON *The Carthusian Order in England* 1930

The volumes of the British Society for Franciscan Studies cover a great deal of ground and include: C. L. Kingsford, *The Grey Friars of London* (Aberdeen 1915) and C. L. Kingsford and A. F. C. Bourdillon, *The Order of Minoresses in England* (Manchester 1926)

R. M. CLAY *The Medieval Hospitals of England* 1909
   The Hermits and Anchorites of England 1914

R. B. DOBSON *Durham Priory* CUP 1973

W. A. HINNEBUSCH *The Early English Friar Preachers* Rome 1951

D. J. A. MATTHEW *The Norman Monasteries and their English Possessions* OUP 1962

H. MAYR-HARTING 'Functions of a Twelfth-Century Recluse' in *History* 60 (Oct. 1976) 337-52

C. PLATT *The Monastic Grange in Medieval England* 1969

E. POWER *Medieval English Nunneries* Cambridge 1922

F. ROTH *The English Austin Friars 1249-1538* 2 vols New York 1961, 1966

A. SAVINE *English Monasteries on the Eve of the Dissolution* Oxford 1909

J. JORGENSEN *St. Francis of Assisi* 1947 (b)

L. VON MATT and W. HAUSER *St Francis of Assisi* 1956—is an attractive pictorial biography (b)

S. WOOD *English Monasteries and their Patrons in the Thirteenth Century* OUP 1955

Detailed local studies include:

B. HARVEY *Westminster Abbey and its estates in the Middle Ages* OUP 1977

R. H. HILTON *The Economic Development of some Leicestershire Estates in the 14th and 15th centuries* Oxford 1947

E. MILLER *The Abbey and Bishopric of Ely* Cambridge 1951

M. MORGAN *The English Lands of the Abbey of Bec* Oxford 1967

J. A. RAFTIS *The Estates of Ramsey Abbey* Toronto 1960

R. A. L. SMITH *Canterbury Cathedral Priory* Cambridge 1945

Texts

Observances in use at the Augustinian priory of Barnwell (LE), ed. J. W. Clark (Cambridge 1897), gives a vivid picture of monastic routine, as does *The Monastic Constitutions of Lanfranc* (LE), ed. D. Knowles (1951). Amongst major monastic chronicles are *The Peterborough Chronicle* (E), tr. H. S. Rositzke (Columbia 1951); William Thorne, *Chronicle of St Augustine's Canterbury* (E), tr. A. H. Davis (Oxford 1934) and the rather hackneyed *Chronicle of Jocelin of Brakelond* (LE), ed. H. E. Butler (Oxford 1953). See also Walter Daniel, *Life of St Ailred, Abbot of Rievaulx* (LE), ed. F. M. Powicke (Oxford 1950) and T. Eccleston, *On the coming of the Friars*, which has been frequently translated. *The Life of Christana of Markyate—a twelfth-century recluse* (LE), ed. C. H. Talbot (Oxford 1959) is a good deal less colourful than the *Life of Wulfric of Haselbury* (L), ed. M. Bell (Somerset Record Society 1933). A number of editions of the *Ancren Riwle* have been published. *Visitations of Religious Houses in the Diocese of Lincoln* (LE), ed. A. Hamilton Thompson (3 vols 1915-29) is a major example of its type. *The Rites of Durham* (E), rev. edn (Surtees Society 107) is a unique and most detailed description of a major monastery and its furnishings. Useful on the economic side are *The Account Books of*

Beaulieu Abbey (L), ed. S. F. Hockey (1975) and *The book of William Mortimer, almoner of Peterborough Monastery 1448-67* (L), ed. W. T. Mellows and P. I. King.

THE SECULAR CHURCH

Amongst the very few useful diocesan histories of any size are to be noted C. M. L. Bouch, *Prelates and People of the Lake Counties* (Kendal 1948), covering the diocese of Carlisle; D. Owen, *Church and Society in Medieval Lincolnshire* (1971); R. J. E. Boggis, *History of the Diocese of Exeter* (Exeter 1922). The *Victoria County Histories of England* provide useful general articles on the ecclesiastical history of their areas, along with short studies of individual ecclesiastical establishments therein, both secular and monastic, but only cover parts of the country. Lists of diocesan officials are given in J. Le Neve, *Fasti Ecclesie Anglicanae*, rev. T. B. Hardy (3 vols Oxford 1854) of which an extensively revised edition by J. M. Horn and others (London University, Athlone Press) is now well-advanced; more detailed studies of this subject have been made for some dioceses. G. Hill, *English Dioceses; a survey of their limits* (1900) is still useful.

Up-to-date lists of English bishops are given in *Handbook of British Chronology*, ed. F. M. Powicke and E. B. Fryde (2nd edn 1961). As to biographies:— W. H. Dixon, *Fasti Eboracenses: lives of the archbishops of York* i (to 1373) (1861) and W. F. Hook, *Lives of the Archbishops of Canterbury* (5 vols 1860-70) are comprehensive, but the latter is somewhat antiquated. Amongst studies of narrower scope are the *Dictionary of National Biography*, which gives brief articles on individual bishops; M. Gibbs and J. Lang, *Bishops and Reform 1215-72* (Oxford 1934); K. Edwards, 'The social origins and provenances of the English bishops during the reign of Edward II' in *TRHS* ix 1954, 51-79 and J. R. L. Highfield, 'The English hierarchy in the reign of Edward III' in *TRHS* vi 1956, 115-38.

For individual bishops see:

E. A. ABBOTT *St Thomas, his Death and Miracles* 2 vols 1898

M. ASTON *Thomas Arundel* 1967

F. BARLOW 'A view of Archbishop Lanfranc' in *JEH* xvi, 163-7

L. H. BUTLER 'Archbishop Melton, his Neighbours and his Kinsmen 1317-40' in *JEH* ii 1951, 54-67

D. A. CALLUS *Robert Grosseteste Bishop and Scholar* OUP 1955

C. R. CHENEY *Herbert Walter* 1967

J. DAHMUS *William Courtenay Archbishop of Canterbury* 1966

D. L. DOUIE *Archbishop Pecham* Oxford 1952

C. DUGGAN 'Richard of Ilchester, royal servant and bishop' in *TRHS* xvi 1966, 1-21

R. FOREVILLE (ed.) *Thomas Becket; Actes du Colloque . . . de Sediéres* Paris 1975

C. H. FRASER *History of Anthony Bek, bishop of Durham 1283-1311* Oxford 1957

M. GIBSON *Lanfranc of Bec* OUP 1978

W. H. H. GREEN *Bishop Reginald Pecock* CUP 1945

R. M. HAINES *The Church and Politics in Fourteenth Century England: the Career of Adam Orleton c. 1275-1345* CUP 1978

'Aspects of the Episcopate of John Carpenter Bishop of Worcester 1444-76' in *JEH* xix 1968, 11-40

A. HAMILTON THOMPSON 'William Bateman bishop of Norwich 1344-55' in *Norfolk and Norwich Arch. Soc. Trans.* xxv 102-37

W. G. HAYTER *William of Wykeham* 1970

W. H. HUTTON *Thomas Becket* rev. edn 1926

E. F. JACOB *Archbishop Henry Chichele* 1967
'Archbishop John Stafford' in *TRHS* xii 1962, 1-23
'St Richard of Chichester' in *JEH* vii 1956, 174-80

A. F. JUDD *The Life of Thomas Bekynton* Chichester 1961

D. KNOWLES *The Episcopal Colleagues of Thomas Becket* CUP 1951
Thomas Becket 1970

C. H. LAWRENCE *St Edmund of Abingdon* Oxford 1960

A. MOREY *Bartholomew of Exeter* Cambridge 1937

D. NICHOLL *Thurstan, Archbishop of York 1114-40* York 1964

E. H. PEARCE *Thomes de Cobham, Bishop of Worcester 1317-27* 1923

F. M. POWICKE 'Robert Grosseteste bishop of Lincoln 1235-73' in *Bull. John Rylands Lib.* xxxv, 482-507
Stephen Langton Oxford 1928

L. B. RADFORD *Thomas of London* Cambridge 1894

A. SALTMAN *Theobold Archbishop of Canterbury* 1956

G. V. SCAMMELL *Hugh de Puiset* CUP 1956

B. SMALLEY *The Becket Conflict and the Schools* OUP 1973

R. W. SOUTHERN *St Anselm and his Biographer* CUP 1963

R. L. STOREY *Thomas Langley and the Bishopric of Durham 1406-37* 1961

W. L. WARREN 'A Re-appraisal of Simon Sudbury, bishop of London (1361-75) and Archbishop of Canterbury (1375-81)' in *JEH* x 1959, 139-59

R. M. WOOLLEY *St Hugh of Lincoln* 1927

In cases where their registers have been published by the Canterbury and York Society, a useful sketch of the career of the bishop concerned usually joins the text.

G. E. AYLMER and R. CANT (eds) *A History of York Minster*—includes R. M. T. Hill and C. N. L. Brooke, 'From 627 until the early Thirteenth Century' 1-43 and D. B. Dobson, 'The Later Middle Ages 1215-1500' Oxford 1977

H. S. BENNETT 'Medieval Ordination Lists in the English Episcopal Registers' in *Studies presented to Sir Hilary Jenkinson*, ed. J. C. Davies 10-34

F. R. H. DU BOULAY *The Lordship of Canterbury* New York 1966

M. BOWKER *The Secular Clergy in the Diocese of Lincoln 1495-1520* CUP 1968

C. N. L. BROOKE 'Gregorian Reform in Action—Clerical Marriage in England' in *Hist. Jnl.* xii 1956, 1-21

C. R. CHENEY *English Bishops' Chanceries 1100-1250* Manchester 1950

I. J. CHURCHILL *Canterbury Administration* 2 vols 1933
and others *Medieval Records of the Archbishops of Canterbury* 1962

G. H. COOK *Medieval Chantries and Chantry Chapels* 1968

E. L. CUTTS *Parish Priests and their People* 1914

W. DANSEY *Horae Decanae Rurales* 2 vols 1835

J. H. DENTON *English Royal Free Chapels 1160-1300* Manchester 1970

J. C. DICKINSON 'The Origins of the Cathedral of Carlisle' in *Trans. Cumberland and Westmorland Arch. Soc.* New Series xlv, 134-43

'Walter the Priest and St Mary's Carlisle' ibid. lxix, 102-14

'Diocesi e Sedi episcopali dell Inghilterra dope la Conquista Normanna' in *Le instituzioni ecclesiastiche della 'Societas Christiana' dei secoli* xi-xii Milan 1974

B. DODWELL 'The Foundation of Norwich Cathederal' in *TRHS* 1957, 1-18

R. M. HAINES *The administration of the diocese of Worcester in the first half of the fourteenth century* 1965

A. HAMILTON THOMPSON *The Cathederal Churches of England* 1928

The Dispute with Canterbury (p)

'Diocesan Organisation in the Middle Ages: Rural Deans' in *Proc. Brit. Acad.* xxix 1948, 3-44

'Notes on Colleges of Secular Canons in England' in *AJ* lxxiv 1917, 139-99

'The College of St Mary Magdalene, Bridgnorth' ibid. lxxxiv 1927, 1-87

'The Statutes of the College of St Mary and All Saints Fotheringay' ibid. lxxv 1918, 241-309

'Introduction to the Registers of the Archbishops of York' in *Yorks. Arch. Jnl.* xxxii 1935, 245-53

F. HARRISON *Life in a Medieval College; the story of the Vicars Choral of York Minster* 1952

R. A. A. HARTRIDGE *A History of Vicarages in the Middle Ages* Cambridge 1930

P. HEATH *English Clergy on the Eve of the Reformation* 1969

E. F. JACOB *Essays in Later Medieval History* Manchester 1968

W. R. MATTHEWS and W. M. AKINS (eds) *A History of St Paul's Cathedral*—includes C. N. L. Brooke, 'The Earliest Times to 1485' 1957, 1-99

K. M. MAJOR 'The Finance of the Dean and Chapter of Lincoln from the Twelfth to the Fourteenth Century' in *JEH* v 149-67

M. RICHTER Introduction to *Canterbury Professions* Canterbury & York Soc. 1973

D. ROBINSON *Beneficed Clergy in Cleveland and the East Riding* Borthwick Papers, York 1969 (p)

W. M. SINCLAIR *Memorials of St Paul's Cathedral* 1909

R. L. STOREY 'Recruitment of English Clergy in the Period of the Conciliar Movement' in *Annuarium Historiae Conciliorum* vii 1975, 290-313

F. W. WEAVER (ed.) *Somerset Incumbents* Bristol 1889—lists of parish clergy

J. F. WILLIAMS 'Ordination in Norwich Diocese during the fifteenth century' in *Norfolk Archaeology* xxxi 1956, 347-58

K. L. WOOD-LEGH *Perpetual Chantries in Britain* Cambridge 1965

B. L. WOODCOCK *Ecclesiastical Courts in the diocese of Canterbury* OUP 1952

C. E. WOODRUFF and W. DANKS *Memorials of the Cathedral and Priory . . . of Canterbury* 1912

Texts

W. BREWYN *A 15th Century Guide Book to the principal Churches of Rome* (E) ed. C. E. Woodruff 1933

G. CHAUCER The Canterbury Tales (E) trs. N. Coghill, Penguin

FELTOE and MINNS (eds) *Vetus Liber Archidiaconi Eliensis* (L) Cambridge 1917

E. M. GOULBURN and H. SYMONDS (eds) *Life, Letters and Sermons of bishop Herbert de Losinga* (LE) 2 vols Norwich 1978

E. F. JACOB (ed.) *The Register of Henry Chichele, Archbishop of Canterbury 1414-43* 4 vols 1943-7

W. LANGLAND *The Vision of Piers Plowman* (E)

St Thomas of Canterbury in English History by contemporary writers (E) trs. W. H. Hutton 1899

A. WATKINS (ed.) *Archdeaconry of Norwich: Inventory of Church Goods temp. Edward III* (L) 2 vols Norfolk Record Society 1947-8

H. WHARTON *Anglia Sacra* 2 vols 1691, repr. 1961 (L)—an extensive collection of texts arranged by dioceses and chiefly concerning their bishops and archbishops.

WILLIAM OF MALMESBURY *Life of St Wulfstan, Bishop of Worcester* trs. J. F. H. Peile (E) Oxford 1934

E. E. WILLIAMS *The Chantries of William Conynges in St Mary Redcliffe* (LE) Bristol 1950

J. F. WILLIAMS *The Early Churchwardens' Accounts of Hampshire* (LE) Winchester 1913

K. L. WOOD-LEGH (ed.) *A small household of the XV century, being the account book of Munden's chantry, Bridport* (L) Manchester 1955

CHURCH AND STATE

G. BARRACLOUGH *Papal Provisions* Oxford 1935

M. BRETT *The English Church under Henty I* OUP 1975

Z. N. BROOKE *The English Church and the Papacy from the Conquest to the reign of John* 1968

N. F. CANTOR *Church, Kingship and Lay Investiture 1089-1135* Oxford 1958

C. R. CHENEY *Pope Innocent III and England* Stuttgart 1976

H. M. CHEW Introduction to *Hemingsby's Register* Devizes 1963

C. DAVIS 'The Statute of Provisors of 1351' in *History* xxxviii 1953, 116-33

C. J. GODFREY 'Pluralists in the Province of Canterbury in 1366' in *JEH* xi 1960, 23-40

G. L. HASKINS *The Growth of English Representative Government* Oxford 1948

R. HILL 'The Theory and Practise of Excommunication in Medieval England' in *History* xlii, 1-11

M. HOWELL *Regalian right in Medieval England* 1962

E. F. JACOB *Essays in the Conciliar Epoch* Manchester, rev. edn 1968

O. JENSEN 'The Denarius Sancti Petri in England' in *TRHS* 1901, 171-247

E. W. KEMP *Canonisation and Authority in the Western Church* OUP 1948
Counsel and Consent 1961
'The Origins of the Canterbury Convocation' in *JEH* iii 1952, 132-4

C. H. LAWRENCE (ed.) *The English Church and the Papacy* 1965

W. E. LUNT *Financial Relations of the Papacy with England to 1327* Cambridge, Mass. 1939

Financial Relations of the Papacy with England, 1327-1534 Cambridge, Mass. 1962
Papal Revenues in the Middle Ages New York 1934
The Taxation of Norwich Oxford 1926

F. MAKOWER *The Constitutional History of the Church of England* 1895

H. MAYR-HARTUNG 'Henry II and the Papacy' in *JEH* xvi 1965, 39–53

C. MORRIS 'William I and the church courts' in *EHR* 82, 449–63

E. PERROY *L'Angleterre et le grand schisme d'Occident 1378–99* Paris 1933

J. E. SAYERS *Papal Judges Delegate in the Province of Canterbury 1198–1254* OUP 1971

G. O. SAYLES *The King's Parliament of England* 1975

P. E. SCHRAMM *A History of the English Coronation* Oxford 1937

A. L. SMITH *Church and State in the Middle Ages* Oxford 1913

W. STUBBS *Constitutional History of England* 3 vols repr. 1926–9

B. TIERNEY 'Grosseteste and the theory of Papal Sovereignty' in *JEH* vi 1955, 1–17

D. B. WESKE *Convocation of the Clergy* 1937

Texts

C. R. CHENEY and W. H. SEMPLE (eds) *Selected Letters of Innocent III concerning England* (LE) 1951

W. STUBBS *Select Charters and other illustrations of English Constitutional History* (L) 9th edn rev. H. W. C. Davis, Oxford 1951

D. WILKINS (ed.) *Concilia Magnae Brittaniae et Hiberniae*, 4 vols 1737, is the classic collection of English conciliar texts

The major local textbook on medieval English church law was the *Provinciale* (L) of William Lyndwood (d. 1446) on whose work see C. R. Cheney in *The Jurist* xxi, 405–34. *Lyndwood's Provinciale* (E) ed. J. V. Bullard and H. Chalmer Bell 1929 translates the canons.

For the medieval Western Church the principal texts of canon law are contained in the *Corpus Juris Canonici* ed. A. Friedberg, 2 vols Leipzig 1879 (b)

HERESY AND PIETY

M. ASTON 'Lollardry and Literacy' in *History* lxii 1977, 347–71
  'Lollardry and the Reformation: Survival or Revival' in *History* xlix 1964

D. BAKER (ed.) *Schism, Heresy and Religious Protest* Oxford 1972

The Cambridge History of the Bible vol. 2, CUP 1969

H. J. CHAYTOR *From Script to Print* Cambridge 1945

M. DEANESLY *The Lollard Bible* CUP repr. 1966
  The Significance of the Lollard Bible 1951 (p)

G. LEFF 'John Wyclif; the path to dissent' in *Proc. Brit. Acad.* 1967, 143–80

R. W. LOVATT 'The Imitation of Christ in late medieval England' in *TRHS* xvii 1968, 97–121

B. L. MANNING *The People's Faith in the time of Wyclif* Cambridge 1919

K. B. MCFARLANE *John Wycliffe and the beginnings of English Non-conformity* 1966

G. R. OWST *The Destructorium Viciorum of Alexander Carpenter* 1952 (p)
   Literature and Pulpit in Medieval England Cambridge 1933
   Preaching in Medieval England Cambridge 1923
B. SMALLEY *The Study of the Bible in the Middle Ages* Oxford 1952
J. A. F. THOMPSON *The Later Lollards 1414-1520* Oxford 1965
M. WILKES 'Predestination, Power and Property: Wyclif's Theory of Dominion and Grace' in *Studies in Church History*, ed. G. J. Cuming 1965
R. WEISS *Humanism in England during the fifteenth century* 2nd edn, Oxford 1957
H. B. WORKMAN *John Wyclif* 2 vols Oxford 1926

Texts

W. BUTLER-BOWDEN *The Book of Margery Kempe (1436); a modern version* 1936
W. HILTON *The Scale of Perfection* tr. G. Sitwell 1953

THE VISUAL ARTS

T. D. ATKINSON *An Architectural History of the Benedictine Monastery of St Etheldreda of Ely* CUP 1933
   Local Style in English Architecture 1947
M. AUBERT *High Gothic Art* 1964 (b)
F. BOND *Gothic Architecture in England* 1906
Catalogue of Seals in the British Museum vol. i 1887
C. J. P. CAVE *Roof-Bosses in Medieval Churches* CUP 1948
A. W. CLAPHAM *English Romanesque Architecture after the Conquest* Oxford 1934
D. H. S. CRANAGE *The Churches of Shropshire* 2 vols, Wellington 1901-3—a most elaborate and comprehensive survey.
F. H. CROSSLEY *English Church Monuments 1160-1580* new edn 1933
J. FOWLER *Medieval Sherborne* Dorchester 1951—a useful study of an interesting small medieval town.
F. A. GREENHILL *Incised Effigial Slabs* 2 vols 1976
J. HARVEY *English Medieval Architects: a biographical dictionary down to 1550* 1954
   The Perpendicular Style 1978
F. E. HOWARD and F. H. CROSSLEY *English Church Wood-work 1250-1550* 2nd edn 1933
F. E. HUTCHINSON *Medieval Glass at All Souls' College* 1949
J. A. KNOWLES *The York School of Glass painting* 1936
H. MUNRO CAUTLEY *Suffolk Churches and their Treasures* Ipswich 1954—a classic local study.
G. L. REMNANT *A Catalogue of Misericords in Great Britain* Oxford 1969
L. F. SALZMAN *Building in England down to 1540* Oxford 1952
A. VALENCE *Greater English Church Screens* 1947
   Old Crosses and Lychgates 1920
G. F. WEBB *Architecture in England in the Middle Ages* 1956
G. ZARNECKI *English Romanesque sculpture, 1066-1140* 1951
   Later English Romanesque sculpture, 1140-1210 1953

Texts

C. R. DODWELL (ed.) *Theophilus, The various arts* (LE) 1961—a curious treatise on the technical side of medieval arts.

The Rites of Durham (rev. edn Surtees Society) is invaluable.

LITERACY AND LEARNING

BORENIUS *St Thomas Becket in Art* 1932

D. G. BREWER *Chaucer in his time* 1963 (b)

R. A. BROWN, H. M. COLVIN and A. J. TAYLOR (eds) *The History of the King's Works* vol. I *The Middle Ages* HMSO 1963—a detailed study of royal building operations.

E. K. CHAMBERS *English Literature at the close of the Middle Ages* 1967

A. B. COBHAM *The Medieval Universities* 1975

S. C. EASTON *Roger Bacon and his Search for a Universal Science* Columbia 1952

A. B. EMDEN *A biographical Register of members of the University of Oxford from 1176-1500* 3 vols 1957-9

A biographical Register of members of the University of Cambridge to 1500 CUP 1963 English medieval wall-paintings of the 12th, 13th and 14th centuries are surveyed by E. W. Tristram, 3 vols 1944, 1950, 1955

A. L. GABRIEL *Summary Bibliography of the History of the Universities of Great Britain and Ireland up to 1800* University of Notre Dame, Indiana 1974

A. GARDNER *English Medieval Sculpture* CUP rev. edn 1951

W. H. GODFREY *The English Almshouse* 1955

J. HARVEY *English Cathedrals* rev. edn 1956—the best modern architectural outline. *The Medieval Architect* 1972

F. E. HOWARD *The Medieval Styles of the English Parish Church* 1936

D. KNOWLES and J. K. St JOSEPH *Monastic Sites from the Air* CUP 1952

W. R. LETHABY *Westminster Abbey and the King's Craftsmen* 1906

A. G. LITTLE (ed.) *Franciscan History and Legend in Medieval Art* Manchester 1937 *Greyfriars in Oxford* 1892

A. R. MARTIN *Franciscan Architecture in England* Manchester 1937

W. OAKESHOTT *The Sequence of Medieval English Art* 1950—on manuscript illumination.

N. ORME *Education in the West of England 1066-1548* 1976

English Schools in the Middle Ages 1973—which has a very full bibliography.

Oxford History of English Art—a pioneer work of rather uneven quality. The relevant volumes are by D. Talbot Rice (871-1100), T. S. R. Boase (1100-1216), P. Brieger (1216-1307) and J. Evans (1307-1461).

W. A. PANTIN 'Chantry Priests' Houses and other Medieval Lodgings' in *Medieval Architecture* iii 1959, 216-58

'Medieval Priests' Houses in South-West England' in *Medieval Architecture* i 1957, 118-46

H. RASHDALL *The Universities of Europe in the Middle Ages* rev. edn F. M. Powicke and A. B. Emden iii, Oxford 1938 is primarily concerned with constitutional development

J. P. C. ROACH (ed.) *Victoria County History of Cambridge* iii, OUP 1959

G. MCN. RUSHFORTH *Medieval Imagery, as illustrated by the painted windows of Great Malvern priory church* Oxford 1936

H. E. SALTER *Medieval Oxford* Oxford 1936

B. SMALLEY *Roger Bacon and the Early Dominican School at Oxford*

R. W. SOUTHERN *Medieval Humanism and other Studies* Oxford 1970

Victoria County History of Oxford ii 1960

C. WOODFORDE *English stained and painted glass* Oxford 1954

Texts

F. C. COPLESTON *Aquinas* 1935 (b)
  A History of Medieval Philosophy 1972

H. CRAIG *English Religious Drama of the Middle Ages* CUP 1956

A. C. CROMBIE *Robert Grosseteste and the Origins of Experimental Science* Oxford 1954

V. H. GALBRAITH 'Nationality and Language in Medieval England' in *TRHS* xxiii 1941, 113-28

F. L. HARRISON *Music in Medieval Britain* 1958

S. S. HUSSEY *Piers Plowman—critical approaches* 1969

G. KANE *Medieval English Literature* 1951

G. H. T. KIMBLE *Geography in the Middle Ages* 1938

W. W. LAWRENCE *Chaucer and the Canterbury Tales* New York 1950 (b)

L. THORNDYKE *University Records and Life in the Middle Ages* (E) Columbia 1944

W. ULLMANN *A History of Political Theory in the Middle Ages* 1965

G. G. WICKHAM *Early English Stages* i (1300-1576), 1959

R. M. WILSON *Early Medieval English Literature* 2nd edn 1951
  'English and French in England' in *History* xxviii 1967, 37-60

R. WOOLF *The English Mystery Plays* 1972
  The English Religious Lyric in the Middle Ages Oxford 1968

F. WORMALD and C. E. WRIGHT (eds) *The English Library before 1700* 1960

C. H. COOPER *Annals of Cambridge* i Cambridge 1842 (E)

The Oxford Historical Society has published an enormous amount of Oxford records, mostly (L).

HEALING AND PILGRIMAGE

E. A. ABBOTT *St Thomas of Canterbury, his death and miracles* (E) 1898—has much valuable textual discussion.

J. C. DICKINSON *The Shrine of Our Lady of Walsingham* CUP 1956

R. C. FINUCANE *Miracles and Pilgrims; popular beliefs in medieval England* 1977
  'The Use and Abuse of medieval Miracles' in *History* 60 Feb. 1975, 1-10

S. RUBIN *Medieval English Medicine* 1974

J. SOMPTION *Pilgrimage: an Image of Medieval Religion* 1975

J. C. WALL *Shrines of British Saints* 1905

E. WATERTON *Pietas Mariana Brittanica* 1879

Texts

ERASMUS *Pilgrimages to Saint Mary of Walsingham and St Thomas of Canterbury* (E) trs. J. G. Nichols 1875—vivid and unsympathetic.

J. O. HALLIWELL (ed) *The Chronicle of William de Rishanger: the Miracles of Simon de Montfort* (L) Camden Soc. xv 1940

J. STEVENSON (ed) Reginald of Durham *Libellus de vita et miraculis S. Godrici* (L) Surtees Soc. xx 1847

(Caesarius of Heisterbach *The Dialogue on Miracles* trs. H. Scott and C. Bland 2 vols 1929 is a continental classic on the subject (b))

ALMSGIVING AND POVERTY

W. K. JORDAN *The charities of London 1480-1660* 1959
Philanthropy in England 1480-1660 1961
The Social Institutions of Lancashire 1962

M. MOLLAT (ed) *Histoire de la pauvreté* 2 vols Paris 1974 (b)

M. M. SHEEHAN *The Will in medieval England* Toronto 1963

J. A. F. THOMPSON 'Piety and Charity in late medieval London' in *JEH* xvi 1965, 178-95

B. TIERNEY *Medieval Poor Law; a sketch of canonical Theory and its application* CUP 1959 (b)

Texts

N. H. NICHOLAS *Testamenta Vetusta* (E) 2 vols 1826—is badly edited but has much interesting material.
Testamenta Eboracensia vols 4, 30, 45, 53 and 59 (mostly (L))—selective but a most illuminating collection, as is
Testamenta Cantiana—extracts, mostly (E), ed. L. L. Duncan 1906

WORSHIP

No useful revaluation of medieval Western worship has yet appeared. Useful descriptive material is to be found in:

T. E. BRIDGETT *The History of the Holy Eucharist in Great Britain* 2 vols 1881 still has its uses.

J. D. CHAMBERS *Divine Worship in England in the thirteenth and fourteenth centuries* 1877

D. ROCK *The Church of our Fathers* rev. G. W. Hart and W. H. Frere 4 vols 1903-4

A. WATKINS (ed) *The Archdeaconry of Norwich: Inventory of Church Goods temp Edward III* 2 vols 1947-8 Norfolk Rec. Soc.—has a very useful introduction on the equipment for parish worship.

J. WICKHAM LEGG and W. G. St JOHN HOPE *Inventories of Christchurch Canterbury* 1902—provides lists of plate, ornaments and vestments owned by the house.

(See also C. Wordsworth and H. Littlehales, *The Old Service Books of the English Church* 1904)

Texts

The Surtees Society has published the texts of *The York Pontifical* (vol. 61), *The York Breviary* (vols 71, 75), *The York Missal* (vols 59, 60) and *The York Manual* (vol. 63). The Henry Bradshaw Society has published a wide range of liturgical texts, and the Alcuin Society various volumes on the history of worship. Here also *The Rites of Durham*, rev. ed. Surtees Soc., 107, is valuable.

J. HARTHAN *Books of Hours and their Owners* 1978

Various

There is no atlas of ecclesiastical history for England. The large but not very accessible diocesan maps published with the text of the *Valor Ecclesiasticus* of 1535 are valuable as is the modern *Map of Monastic Britain* (Ordnance Survey). R. N. Hadcock's 'A map of medieval Northumberland' in *Archaeologia Aeliana 4th Soc.* xvi 1939, 148–218 is useful for its area. See also E. Ekwall, *The Concise Dictionary of English Place-names*, Oxford 1947; N.P. Ker, *Medieval Libraries of Great Britain*—a list of surviving books, 2nd ed. 1964; *Handbook of Dates for Students of English History*, ed. C. R. Cheney 1948.

INDEX

*Denotes reference to a monastery.

†Refers to a definition of the term concerned.

Bishops and archbishops are indexed under their surnames, academic colleges under the university to which they belong.